Seeing Like an Activist

Seeing Like an Activist

*Civil Disobedience and
the Civil Rights Movement*

ERIN R. PINEDA

Oxford University Press is a department of the University of Oxford. It furthers the University's objective of excellence in research, scholarship, and education by publishing worldwide. Oxford is a registered trade mark of Oxford University Press in the UK and certain other countries.

Published in the United States of America by Oxford University Press
198 Madison Avenue, New York, NY 10016, United States of America.

© Oxford University Press 2021

All rights reserved. No part of this publication may be reproduced, stored in a retrieval system, or transmitted, in any form or by any means, without the prior permission in writing of Oxford University Press, or as expressly permitted by law, by license, or under terms agreed with the appropriate reproduction rights organization. Inquiries concerning reproduction outside the scope of the above should be sent to the Rights Department, Oxford University Press, at the address above.

You must not circulate this work in any other form
and you must impose this same condition on any acquirer.

Library of Congress Cataloging-in-Publication Data
Names: Pineda, Erin R., author.
Title: Seeing like an activist : civil disobedience and the civil rights movement / Erin R. Pineda.
Other titles: Civil disobedience and the civil rights movement
Description: New York : Oxford University Press, 2021. |
Includes bibliographical references and index.
Identifiers: LCCN 2020043416 (print) | LCCN 2020043417 (ebook) |
ISBN 9780197526422 (hardback) | ISBN 9780197526439 (paperback) |
ISBN 9780197526453 (epub)
Subjects: LCSH: Civil rights movements—United States—Historiography. |
Critical race theory—United States. | Civil disobedience—United
States—Philosophy.
Classification: LCC E185.615 .P538 2021 (print) | LCC E185.615 (ebook) |
DDC 323.0973—dc23
LC record available at https://lccn.loc.gov/2020043416
LC ebook record available at https://lccn.loc.gov/2020043417

DOI: 10.1093/oso/9780197526422.001.0001

for R., obviously

come let us build a new world together

        Student Nonviolent Coordinating Committee Poster (1963)

Contents

Acknowledgments — ix

Introduction: Civil Disobedience and the Civil Rights Movement — 1

1. Seeing Like a White State — 22
2. An Entire World in Motion — 53
3. Incarceration as Liberation — 91
4. Forcing the Better Argument — 127
5. The Techniques of Disavowal — 159

   Epilogue: To Build a New World — 192

Notes — 203
Index — 255

Acknowledgments

During graduate school, I received two pieces of advice about writing a book. The first was that the process is circular, not linear. The second was that books are not written alone. It sounded right to me, but I couldn't fully appreciate what it meant. Now I do. This book is something quite distinct from the project that I started in 2012, and I could not have predicted then where it is now. I had to circle around to it. As for the second part, this book would not be a book at all but for the generosity and creativity of many others; it is a product of years of conversation and collaboration. Here, I would like to briefly express my gratitude to all the individuals whose ideas and friendship live between the lines of these pages, and whose guidance and input marked the circuits I traveled to get here.

The earliest version of this project was my dissertation, which benefited from the guidance, mentorship, and support of my committee members: Seyla Benhabib, Karuna Mantena, and Jim Scott. I thank Seyla for her incisive comments, keen insights, and challenging questions; and for being the kind of adviser who brings together a diverse set of graduate advisees. She gave us each space to do the kinds of political theory we wanted most to do and guided a truly dizzying array of projects, some of which fell far afield from her own substantial scholarly interests. Jim's unwavering enthusiasm for the animating theoretical and historical impulses behind this project, and his encyclopedic knowledge of an astounding range of subjects and texts was—in equal parts—inspiring, rewarding, and intimidating. My deepest thanks go to Karuna: her investment in my project, and its articulations with her own work on Gandhi, indelibly shaped the course of this work. It has been my enormous good fortune to have had the opportunity to work with and learn from her, and to have benefited from her unmatched combination of intellectual rigor and interpersonal generosity. She modeled for me the kind of adviser and mentor I hoped to become.

Beginning at Yale and in the years since I left, I have been lucky in the colleagues who have surrounded me. They have been generous readers, valuable interlocutors, and genuine friends: Umur Basdas, Alyssa Battistoni, Charles Decker, Carmen Dege, Stefan Eich, Blake Emerson, Lucas Entel,

Ted Fertik, Lisa Gilson, Devon Goure, Aaron Greenberg, Mie Inouye, Lizzie Krontiris, David Lebow, Matt Longo, Michelle Morgan, Tatianna Neumann, Shmulik Nili, Travis Pantin, Celia Paris, Kristin Plys, Hari Ramesh, Paul Linden-Retek, Brandon Terry, and Rory Truex. Adom Getachew and Anurag Sinha provided invaluable feedback and support—each suffering through multiple versions of my practice job talk, and reading many drafts of my chapters. Adom, in particular, modeled for me how to combine political theory and archival work, and how to transform a dissertation into a book. Anna Jurkevics, Michael Weaver, and Dawn Teele have been like family to me, and their own projects have left significant marks on mine. Additional thanks to other faculty in the Political Science and Sociology Departments who have shared their time and expertise with me at various points in this process, from the prospectus through a finished dissertation: Bryan Garsten, Phil Gorski, Hélène Landemore, Andrew March, Paulina Ochoa, Ian Shapiro, and Libby Wood.

My time at Yale and my understanding of direct action was shaped by my experiences being organized by—and learning to organize with—my colleagues and comrades at GESO/UNITE HERE 33. Their visions for a more just, equitable university—and for the promise of a revitalized, radicalized labor activism on campus and beyond—were energizing and challenging, and I was (and am) deeply humbled by their skill and depth of knowledge. I admit, much to my present-day embarrassment, that I was not always the most enthusiastic participant in these efforts, nor the easiest individual to organize. I am grateful that they never gave up on me and continued to welcome me in: Alyssa Battistoni, Charles Decker, Ted Fertik, Adom Getachew, Aaron Greenberg, and Gabe Winant.

Political theorists don't often receive training in archival work, and when asked, I often say that I had to teach myself. That's not quite true and fails to give credit to the archivists and library staff whose expertise and boundless patience helped me learn how to work in archival collections. In particular, I'd like to thank Tal Nadan at the New York Public Library, Alla Roylance at the Brooklyn Public Library, Andy McCarthy at the Brooklyn Historical Society's Othmer Library, Cynthia Lewis at the Martin Luther King Center for Nonviolent Social Change in Atlanta—who also showed me where to get the best fried fish sandwich in Sweet Auburn—and too many staff members, reference librarians, and archivists to name at the Schomburg Center for Research in Black Culture and the Beinecke Rare Books & Manuscripts Library. My trips to these locations involved more than just time in the libraries, and I am enormously grateful to those who made new cities feel like home. I owe a debt of gratitude, especially, to Derrick Jordan for opening his home to me in Atlanta, and to Nedra Deadwyler for her warmth and hospitality in the Old Fourth Ward.

This project might have ended up as something else entirely but for the two years I spent in the Center for the Study of Race, Politics, and Culture at the University of Chicago, and for the past three years at Smith College. The interdisciplinary space of the CSRPC was an incredible intellectual home, and I am so grateful to Dara Epison and Tracye Matthews for making room for me there, and for all their work in running the center and in making it such a vibrant place. I benefited immeasurably from conversations and support from faculty, graduate students, and postdoctoral fellows at Chicago, most especially Cathy Cohen, Alex Hastings, Annie Heffernan, Michael Dawson, Adom Getachew, Alfredo Gonzalez, Emily Katzenstein, Marcus Lee, Emma Stone MacKinnon, Patchen Markell, John McCormick, Tejas Parasher, Nazmul Sultan, Sylvia Zamora, and Linda Zerilli. I completed this project while settling in to a new position at Smith College, and I am grateful for my colleagues at Smith for helping me make this my home: Donald Baumer, Mlada Bukovansky, Pat Coby, Kim Dionne, Brent Durbin, Velma Garcia, Howard Gold, Alice Hearst, Steve Heydemann, Gary Lehring, Marc Lendler, Greg White, and Dennis Yasutomo. Velma has been a wonderful, supportive mentor from my very first days at Smith, and I am appreciative of her advocacy, encouragement, and no-nonsense advice. I am particularly grateful to my junior colleagues—Anna Mwaba, Boz Welborne, and Sara Newland—for the friendship and camaraderie extending out of many happy hours; to those who have supported and encouraged me from outside my department, particularly Lisa Armstrong, Patricia DiBartolo, Liz Pryor, and Kate Queeney; and to the community built through the Five College Seminar in Political Theory for challenging and thinking with me—Ali Aslam, Angelica Bernal, Joan Cocks, Barbara Cruikshank, Adam Dahl, Liz Markovitz, Rob Martin, Sam Ng, Mike Stein, and Anna Terweil. I continue to be thankful for the space and time to write at the gorgeous MacLeish Field Station in Whately, Massachusetts, and am thankful for Liz Klarich for organizing our retreats and to Paul Wetzel for generously allowing us to use it. Finally, I thank my students and advisees, especially those in my Spring 2020 seminar on Dissent, whose humor, earnestness, kept me motivated and kept me thinking, even as the world seemed to close in around us: Jassandre Berlus-Jacques, Dana Chen, Rose Hatem, Madeleine Hoecklin, Madeline McCurry, Annika Miller,

Taegan Mullane, Caitlyn Perrotta, Maddy Troilo, Anna Bethmann-Hollweg, Destiny Wiley-Yancy, and Anny Wysocki.

This book has benefited enormously from the opportunity to present parts of it, over the years, at numerous workshops, colloquia, and conferences: the Manchester Center for Political Theory Workshops; the Political Theory and Center for the Historical Enquiry & the Social Sciences workshops at Yale; UC Berkeley's Haas Institute for a Fair and Inclusive Society; the Globalizing Race Studies conference at Northwestern University; the UPenn Political Theory Workshop; the Political Theory and Reproduction of Race & Racial Ideologies Workshops at the University of Chicago; the Transformations of Civil Disobedience conference hosted at my alma mater, Barnard College; the colloquia series on Rethinking Civil Disobedience at Cornell University; the Five College Seminar in Political Theory; the Five College Program for Crossroads in the Study of the Americas; the conference on Seeing Beyond the Veil: Race-ing Key Concepts in Political Theory at Brown University; and the program on Philosophy, Politics, and Economics at Northeastern University. At a few of these events, a single interaction with a fellow panelist, discussant, or audience member made all the difference: Anne Norton asked me a question in 2016 that I could not answer convincingly; and wrestling with that troubling fact prompted me to write Chapter 2 and rethink the entire argument (for the better, I hope). Conversations with Joel Schlosser and Robert Vitalis enabled me to dig in to the argument in Chapter 1; and a brief exchange with Bonnie Honig helped me find my way to a title. Across the years, generous funding from Yale University, the Beinecke Rare Books & Manuscripts Library, the Provost's Career Enhancement Postdoctoral Fellowship at the University of Chicago, and the Picker Fellowship at Smith College enabled me to see this project through each stage of research and writing.

Books, as it turns out, really are collective enterprises, and this one took shape thanks to years of exchange with a number of others writing and thinking about civil disobedience, political action, and race and politics, including: Lawrie Balfour, Alyssa Battistoni, Robin Celikates, Çiğdem Çidam, Cathy Cohen, Michael Dawson, Candice Delmas, Jason Frank, Adom Getachew, Lisa Gilson, Alex Gourevitch, Laura Grattan, Barnor Hesse, Juliet Hooker, Mie Inouye, Jane Junn, Jennet Kirkpatrick, Ainsley LeSure, Alex Livingston, Daniel Markovits, Karuna Mantena, Patchen Markell, Julie Lee Merseth, Charles Mills, Thea Riofrancos, Melvin Rogers, Bill Scheuerman, Brandon Terry, Al Tillery, and Deva Woodly. I am indebted, especially, to

Ali Aslam and Lida Maxwell, who served as reviewers for Oxford University Press, as well as two anonymous reviewers for Cambridge University Press. They provided detailed and enormously constructive criticism of the final versions of this manuscript; I'm not sure I would have been able to fully articulate what I wanted to say without first seeing my argument through their eyes.

I thank my editor, Angela Chnapko, for her enthusiasm for and commitment to this project; and Vanessa Tyson, for her advocacy and for introducing me to Angela. The production team at Oxford University Press brought this book across the finish line and guided me, with generosity and expertise, through the process. I finished revisions of this manuscript in the midst of the COVID-19 pandemic; I am thankful to those who fielded last-minute emails from a stranger and responded with kindness during those dark weeks—especially Brian Purnell, who shared the wealth of his own intellectual labor with me in the form of many interview transcripts. Finally, I thank University of Illinois Press for allowing me to reprint material from my 2015 article, "Civil Disobedience and Punishment: (Mis)reading Justification and Strategy from SNCC to Snowden" as part of Chapter 3; and the estate of Jack Whitten for allowing the use of his marvelous painting "Birmingham (1964)" on the cover.

The love of my extended family—especially my parents, Charlie and Claire; my siblings, Lauren and Simon; and their partners and children, Jessie, Mathilde, Jeff, Asher, and Mae—has enabled this entire enterprise, from the early and uncertain days of graduate school to the present. My in-laws, too, have been unfailingly kind and supportive and have always welcomed me into their family: Candy, Larry, Jordan, Angie, Max, and Tilly. At all stages of this process, I always knew I could rely on their affection and support. For that, I will be forever grateful. A special word of thanks goes to Marissa Nicosia, who is not family in any official sense, but *is* and has long been family in a real sense, for years spent as a fellow-traveler—and for her wisdom, advice, and exceptional sense of humor. Finally, I cannot express enough thanks to Ryan Ourada, my partner and best friend, whose intellectual curiosity and creativity daily put me to shame and keep me honest. (He also supplied expert copy-editing for almost all of this manuscript; if this book finds its way into readers' hands a little bit easier to read, it is thanks to his efforts.) Ryan believed in this undertaking even when I thought its prospects looked grim and uncertain—and reminded me, whenever I grew to doubt it, why this project matters to me. I dedicate what follows to him.

Introduction

Civil Disobedience and the Civil Rights Movement

In popular American discourse, the civil rights movement operates not merely as a powerful example of civil disobedience but also as the horizon of judgment for *all* civil disobedience—one that is constantly receding and impossible to meet. In the 1980s, when anti-abortion activists prayed outside health clinics and "went limp" upon arrest, forcing police to drag them from the scene, some asked whether they were practicing the kind of humility required of the civilly disobedient—the kind of humility displayed by the sit-in campaigns of 1960, in which protestors went cheerfully to jail.[1] The 1999 protests at the World Trade Organization in Seattle seemed too angry, too uncivil, too unwilling to embrace nonviolence for more than tactical reasons to live up to the proud tradition of American civil disobedience most iconically represented by the struggle for civil rights.[2] When, in 2011, the Occupy Wall Street movement took over New York City's Zuccotti Park—and subsequently spread to cities all over the country—the actions of occupiers were judged according to the standard set fifty years prior, by civil rights activists in Montgomery, Greensboro, Jackson, Birmingham, and Selma.[3] Despite rather apparent disanalogies between the mass mobilization of thousands of civil rights activists and a singular act of whistleblowing, when Edward Snowden leaked classified National Security Administration documents in the summer of 2013, his decision to flee the country for exile was measured—and found wanting—according to the terms of Martin Luther King, Jr.'s "Letter from a Birmingham Jail."[4] And so it felt all but inevitable, after protests erupted in the wake of the murders of Trayvon Martin, Michael Brown, and Freddie Gray, that commentators across the political spectrum would come to chastise the emerging Movement for Black Lives for stepping beyond the boundaries of decorum supposedly laid down by their civil rights movement predecessors. Swift criticism from the right was perhaps to be expected—the idea of the nascent movement as nonviolent at all was roundly mocked on *Brietbart*, and presidential hopeful Mike Huckabee spared no time in proclaiming the tactics appalling and out of step with King's legacy (as if he were a credible spokesperson for, or guardian of, that legacy). But there were plenty on the left, too, including veterans of the 1960s movement, who saw things in similar terms: Black Lives Matter was, according to at least one former activist, a "divisive," "confrontational" and altogether unrespectable movement that blatantly rejected or "ignored" the history of civil rights activism based in "love and unity."[5] As Jeanne Theoharis has remarked, by the turn of the twenty-first century, invoking the civil rights movement to discipline new movements had become an American past-time—"a clever suit to assert one's enlightened bona fides. It crossed party and ideology. Simply everyone was doing it."[6]

What is most striking about these linkages, and the way they circulate through the American public sphere and through the halls of political power, is their sheer *obviousness*—that is, the pervasive presumption that civil disobedience is distilled in a single example that we call "the civil rights movement"; that we already know what this example means and contains; and that this singular example applies directly to all cases of activism, no matter how different the contexts, aims, and tactical forms. It is an object lesson offering clear moral imperatives, and no one fares very well standing next to it.

The "civil rights movement," in these narratives, refers not to a complex decades-long assemblage of *movements*, but to a movement in the singular, defined by a clear trajectory from denial to fulfillment, from the aberrant national sin of racial segregation to its ultimate redemption and peaceful overcoming. As President Obama put it on the fiftieth anniversary of the 1963 March on Washington, "blacks who longed for freedom and whites who could no longer accept freedom for themselves while witnessing the subjection of others" came together "to awaken America's long-slumbering conscience":

> In the face of hatred, they prayed for their tormentors. In the face of violence, they stood up and sat in, with the moral force of nonviolence. Willingly, they went to jail to protest unjust laws, their cells swelling with the sound of freedom songs. . . . Through setbacks and heartbreaks and gnawing doubt, that flame of justice flickered; it never died. And because they kept marching, America changed.[7]

Two years later, standing on the site of the 1965 "Bloody Sunday" march across the Edmund Pettus Bridge in Selma, Alabama, and speaking amidst growing public protests over police brutality, Obama affirmed the events at Selma and the sweep of the civil rights movement as "the manifestation of a creed written into our founding documents"—a struggle to "remake this nation to more closely align with our highest ideals."[8]

This narrative—which charts the course from the nonviolent, moral civility of black protestors through an appeal to the majority's conscience, and ultimately to concrete social change—proves the efficacy, the moral force, of civil disobedience, even in the entrenched and brutal conditions of the Jim Crow South. Protestors went willingly to jail; they refrained from violence and oriented themselves toward brotherhood and understanding; they spoke in rhyme with "self-evident" American truths, of liberty and justice for all. They were dissenters, but perfectly *domestic* and *domesticated* ones; they challenged not the American state or systemic white supremacy, but a simple failure of American citizens to live up to the best version of themselves, awakening conscience to truths that were always already there, though slumbering deeply. They were paradigmatically *civilly disobedient*.

If, as Jacquelyn Dowd Hall reminds us, "remembrance is always a form of forgetting," there is much about the history of the civil rights movement, as an enacted and lived struggle, that is obscured by this account—that is displaced by its obviousness.[9] Yet insofar as the civil rights movement provides a crucial motivating example for political and philosophical intuitions about what civil disobedience must be, the standard cultural narrative of the movement does more than misremember history; it also distorts our political judgments about how civil disobedience might fit into democratic politics more generally, in the political present and beyond. As revealed by the myriad contemporary references to King and civil rights in the midst of other protest campaigns, the moral boundaries of legitimate dissent are continually assessed and debated in terms set by shared understandings of exemplary protest during the sit-ins, the Freedom Rides, and the iconic confrontations in the streets of Birmingham and Selma. This "official reading" of civil rights disobedience is not merely inaccurate; as Candice Delmas has recently articulated, it "also functions, thanks in part to this inaccuracy, as a counter-resistance ideology."[10] The intuition at the heart of this book is that there is therefore something crucial to be gained for our political and philosophical thinking about civil disobedience by re-examining its emergence within the civil rights movement—that is, by reconsidering the example we already think we know so well.

Indeed, as I will argue, the recurrence of the civil rights movement as disciplining example and moral exemplar amid debates over civil disobedience is neither accidental nor random. The iconic, disobedient activism of the movement was in fact deeply influential in the formation of predominant ideas about civil disobedience, both within academic philosophy and in public discourse. *Seeing Like an Activist* charts the emergence of mainstream theories of civil disobedience in the midst of 1960s debates over law, order, and the limits of racial justice, and demonstrates their entanglement with and reliance on a stylized, politically expedient narrative about the civil rights movement in which black civility triggered white empathy and ultimately legal redress. This nascent understanding of civil rights protest shaped the normative contours of the concept of civil disobedience and generated an increasingly solidified script for action: civilly disobedient protestors must appeal to constitutional principles recognized by the majority, submit to legal punishment, and use persuasive rather than coercive means, all of which are meant to signal acceptance of the system's legitimacy. In this way, philosophers of civil disobedience saw the subjects of their analysis *like a white state*: taking for granted the legitimacy of the constitutional order, assuming as primary the ends of constitutional integrity and stability, centering the white citizen as the normative ideal, and figuring the problem of racial injustice as limited, exceptional, and all-but-already solved. Seeing civil disobedience from this perspective, I contend, has significant consequences not only for how the example of civil rights disobedience is read and interpreted—shaping the questions we believe activists are posing, and the answers we find in their words and deeds—but also our expectations for how civil disobedience ought to unfold in the present.

Seeing Like an Activist responds by reinterpreting the forms of action, strategic decisions, and ethical claims posed by the enactment of civil rights disobedience in the 1950s and 1960s as generative sites of political theorizing—ones that suggest different analyses of the problem of racial injustice; that pose contrasting accounts of how disobedient action responds to and redresses the problem; and that raise different dilemmas about the possibilities for persuasion, the uses of coercion and disruption, and the limits of disobedient activism. Building on archival and historical research, this book details how civil rights activists devised strategies of mass jailing, civil disruption, and crisis-generation to exercise novel forms of agency, disclose the nature of systemic injustices, dispute settled norms, and destabilize the bases of state legitimacy. From the students at the forefront of the 1961 "jail, no bail" campaign to the citizens of Birmingham mobilized by the Southern Christian Leadership Conference and the Alabama Christian Movement for Human Rights, activists experimented with tactics that embodied principles of self-liberation, multiplied protest across new arenas, complicated easy understandings of what "nonviolence" looks like, jeopardized the smooth functioning of institutions both local and national, and grappled with the problem of how to transform the moral perspective of white citizens—whose intuitions about civility, responsibility, justice, equality, and order had been forged within the crucible of white supremacy. In so doing, activists devised accounts of the problem of racial injustice utterly at odds with the one operating between the lines of mainstream analyses of civil disobedience. Recovering this alternative perspective on civil rights disobedience as substantive political theory both reveals the racially marked assumptions that structure mainstream civil disobedience theory and recuperates the "short" civil rights movement—the nonviolent direct action movement between the years of *Brown v. Board of Education* and the Selma campaign—as a surprising resource for radical critique and disruptive, disobedient action.

In what follows, I provide a brief overview of the literatures on civil disobedience—old and new—tracing the way that the debate has shifted since the mid-century (moving from a decidedly liberal framework to various democratic ones) as well as broadened (bringing attention to new movements and forms of action). As I show, however, and despite the important insights generated out of what Guy Aitchison has characterized as the "new civil disobedience debate," the civil rights example remains at once *central* and *marginal*—operating as a key proving ground for the political purchase of liberal and deliberative theories but also attesting to their limits, without making the movement itself the subject of sustained analysis or theoretical interest.[11] In many ways, the new literature on civil disobedience makes a compelling and convincing case for moving beyond the civil rights example; yet it often does so without first asking if we have really understood the example, and the historical, theoretical, and political stakes of its entanglement with the liberal theory that claims to describe it.

Civil Disobedience Theory and the Civil Rights Movement

Although the subject of civil disobedience has long generated discussion and disagreement, out of the 1960s and 1970s emerged a remarkably durable academic and popular consensus over the basic forms of action that define civil disobedience—a consensus evident in the influential work of John Rawls, Hugo Bedau, Peter Singer, and Michael Walzer and echoed in the uptake of civil disobedience by deliberative democrats in the 1980s and 1990s, notably Jürgen Habermas. By these accounts, civil disobedience, despite its hallmark defiance of particular laws, is distinguished from ordinary criminal lawbreaking, on the one hand, and full-scale rebellion, on the other hand, by its commitment to a certain kind of "civility."[12] By engaging in actions that are at once public, nonviolent, conscientious, and limited, protestors draw public attention to unjust laws, discriminatory policies, or pervasive rights violations, while expressing their desire to remain, as Rawls phrases it, "within the limits of fidelity to the law."[13] Protestors, therefore, must conform to a particular code of conduct: they must submit willingly—some say "eagerly"—to legal punishment, use persuasive rather than coercive means, and phrase their appeal in terms of core principles affirmed by a majority of their fellow citizens. In so doing, those who undertake civil disobedience express their commitment and sincerity, reveal the common values animating their actions, and signal their acceptance of the system's underlying legitimacy—thus staging a compelling appeal to the majority's conscience. For the civilly disobedient citizen, the basic architecture of the constitutional order is presumed legitimate and commands respect, despite the serious rights violations or persistent injustices that motivate and justify protest. Civil disobedience thus provides a crucial mechanism for change but also ensures its limit.

As Chapter 1 demonstrates, the apparent narrowness of this understanding of civil disobedience is intentional; it is the product of its particular political context. Writing, by and large, in the midst of two decades of intense social, political, and cultural upheaval, liberal political and legal theorists like Rawls, intent on defending the civil disobedience of the civil rights and antiwar movements, nevertheless had to answer the claim of critics that lawbreaking, no matter how conscientious, was directly tied to a general degradation of the state's authority that would lead to violence, criminality, and anarchy. Hundreds of urban riots in cities nationwide, scores of uprisings and clashes on college campuses, and unrepentant segregationist mobs spurred on by officially sanctioned "massive resistance" seemed proof enough that civil disobedience was dangerous, and opened the door to violence. In response to those who charged civil disobedience with instigating widespread lawlessness and disorder, its defenders argued that civil disobedience is in fact self-limiting, remaining within the law even while breaking it. While the fact of public lawbreaking signals the radical nature of the protestor's intervention, the way in which that lawbreaking is undertaken—as nonviolent, noncoercive, persuasive, and oriented toward common, constitutional principles—ensures that it remain governed by the impulses of public reason and the norms of citizenly conduct within the constitutional democratic state. The civil rights movement, and principally, the arguments within King's "Letter from a Birmingham Jail," often proved to be the crucial case in point here.

Although the Rawlsian account continues to resonate in popular discourse, a variety of democratic theorists have more recently taken issue with the restrictive nature of the liberal theory of civil disobedience. In particular, deliberative democrats and neorepublican theorists have challenged the idea that disobedience is only justified when basic rights and liberties are violated, drawing attention to the problems of democratic processes that can become the legitimate target of disobedient action. Though otherwise echoing the core features of liberal, Rawlsian civil disobedience, in an influential 1985 essay, Jürgen Habermas argued that there may be situations in which bare parliamentary majorities serve as an insufficient basis for legitimate, democratic decision-making. Commenting on protests in response to the installation of Pershing II missiles in Germany, Habermas—quoting constitutional jurist Helmut Simon—raised the following questions: "'Does the principle of simple majorities (outside the realm of inalienable rights) really *always* suffice? Is it also adequate for momentous decisions of an irreversible nature, i.e., for those which can no longer simply be revoked after a shift of majority opinion and which could have deadly consequences for everyone if they are wrong?'"[14] In such situations, then, ordinary citizens—acting in their "plebiscitary" and sovereign function, may need recourse to civil disobedience as a means of last resort to intervene in decisions with a crucial legitimacy deficit, even where "the kind of injustice against which Martin Luther King and the American Civil Rights movement took action" is not at stake—"i.e., of the obvious violation of civil rights."[15]

More recently, extending and deepening Habermas's important insight, William Smith and Daniel Markovits have both compellingly argued for theorizing civil disobedience in specifically democratic (rather than liberal) terms. Markovits attends to the republican principle of popular sovereignty, requiring that citizens act as the collective authors of the laws and decisions that bind them, by participating in modes of "democratic engagement" beyond the simple aggregation of individual votes. In contrast to the liberal theory of civil disobedience—espoused by Rawls and epitomized by the civil rights movement—"democratic disobedience" arises in the face of political decisions that cannot be meaningfully recognized by citizens as the product of their own wills. Such decisions run "democratic deficits": they are the products of special interest and lobbying influence, or they are bogged down in institutional processes that render them ineffective, inattentive, or out of step with addressing the political problems that necessitated them in the first place.[16] Similarly, though in deliberative rather than republican terms, Smith views civil disobedience as responding to deliberative failure—"a means of contesting discursive blockages that inhibit the proper functioning of the *public sphere* in a deliberative democracy." On this reading, disobedience "can be justified as part of a broader campaign to publicize urgent and important agendas—or 'discourses'—that receive insufficient consideration in the public sphere due to the pervasive effects of *deliberative inertia*."[17]

While broadening the potential sites for disobedience and reinterpreting civil disobedience beyond the bounds of a liberal theory of political obligation, these deliberative and republican interventions nevertheless hew closely to the standards for comportment required for civil disobedience by their liberal predecessors. On the deliberative reading, protest and disobedience may arise under conditions of deliberative failure, but they remain in many ways subject to deliberative standards of discourse; they operate not *outside* deliberative democracy but as important mechanisms of it. As with other forms of deliberative communication, civil disobedience and social protest must act, to cite Smith's formulation, "in such a way that they respect the principles of public deliberation, in particular that deliberation is geared in the first instance towards reason-giving and persuasion, only in the final instance towards strategic compromise, and never towards coercion."[18] The civilly disobedient are thus understood as communicative collective actors, whose primary purpose is to publicize grievances and persuade "the state to engage in deliberative uptake."[19] Though a particular act of civil disobedience—a sit-in or a march—may be spectacular or disruptive, it operates through the same mechanism as more traditionally dialogic deliberation, which is to say, persuasion and the "unforced force of the better argument."[20] For his part, though not adopting the language of deliberation, Markovits similarly circumscribes the boundaries of "democratic disobedience," providing familiar—though meaningfully reinterpreted—standards for non-coercion, nonviolence, and an orientation toward communicative persuasion.

Yet communication need not be nonviolent, nonconfrontational, or particularly civil—and there are good reasons to theorize disobedience beyond these bounds. Occupy Wall Street, digital "hacktivism" by groups like Anonymous, anti- and alter-globalization movements, transnational environmental activism—these contemporary movements are neither motivated by the moral-political language of liberal constitutionalism nor willing to remain within the parameters of respectful deliberative engagement. In response, some scholars have taken a more radically inclusive approach to theorizing civil disobedience's democratic dimensions—critiquing the inability of existing liberal and deliberative theories to address the dynamics of protests that do not seem to follow the script provided by paradigmatic civil rights mobilizations from Montgomery to Selma.[21] Like Smith, Kimberley Brownlee conceives of civil disobedience in communicative and conscientious terms; in contrast to the deliberative account, however, she insists that the dialogic interaction between protestors and the state inaugurated by civil disobedience may not require—or be best served by—standard presumptions in favor of nonviolence or accepting legal punishment.[22] Relatedly, in an important set of articles, Robin Celikates has disputed the liberal approach to disobedience by pointing to the way that calls for civility, reasonableness, rationality, and nonviolence can function in a restrictive, ideological, and disciplining fashion. In his view, the liberal account neither captures seemingly easy cases like the civil rights movement nor more contemporary movements in the face of "the crises-ridden globalization of neoliberal political and economic power structures, the rise of the Internet both as a tool of political action and as a politically contested space, and the troubled resurgence of radical opposition to the status quo, for example, in the form of the Occupy movement."[23] Such movements, Celikates contends, force us to see the widely accepted, liberal definition of civil disobedience— a public appeal to the morality of the majority, expressing fidelity to the law through nonviolence and acceptance of punishment—as politically constructed and inherently contested (and therefore, neither *definitive* nor obvious). Instead, Celikates offers a more stripped down definition, one that "leaves open whether civil disobedience is public, nonviolent, conscientious, appealing to the majority's sense of justice, and restricted to transforming the system within its existing limits."[24] Thus, as for Brownlee, civil disobedience could plausibly include more militant, violent forms of action than are usually associated with the term.

Expanding the scope of what can count as civil disobedience is only one way of moving beyond the liberal paradigm, to account for—and do justice to—contemporary movements that eschew civility or acceptance of punishment as binding normative standards, powerful modes of communication, or effective means. Candice Delmas takes the inverse approach: opting for a relatively constrained, broadly liberal interpretation of *civil* disobedience, while making the case that specifically *uncivil* forms of disobedience are not only potentially justifiable but, under some conditions, are also morally required. The civil disobedience that characterized the civil rights movement—action that is illegal but public, non-evasive, nonviolent, and decorous—has its place in the spectrum of resistance; but it is not all there is. Indeed, on Delmas's account, owing to the strictures of decorum—which requires that "citizens who want to enter the public sphere ought to behave in a dignified and polite manner and avoid causing offense"—civil disobedience may be inappropriate, ineffective, or impossible in many situations of peril, violence, exploitation, or injustice.[25] In a different register and to different effect, Bernard Harcourt's argument for the category of "political disobedience" deploys a similar strategy—putting civil disobedience in its place in order to make space for newer, more radical alternatives. Whereas civil disobedience "accepts the legitimacy of the political structure and of our political institutions" while resisting "the moral authority of the resulting laws," Harcourt writes that political disobedience "resists the very way in which we are governed. . . . It rejects the very idea of expressing or honoring 'the highest respect for law.' It refuses to willingly accept the sanctions meted out by our legal and political system. It challenges the conventional way in which political governance takes place and laws are enforced. It turns back on the political institutions and actors who govern us. And, beyond that, it resists the very ideologies that have dominated the postwar period." The paradigmatic case of civil disobedience is the familiar terrain of King's "Letter" and the civil rights movement, while Occupy Wall Street provokes Harcourt's thinking about the political disobedience that defies this logic.[26]

It is instructive to track how the civil rights example moves in and out of these more recent accounts—operating sometimes as the example that undercuts the liberal theory's utility and plausibility, while at other times serving as the crucial illustration in favor of it. In Celikates's critique of Rawls, he effectively—and quite artfully—returns again and again to the civil rights example to demonstrate how out of step with political practice the Rawlsian theory is. Echoing David Lyons's insightful analysis of the ways that liberal disobedience theory systematically mischaracterizes the historical claims of its most celebrated practitioner-theorists—Henry David Thoreau, M. K. Gandhi, and Martin Luther King, Jr.—Celikates systematically undermines the definitional and justificatory underpinnings of Rawls's theory by wielding the example that Rawls seems best equipped to theorize.[27] In contrast, many others—Markovits, Harcourt, and Delmas among them—deploy the civil rights example to fix intuitions about what a classic case of civil disobedience looks like. Here, the emphasis is on showing how King's ideas or the activities of the movement are cognizable in liberal or Rawlsian terms, thereby clearing the way for an analysis of movements and actions that the standard conception cannot so easily contain: "The civil rights movement," Markovits contends, "represented the heyday of liberal disobedience. In the subsequent years, the most prominent cases of political disobedience have increasingly not emphasized liberal rights to equal treatment or to basic liberties." The shift from liberal disobedience began in the late 1960s with the antiwar movement; its trajectory runs through the antinuclear campaigns and ultimately through "the most prominent cases of political disobedience in the United States and Europe today, which arise in connection with protests against globalization." It is such cases, Markovits concludes, those that "cannot be fit into the liberal model—which represent the future of political disobedience."[28]

The new literature on disobedience—civil and uncivil; liberal, democratic, and political—has, over the past decade, broken new ground in analyzing an enormous range of movements and actions, while reinvigorating a debate over civil disobedience that had gone stale (or largely silent). Yet the apparent flexibility—and ubiquity—of the civil rights example within these accounts ought to give us pause. The circulation of the civil rights example in this way is evidence of questions not yet fully asked or answered; it points to a problematic tendency for theorists to use the civil rights movement as an argumentative device or object lesson—a means of clearing ground or fixing ideas about existing bodies of theory—rather than a generative source of theoretical insight. This pattern of symbolic centrality alongside "intellectual marginalization," as Brandon Terry and Tommie Shelby have argued, places civil rights activists in a secondary role as tacticians or symbols—demonstrations in the service of someone else's theory, struggling to fulfill already extant ideals—rather than centering them as primary producers of political thought.[29] What seems clear, from Rawls through the present, is that there is an important relationship between theorizing civil disobedience and thinking through the civil rights movement—but the nature of that relationship remains unexplored. Why do we return, again and again, to King's "Letter," to the student sit-ins and Freedom Rides, to Birmingham and Selma, as a means of unsettling or solidifying our thinking about civil disobedience? How does that practice of theorizing relate, in turn, to the political theorizing—"thinking in the streets"—undertaken by civil rights activists themselves?[30] These are the principle questions that motivate the book that follows.

The Long and Short of It

The theoretical framework of this project and its historical research is deeply indebted to recent work on the histories of the "long," "local," and "Northern" civil rights movements, as well as to critical race theorists, who have challenged the tidy consensus around civil rights on its historical merits and for its political, legal, and ideological implications. The prevailing narrative of the civil rights movement—the narrative "distilled from history and memory, twisted by ideology and political contestation, and embedded in heritage tours, museums, public rituals, textbooks, and various artifacts of mass culture," as Jacquelyn Dowd Hall writes—has obscured a history of radical activism with its origins in the 1930s. In 2005, Hall issued an agenda-setting plea for a shifted perspective—a longer view of the civil rights movement that could do justice to the bold, progressive potential of this earlier moment, while making the civil rights movement as a whole "harder to cast as a satisfying morality tale" and "harder to simplify, appropriate, and contain."[31] Taking up her challenge (as well as those of others), a generation of historians has redefined the time, space, and scale of what we mean by "the civil rights movement": stretching its temporal bounds to encompass the 1930s through the 1970s; displacing the locus of activity from the South to cities of the North, industrial Midwest, and West; changing scale downward from national organizations to local organizing and activism, or upward from a domestic project of constitutional reform to a transnational struggle against white supremacy and global capitalism. They have also reworked the narrative arc from a romantic, victorious legal battle for rights into the tragedy of a capacious, unfinished project for liberation and racial justice.[32]

Taken together, these altered perspectives lay bare the limitations of viewing the "short" civil rights movement in isolation, outside of its own more expansive and contested history, geography, and ideational constellation. From the standpoint of earlier decades of activism, the legal victories of the mid-1960s appear more partial and less definitive; viewed from urban struggles outside the South, or from within the horizon of a transnational anticolonial movement, the problem of Jim Crow rule appears at once more specific and less regionally confined. In particular, scholars of the long movement have revealed the ideological skew of the prevailing narrative—its reliance on ideas of a backward South in an otherwise exceptional nation; its depiction of a well-known cast of characters who sang and held hands, limiting their efforts to inclusion and formal rights, while eschewing radical critiques of capitalism and colonialism—as well as its disciplinary power. This narrative of the civil rights movement is not a simple matter; it is not mere misremembering, but a complex reimagining of the past to suit different political objectives and needs—one that cuts both ways, legitimizing the activism of the civil rights years (narrowly understood) while simultaneously taming its implications, universalizing its meaning while draining its contemporary relevance. Read as a movement that triumphed over a Jim Crow order of legalized segregation that has by definition ended, "*the* civil rights movement" is of little relevance in an era of putatively color-blind law, "de facto" segregation, and racial exploitation produced by and naturalized as the workings of "the market." Viewed as a movement that remained carefully and civilly within the bounds of prevailing values, norms, and modes of comportment, the forms of protest underwritten by the official memorialization of civil rights offer a fundamentally nonreplicable standard for activism—appearing to legitimize dissent while insisting that *these* protestors are never as well-behaved as we know they ought to be, as we know civil rights protestors always were. In short, as Hall argued, the consensus narrative can stand in the way of locating within the civil rights movement a "useable past"—preventing "one of the most remarkable mass movements in American history from speaking effectively to the challenges of our time."[33]

However, despite the critical resources that I draw from this work, my focus in this book remains on events and actions well within the bounds of the "classical phase" of the civil rights movement. In most chapters, I train my attention on episodes and figures so familiar and canonical as to appear in need of no further attention—the student sit-ins, the Freedom Rides, the Birmingham campaign, the writings of Martin Luther King, Jr. In working through this material, I want to insist—alongside others—that there is more to be gained from retracing these well-traveled roads than is encapsulated within the consensus narrative. Indeed, within some work in the "long civil rights" paradigm, there is a tendency (often implicit, sometimes explicit) to treat the activism of the "short" civil rights movement as something of a wrong turn—or simply as the residue of an earlier, more radical phase, cut short by the imperatives of an increasingly paranoid and dogmatic nationalism. Hemmed in by Cold War conventionalisms, cut off from radical predecessors, and dominated by a middle-class politics of respectability, in some accounts the civil rights movement of this short period comes fairly close to fulfilling the expectations set for it by the consensus narrative. For some, it seems, recovering the radical nature of civil rights critique and civil rights activism means putting this era in its place as a "casualty" of McCarthyite politics and narrow geopolitical considerations—displacing its importance and exemplarity in favor of a different era of "civil rights unionism" and cross-racial labor organizing.[34] The upshot here is that pushing beyond anodyne, feel-good truisms about integration—and confronting less anodyne, cynical appeals to color-blindness and post-raciality—requires dismissing the activism of integrationism that supposedly dominated the late 1950s and early 1960s, with its focus on civility, mainstream values, and civic belonging, in order to seek more promising but forgotten alternatives elsewhere.[35] Civil disobedience, as the most prominent vehicle for this activism, becomes likewise suspect—constraining, contained, and moribund.

The tendency, then, is to conflate the ideological and triumphalist appropriation of the "short" movement with the movement's own political claims—losing "the opportunity to retrieve crucial resources for a resurgent emancipatory politics" from within them.[36] As Thomas Holt has argued, this view is undergirded by a set of assumptions about the movement's focus ("the integration of public accommodations and civic belonging") and its impact (a "disastrous wrong turn" that failed to meaningfully challenge the sociopolitical order of Jim Crow, despite a successful drive for legal reform). Together, these assumptions "[misread] the significance of what did happen as well as what was possible in the populous core of the black South." Far from being narrow—let alone fully contained within middle class, consumerist, or nationalist ideologies—Holt contends that the "antiracist strategy [of the 'short' civil rights movement] was impressively multifaceted, its foci embracing labor, job discrimination, voter registration, and cross-racial political alliances, as well as the newly relevant targets of segregated public accommodations, which the massive war-time and postwar growth of black populations in southern cities made flashpoints of contention."[37] Embedded within this multifaceted strategy, and as part of a wider—indeed, global— conversation about the expanse of racial hierarchy and the power of political action to transform it, civil disobedience at the lunch counter, at bus depots, or outside storefronts no longer appears as an obviously limited means of demanding entry to an existing consumer society, an already legitimate democratic order.

This project, then, attempts to confront the consensus narrative where it lives: in the years between Montgomery and Selma, and within the campaigns devised by a predominantly Southern movement making creative use of nonviolent direct action and civil disobedience. To be sure, the choice of the "short" civil rights movement as my case material is one driven by practicality as much as by concept and argument: the early to mid-1960s, after all, represented the high-water mark of civil rights disobedience. Yet as suggested by the myriad contemporary references to King and the civil rights movement in the midst of other protest campaigns, the boundaries of dissent are continually assessed and debated in terms set by shared understandings of exemplary protest during the sit-ins, the Freedom Rides, and the Birmingham campaign. *Seeing Like an Activist* revisits these protest campaigns of the early 1960s with careful attention to the ways civil rights activists constructed the problem of white supremacy; devised strategies for effective action; and challenged the meaning of democracy, equality, freedom, and citizenship. Specifically, this book examines how activists explored the connections between theory and action: civil disobedience expressed activists' understanding of how racial domination was produced and maintained, and at the same time offered a practice for remaking those oppressive structures, subjectivities, and relations. In this, the disagreements between individual organizers over the scale and nature of the problem and the best methods for protest—ethically and strategically—emerge not as questions about the boundaries of legitimate lawbreaking but as part of an ongoing, contested discourse about how to build a new world. Focusing on this material and the handful of years that seem so familiar reveals not just that the "short" civil rights movement contains more substance (and is, perhaps, less familiar) than the consensus narrative suggests. Doing so also makes plain the conditions under which this narrative was generated—and made both plausible and popular—in the first place.

Theorizing Disobedience in the Streets

How can we see civil disobedience—and with it, the activism of the "short" civil rights movement—differently? I suggest we start with the words and deeds of the activists themselves: those theorizing disobedience out loud, out of doors, and in the streets. If the operative framework for civil disobedience in academic philosophy is one of race-neutral moral justification—*Under what conditions can citizens justify breaking the law in protest? What are the obligations citizens owe to the state and to other citizens?*—the questions that emerge from the civil rights disobedience in the streets are consummately race-relational, political ones, attuned to the particularities of democratic life within a racial order: *How does white supremacy function, and how is it maintained? What kinds of action can dismantle it? What kinds of action can build a radically democratic, multiracial order? What are the dilemmas and costs of activism in a racist society that also understands itself to be a democratic one— and who bears those costs?*[38]

Building on archival and historical research, this book details how civil rights activists—in concert with anticolonial activists across the globe— constructed civil disobedience as a *decolonizing praxis*. Constructing white supremacy as a global structure of domination that linked colonial rule to "domestic" segregation and racism, activists across a world in motion theorized and deployed civil disobedience as a practice of self-liberation that could disclose the profound reach of racial hierarchy, disrupt the practices that maintain and reproduce it, and transform relations premised on domination into the bonds of multiracial, democratic citizenship. Put to use as disobedience in the streets, activists' decolonizing praxis resisted the separation of ethics from tactics—drawing together an *inward-facing* politics of self-making (liberating oneself through fearless action, and refusing the performance of submission demanded by racial domination) with *outward-facing* uses of disclosive, disruptive, coercive, and persuasive power to transform structures and relations with white citizens—to "turn [democracy] up side down and right side up," as Martin Luther King, Jr. once remarked.[39] These *inward-facing* and *outward-facing* purposes were inextricably linked. The disruption of the everyday ordinary of racial hierarchy, which required the use of coercive power and the making of persuasive political claims, was also simultaneously the means of enacting self-emancipation. Likewise, the dramatic work of protest—staging public confrontations to reveal the scale and nature of racial injustice—was also necessarily an invitation to white citizens to reconsider their own ethical commitments and obligations to others—and thus, to turn inward and be transformed through action. In this way, the decolonizing praxis of civil disobedience was meant to undermine the conditions that enabled white supremacy and constitutional democracy to coexist. By exposing the violence that underpins every racial order, civil disobedience could unsettle the frames and imaginaries that enable citizens to see their society as a nearly just one—not a racial order at all, but a legitimate constitutional democracy, in which segregation is a domestic problem of imperfect implementation; an important but remediable exception.

Reading civil disobedience as a decolonizing praxis offers a direct challenge to modes of political theorizing that participate in the production—and justification—of these frames and imaginaries. This is also the problem at the heart of the relationship between theorizing civil disobedience and mobilizing the civil rights example. Even while drawing on the civil rights movement, some of the most influential theorists of disobedience (Rawls chief among them) routinely evaded sustained engagement with the racial order—*qua* racial order—within and against which black activists mobilized. This decontextualizing maneuver, as Kimberlé Crenshaw and Gary Peller suggest, performs ideological work, as an insistence on "formal legal equality—[on] the objectivity of 'the rule of law' " helps "obscure the everyday character of racial power."[40] In theories of civil disobedience, the imposition of a race-neutral framework of political obligation presupposes the achievement of a liberal democracy that can rightly demand a uniform "fidelity to law" or a performance of constitutional patriotism from all its citizens. The problem is not only that such an achievement cannot be taken for granted, but that doing so further obscures the constitutive role of white supremacy in democracy's central categories of practice and analysis—reinforcing, Lawrie Balfour argues, "a view of racial hierarchy as tangential rather than fundamental," and shoring up the normative resources through which racial hierarchy renders itself invisible.[41]

It is these discursive practices that I have in mind when I argue, in Chapter 1, that liberal theorists in the 1960s saw civil disobedience *like a white state*.[42] In pressing this charge, I point to the ways theorizing can itself perform racial power—lending racial states the normative validity vested in the deracialized terms of constitutional democracy, and discursively disciplining protestors who refuse the limits imposed by these terms. Political theory sees like a white state when it adopts the state's interest in maintenance and stability as its own normative end, when it centers the white citizen by treating racial injustice as aberrational rather than constitutive, and when it obscures racial hierarchy behind the language of constitutional democracy.[43] It is not incidental that such a view simultaneously conscripts the bodies of black activists as ahistorical object lessons, while also diminishing their intellectual labor and creative contributions to the history of democratic thought. Indeed, in so doing, it fails to take them seriously as *thinkers* at all.

Thus, this book's two primary methodological commitments—to reading political theory texts in context, and to reading activists themselves as engaged in the work of political theory—are linked to each other and to the substance of my argument. The critical practices of seeing like a white state suggest *seeing like an activist* as an important alternative starting point; at the same time, the critical practices of seeing like an activist supply the tools we need to fully understand the implications—and stubborn appeal—of *seeing like a white state*.

Here, however, I want to take care to note what I am, and am not, claiming to accomplish in proposing to see civil disobedience like an activist. This book does not endeavor to present "authentic," unmediated material from within the annals of the archives. I make no claims to accounting for these particular activists' original intentions or true self-perceptions—as if I could somehow convey without interpreting, make present without representing, or cut through the layers of representation already thick within oral histories, interviews, and scholarly monographs, to access some original, newly transparent reality. In taking up the visions of activists, moreover, I am not juxtaposing their "truth" to the academic theorist's "falsehood." Instead, this book tries to think more deliberately about what political theory—whether produced by scholars or by activists—does in the world: how the practice of theorizing frames and envisions political possibilities, and how these visions shape the contexts in which states and citizens act. In keeping with this ambition, and following David Scott, what I am interested in is the "problem-space" inhabited and enacted by civil rights activists, as well as by mid-century liberal theorists of civil disobedience: the "ensemble of questions and answers around which a horizon of identifiably stakes (conceptual as well as ideological-political stakes) hangs."[44] What we see, then, by looking through a different lens than the one adopted by many academic theorists of civil disobedience, is not the activist's *truth*, but a distinct set of questions and answers—*arguments* about what the problem of racial injustice and white supremacy is, and how different forms of action (civil disobedience among them) could answer that problem.

This work begins in Chapter 1 by placing influential mid-century theories of civil disobedience within their "context of argument" (to use Scott's terms)—1960s debates over law, order, and the limits of racial justice—to understand their relationship to the civil rights example and the discursive practices that led them to view civil disobedience as a "stabilizing device."[45] Chapter 2 proposes an alternative framework for understanding the civil disobedience of civil rights activists: a decolonizing praxis that linked their dissent to that of anticolonial activists, and tied the context of Jim Crow to a wider world of global white supremacy. As I argue, the receptiveness of African American civil rights activists to the means of nonviolent direct action and civil disobedience was crucially informed by the deployment of nonviolence in the midst of anticolonial struggles around the world, and perceptions about its potential efficacy as a means of self-emancipation and colonial liberation. If the constitutional, democratic state formed the normative horizon for Rawls's understanding of civil disobedience, activists' horizon was defined by processes of *imaginative transit*—the process of thinking and traveling across boundaries and disparate contexts, though which activists in motion constructed civil disobedience as a means of transforming worldwide structures of racist imperialism, colonial rule, apartheid, and Jim Crow. Between 1920 and 1960, African American, Indian, South African, and Ghanaian activists proposed, debated, and wielded nonviolent direct action as a means of self-liberation from white supremacy's structures of fear and violence—and a way of disrupting and transforming the practices that held those structures in place.

Subsequent chapters explore the dynamics of this decolonizing praxis on the ground and in the streets of the United States, during key moments of the "classic phase" of the civil rights movement. Chapter 3 focuses on the *inward-facing* purposes of civil disobedience by revisiting the student-led campaign of "jail, no bail" pioneered by the Student Nonviolent Coordinating Committee (SNCC) and the Congress of Racial Equality (CORE). Building on Bernard Boxill's reading of Martin Luther King, Jr. as part of the philosophical lineage of abolitionism and black republicanism—those "more-than-half-free slaves" struggling to liberate themselves—I read the practice of accepting arrest as one of "comparative freedom," through which activists reframed the experience of incarceration as one of liberatory self-making.[46] The point of "jail, no bail"—withholding bail money and voluntarily staying in jail—was not to signal fidelity to law, stabilize state authority, or contain the unruly potential of dissent. Rather, through "jail, no bail" student activists transformed an experience defined by fear, stigma, and vulnerability into an enactment of courage, dignity, and freedom. They used their time in jail to multiply and extend their protest into new arenas: the jail cell was a site of solidarity building and a mechanism for mobilizing local and national black publics. Accepting arrest was thus a means of withholding collective and individual cooperation from illegitimate power, and thereby refusing the rituals of submission and domination that defined Jim Crow. Reading "jail, no bail" in this way links the geographic imaginative transit of Chapter 2 (across the global expanse of the decolonizing world) with a temporal imaginative transit that tied civil rights activists to struggles for emancipation from slavery—struggles still unfinished and continuous with their own.

Chapter 4 turns to the *outward-facing* dynamics of civil disobedience by examining the tactics employed in the 1963 Birmingham Campaign. Though Birmingham is often memorialized as the pinnacle of nonviolent and properly *civil* disobedience in the United States, the tactics that the Southern Christian Leadership Conference (SCLC) deployed there trouble the easy distinction between persuasion and coercion, nonviolence and force. Activists in Birmingham described and defended their actions as crisis-generating—as mechanisms of what I call the *tactics of disruption* and the *tactics of disclosure*. In a society shaped by white supremacy, black activists knew that they would have to arrest the attention of white citizens—disrupt everyday routines, violate norms of comportment, and involve spectators in a dramatic conflict—in order to create the space for persuasion to do its work. The dilemma is contained in the idea that activists had to somehow *force* the better argument: forms of disruption, confrontation, crisis-generation, and coercion are not best understood as persuasion's opposites, but as the tools that—in the midst of persuasion's systemic failure—"spark the imagination of the politically, economically, and socially disenfranchised and reveal possibilities that exist outside the legal boundaries of our current culture, so long as one is willing to venture beyond those boundaries," as Jarrett Lovell compellingly writes.[47] What Brandon Terry identifies as the "pedagogical" aspect of protest action—its ability to reveal alternative possibilities and disclose invisibilized realities—is both reliant upon and complicated by the mechanisms of disruption, coercion, and provocation.[48]

The direct action activists of SNCC, SCLC, and CORE were neither naïve nor particularly sanguine about the potentialities of transforming white citizens. But the political possibilities of civil disobedience relied on the notion that the disclosure of white supremacy's violence (latent and overt) and the disruption of both everyday institutional functioning and everyday routine would serve as a forceful but effective invitation to white citizens to recognize their own responsibility for establishing relations of equality and remaking a world in common. This optimistic and fundamentally democratic possibility foundered, time and again, on the stubborn shoals of what Charles Mills and Elizabeth Spelman call "white ignorance"—the ways of seeing and habits of interpretation produced by the political context of the white state that continually shore up its normative resources. By chronicling a "failed" protest at the 1964 World's Fair and its public reception, Chapter 5 attends to the discursive *techniques of disavowal* that white citizens and state officials used to dismiss black activism as inappropriate, irresponsible, gratuitous, and violent—thereby avoiding the claims such protest made upon them while preserving their own innocence and moral standing. In stepping outside the South and the familiar set of events that make up the public memory of the "short" civil rights movement, the chapter also suggests that some aspects of campaigns like the one in Birmingham were enabled—and publicly legitimated—by the very techniques of disavowal that limited the movement's radical potentialities. Seeing like an activist uncovers a novel account of civil disobedience's power, but it also suggests new limits—limits that can neither be seen nor assessed when disobedience is viewed like a white state.

The analysis of Chapter 5 returns us, anew, to the problem of vision: the ways of seeing, knowing, and theorizing that safeguard the racial order, and enable citizens and state actors to deny that such an order exists. In the epilogue, I suggest that this was the problem that dogged direct action through the 1960s and contributed to the exhaustion of civil disobedience's decolonizing praxis. In light of this history, I conclude by considering the political effects of demanding that contemporary protests against racial injustice endlessly replicate the *civil*-ized, *domestic*-ated script for civil rights disobedience. Such demands suggest a limited political imagination around protest and an unwillingness to engage with the present conjuncture on its own terms—in particular, the way that present conditions relate to the failures and limitations (as well as the successes) of past activism. The problem is not merely that recycling the civil rights struggle as a peaceful petition for reform misunderstands the past. It also fundamentally misrecognizes the work of activism as the repetition of given repertoires, rather than an imaginative enterprise—imperfect and always incomplete—of rebuilding the world through action.

1
Seeing Like a White State

> This exploitation of so many angry and sincere people, whose indignation was misrepresented as some kind of testimonial for the system that had oppressed them, and against which they were protesting, must qualify as one of the greatest and most shameless manipulations of recent years.
> —Michael Thelwell, "The August 28th March on Washington" (1964)[1]

Civil disobedience is a notoriously disputed concept: for as long as we have had a notion of civil disobedience, we—scholars, activists, journalists, politicians, ordinary citizens—have been arguing about its purpose, meaning, and legitimacy, as well as which examples qualify as properly *civil* or properly *disobedient*. Nevertheless, over time something of a consensus has emerged—albeit an "uneasy" one, as Tony Milligan observes—over the *set of behaviors*, the modes of comportment, that function as defining hallmarks of civil disobedience.[2] Indeed, across diverse bodies of political theory, as well as in popular American discourse, the forms of action that define civil disobedience are remarkably stable: to be considered truly and legitimately civil, disobedient protestors must willingly face legal sanctions for their actions; restrict their methods to those that are persuasive, noncoercive, and nonviolent; and frame their appeal to the broader society in terms of core, shared values that they affirm and accept. In this way, civil disobedience distinguishes itself from militancy and rebellion; it affirms, rather than undercuts, the normative legitimacy of the existing constitutional order. The terms of these requirements are thus general, universal—they are meant to apply across a range of contexts in which citizens face injustice of a serious and fundamental sort that requires redress or reconsideration, but that falls short of justifying the violent overthrow of the regime. With an eye toward safeguarding the rights of others and the stability of the existing legal-political order, the architecture of the theory of civil disobedience promises significant reform and change *without* significant disorder, unrest, or revolutionary upheaval.

Theories of civil disobedience do not, as a whole, read as case studies; theories supply abstract standards with wide applicability. But in between the lines of theory there lies history, and here the example of the civil rights movement looms large. The ideas of nonviolent action espoused by those like Martin Luther King, Jr., and practiced throughout the course of the civil rights struggle, serve as key legitimating examples for theoretical treatments of disobedience—demonstrating that their parameters are not only plausible but also effective even in the context of the horrors of Jim Crow segregation and violence. The civil rights movement also serves as a crucial reservoir of inspiration, based on shared understandings of what the movement was, how it worked, and what it meant. The received wisdom about how civil disobedience ought to function points to a common reference point—in which a commitment to civility amongst black protestors solicits white empathy across the nation, arousing conscience and triggering legal redress. Because protestors went joyfully to jail after breaking the law, because they refrained from coercing both bystanders and the targets of their protest, because they remained resolutely nonviolent, and because they spoke in the refrains of "We, the people," and a right to "life, liberty, and the pursuit of happiness," white Americans recognized their own moral and national selves in black demands and were persuaded to engage in the work of legal reconstruction. As Jim Crow came tumbling down, a recalcitrant South was brought into alignment with national, democratic values.

Of course, few would argue that reality is so simple or neat. The iconic photographs that populate the American political imaginary give powerful testimony to this fact—as does the assassination of the civil rights movement's most visible and celebrated figure. Yet in its broad outlines, the mainstream narrative of civil rights disobedience enjoys such wide credibility that even those who challenge standard theories of civil disobedience as too limited and narrow often presume that the movement is well described by the account of punishment, persuasion, and principle—even if this model fails to capture other, more contemporary, uses of disobedience.[3]

But the definition and justification of civil disobedience has its own political history—one that is not really about the way that civil rights activism unfolded in its own time and place, nor even about the derivation of normative principles from a priori theoretical premises. This chapter details part of this political history and traces the origins of a dual-consensus—on the one hand, a particular telling of civil rights history, and on the other hand, a parallel theory of legitimate civil disobedience. As civil rights disobedience was still unfolding in the mid-1960s, a political struggle was simultaneously underway about how to both conceptualize and domesticate the disorder in the streets. Against the charges of those conservatives like Barry Goldwater who sought to link civil disobedience with violent crime, riots, and the breakdown of order, liberals understood their task as decoupling disobedience from disorder in order to defend both its necessity and its achievements.[4] In this moment, liberal political leaders struggled to affirm the civil rights movement's goals while restraining its means and limiting its repercussions—authorizing certain terms of the struggle while sidelining others, and attempting to recognize key goals while moving the action off the streets and into the courts and legislature. In the course of this discursive struggle, a particular version of civil rights action was legitimized—providing a compelling way to distinguish King from more "militant" actors, and absorb the triumphs of the civil rights movement into the fabric of mainstream American politics while limiting the boundaries for further extra-institutional action. This resolution entailed a reconstruction of the means and ends of civil rights protest: if the problem of racism was fundamentally one of individual prejudice and Southern backwardness, then the means of persuasion and the appeal to mainstream (national) values would be all that redress required; if black Americans were not dominated by complex systems of economic, social, and political institutions, but excluded from an otherwise healthy public sphere, then legal and legislative mechanisms assuring their entry would be satisfactory to dissolve racial inequality in America.

The theories of civil disobedience that initially emerged out of the 1960s bear the imprint of this history. These same arguments played out, albeit in philosophical rather than political form, as conservative critics of civil disobedience like Herbert Storing and jurist Abe Fortas faced off against its liberal defenders, from Hugo Bedau to John Rawls, Carl Cohen, and Michael Walzer. These debates, too, drew on a nascent cultural understanding about how the civil rights movement was acting to provoke change, and—implicitly and explicitly—appealed to its power as an example of how some kinds of lawbreaking could nevertheless serve a vital role in democratic processes of lawmaking.

By revealing the political formation of the intertwined narratives of civil rights and civil disobedience and detailing their relationship to the 1960s and 1970s conservative push for "law and order," I trace the significant ways that this context shaped the conceptualization of civil disobedience as a means of realizing and strengthening already extant constitutional principles. As I contend, theorists like Rawls saw civil disobedience—and with it, the problem of racial injustice—from the perspective of *a white state*: taking for granted the legitimacy of the constitutional order; assuming as primary the ends of constitutional integrity and stability; and figuring the problem of racial injustice as limited, exceptional, and all-but-already solved. Such a stance, I suggest, takes the state's perspective by theorizing within the bounds of a presupposed legitimacy, thereby prioritizing stability and maintenance of an existing system. It also centers white citizens while abstracting away from their enmeshment within structures of domination, delivering standards of judgment that tend to bolster rather than undermine the foundations of white supremacy.

"A Climate of Lawlessness"

In the wake of the assassinations of Martin Luther King, Jr. and Robert Kennedy and the outbreak of mass violence in 175 cities across the country in 1968, President Lyndon Johnson signed Executive Order #11412, establishing the National Commission on the Causes and Prevention of Violence (NCCPV). Chaired by Dr. Milton Eisenhower and comprised of thirteen legislators, judges, and religious and civic figures, the Commission was tasked with examining "the causes and prevention of disrespect for law and order, of disrespect for public officials, and of violent disruptions of public order by individuals and groups" in order to make policy recommendations to the administration.[5] With the ink still drying on the decade's landmark civil rights legislation, and the roar of the putatively illegal protests that catalyzed those laws still reverberating in their ears, the Commission reached the conclusion that disobedience "is disastrous from the standpoint of the maintenance of a democratic society": no matter how conscientious or nonviolent, the violation of law by protestors inevitably chips away at the foundations of a lawful democratic order and encourages "a climate of lawlessness" and violence.[6] Using the language of "contagion," the report moves quickly from references to the legitimacy of dissent to concerns about disorder and violence—tying disobedience to law to violent destabilization, revolution, and the unleashing "of some of the most destructive elements in American society"—forces that "might otherwise [have lied] quiescent beneath the surface of national life."[7] Invoking Martin Luther King, Jr. to argue *against* civil disobedience, the report slyly equates protest with violence and degradation, observing that "violence against an oppressor only tends in the long run to justify oppression. Repeatedly putting one's body 'on the line' does not enhance, but diminishes, the worth of that body to the dominant society."[8]

Paradoxically, from out of the civil rights struggle, the members of the NCCPV drew a lesson about the power of existing, institutional avenues for redress, to which they credited the arrival of "significant change in recent years." The "remedy for the discontented," then, "is to seek change through lawful mechanisms."[9] Despite the upheaval of the late 1960s, the commissioners doubled down on the American ideal of peaceful progress, while failing to register the cruel irony of the argument or offering any tangible means for rendering its vicious circularity more virtuous. Indeed, warnings of the Commission's own task force on protest—that "the myth of peaceful progress offers intellectual support for existing political arrangements and validates the suppression of protest" while serving "to conceal the role of official violence in the maintenance of these arrangements"—go spectacularly unheeded, as several sections of the report move to advocate for more effective policing as a prime solution to urban violence and mass protest.[10] Justice will have to wait for the long haul; domestic tranquility represents an immediate necessity.

Given the unprecedented eruption of unrest that followed King's death in April 1968—as well as the urban riots that had arrived in successive waves, one "long, hot summer" after another since 1964—the Commission's focus on the risk of widespread disorder is perhaps understandable.[11] Yet the urgency of the Commission's immediate context—the assassinations, the riots, rising crime—belies the political construction of the problem of violence and disorder, and the tendentious and empirically questionable thesis that civil disobedience, riots, and violent crime are somehow of a piece, each one bleeding inevitably into the next. In fact, far from being merely given, these linkages were years in the making: the tangled threads connecting political protest to street crime were racially marked, politically forged, and strategically deployed in the midst of a conservative resurgence against racial equality and New Deal liberalism. In civil disobedience, the thirteen commissioners perceived a dilemma—one familiar to Johnson-era liberals at the close of the 1960s: How to claim ownership over the victories of the civil rights era while discrediting the forms of social disorder that seemed to follow in their wake—or brought them about in the first place?

This predicament became acute not merely by the fact of rising crime or urban riots but by the discursive links that political elites constructed, connecting "civil rights" to a diffuse and menacing idea of "civil disorder." As recent scholarship has shown, conservative opponents of the civil rights movement had been working for years to connect the pursuit of racial equality to violence, rioting, street crime, and ultimately the complete breakdown of "law and order." While throughout the 1940s and 1950s, defenders of segregation enjoyed broad discursive leeway to take on the idea of racial equality as such, by the time the 1964 and 1965 civil rights legislation passed, a direct assault on integration itself gave way to a coded discourse about crime and disorder. Thus, the kinds of claims that Senators Strom Thurmond or James Eastman made freely amidst congressional debates in the late 1950s— warning that "political demands for the integration of the races" would necessarily bring with them a "wave of terror, crime, and juvenile delinquency," or contrasting the "peaceful" segregated South with Northern cities plagued by "rape," "murder," "muggings," and "crime on the streets"—became, by the mid- to late-1960s, less politically acceptable.[12]

In this context, the issue of civil disobedience took on critical importance: not racial equality per se, but the lawlessness of black protestors in pursuit of civil rights became the new problem in need of address. Less a single coherent argument than a shifting set of overlapping, interlocking rhetorical maneuvers, these appeals allowed for a subtle but pernicious conflation of distinct phenomena from political protests to rape and homicide—rolling them all into a single, menacing threat to democratic stability, social harmony, and American values of decency, civility, and lawful order. By insisting that organized, disobedient protest was definitionally both criminal and violent—as intentional violation of the law, so the argument goes, disobedience simply *is* crime; as action that operates outside of legitimate procedures, it simply *is* violence—critics recast protestors as lawless criminals wreaking havoc on society. For many a segregationist, "the rise of black civil disobedience in 1961 and 1962 only further reinforced the idea that black civil rights activists were disrespectful agitators and deliberate lawbreakers." As Naomi Murakawa explains, "In this calculus, black protest is a form of criminal extortion, and therefore civil rights legislation is misguided federal capitulation to extortion."[13] In a 1964 presidential campaign speech, Arizona Senator Barry Goldwater argued the point quite directly: "Choose the way of this present Administration and you have the way of mobs in the street, restrained only by the plea that they"—that is, black protestors and civil rights demonstrators—"wait until after election time to ignite violence once again." The result, he bemoaned, is that "crime grows faster than the population, while those who break the law are accorded more consideration than those who try to enforce the law."[14]

The conceptual leaps that Goldwater makes in these lines—from crime to protest to violence and back again—did significant discursive work in refiguring political protest as generalized criminal lawlessness. For critics offered not just *definitional* but *causal* links to further fuse disobedience to violence and crime. Civil disobedience, critics contended, is not civil at all; it leads to the violation of others' rights, encourages others to break laws as they see fit, and escalates inevitably to violent clashes between protestors, other citizens, and police. Conflating demonstrations with riots, and charging that civil disobedience causes other forms of lawbreaking, conservatives effectively placed the blame for rising crime and proliferating riots on civil rights protestors themselves—as well as those officials within the Johnson administration who had apparently encouraged and rewarded them with legislation. J. Edgar Hoover made these connections explicit in a 1965 speech: "To my mind, there are two frightening aspects to civil disobedience. One, sowing contempt for law and order and promoting pride in lawbreaking among the Nation's youth can only result in the acceleration of our serious crime problem. . . . Secondly, where is the line to be drawn against the snowball effect of civil disobedience? Willfully disobeying misdemeanor statutes today and committing felonies tomorrow is a logical regression from a government of law to an anarchic society."[15] As Hoover charged, "rioting, looting, burning, and killing—deliberate crimes—are outrages spawned under the banner of civil disobedience, a dangerous philosophy based on shallow reasoning." Crime would decrease when support for disobedience, and the black protestors wielding it, was resoundingly repudiated.[16]

While the association of civil disobedience with violence would seem to cut against the most obvious evidence to the contrary—the fact that civil disobedience re-entered the American stage mid-century under the banner of nonviolence—it both identified and reinforced a feeling amongst white Americans that violence, not nonviolence, had become the watchword of the decade. In response to a September 1964 poll inquiring whether "most of the actions" taken by "Negroes . . . to get the things they want" had been violent or nonviolent, 57% answered that "most" had been violent. By the end of the decade, concern about the riots, violence, and disorder associated with the fight for racial equality had only increased—alongside and linked to pervasive public anxiety about rising crime.[17] It was thus to many sympathetic ears that Richard Nixon issued the following words in a 1968 radio address:

> The old violence today parades in a new uniform. Both at home and abroad, it has wrapped itself in propaganda. At home, it may masquerade as "civil disobedience," or "freedom," and sometimes it marches under the banner of legitimate dissent.... The sloganeering of the new violence confuses many people. That's what it intends to do. But when the slogans are stripped away, it is still violence plain and simple, cruel and evil as always, destructive of freedom, destructive of progress, destructive of peace.[18]

At the end of the speech he concluded that the "uncomplicated task" facing Americans at the end of the 1960s was "to damp the fires of violent change, to cement our mastery of the pace of change, and to make the most of our opportunity for constructive change."[19]

The strategic deployment of these "law and order" claims effectively depoliticized the struggle for racial equality while simultaneously drawing on a long tradition of racializing crime, as Vesla Weaver persuasively demonstrates.[20] In the process, civil disobedience operated as both the cause and effect of a general moral malaise, for which Great Society governance itself—with its social welfare programs, appeasement of rioters, encouragement of lawless demonstrations, and protections for the civil liberties of criminals—was ultimately to blame. While Weaver, Murakawa, and others have shown the effects of this new politics of law and order on developing crime policy, what has been less thoroughly reconstructed is the way in which the discourse around civil disobedience and organized protest was durably shaped by the same political forces and dynamics. In essence, many white supporters of the 1960s civil rights agenda viewed the issue as a binary choice: reject civil disobedience, despite its very recent achievements (as did the members of the NCCPV), or find a way to reclaim it as a politics of *order*, at home within the established legal structure, and posing no intrinsic threat to stability and lawful democracy. The alternative suggested by many black activists and intellectuals—that undercutting the stability of a democracy built on the grounds of white supremacy was precisely the point, and that in this regard, the work of reconstruction had only just begun—was often not seriously entertained.

It was in this political context that much of the contemporary literature on civil disobedience in political and legal theory developed. A young generation of liberal and left scholars, including John Rawls, Michael Walzer, Carl Cohen, and Hugo Bedau, not only identified with the causes driving contemporary civil disobedience—particularly civil rights, but also the antiwar movement—they also sought to defend the means of protest from the sort of criticism that ran through the Commission report and the conservative critique. Their collective response required distinguishing civil disobedience from the forms of disorder, violence, and force with which critics associated it; it meant redefining civil disobedience not as a strategic use of disruption and the power of numbers, but a moral appeal to the majority's conscience, in the shared terms of principles affirmed by all. However, in so responding, liberal theorists tended to accept the premises of the conservative argument—that disruption and disorder mark the boundaries of democratic society; that American political institutions are basically just and require external provocation only rarely and on narrow terms; and that peaceful mechanisms of law, reason, and persuasion remain sufficient for ushering in necessary social and political change. With recourse to a morally powerful example of Martin Luther King, Jr. as a prophet of core American values and the gentle way of nonviolence, civil disobedience was thus remade, from a risky mechanism of illegal, extra-institutional action, into a means of reform *internal* to legal and political institutions.

Civilizing Disobedience

While dissent and disobedience had long been subjects of interest for philosophy, it was the political and social events of the 1960s that prompted their return to center stage, as the locus of a vital and contentious debate both within and beyond the academy. In response to those like the members of the NCCPV who viewed civil disobedience as promoting lawlessness, riots, crime, and worse, liberal legal and political theorists sought to define and justify disobedience in such a way as to place it firmly within the bounds of liberal, constitutional democracy, even if at its margins. What emerged from this effort has been a remarkably stable set of ideas about civil disobedience—the forms of action and sets of attitudes entailed by it—that have remained central to the way that political theory, as well as the American political public at large, reasons about the definition, role, and justification of disobedient protest.

Early in the decade, philosopher and anti-death penalty activist Hugo Bedau laid the groundwork for what would ultimately become the standard, consensus view of the subject amongst liberal philosophers and legal theorists.[21] Owing, undoubtedly, to the political context at the time—and perhaps the demands of his own advocacy efforts—civil disobedience captured Bedau's interest in the early 1960s, leading him to author a series of articles, compile an extensive bibliography, and edit several volumes on the topic, all of which would provide a common starting point for subsequent work by many others, including Rawls's influential discussion.[22] In contrast to other, broader discussions of direct action, nonviolent resistance, or noncooperation, Bedau's account placed special emphasis on the relationship between those who undertake civil disobedience and the law. "Civil disobedience," Bedau argued in a paper delivered at the 1961 meeting of the American Philosophical Association, "is not just done; it is committed. It is always the sort of thing that can send one to jail."[23] On his reading, an act qualifies as civil disobedience only when it is done "illegally, publicly, nonviolently, and conscientiously with the intent to frustrate (one of) the laws, policies, or decisions of [the] government."[24] Because of its specifically illegal nature, therefore, civil disobedience requires a certain set of actions and attitudes from those who undertake it. As Bedau specifies, it typically entails that "the dissenter acknowledge that the law, no matter what it is, makes some claim on his obedience," and that he acts without "disloyal, seditious, traitorous, or rebellious intent"—and thus is willing to accept, without further resistance, "the legal consequences of the act."[25] What emerges from Bedau's discussion, then, is a paired emphasis on *law* and the modes of *civility* that keep disobedience within its bounds—if barely.

Nevertheless, Bedau remained ambivalent about the possibility of grounding disobedience fully within a theory of political obligation. Law, on his argument, proves insufficient for generating an obligation to obey it, while the dictates of conscience cannot alone justify disobedience. Caveats and qualifiers like "typically," "ordinarily," and "in most cases" mark the 1961 essay; in the end, he stops just short of providing general criteria for when disobedience is legitimate.[26] Yet his focus on the dissenter's attitude toward law—and on the forms of action that follow from this attitude—provided a ready framework for other theorists to do just that. Indeed, in the throes of a decade of upheaval, the political stakes of not only defending civil disobedience but also limiting it by carefully specifying its boundaries, proved to be rather high. John Rawls, whose account of civil disobedience has been amongst the most influential to come out of the period, followed Bedau's definition closely, but shifted his approach dramatically.[27]

"I shall assume, as requiring no argument, that there is, at least in a society such as ours, a moral obligation to obey the law."[28] This is the striking claim offered by Rawls in his earliest foray into the subject of political obligation and its limits. The condition he places on the obligation to obey—that it obtains in a "society such as ours"—is a crucial one, because it not only suggests that citizens might be morally obligated to comply with laws in real-world situations that fall short (perhaps considerably so) from ideally just ones but also that this assumption of obligation is relatively unproblematic within the political horizons of Rawls's own time. For Rawls—and he is hardly unique amongst his contemporaries on this point—disobedience offers a discrete exception to the general rule of obligation.[29] Within the horizon of what he calls the "fundamentally" or "nearly" just state, in which there exists a "legitimately established democratic authority" and a relatively "well-ordered" constitution recognized by the citizenry, the problem created by civil disobedience is that political obligation cannot simply be dissolved by the existence of an unjust law.[30] Laws are the product of imperfect, human institutions, and there is no procedure that can guard completely against injustice; if the injustice of any particular law (or its implementation) were enough to dissolve the obligation to comply with it, the idea of obligation itself might lose all political and moral relevance. Worse still, disobedience to every unjust law might do more harm than good, undermining the institutions and procedures that guarantee rights and liberties in the first place. Consequently, citizens of constitutional democracies are sometimes required to obey bad laws and even significantly unjust ones; as Rawls writes, citizens must simply "[suffer] the defects of one another's knowledge and sense of justice."[31]

Yet there are limits to the forbearance that citizens must show in the face of injustice. If we are sometimes obligated *not* to resist, surely there must be situations in which the gravity and scope of injustice is so great to allow for, if not require, disobedience. Rawls's interest in civil disobedience thus sits at a very peculiar point between justice and its opposite: within a state that is "well-ordered for the most part"—that is, one that citizens not only have an interest in maintaining but also recognize as legitimate—"but in which some serious violations of justice nevertheless do occur"—injustices that are sometimes serious enough to justify disobedience.[32] Rawls provides two indications of the sort of violations he has in mind here, which qualify as a "serious breakdown."³³ "Roughly speaking," he argues, "in the long run the burden of injustice should be more or less evenly distributed over different groups in society, and the hardship of unjust policies should not weigh too heavily in any particular case." That is, the ordinary injustice of the nearly just state shows no patterns—it is as likely to affect one group as another, and so all citizens are, on average, equally burdened by it. What this means, for Rawls, is that the general presumption of a moral obligation to obey is "problematic for permanent minorities that have suffered from injustice for many years," and who are made to endure a disproportionate share of losses, insults, and injustices made into law.³⁴

The other manner of injustice that concerns Rawls, and which opens the door to justified, conscientious lawbreaking, is the "denial of our own or others' basic liberties."³⁵ Specifically, Rawls is interested in those "instances of substantial and clear injustice" represented by "serious infringements" of the principle of equal liberty and "blatant violations" of "the principle of fair equality of opportunity." His intuition is that these kinds of injustices not only cut to the heart of the basic principles that are supposed to order institutions; the violation of liberty and equal opportunity also tends to generate other kinds of injustice, constraining citizens' ability to participate freely and equally in the institutions that order their lives. Rawls's key example here should not surprise us, given the context in which he was writing: "Thus when certain minorities are denied the right to vote or to hold office, or to own property and to move from place to place, or when certain religious groups are repressed and others denied various opportunities, these injustices may be obvious to all. They are publicly incorporated into the recognized practice, if not the letter, of social arrangements."³⁶ Only when there are embedded, pervasive institutional injustices that emanate from the "basic structure of society" is the moral duty to obey negated; as David Lyons puts it, such an obligation "cannot coexist with significant, systematic injustice that is deeply entrenched."³⁷

Given the rather thorny question of determining whether a system is "reasonably" or "nearly" just, there is something of a puzzle created by Rawls's account: What exactly are the liberal and democratic credentials of a system that is guilty, in an entrenched way, of denying the basic rights and liberties of some section of the population? What manner of state does Rawls have in mind? Most troublingly, Rawls's designation of the "nearly just" state appears to include the United States under Jim Crow; indeed, he seems to have constructed his examples to speak to just such a case.[38] As we have seen, the kinds of injustice that occur within the "nearly just" state are not necessarily accidental or mistaken but may be "more or less deliberate" violations of basic rights and liberties, enforced "over an extended period of time." They may persist, according to Rawls, in the face of repeated appeals for redress, to which a "wantonly unjust," "overly hostile," "immovable," or "apathetic" majority has proven "indifferent."[39] Such a system nevertheless qualifies as "nearly just" for Rawls—but why?

Answering the question requires examining in more detail how Rawls thinks civil disobedience can function to address and remediate these particular forms of injustice. Following Bedau's foundational account, civil disobedience, properly distinguished from both criminal lawbreaking and revolutionary action, requires a commitment to a certain kind of *civility*— understood not just in the colloquial terms of courteousness or restraint, but as a form of civic-mindedness that entails particularly modes of reason giving and justification. By engaging in civil disobedience, protestors attempt to "address the sense of justice of the majority of the community" while expressing "a respect of legal procedures" and continuing to act "within the limits of fidelity to the law," even as they break individual laws.[40] This "fidelity" is, in turn, manifested through adherence to particular modes of action: protestors must appeal to "a common conception of justice" held by the majority and enshrined within the constitution of the "nearly just" state; they must accept the stipulated legal punishment for their acts without further resistance; and they must orient themselves to persuading others of the justice of their cause rather than coercing others in order to get their way.

Rawls's central claim—one which he shares with many others—is that there is a core expressive element in these "civil" acts: the performance reveals the moral judgment of the protestor, demonstrating that though they may break a particular law, they partake in a view of justice shared by the majority of citizens, which is embedded within the polity's central institutions and ideals. "Civil disobedience, so understood, is clearly distinct from militant action," argues Rawls. "The militant, for example, is much more deeply opposed to the political system. He does not accept it as one which is nearly just or reasonably so; he believes either that it departs widely from its professed principles or that it pursues a mistaken conception of justice altogether." Consequently, in the face of an unjust "basic structure," the militant believes "that one must try to prepare the way for radical or even revolutionary change."[41] In contrast, the civilly disobedient accept legal punishment, eschew the use of violence and coercion, and appeal to the majority's own foundational principles in order to signal sincerity, conscientiousness, and a basic acknowledgment that the overall structure of the existing order is legitimate and "reasonably" just. Thus while disobedient lawbreaking is indeed a risky form of activism that may, at the margins, give way to "serious disorder," it can be justified when used as a "last resort" against the kinds of grave injustices outlined earlier.[42]

Thus in locating civil disobedience as the "last resort" of those who are the victims of serious, entrenched injustice in the context of a nearly just state, Rawls means to convey several key ideas. Centrally, he means to limit the occasion for civil disobedience to only the most egregious cases in which core constitutional principles are at stake, and the need for reform cannot be disputed in seriousness. In these cases, he argues, the injustices "may be obvious to all."[43] Tellingly, Rawls's conceptualization of civil disobedience excludes claims to social and economic policies, which relate only indirectly to "fundamental equal liberties." On Rawls's account, only "serious infringements" of the principles of equal liberty (the more or less standard set of liberal political and civil rights) and fair equality of opportunity count as "instances of clear and substantial injustice." He explains that this is so because, unlike infractions of equal liberty and fair equality of opportunity, claims on "economic and social institutions and policies" are too difficult to evaluate, depending not on the "public's conception of justice" but on "a wealth of statistical and other information, all of which is seasoned with shrewd judgment and plain hunch."[44] Rawls is no doubt overly sanguine about the obviousness of violations of basic liberties, and their separability from the social and economic issues he deems to thorny to touch; his thinking here reveals a great deal about his own certainty—prior to *Political Liberalism*—that his liberal conception of justice could be universally affirmed and rationally accepted. The issue of clarity is, however, essential for him; without the clarity of the wrong under protest and the clarity of the relationship between the protestor's appeal and the majority's sense of justice, civil disobedience is a recipe for instability, strife, and perhaps violence.

Rawls is careful, however, not to put too severe a restriction on the form that this shared conception takes. While the "collective force" of the principles of justice needs to be sufficiently effective and present in society, routine violations will nevertheless occur. A shared sense of justice, therefore, may become evident only in a negative fashion, when a majority reveals itself to be "unable to undertake the measures required to suppress the minority and to punish as the law requires the various acts of civil disobedience. The sense of justice undermines the will to uphold unjust institutions, and so a majority despite its superior power may give way."[45] For this to occur, it need only be the case that "those who perpetrate injustice can be clearly identified and isolated from the larger community," and that the public consensus over the principles of justice—though neither perfect nor complete—is such that the views of all sides "support the same judgment in the situation at hand, and would do so even should their respective positions be interchanged."[46] Whenever this is not the case—whenever distinct, opposed communities of opinion form, espousing different ideals of the public good—then "the wisdom of civil disobedience" becomes "highly problematic": instead of supporting and strengthening the existing constitutional consensus, civil disobedience threatens and invites anarchy.[47] A shared conception of justice is therefore absolutely essential in differentiating between the valid claims of citizens, enacted disobediently, and the unbridled will of the mob.[48]

Embedded here within a normative claim about the bounds of political authority and moral obligation, then, is a descriptive claim about the nature of systemic injustice and its associated avenues of redress. By so describing civil disobedience, Rawls provides the outlines of what injustice looks like in a nearly just state: a gap between principle and practice, enforced by a clearly identifiable group, such that an appeal to what is truly foundational—the principle at the heart of the established order—provides both the avenue for meaningful change and its limit. For Rawls, "when laws and policies deviate from publicly recognized standards, an appeal to the society's sense of justice is presumably possible to some extent." This is the "condition ... presupposed in the undertaking of civil disobedience."[49] Thus, as Andrew Sabl illuminates, what Rawls has in mind for the "nearly just" state is one in which "fair treatment, mutual cooperation, and a sense of justice" exist and even thrive within a "ruling group with respect to its own members," alongside a "cruel and near-absolute tyranny towards people outside its own membership."[50] Civil disobedience, in such a society, serves the purposes of pointing out the hypocrisy according to which the polity is ordered and appealing to those principles that are proclaimed but not practiced. "The key consideration," on Sabl's gloss, "is whether the targets of disobedience are likely to have the sentiment—even as a background or tacit belief, held only sporadically or hypocritically—that fair cooperation is the normal basis for political life and arbitrary domination cannot normally be justified."[51] The remediation of injustice, demanded by disobedience, entails addressing the formal exclusion of a portion of the population from the rights and privileges that ought to belong to all citizens but are currently enjoyed only by some. And it entails appealing to the majority to persuade them to live up to their own ideals.

To be sure, Rawls's account is particular to him in many ways, dependent as it is on the architecture of his broader theory of justice. But for all the differences in details between Rawls and his interlocutors, the script for civil disobedience—the forms of behavior and comportment required of those who undertake it, from going to jail to engaging in nonviolent persuasion and moral appeal—remains remarkably stable across a wide range of texts, beginning in the 1960s and stretching into numerous more recent accounts. Though situated in an altogether different account of political obligation, Michael Walzer's explication of the problem of "democratic oppression" nevertheless traces a similar conceptual trajectory: those formally recognized as citizens but substantively excluded from certain rights and privileges must use the rules of the system against itself in order to point out its hypocrisy. But insofar as their goal remains inclusion in a state that is, in some nontrivial way, democratic, the "democratically oppressed" have the responsibility not to threaten the "existence of the larger society" or wage revolution on it. Equal rights "cannot be won by a revolutionary attack upon the social and political structures within which equality is being sought."[52] The underlying conceptual point is summarized by Carl Cohen in the following terms:

> [Civil disobedience] does not seek to unseat an existing government and does not destroy the order or stability of national or community life. It *is* a serious matter, in being a deliberate violation of the law, but it is a shallow (although common) mistake to confuse it with revolution or to view the civil disobedient as a revolutionary.
>
> The essential difference between the two lies in this: the civil disobedient does, while the revolutionary does not, accept the general legitimacy of the established authorities. While the civil disobedient may vigorously condemn some law or policy those authorities institute, and may even refuse to comply with it, he does not by any means intend to reject the larger system of laws of which that one is a very small part.[53]

In short, the civilly disobedient dispute a single law or a small set of them; they do not question the legitimacy of the state, nor do they seek to transform it in any expansive way. No sweeping transformations are sought, and no revolutionary critiques are offered: civil disobedience is an appeal to conscience in terms we already know and accept. As such, disobedience offers not a disruptive challenge to the prevailing order, but rather a necessary progression in its own core values—more a communicative act than direct action.[54] Far from being a destabilizing force, then, disobedience (properly understood, and properly civilized) both affirms and stabilizes the constitutional order. It marks the border of, but remains within, a politics of *order*.

To a large extent, the terms set by the debate in the 1960s and 1970s have dominated discourse about civil disobedience to this day. Even while some theorists of deliberative democracy have disputed the narrowness of the Rawlsian account and argued for a specifically *democratic* defense of disobedience, they have tended to reiterate the main definitional and historical moves that I have described here: civil disobedience is an essentially communicative appeal to democratic majorities, relying on both nonviolence and the acceptance of punishment for its persuasive force.[55] And for the liberal-democratic theorists of fifty years ago—as well as many who have written on disobedience since—the civil rights movement seems to provide the key legitimating example, lending historical and political credibility to abstract philosophical claims. Indeed, at first glance, "Letter from a Birmingham Jail"— and the movement it references—seems to tell just such a story. After all, King wrote from a jail cell that "an individual who breaks a law that conscience tells him is unjust, and willingly accepts the penalty by staying in jail to arouse the conscience of the community over its injustice, is in reality expressing the very highest respect for law."[56] The imperatives of action, as well as the mechanisms of social change, appear clear: practices of civility and self-sacrifice (like willingly going to jail) will arouse community conscience amongst the majority, triggering redress, while continuing to uphold legitimate order.

For this reason, perhaps, Rawls thought of his own efforts to theorize civil disobedience as providing a "wider framework" for the account provided by King's "Letter."[57] Rawls's notes and lectures from the years spent writing his essays on political obligation and civil disobedience, including the sections on these topics that appear in *A Theory of Justice*, give further evidence to the weight of the civil rights example in his thinking. Reasoning out of the student sit-ins in the early 1960s, Rawls argued that it is only "because our Constitution is *just*" that civil disobedience "can be interpreted, not as an appeal to the [sense of justice] of the majority as an extra-legal conception, but as an appeal to the Constitution itself—or to the ideals which it expresses & which it is believed would dictate repeal or reform of existing lower (or local) authorities."[58] This, for Rawls, distinguishes the civil disobedience of civil rights protesters—elaborated by King as the "classical theory of the civil rights movement"—from revolutionary action.[59] Years later, in *Political Liberalism*, Rawls would continue to maintain that King—and the civil rights movement he led—appealed to public reason in just the way his theory lays out. "King's doctrines," he argued against his critics, "were in accord with the constitutional values of a liberal regime."[60] Unlike the abolitionists, who waged their fight against a slavery-era constitution, "King could appeal . . . to the political values expressed in the Constitution correctly understood."[61]

Rawls has long been in good company in interpreting the civil rights movement, and King particularly, in this way. Contemporaneous with his own theorization of civil disobedience, Walzer's coverage of the civil rights movement in the pages of *Dissent* magazine reinforced the idea that the movement was aimed at "[winning] entrance into American (white) society"—an aim that required the tools of civility, nonviolence, and a conscientious appeal to the Declaration of Independence.[62] Although a number of academic historians and theorists of black politics have repeatedly drawn attention to more radical dimensions of civil rights activism, it is still all but commonplace—in both political theory scholarship and everyday political discourse—to suggest that the success of the civil rights movement, particularly in the years between the 1956 Montgomery bus boycott and the 1965 Selma campaign, can be attributed to activists' commitment to the civility of civil disobedience and their affirmation of the majority's normative commitments.[63] In his more recent account of King as a "moral activist," for example, Andrew Sabl describes the early King as someone who "aim[ed] at achieving social change not through pressure tactics but primarily through moral and rhetorical appeals based on principles widely accepted by the political system and its citizens."[64] For Sabl, the lesson taught by King's style of "moral activism" is that the activist "does not claim a license to impose *new* principles on the listeners, nor even to question their old ones, but only to practice what the audience already believes."[65] The early civil rights years were paradigmatic in these terms—involving "simple pleas to let blacks pursue their interests in private life, and vote their interests in public life, just as whites did."[66] The seemingly perfect fit between these theoretical accounts and the claims of the civil rights movement works to lend historical credibility, explanatory power, and moral weight to the theories.

As I will argue later in the chapter, however, this mobilization of the civil rights example is premised on viewing civil disobedience from a very particular perspective—one that has the problematic effect of drafting the civil rights movement into a theory that reinforces the tacit presumptions of white supremacy.

Seeing Like a White State

It is worth pausing to consider what this deployment of the civil rights example implies—what historical and social-theoretic assumptions are being made—and what its consonance with the Rawlsian theory of civil disobedience suggests. What must we assume about the nature of racial injustice to render this historical and theoretical narrative plausible? I take it that the assumptions at work go something like this: First, the nature of the injustice is a gap between principles and practice—a matter of inconsistency or hypocrisy that most people would not find acceptable if pointed out to them in just this way. Thus, the problem is both a technical one (principles unevenly applied or misapplied) and an epistemological one (most white citizens remain ignorant of the disconnect but would have a problem with it if they only knew). Second, as this gap is institutionalized and lived, principles are free-floating and relatively independent of practices, in that principles retain their integrity, meaningfulness, and normative power despite ongoing practices that countervail, undercut, or contradict them. In this way, it is the principles (no matter how abstract and unrealized) that are fundamental to the political order, and not the way those principles are lived (or are not lived). Consequentially, racial injustice lives in isolated elements of a social order that is otherwise relatively well-ordered, just, and sound—such that remedying injustice requires bringing particular institutions, laws, or elements of society into line with the whole. Therefore, the stability and maintenance of the existing order—not in its details, but in its broad strokes (its "constitutional essentials")—is the primary thing.

To see civil disobedience this way, I suggest, is to see it like a state, and particularly, to see it like a white state. By "seeing like a state," I mean to invoke—but nevertheless, substantially alter for my own purposes—James C. Scott's evocative claim about the ways modern-state projects seek to rationalize, standardize, and make citizens legible subjects in pursuit of ambitious projects of social transformation.[67] While the sorts of projects that Scott critiques are well beyond the bounds of what I am talking about here—in terms of scale, ambition, and effect[68]—there are three key moves made by theorists of civil disobedience that resonate with Scott's analysis: the adoption of the ends of the state as the normative starting point; the rationalization and standardization of the citizen; and the abstraction away from the concrete conditions of political life, effectively silencing forms of "local knowledge." Taken together, these three elements contribute to a theory that does not simply describe a given political reality, despite references to the civil rights example that may suggest otherwise. Instead, these theories of civil disobedience offer standards of judgment and parameters for action that can be instrumental in disciplining those citizens who do not fit the script.

While many of the key actors in Scott's narrative are state planners and political officials—those for whom seeing like a state is essentially a job requirement—what is crucial here is the way that liberal philosophers of civil disobedience, who presumably have no official or direct role in the charting of state policy, adopt the ends of the constitutional nation-state as their philosophical starting point. Beginning, as they do, with the presumption of a (mostly) legitimate constitutional order, and thus a prima facie obligation to obey the law, civil disobedience only becomes a question at all—a puzzle worthy of philosophical elaboration and demanding normative justification—when the law can be presumed to be the product of legitimate institutions that citizens have an interest in maintaining. Under these conditions, and only these conditions, breaking the law in protest becomes normatively troubling and requires special justificatory work. The stance that these theorists adopt and defend, working within this philosophical framing and responding—as I have argued—to a conservative critique of disobedience as violent disorder, takes as primary the stability and maintenance of the existing order. A "society such as ours" is one that is *not just*, and so disobedience might be justifiable; and yet it is *just enough*, such that disobedience can be recast as a stabilizing force for the normatively defensible parts of the existing order. To view civil disobedience this way is, I think, to see it like a state: to view the boundaries of dissent and activism as determined by the presumption of state legitimacy and constitutional integrity.[69] The invocation of sight here is useful, though less material than Scott's reference to the kinds of state vision materialized in cadastral maps and rationalized forests. Thinking with Sheldon Wolin (as well as Scott), my claim is that "political philosophy constitutes a form of 'seeing' political phenomena and that the way in which the phenomena will be visualized depends in large measure on where the viewer 'stands.'"[70] Seeing, in this context, invokes particular visions of the social order, the ways that bodies in dissent are perceived as they move within and against this order, and the imaginative practices that enable and constrain critique. Crucially, this implicates forms of racialized "vision" in the way that the physical bodies and concrete actions of activists are interpreted as threatening to or supportive of the existing constitutional structure and modes of citizenship.

Thus far, I have made the case that liberal philosophers of disobedience were motivated by more than just an abstract philosophical problem: they were responding to a particular political context, in which the problem of racial injustice loomed large. Consequently, I would suggest that the theories they devised also made assumptions about the nature of racial injustice. Specifically, the Rawlsian theory explains how such injustice persists within a *legitimate* constitutional order by figuring it as a problem of uneven application: the basic structure is premised on fundamentally sound principles that are, nevertheless, only partially realized. In terms suggested by Danielle Allen and Charles Mills, this renders racial injustice as a problem of exclusion that is aberrational within an otherwise coherent, legitimate, or desirable whole. As Allen elaborates, to view racial injustice as exclusion is to assume that "under segregation, some people lived inside an essentially healthy political sphere although others lived outside it." Therefore, to understand what normative standards can be used to critique and redress the situation, one can rely on the principles and "the activities of those who are 'within the pale' of the people."[71] In essence, this means that once those practices of exclusion are exposed and formal barriers are removed, the excluded can be brought fully "within the pale" of white citizenship—they can be included in the public realm as it already exists amongst white citizens. From the perspective of the "nearly just" but "democratically oppressive" white state, "[i]f exclusion is the basic injustice perpetrated by segregation, the segregating regime is a fundamentally sound political order, but for the unfortunate exclusion of black people."[72] The account of civil disobedience, then, constructed in conversation with and in some ways deployed to explain the actions of civil rights movement activists, unreflexively adopts the view that racial injustice is a limited exception—an almost technical problem that can be readily solved if aberrational laws are amended, racist beliefs are revealed as hypocritical, and principles are evenly applied.[73]

This is not just civil disobedience seen like a state; it is civil disobedience seen like a white state—one in which the normative ideal of the citizen is figured not simply in standardized terms, but in implicitly racialized ones as well—that is, as white. It is a view that significantly minimizes white entanglement with, and deep investment in, a racial hierarchy that systematically privileges them, and thereby drastically overestimates the power of abstract commitments to equality or fairness. It is a view that centers white citizens as the presumed audience for disobedience, even as race is made to disappear within unmarked invocations of "the majority." In this way, political theorists who saw disobedience like a white state lent *epistemic authority* to a framework of a democratic, constitutional state that reaffirms its own legitimacy precisely by *disavowing* its existence as a racial state. They theorized from within, and shored up the theoretical and epistemic resources for, what theorist Joel Olson called "white democracy."[74] Following Olson, "white" names a historically produced political category inseparable from the modern structures of racial domination. As Olson argues, whiteness confers simultaneous "equality and privilege" on its bearers: white citizens enjoy equality with one another, while dominating those outside the bounds of whiteness. The problem, therefore, is not inclusion and exclusion, but the construction of citizenship and democracy *through* status hierarchy and practices of domination and submission. The ideological structure of white democracy—equality secured through inequality—hides its own tracks: racial injustice can be acknowledged and condemned, but only as aberrational. This form of simultaneous acknowledgment and disavowal bolsters the legitimacy of the constitutional order—confirming its democratic *bona fides* by obscuring the centrality of white supremacy.[75]

This critique, I suggest, offers a complementary approach to that taken by Charles Mills (and others), who suggest that Rawls's analysis evinces a profound blindness to realities of race and racial injustice—a blindness derived from his commitments to ideal theorizing.[76] Like Mills, I view the decontextualizing work of Rawls's theorizing as both erasing the centrality of white supremacy to the categories of Western political thought and implicated in the reinscription of racial hierarchy—insofar as abstract commitments to the rule of law or to the duties of civility both mask and perform racial power. In distinction to Mills, however, my claim is not that Rawls is *inattentive* to racial injustice, but that he theorizes it in a particular way—and along with it, civil disobedience, conceived as a means of political redress for the harms of racial exclusion and segregation. Indeed, what is interesting about Rawls's engagement with civil disobedience is that it is explicitly an attempt to step outside of the bounds of ideal theory in order to think about the kinds of actions and claims available to democratic citizens who have been made to suffer a disproportionate share of the burdens, political losses, rights violations, and dignitary harms that sometimes result from imperfect political institutions. Thus, the problem is not a race-blind "ideal theory," but the implicit adoption of a social, political analysis that centers racial injustice even while it denies the significance of its structuring effects on core constitutional principles, central political institutions, everyday relations between citizens, and political subjecthood—a way of seeing that enables a valorization of civil disobedience as both powerfully effective, and substantially circumscribed.[77]

These dimensions of civil disobedience seen like a white state, not surprisingly, nestle comfortably within the bounds of American exceptionalism. It is not at all difficult, in fact, to see mid-century theorists of civil disobedience as inspired by—or captive to—a particular faith in peaceful American progress, directed by the power of universal ideals already held by a majority of American citizens. Preempting, by more than twenty years, Rawls's own elaboration of a majority "sense of justice" oriented toward the core constitutional essentials and basic structure of a democratic constitutional order, Gunnar Myrdal's 1944 *An American Dilemma: The Negro Problem and Modern Democracy* posited a foundational "American Creed" of "liberty, equality, justice, and fair opportunity for everybody" operative at the heart of American political life.[78] "The American Creed is not merely—as in some other countries—the implicit background of the nation's political and judicial order as it functions," Myrdal reported in his influential, multi-volume study of American race relations. "To be sure, the political creed of America is not very satisfactorily effectuated in actual social life. But as principles which *ought* to rule, the Creed has been made conscious to everyone in American society."[79] Despite the core ethical and intellectual commitments that, in Myrdal's assessment, distinguish American political culture—"moral concern," "rationalism," "liberalism," and "optimism"—by the 1940s, anachronistic, illiberal, and irrational beliefs continued to hold sway over public life.[80] And therein lay the dilemma: though the Creed existed in principle (and in law), it was often defied in practice, most glaringly in the form of the "Negro problem."[81]

As Myrdal and his collaborators described it, the "Negro problem" is a problem rooted in the hearts and minds of white citizens—in localized prejudice and individual, sometimes willful, ignorance. The book's central premise is based on the clash between the enlightened, rational, and universal American Creed, on the one hand, and the "personal and local interests," "considerations of community prestige and conformity," "group prejudice," and "all sorts of miscellaneous wants, impulses, and habits" that come to dominate in local contexts, on the other.[82] Myrdal's analysis centered on a cycle of self-confirming, but ultimately baseless and backward, racial animosities.[83] Years of prejudice and discrimination had kept black Americans in subservient positions, promoting poverty, undereducation, and pathological cultural reactions, all of which only seemed to confirm the basis of prejudice in the first place; meanwhile, the hardening of segregation ensured that whites were not often confronted with the real effects of racial prejudice and the conditions of black life in America. If they were, the continued attachment to fundamentally contradictory principles—an egalitarian Creed alongside racially prejudicial beliefs—would become untenable both psychologically and socially. "A great many Northerners, perhaps the majority," Myrdal argued, "get shocked and shaken in their conscience when they learn the facts. The average Northerner does not understand the reality and the effects of such discrimination as those in which he himself is taking part in his routine of life." Furthermore, Myrdal surmised, "I have become convinced . . . that a majority even of Southerners would be prepared for much more justice to the Negro if they were really brought to know the situation."[84] In the contest between a rational principle and irrational prejudice, universal ideals and local jealousies, the American Creed would win out. The Creed had a corrective power—an "unforced force," to deploy Habermasian terms *avant le lettre*—all its own.

As Ralph Ellison's early, scathing critique of Myrdal readily pointed out, the account of the dilemma centered white citizens, while marginalizing and pathologizing black citizens. Fundamentally, for Myrdal, the principles of the Creed were Euro-American creations; they represented the fruits of European Enlightenment thought transplanted onto American soil. When black Americans (or the other "disadvantaged groups" Myrdal lists) espoused allegiance to national ideals, it was an act of necessary appropriation rather than original authorship. In the end, "the Negro's entire life and, consequently also his opinions on the Negro problem are, in the main, to be considered as secondary reactions to more primary pressures from the side of the dominant white majority."[85] Yet this turns out to be quite fortunate, for in the Creed, black Americans could find the means for addressing their needs and combatting racism; those stuck at the losing end of the white citizen's dilemma "could not possibly have invented a system of political ideals which better corresponded to their interests."[86] The Creed was a tool that well-conceived black protest movements could readily mobilize:

> They will have a powerful tool in the caste struggle against white America: the glorious American ideals of democracy, liberty, and equality to which America is pledged not only by its political Constitution but also by the sincere devotion of its citizens. The Negroes are a minority, and they are poor and suppressed, but they have the advantage that they can fight wholeheartedly. The whites have all the power, but they are split in their moral personality. Their better selves are with the insurgents. The Negroes do not need any other allies.[87]

This is the kind of narrative that Vincent Harding would later lambast as "White History"—the "history of affirmation of the society . . . the history that finds basic justification and basic goodness in the very nature of American society"—and that I am identifying as a central pillar of what it means to see like a white state.[88]

Myrdal's commitments shared in a set of ideas pervasive and influential in American political culture—that is, as historian David Kennedy writes, "the simple belief that a factual appeal to the better angels of their nature would induce [white] Americans to do the right thing."[89] Indeed, part of the success and long-term impact of *An American Dilemma*, then, was how it "complimented and comforted [white] Americans even as it criticized them"—promising that the recipe for remedying the vexing "Negro problem" was not only at hand but an intrinsic and central part of American political life as well. As Kennedy observes, the book "held out the prospect of a virtually painless exit from the nation's racist history."[90] With white Americans made to face the truth, with black Americans resolutely and sincerely committed to the Creed, and with both living in a nation whose fundamental structures and principles remained sound, change could come without upheaval, crisis, or violence. The ultimate conclusion Myrdal reached was this: "In principle the Negro problem was settled long ago; in practice the solution is not effectuated."[91]

This central idea inhabits liberal theory's assertions about civil disobedience, though little of this is directly articulated—a silence that, in itself, provides a rather revealing indicator of the extent to which these theorists viewed racial injustice as exceptional rather than fundamental, even as the civil rights movement unfolded around them. Yet there are some explicit indications that this view was at work behind the scenes. In one of Rawls's undergraduate lectures from the mid-1960s, delivered in the same years that he was writing his first essays on political obligation and civil disobedience, he sounded a distinctly Myrdallian note, suggesting that liberal political philosophy had essentially "settled" the "major political questions" pertaining to "political liberty & civil rights," including the problem of segregation; and that therefore, all that was left was to apply the solution to the real world.[92] Walzer, too, theorized the civil rights struggle as one that successfully "utilize[d] the possibilities of an open political system": as *formally* free" but substantively "oppressed *citizens*," they worked to take "advantage of democratic rules in order to expose their hypocrisy." The success of this strategy during the civil rights movement revealed that the rules were "not entirely hypocritical," after all: the "rules yield[ed] advantages," and so the state, though imperfect, was necessarily and meaningfully democratic.[93] In later writings, Walzer would later emphasize the "severe but episodic" and exceptional nature of American racism, while affirming the "American civil rights struggle" as "a nice example of a conflict for which our moral/political language was and is entirely adequate." [94] The victory of liberal values, then, is given from the beginning: in appealing to true principles, core constitutional ideals (properly understood), or the majority's "sense of justice," civil rights protestors had to merely point out what white citizens must already believe.

This is the narrative of civil rights that undergirds, and is partly constitutive of, theories of civil disobedience—in which activists' use of nonviolence, willingness to serve jail time, and persuasive appeal to shared ideals "evoked a palpable tradition, a set of common values such that public disagreement could focus only on how (or how quickly) they might be realized."[95] Indeed, the civil rights movement—or rather, the story we often tell about it—appears to conform so closely to the liberal theory of disobedience because the two are cut from the same cloth. Out of the political and cultural struggle unleashed by the mobilization of the civil rights movement—as an attempt both to understand it and confine it—a compromise developed, allowing racial rule to be criticized to the extent that it could be exceptionalized. A broad range of political figures and intellectuals identified the problem of the Jim Crow order as a mismatch between true, national democratic ideals, and an outmoded, Southern racial authoritarianism, rather than something more complicated and pernicious: not a mismatch at all, but a particular institutional expression of the ways violent racial rule and American democracy had long constituted each other. With the South as an exception to rather than reflection of prevailing American values, norms, and systems of order, the demands of the civil rights movement could be contained, limited to "terms that excluded radical or fundamental challenges to status quo institutional practices in American society by treating the exercise of racial power as rare and aberrational rather than as systemic and ingrained."[96] Under this compact, the trajectory of the civil rights era came to be understood in terms as narrow as the theory of civil disobedience based upon it: black protestors targeted local, Southern segregation laws out of step with federal law and constitutional principle; they conformed to strict nonviolence and the means of moral suasion, going cheerfully to jail in order to signal "fidelity" to the law; they aroused the conscience of white Americans and ultimately the state, generating legislative change. In this way, as Kimberlé Crenshaw has powerfully argued, "the deeply transformative potential of the civil right's movement's interrogation of racial power was successively aborted as a piece of mainstream American ideology."[97]

When theorists of civil disobedience like Rawls drew authority from the example of the civil rights movement, they transformed the disruption, risk, and uncertainty of a decades-long struggle for black freedom into a consensual endorsement of existing institutions and ideals—a "testimonial for the system" made possible precisely through the educative force of disobedience's civility.[98] Even as they turned their attention to defending the civil rights movement's disobedient activism from conservative "law and order" criticism, these theorists did more to erase than amplify the agency, arguments, and creative political practices of the movement's activists. In sum, they failed to seriously entertain the possibility that the very activists who inspired their theorizations might construe the problem differently. This is part and parcel of what it means to see civil disobedience like a white state and indicative of what is consequently obscured from view: the questions, analyses, claims, and forms of action developed by activists on the ground—in Scott's terms, the forms of contextualized, embedded "local knowledge" developed in the midst of political action. How did the activists that made up the decades-long struggle against Jim Crow think about the nature of racial injustice? How did they conceive of civil disobedience, and why was it a meaningful way to fight against racial injustice? What forms of remediation did civil disobedience offer to a society structured by white supremacy, and what conclusions did activists want spectator citizens to draw from their actions? These questions are not posed at all; they are effectively ruled out in a framework for civil disobedience that adopts the perspective of an already legitimated state. Instead, the civil rights movement (and its multitude of activists) operates between the lines of theory as an object lesson—a ready-made example that proves the moral purchase of the theory, rather than a live source of novel theoretical insights and political claims. This, indeed, is the final silencing slight of a theory that sees like a white state: civil rights activists cannot tell us anything new about racial injustice or the struggle against it that white citizens (or academic philosophers) do not already know.

There are hints of an alternative reading of civil disobedience in the so-called classical phase of the civil rights movement, available within the very document most ubiquitously cited as proof of the Rawlsian version of disobedience: King's "Letter from a Birmingham Jail." On King's account, the demand that those breaking an unjust law do so "openly" and "lovingly" with a willingness to accept punishment for their actions serves to rouse the conscience of the broader community while also expressing "the very highest respect for law"[99]—just as liberal theory demands. Yet moving beyond these few lines, we should note how King frames the entire problem of civil disobedience at the beginning of the "Letter." He writes the following: "Nonviolent direct action seeks to create such a crisis and establish such creative tension that a community that has constantly refused to negotiate is forced to confront the issue. It seeks so to dramatize the issue that it can no longer be ignored. . . . So the purpose of the direct action is to create a situation so crisis-packed that it will inevitably open the door to negotiation."[100] The language is unmistakably the language of crisis, destabilization, and even coercion (though nonviolent). It is also a language of action, which addresses not just the normative commitments behind nonviolent protest but also its functions: to affirm and enact the capacities for self-liberation among the oppressed, to disclose the ongoing oppression faced by black citizens, and to "force" a confrontation with systematic injustice in order to build a new polity. King's treatment of civil disobedience raises the question of *how* activists go about doing this—the concrete forms of action they employ.[101] Exploring this account requires a shift in perspective—seeing civil disobedience not like a white state, but like an activist.

As will become clear in the pages that follow, moreover, to the extent that activists made use of the kinds of appeals required of them by theories of civil disobedience, they found the approach simultaneously enabling and limiting. Even as it eventually produced a new social consensus rejecting legalized segregation as antithetical to core national values, it deferred and deflated a serious consideration of the costs of racial justice for a society invested in white supremacy—and complicated activists' own attempts to articulate more expansive notions of equality beyond formal desegregation or freedom beyond private liberty, let alone to stipulate their practical entailments. Choosing, at times (and before particular audiences) to place the movement in the sweep of American exceptionalist discourse—aligned with the romance of national destiny, a new step in the inevitable and progression of American values—activists were sometimes able to compel political elites within the Kennedy and Johnson administrations to authorize and legitimate the movement and (some of its) goals. Yet this rhetorical device also hindered activists' attempts to disclose and disrupt more subtle systems of racial subjugation that implicated not just the legal code of the Jim Crow South but also a complex network of social, cultural, economic, and political institutions that were national and in some cases global in scope—narrowing, as historian Mary Dudziak notes, "the field of vision to formal equality, to opening the doors of opportunity, and away from a broader critique of the American economic and political system."[102] In this way, movement activists sometimes appealed to a vision of primarily persuasive, nondisruptive action while simultaneously deploying the mechanisms of nonviolent coercion to precipitate political and moral crises—a gap between rhetoric and reality that could be exploited by critics of the movement and enthusiastic proponents of "law and order" politics, furthering the conceptual collapse between "civil disobedience" and "civil disorder."[103]

It is just this sort of nuance that becomes increasingly obscured in the ways of talking and thinking about civil disobedience—the ways of *envisioning* it—that emerged among many political theorists out of the tumult of the 1960s and 1970s. In imagining racial injustice as a gap between principle and practice, between oppressed minority and a singular majority, the social theory that lives between the lines of the mainstream, liberal ideals about civil disobedience flattens the social context in which civil rights activism was happening. Activists did not engage with civil disobedience as a limited justificatory enterprise—when it is permissible to break the law in a liberal democracy?—but a dynamic political practice beset by the peculiar dilemmas generated by trying to act within and against the structures of white democracy. Without engaging with the particular "problem space" civil rights activists inhabited, it is hard to appreciate the opportunities found—and lost—in the "classical phase" of civil rights disobedience.[104]

Civil rights activists were engaged in a vibrant, contentious debate about how to understand the problem posed by the mid-century American racial order; how to construct the meaning of the sacrifices and risks of collective action; and how to devise strategies that would best confront, combat, and reconstitute the polity as a multiracial democracy. Though there was never a convergence on any one set of answers—there is no such thing as *the* civil rights movement, in the singular—the political theories crafted by and debated among activists do, collectively, pose a striking contrast with the view from the white state that defines liberal disobedience theory. Indeed, far from being wholly captured by and subsumed within the bounds of the presumptively legitimate, democratic constitutional order, civil disobedience circulated among figures such as Bayard Rustin and Martin Luther King, Jr. as a specific tool in the struggle against a global white supremacy that encompassed colonialism as well as segregation. As such, Jim Crow was understood not as a regime of exclusion or legalized segregation, but as systemic domination: a regime of extreme violence premised on pervasive fear (both white status anxiety and black terror), shaping practices, relations, and subjects across the whole of American society. Nonviolent direct action, these figures suggested, offered a *decolonizing praxis*: it could serve as a powerful means of self-emancipation from white supremacy's empire of fear and violence, transforming both the activist and the world around them without risking the most aggressive and total forms of white retaliation. This last proviso was crucial, securing not just survival but also the eventual transformation of white oppressors into fellow citizens. The work of *democratic* decolonization demanded no less.

Consequently, when deployed on the ground, civil disobedience did not cleave faithfully to the standards of public reason and constitutional principle that philosophers like Rawls read out of these engagements. As I detail in subsequent chapters, civil disobedience instead espoused a vocabulary of liberation and grappled with Jim Crow in expansive rather than limited terms: a local instantiation of a global system of violence and fear; a regime whose practices of racial domination crisscrossed jurisdictional, geographical, and institutional lines, as well as those between public and private; and a system based not on the monopolization of force by the state, but the democratization of force among white citizens, empowered to maintain the status quo with whatever means necessary. Persuasion, then, was simply and avowedly not enough: forms of disruption, forms of coercion, forms of crisis-generation were also operative in pressing claims and forcing responses, and in raising the idea that all citizens, as well as state officials, bore responsibility for the maintenance and therefore the dismantling of racial hierarchy. Not the removal of barriers to entry, but the collaborative construction of a new social order would thus be required—one that, as Danielle Allen puts it, "in no way relies on domination to stabilize itself."[105] At stake in civil disobedience, then, was nothing short of transforming the world.

2
An Entire World in Motion

This is a period of acceleration. The entire world is in motion. If Negroes hope to win equality, justice and liberty, they must get into motion in great masses in world-shaking maneuvers and strategy.
—Philip Randolph, Speech at Madison Square Garden (1942)[1]

If non-cooperation brings the British to their knees in India, there is no reason why it should not bring them to their knees in Africa, nor is there any reason why it should not bring the white man to his knees in the South.
—James Weldon Johnson, "Gandhi a Prisoner" (1922)[2]

... we belonged to a whole world
nkrumah was no foreigner
virgil aikins was not the only fighter
—Ntozake Shange, "Mood Indigo" (1983)[3]

Disobedience, Domesticated

At the tail end of five decades that had witnessed coordinated, mass non-violent protests across the globe—from India, South Africa, and Ghana to Czechoslovakia and cities across Western Europe—Hannah Arendt pronounced civil disobedience a strictly American affair. "Although the phenomenon of civil disobedience is today a world-wide phenomenon," she argued in 1972, "it is primarily American in origin and substance." Based on this premise, she pressed the striking claim that "no other country, and no other language, has even a word for it, and that the American republic is the only government having at least a chance to cope with it—not, perhaps, in accordance with the statutes, but in accordance with the *spirit* of its laws."[4] On Arendt's distinctive reading of civil disobedience, the conceptual lineage of the practice is defined by specifically American traditions of voluntary association and a history of ideas rooted in a robust understanding of consent—a consent that operates horizontally between fellow citizens and that is constituted by the permanent possibility of dissent. On this basis, Arendt concluded, the practice of civil disobedience finds a natural home in American political tradition, and should have a corresponding place in the American constitutional order.

While Arendt's essay railed against much of the civil disobedience orthodoxy that was then circulating through philosophy journals, legal discourse, and the public sphere, in her insistence on disobedience as inherently *domestic*—and inherently American—in both "origin and substance," she shared something rather substantial with many of the theories that otherwise drew her ire. Indeed, she made explicit a basic premise that underlay the entire framework for conceptualizing disobedience within liberal and democratic theory: that civil disobedience is defined by, and operates entirely within, the normative landscape of the democratic, constitutional nation-state.

This "domestic" presumption emerges from the way philosophers in the 1960s and 1970s approached the very subject of disobedience—and the way that many scholars have approached it since. As we saw in Chapter 1, for theorists such as Rawls or Walzer, civil disobedience only becomes a *problem* for philosophy—rather than a feature of political life or a subject for history or a tactic for activists—within constitutional democracies. Civil disobedience might occur everywhere, but in democracies—in a "society such as ours"—where the law is presumed to be the product of legitimate institutions that citizens have an interest in maintaining, breaking the law in protest—even for good reasons—becomes normatively troubling.[5]

This way of framing the philosophical question of civil disobedience—the contexts in which it does, and does not, pose a normative problem—likewise shapes the kinds of claims, the forms of action, and the normative vocabulary presumably available to disobedients within the constitutional nation-state. If the philosophical space of disobedience is defined by constitutional order, then the boundaries of action are shaped by the imperative of stabilizing that order and actualizing its "real meaning." In the context of the democratic state, this requires sticking to what philosopher Candice Delmas has referred to as "the template of civil disobedience"—the script for action that dictates what activists must do if they wish to be received by their fellow citizens as sincere constitutional patriots and not rebels.[6] The entire theoretical imagination of what civil disobedience is and looks like is, in these accounts, determined by a particular way of understanding the obligations generated by domestic democratic institutions.

This domestic framing, so familiar and commonplace within the philosophical debates over civil disobedience, sits quite uneasily within a history of civil disobedience that is overwhelmingly transnational. Of course, it is not as if these theorists were somehow ignorant of the fact of disobedience as "a world-wide phenomenon," outside of the orbit of those states categorized as constitutional democracies. Civil disobedience obviously lived other lives elsewhere, where it traveled different trajectories, pursued different ends, and articulated different theoretical vocabularies. It is just that—for Rawls, Walzer, and even Arendt—those trajectories and vocabularies had little to do, at a philosophical level, with what civil disobedience meant, and should mean, *here*. *Here*—a "society such as ours"—is decidedly democratic; its disobedience decidedly domestic.

Yet the idea of such bounded disobedience is historically untenable—at least insofar as the civil rights movement, the supposedly paradigmatic example of domestic disobedience, is concerned. Indeed, the central questions posed by mainstream philosophical accounts of civil disobedience run in precisely the opposite direction of the ones that historians and sociologists tend to ask about the global history of civil disobedience and its parent category, nonviolent direct action. A primary question for historians and sociologists of the civil rights movement has been about the paths of conceptual migration leading from Mahatma Gandhi's *satyagraha* to American civil rights disobedience—that is, to borrow Richard Fox's words, "how do we explain [the] local U.S. replication of an originally Indian protest method?"[7] This question about transnational transmission—about the lines connecting the American civil rights movement to its noteworthy predecessors, Gandhi and the campaign for Indian independence from British colonial rule—does not figure as relevant at all in the predominant political theories of civil disobedience crafted in the wake of the civil rights movement.[8] In fact, it is a question effectively ruled out by a framework in which only those instances of disobedience that occur within the bounds of a certain kind of polity—a constitutional democracy—can be subjects for serious theoretical reflection; or when the problem of racial injustice is figured as a purely domestic one—a problem of national minorities petitioning for full inclusion within the polity. An entire geography of political claim-making is rendered invisible—or simply irrelevant—when we see civil disobedience like a white state.

This chapter is an attempt to step beyond those narrow parameters. Drawing on recent work in international history, and on the evidence I see in the civil rights archives, the pages that follow chart the movement of ideas about civil disobedience and nonviolent direct action as they traveled between the United States, India, South Africa, and Ghana through four decades of the twentieth century. As I argue, the receptiveness of African American civil rights activists to the means of nonviolent direct action and civil disobedience was crucially informed by the deployment of nonviolence in the midst of anticolonial struggles around the world and perceptions about its potential efficacy as a means of self-emancipation and colonial liberation. Between 1920 and 1960, the idea of nonviolent resistance was in *imaginative transit* across disparate contexts, as African Americans, Indians, South Africans, and Ghanaians explored the relationship between systems of colonialism and segregation and found common cause in waging nonviolence against local instantiations of a global white supremacy. By *imaginative transit*, I mean to capture the creative, constructed linkages between disparate contexts, the forged solidarities and notions of shared struggle, and the actual, literal transit of activists across a world in motion. While the notion of *imagination* is intended to underscore the intellectual labor and conceptual innovation required to construct a world of colonized and racially oppressed peoples for whom nonviolence could provide an answer, the notion of *transit* emphasizes the work of boundary crossing—of bodies in motion across continents, in order to set bodies in motion in protest—that enabled and emerged from such an enterprise.[9] These lines of transit, I contend, embedded civil rights activists in the United States in a wider geography, and a larger normative universe, than a conception of a purely domestic disobedience can hope to capture. The constellation of animating ideas about what civil disobedience was—and what it was good for here in the Jim Crow United States—took shape transnationally, through the movement of activists exploring nonviolence and amid a set of arguments about what the conditions of segregation and colonialism shared. By the mid-1950s and the emergence of mass, grassroots nonviolent action against segregation—a decade before the recognized rise of Black Power and Third World solidarity within the civil rights movement—the concept of civil disobedience already betrayed an "imagination that had long overflowed the bounds a of a staid Americanism."[10] Through these years, activists cultivated and readily mobilized a language of self-liberation from white supremacy's structures of fear and violence—a language effectively erased when domestic constitutionalism is the only plausible framework for comprehending the idea of civil rights disobedience. Attending to these circuits of transit and the concepts forged along them, then, is an interpretive strategy intended to counter the simultaneous de-contextualizing and domesticating maneuvers identified in philosophies of civil disobedience—the maneuvers that enable those philosophies to see like a white state.

Even as I build on recent historical work on black transnationalism and international history to construct this account, I also aim to push back against two key interpretive moves made within that literature. First, for many writing within the revisionist tradition of the "long civil rights movement," the early Cold War years represent an effective foreclosure of the radical potentialities of the black transnational activism that was so alive during the 1930s and 1940s. In historian Penny Von Eschen's estimation, as civil rights activists "negotiated an international and national terrain dominated by the Cold War," they were forced to do so in ways that often parroted US foreign policy objectives, and exacerbated "the severing of international and domestic politics" and "the silencing of antiimperialist and anticapitalist politics" that had erstwhile thrived.[11] The force of repression during the late Truman and early Eisenhower years was, of course, real, and it took a serious toll on anticolonial and antiracist activists within the US and abroad, shutting down lines of transit and avenues of critique that had once seemed promising and potent—both for those seeking to dismantle Jim Crow in the US, as well as those pushing the US to support anticolonial and antiapartheid movements worldwide. Yet I want to insist that the activism of the figures within the story I tell here—those like A. Philip Randolph, Bayard Rustin, Bill Sutherland, and Martin Luther King, Jr.—was not so wholly captured by the logic of "Cold War civil rights," and that the particularly paranoid style of McCarthyite politics shifted, but did not doom, the possibilities for transnational anticolonial activism. The approach to nonviolence developed by this set of activists was both distinctly *anticolonial* and *transnational*; and for them, nonviolent direct action and anticolonial liberation were an intimately associated pair. This framework, I argue, had real consequences for the way they imagined civil disobedience would unfold—the dynamics they attributed to it, and the potential they thought it offered for tackling racial hierarchy in its multiple forms.

Second, this chapter works to broaden the geographical focus of the literature on the transnational dimensions of the civil rights movement by questioning the extent to which the movement's uptake of nonviolence is adequately or accurately characterized as a process of adapting Gandhian nonviolence from its British colonial context for the fight against Jim Crow. Seminal works by Sudarshan Kapur, Gerald Horne, Sean Chabot, and, most recently, Nico Slate establish the vital links that were forged between movements in the United States and India in the first half of the twentieth century, and they illuminate the creative, generative, and fraught process of translating the dynamics of nonviolent action from one freedom struggle—and one racialized hierarchy—to another.[12] While the relationship between Afro-America and the Indian independence movement is indeed crucial, and figures prominently in this chapter, the process of imaginative transit that I attempt to capture here was the product of, and productive of, a genuinely *global* anticolonial imaginary.[13] This complicates the idea of the civil rights movement as simply translating Gandhism as such; instead, I suggest, these activists were immersed in broad processes of thinking about a shared condition of racialized unfreedom that was playing out globally, in the form of colonialism, segregation, and violence.

None of this is meant to deny the fact that civil rights activists, particularly in the decade between the Montgomery bus boycott and the Selma voting rights campaign, mobilized the language of American constitutionalism and the founding principles of the Declaration of Independence. My claim here is not that these appeals did not exist; but that they were nested within, and only fully cognizable through, a normative geography of anticolonial nonviolence—a network of specific activists in transit across the globe, connected by a constellation of ideas. Their transit rendered nonviolence plausible as antiracist, *decolonizing praxis*: a means of acting directly on the psychological, structural, and relational bases of white supremacy in order to transform them.[14] In this way, I wish to make the strong claim that the specific form of anticolonialism charted within these pages is normatively prior to the domestic and constitutional appeals that are typically privileged in accounts of the "short" years of the civil rights movement. That is, we cannot understand the concept of civil rights disobedience as it emerged *within* the United States in the 1960s—how activists conceptualized the problem of racial domination, and the transformative work they believed nonviolence could perform under Jim Crow—without appreciating how the concept was formed through transit, *across* and *beyond* its borders, in the decades before.[15]

The idea of transit brings into view the shape of the world imagined and constituted by these networks of anticolonial and antiracist nonviolent activism—and signals the limitations of this imaginary. The anticolonial transnationalism of Rustin or King does not replicate the projects undertaken in earlier decades; nor is it a draft version of the forms of Third World solidarity that developed after 1965, which figured black America as the "internal colony" of the United States. The geographies of transit are distinct, and concomitantly the analyses of colonialism, empire, and white supremacy that emerged from them. The lens of nonviolence forged particular alliances and connections, enabling a diagnosis of colonialism and segregation as a shared condition—subjection to the racial rule of fear and violence—that could be countered and transformed through the creative use of nonviolent direct action. Here, I trace the formation of these ideas to push back against the decontextualization of civil rights disobedience and its domestication as race-neutral constitutional patriotism. The imaginative transit of these activists undercuts the kind of epistemic authority philosophers of disobedience lend to the racial state when they refigure it as "nearly just," "democratic," and "constitutional," and when they position such a state as the normative horizon for political action—a slippage and itself a form of transit that hides racialized "imperialist intent" within a discourse about the rule of law.[16]

This vision of nonviolence as a decolonizing praxis has its limitations, however, made visible in the geography of colonialism imagined through it. For Jodi Byrd, "transit" denotes the enmeshment of systems of racialization and colonization in the United States, such that "racialization in the United States now often evokes colonization as a metonym," obfuscating "the distinctions between the two systems of dominance and the coerced complicities amid both." Transit, in this sense, erases "the territoriality of conquest" and reinscribes the original injury of settler colonialism by collapsing Indigenous claims to sovereignty into appeals for racial equality among citizens.[17] In other words, even as African American activists located themselves in a world in motion beyond the nation-state, the same analytic that enabled them to relate and analogize (domestic) segregation to (foreign) colonialism simultaneously erased the expropriated, colonized ground on which they already stood. Though I cannot further detail these connections here, it is important to mark the ways in which civil disobedience as a decolonizing praxis illuminates new possibilities, even as it obscures others.

Before I proceed, a brief word on terminology. In what follows, I often use the terms "nonviolent direct action" and "nonviolent resistance" as if they were more or less interchangeable with civil disobedience. I recognize that these terms are not interchangeable and that the former are far broader than the latter. For political theorists, the distinction between civil disobedience and the larger category of nonviolent direct action—which might include a wide array of legal and illegal tactics—is an important one because of the normative conundrum posed by purposeful lawbreaking. "Civil disobedience," as philosopher Hugo Bedau once wrote, "is not just done; it is committed. It is always the sort of thing that can send one to jail."[18] While recognizing, in the abstract, the analytical purchase of distinguishing between tactics that violate the law from those that do not, I nevertheless treat civil disobedience and nonviolent direct action as if they were cognate terms because, by and large, the individuals at the heart of this story tended to do so.[19] Moreover, I contend, the fact that they did so is instructive for understanding the context in which black civil rights activists undertook nonviolent resistance. Jim Crow was, among other things, a system through which white Americans sought to dictate the placement of black bodies in space—who could go where, and when, and under what conditions—for the purposes of racial control. Under these conditions, when black citizens rebelled against the racial order, putting their bodies in spaces where they were out of place—sitting at all-white lunch counters or in the front seats of the city bus; marching in open defiance of the reprisal that was sure to come—they posed a threat to the order of Jim Crow. Whether their actions were fully legal, began as legal but crossed into a gray area when they were told to leave but did not, or were purposely designed to break the law, activism tended to end in arrest. In other words, for black activists in the South, civil rights protest was usually "the sort of thing that [could] send one to jail," no matter where the line of the law really lay. Nonviolent direct action was always, at least potentially, disobedient.

"Suppose There Should Arise a Negro Gandhi"

In the twentieth century, the conversation about whether civil disobedience should be used to fight Jim Crow in the United States began in earnest, at a national level, with India. The Indian independence movement was a matter of sustained, decades-long interest amongst black Americans. News frequently circulated through the African American press, particularly after World War I and the escalation of anticolonial activism, and generated considerable debate about the meaning of nonviolent resistance and its relevance for the racial order in the United States—a debate that tended to rise and fall in intensity alongside Gandhi's main mass actions, from the noncooperation campaign of 1920 through the Salt March and nationwide disobedience in 1930, to the Quit India campaign of 1942.[20]

For many people in the United States, it was in the context of the noncooperation campaign that they first became familiar with "the Mahatma." Gandhi proposed noncooperation as a response to the April 1919 massacre at Amritsar, in which British colonial officers fired on thousands of demonstrators convened in violation of a ban against political gatherings, killing hundreds. In the months after the massacre, the Indian National Congress adopted *swaraj*—self-rule—as its goal for the first time, and Gandhi announced the launch of a large-scale noncooperation campaign. In concert with the Congress and the Islamic Khalifat movement, Gandhi devised a multistage program of withdrawal from British-controlled institutions— beginning with the surrender of titles and offices and the boycott of foreign and imported goods; followed by mass resignation from jobs with the government, military, and police; and concluding, if necessary, with societywide tax revolt and other forms of civil disobedience. The campaign earned considerable support across Indian society, but its victories were in the end more symbolic than practical. The campaign generated massive support throughout the subcontinent, but only a handful elite Indians actually ceded their posts in India's colonial government; those without offices to give up in protest—the majority of the population—were "highly excited but unable to do much more than shout 'Mahatma Gandhi ki jai' ('victory to Mahatma Gandhi')."[21] When Gandhi issued the call to escalate the campaign to its final stage of tax disobedience in early 1922, demonstrators in Chauri Chaura clashed with police, who opened fire. In response, thousands of villagers in descended on the police station and burned it, killing the policemen trapped inside. Gandhi and the Congress immediately suspended the campaign. The British colonial government, meanwhile, arrested Gandhi in March for his role in leading noncooperation and sentenced him to a six-year term.[22] The movement was, for the time being, over.

Even so, Indian noncooperation generated widespread interest in the United States, as news circulated through the mainstream and black presses, igniting a conversation about its relevance to the problem of American racial hierarchy. To be sure, there existed vibrant and long-standing traditions of African Americans and allied whites using noncooperation, boycotts, and disobedience to fight against slavery, racial segregation, and discrimination. As George Frederickson notes, "Boycotts of segregated facilities and disobedience to Jim Crow laws and customs had been a feature of the antebellum abolitionist campaign against racial discrimination in the northern states and had also been part of the spontaneous response of the Southern African Americans to white attempts to impose streetcar segregation during Reconstruction and again around the turn of the century."[23] Novel, however, was Gandhi's philosophy of nonviolent action—what Gandhi dubbed "*satyagraha*," literally translated as "truth force" or "holding fast to truth"—which represented nonviolence not only as a means to political ends but as an end in itself, a prefigurative politics that would refashion both self and society along new lines. Novel, as well, was the idea of using nonviolent direct action on such a large scale, as a means of sustained, coordinated resistance to white colonial power. The combination of these two ideas stirred many an imagination with the possibilities for fighting the color line here at home.

In the midst of the noncooperation campaign, Alexander Louis Jackson, general manager of the *Chicago Defender* and former educational secretary for the National Urban League, published a glowing report of Gandhi's use of nonviolent methods. "The Indians have experimented with some of the other well-known methods of fighting foreign rulers and oppressors," Jackson wrote, including "mutiny." Yet armed uprising has proven "disastrous" for Indians: "The Indians were 'licked' not only by superior war weapons, but by their inability to arrive at any common bases of understanding or action," allowing the British to divide and conquer. According to Jackson, "Gandhi has turned his back on all this," by rooting the struggle in "self-control," "self-mastery," and the "doctrine taught by Christ . . . [to] turn the other cheek twice and yet again if necessary." For Jackson, the potential relevance for the rest of the colonized world—"our Egyptian friends and African brothers"—was immediately obvious. But equally clear was the association between the Indian fight and the African American one. Slyly observing that eventually Gandhi's efforts were going to "worry someone," Jackson seemed to foresee the Montgomery Bus Boycott of the mid-1950s when he suggested that "some empty Jim Crow cars will some day worry our street car magnates in Southern cities when we get around to walking rather than suffer insult and injury to our wives and children." Thus, he concluded, it would behoove black America to take note—to "turn our eyes from the South for awhile toward India that we may know that the task is world wide and equally important. Heaven send us prophets equal to the task."[24]

Jackson was not the only one to locate the fight against Jim Crow in a wider world of anticolonial struggle and to see more local possibilities in the Indian example. In March of 1922, James Weldon Johnson—then serving as the first black executive secretary for the NAACP—wrote about Gandhi's noncooperation campaign with "absorbing interest" in the pages of the *New York Age*. Less than a year after the conclusion of the Irish War of Independence and on the heels of Gandhi's arrest, Johnson wondered whether Gandhi's methods would, in the end, prove as effective as armed struggle. "It remains to be seen what the effect of Gandhi's arrest will be on the movement launched by him," he offered. "But what should interest observers more than anything else is what will be the final result." Should Gandhi prove successful, Johnson suggested, "it will mean a new hope for independence and self-determination on the part of those peoples and groups who are prohibited the possession of the implements of force." The triumph of nonviolent resistance over the British in India could signal nothing less than the end of white domination: "If non-cooperation brings the British to their knees in India," he concluded, "there is no reason why it should not bring them to their knees in Africa, nor is there any reason why it should not bring the white man to his knees in the South."[25]

Prophetic as Johnson's words now seem, however, there was nothing inevitable about the uptake of Gandhian methods by African Americans fighting Jim Crow. Despite sharing in the experience of oppression, "Gandhi and India represented worlds which were in many ways different from the reality of Afro-America," as Sudarshan Kapur indicates. "Therefore imagination and creativity were needed to draw upon Gandhi" and his methods of struggle.[26] Indeed, it required considerable political work to transform the Indian example into an exemplar—from a matter of interest for black Americans into a model that might meet their needs. This task was complicated by the way that Gandhi himself was received and depicted in public discourse. As historian Sean Scalmer has detailed in his study of the reception of Gandhi in the UK and US, initial responses to Gandhi in the mainstream American press tended to draw on racialized tropes, presenting Gandhi as an "Oriental" mystic garbed in a loincloth.[27] While this coverage was often dismissive and pejorative, sympathetic coverage also tended to mobilize a discourse of "hyper-difference," describing Gandhi's methods as rooted in Hindu religious practices and beliefs that were essentially foreign to the social context of the West, and portraying Gandhi himself as a mystic and a saint. When interpreting *satyagraha*, Scalmer writes, the "consensus was that this was a 'revival' of an 'ancient Hindu practice,' to use the words of the *New York Times*, and that it was therefore based upon an 'underlying psychology' that was 'peculiarly Indian or Hindu.' "[28] The cultural makeup of Gandhian nonviolence seemed, in these accounts, inescapably foreign, rendering an American reprisal unlikely.

Perhaps more consequentially, some raised concerns that structural differences in context would prevent nonviolent resistance—so compellingly waged against the British empire—from ever being effective against the "empire of Jim Crow."[29] In particular, the routine reality of violence and racial terror wielded against black Americans cast doubt on the efficacy and prudence of embracing a Gandhian principle like *ahimsa,* or non-harm. Responding, perhaps, to James Weldon Johnson's interest in the power of Gandhi's methods to "bring the white man to his knees in the South," sociologist E. Franklin Frazier published a fiery editorial in the March 1924 issue of *The Crisis,* the official journal of the NAACP, founded and edited by W. E. B. Du Bois. Though he did not reference Gandhi by name, Frazier took to task those who offered ideas of "Christian humility," "love," or "non-resistance" as meaningful ways to fight racial oppression. "They go about saying that Southern white people love us when they lynch us and deny us an opportunity for education and even primitive justice," Frazier wrote. Reminding his readers that "a man may love his dog" and still mistreat him, he concluded that "the question of love" is ultimately "irrelevant" to the question of racial justice. "It is foolish to go about asserting in the face of facts to the contrary that white people love us, unless perchance some think that by a sort of suggestion white people will be hypnotized into loving us. The Negro does not want love. He wants justice."[30] To fight for justice in the context of Jim Crow, Frazier implied, required something much more forceful than turning the other cheek.

Frazier's essay shocked at least some partisans of nonviolence, prompting "one or two" letters to the editor, according to Du Bois.[31] Ellen Winsor, a Quaker and suffragist who had served a five-day jail sentence for her participation in the 1919 "Watchfire" demonstration, wrote to Du Bois on March 2 to express her disagreement with Frazier's critique of nonviolence.[32] While Frazier worried that nonviolence would leave African Americans ever more vulnerable, Winsor sounded the opposite alarm: "Not that I am one of those who desire to keep the Negro happy and contented in his present lot to which it hath pleased the white over-lord to call him, but because the evidence is so strong that a spirit of rebellion fostered on personal hatred will lead black and white alike into a pit as wide and deep as gaping hell." War and violence, Winsor argued, have only spread "the poison of disease, poverty, famine and bitterness . . . over the nations of the earth." In seeming to defend the use of force, then, Frazier was "willing to offer the same up again to his people." Noting that Gandhi "has not one drop of white blood in his veins," Winsor thus pointed to hope for a future in which "a Gandhi will arise in this country to lead the people out of their misery and ignorance, not by the old way of brute force which breeds sorrow and wrong, but by the new methods of education based on economic justice leading straight to Freedom."[33] Du Bois declined to publish Winsor's letter, expressing broad agreement with Frazier's stance and sounding his own note of skepticism about nonviolence—"I am," he replied to Winsor, "compelled to smile at the unanimity with which the great leader, Mr. Gandhi, is received by those peoples and races who have spilled the most blood."[34] He did, however, show the letter to Frazier and invited him to provide a response.

In his second editorial, Frazier was even more pointed. He clarified that his concerns centered on the vulnerability of black Americans and the need to preserve all available means, particularly armed self-defense, in the face of an intransigent and violent racial order. Noting that a world war had done little "to achieve democracy and make an end of wars," Frazier nevertheless insisted—in a particularly prescient moment—that "however much we may lament war, it appears that a disillusioned, but stupid world must undergo another war before white men will learn to respect the darker races." Even so, Frazier's principal object was not to advocate "wholesale violence" as a means of winning freedom for African Americans. Instead, he emphasized the importance of "violent defense in local and specific instances" in making "white men hesitate to make wanton attacks upon Negroes." How else, he asked, "are we to meet the attitude of those supposedly civilized intellectuals of the South, who, according to Frank Tannenbaum, would resort to a general slaughter of Negroes rather than give them justice, but show a greater reluctance in the face of the growing disposition on the part of Negroes to retaliate?" Frazier's reference here is to *Darker Phases of the South*, Tannenbaum's 1922 investigation of the Ku Klux Klan in which he argued that white racial violence was based on a deep-seated fear. "There is an underlying current of apprehension that the South will be outstripped in population by the colored against the white," Tannenbaum wrote in that work. "It is fear of losing grip upon the world, of losing caste, of losing control. The fear is not always conscious. It is not always evident. But it is the force back of the generous condemnation of the negro [sic]. It is the factor that underlies much of the talk of inferiority—of pointing a moral why it [desegregation] must not, why it cannot, why it may not happen." In Tannenbaum's estimation, it was this bedrock fear that animated the persistent racial terror of Klan rule—a fear so powerful and yet so disconnected from social reality that it continually overwhelmed the potential of moral suasion, education, or law to restrain it. As he reported, "I recall talking to a man—a man of high standing in his State, a scholar of much learning, and he said to me: 'We will paint this State red before we paint it black.' . . . It is this fear that colors all talk about the negro [sic], and as long as it exists there is no possibility of securing in the South a general program that will lead to an amelioration of the situation."[35]

It was this precise coupling of fear and violence that convinced Frazier of the inadequacy of nonviolent resistance. Taking up Winsor's prediction that an American Gandhi might someday arise, Frazier painted an alternative outcome: "suppose," he granted, "there should arise a Negro Gandhi to lead Negroes without hate in their hearts to stop tilling the fields of the South under the peonage system; to cease paying their taxes to States that keep their children in ignorance; and to ignore the iniquitous disenfranchisement of Jim-Crow laws." The result, Frazier suggested, would not be the bold and hopeful march to "Freedom" Winsor promised, but a bloodletting of unrivaled brutality: "I fear we would witness an unprecedented massacre of defenseless black men and women in the name of Law and Order and there would scarcely be enough Christian sentiment in America to stay the flood of blood."[36]

In the midst of decades of lynch laws and at the height of Jim Crow, Frazier's concerns were certainly weighty ones—concerns that were likely more common than any enthusiasm for a reprisal of Gandhian nonviolent resistance stateside. The plausibility of nonviolent struggle in the context of the American racial order—with its nightrider vigilantes and official acceptance of extreme antiblack violence—was neither obvious nor inevitable. As James Weldon Johnson made perfectly clear, even as he perceived the potential of Gandhi's methods, the evidence was not yet in regarding the efficacy of nonviolence as a mode of anticolonial resistance. In particular, Frazier's pressing concern demanded an answer: If white Americans fundamentally feared black power, and that fear routinely led to violence, how could nonviolence offer a way to press demands without leaving black communities thoroughly disarmed in the face of reprisals? Given the nontrivial differences between the conditions of the South and the conditions of British colonial rule, making the case for an American Gandhism would require a significant amount of work in order to establish a basic commonality between the plight of Indians and African Americans: a shared state of subjection to racialized oppression, and thus shared participation in a task that was "world wide," even as local conditions varied. It required nothing less than the imaginative transit necessary to construct and sustain such a world.

Charting the "Common Cause"

In a 1959 article for *Ebony* magazine, Martin Luther King, Jr.—newly returned from a trip to India—recounted the warm reception he received there in the following terms: "We were looked upon as brothers with the color of our skin as something of an asset." This seemingly simple statement of racial fraternity in fact reflected years of imaginative transit—years of forged solidarities, experimental activism, and political exchange—between black America and India. The affinity King expressed was therefore more than just skin deep. His statements tapped into an idea of a shared struggle against linked problems— making common cause against a common cause—that had been decades in the making. As he continued in his article, "[t]he strongest bond of fraternity was the common cause of minority and colonial peoples in America, Africa, and Asia who now struggle to throw off racialism and imperialism." While referencing, in brief, the potential structural differences between "minority" and "colonial" peoples, King nevertheless depicted them as united, joined in a common fight against a shared set of problems—"racialism" and "imperialism." King was one of a long line of prominent African American leaders to think in these terms; many perceived in the Indian independence movement "a struggle that was also theirs."[37] For King, moreover, the lessons of this bond were clear: "I left India more convinced than ever before that nonviolent resistance is the most potent weapon available to oppressed people in their struggle for freedom."[38]

King's statements are reflective of what historian Nico Slate has called "colored cosmopolitanism," a project that linked African Americans and Indians from the First World War through Indian independence. In these years, as Slate argues, "African Americans and Indians helped engineer one of the most creative and politically significant redefinitions of racial borders in the twentieth century—the invention of the colored world."[39] Tying black Americans to Indians through a common racial identification—as "colored," "black," or "dark"—enabled a reconstruction of colonization and Jim Crow as related conditions, Slate demonstrates; ultimately, I argue, this also enabled the reception of nonviolent direct action as a plausible weapon against both.

Few individuals were as persistently involved in the "invention of the colored world" as Du Bois.[40] Though skeptical of Gandhism as such, and particularly its application in the US, Du Bois was nevertheless invested in Indian independence as a movement of resistance to the global forces of racism and imperialism. Even as he expressed misgivings at the idea that boycotts and civil disobedience could work in the South, he consistently lauded Gandhi as a "great leader" and a "great man." And, most importantly for my present purposes, he frequently worked to present Gandhi as a leader of "dark" men against white oppressors, painting Indian independence in terms with which African Americans could identify. When, in 1929, the NAACP celebrated its twentieth anniversary, Du Bois wrote to Gandhi to solicit an article for the anniversary issue of *The Crisis*—a "message" from Gandhi "to these twelve million people who are the grandchildren of slaves, and who amid great difficulties are forging forward" in the United States. "I know how busy you are with your own problems," Du Bois said in closing his letter, "but the race and color problems are world-wide, and we need your help here."[41] Gandhi declined to write an article and instead sent Du Bois what he called a "little love message," which was subsequently published in the July issue:[42]

> Let not the 12 million Negroes be ashamed of the fact that they are the grandchildren of the slaves. There is no dishonor in being slaves. There is dishonor in being slave-owners. But let us not think of honor or dishonor in connection with the past. Let us realize that the future is with those who would be truthful, pure and loving. For, as the old wise men have said, truth ever is, untruth never was. Love alone binds and truth and love accrue only to the humble.[43]

While Gandhi's note focused on truth and love, Du Bois's introduction to the "little love message" pointed to Gandhi as "the greatest colored man in the world" and introduced readers to his biography by recounting how he "toiled in South Africa to remove race prejudice."[44] In Du Bois's rendering, "Agitation, non-violence, refusal to co-operate with the oppressor" were the tools with which Gandhi was "leading all India to freedom," not truth and love. It was through these that he "stretch[ed] out his hand in fellowship to his colored friends of the West."[45]

Acknowledging the difficulties of translation and cross-cultural identification that the Indian movement presented, across a number of articles Du Bois engaged with Gandhi's work in terms that placed Gandhi on a familiar field of struggle against disenfranchisement and oppression, and that drew on a language of shared racial identification. Introducing India to the readers of the *New York Amsterdam News* in 1931, Du Bois described a subcontinent that had witnessed the rise of "many black civilizations"—a diverse place of many races, in which the "great mass of [people] are brown people, with wavy hair ... allied more nearly to the peoples of Africa and Asia than to those of Europe." Quoting his own *Dark Princess,* he concluded the article: "India! India! Out of black India the world was born. Into the black womb of India the world shall creep to die."[46] This pronouncement is, perhaps, particularly Du Boisian; yet beyond Du Bois many writers and editorialists took to the pages of the African American press to engage in a similar discourse. A May 1930 *Pittsburgh Courier* editorial called out Britain as "the foremost exploiter of black labor in the world" while praising Gandhi's leadership of "300 million dark people" in defying "the power of the British Empire with his program of civil disobedience."[47] In the *Chicago Defender,* labor organizer O. R. Burns raised the question of why "[repression must] always and everywhere be the lot of the fine souls housed within dark-colored bodies" and suggested that the American iteration of this question might at last be laid to rest if African Americans followed Gandhi's lead.[48] Over the course of two decades, articles like these reinforced the existence of a shared problem of racial subjugation and reported on the success of nonviolent struggle in forging a path to freedom from one instantiation of it—colonial domination in India.

Travel between the United States and India to meet the Mahatma reinforced and strengthened these connections, allowing a series of influential African Americans centered on Howard University—those far less ambivalent about nonviolence than Du Bois—to press Gandhi on some of the finer points of nonviolent resistance. In the fall of 1935, Howard Thurman, dean of Howard University's Rankine Chapel, and his wife, Sue Bailey Thurman, social historian and staff member at the Young Women's Christian Association (YWCA), led a delegation to India; Benjamin Mays, dean of Howard's School of Religion and later president of Morehouse College, followed at the close of 1936; William Stuart Nelson, who became dean of the School of Religion after Mays, made his own trip in 1946, and would return several times in subsequent years.[49] While there, they engaged in lengthy conversations with Gandhi about the practical and philosophical dimensions of nonviolence, particularly those areas most pertinent to the American context—the relationship between nonviolence and direct action, the difference between passive and active resistance, the kind of training and preparation required for mass action, the realities of responding to a violent oppressor, and the possibility of a minority wielding nonviolent action against a majority. In these exchanges, Gandhi asked his own barrage of questions about life in black America. "Never in my life have I been part of that kind of examination," Howard Thurman reported of his conversation. Gandhi, he said, asked "persistent, pragmatic questions about American Negroes, about the course of slavery, and how we survived it." When Gandhi and the Thurmans parted ways, Gandhi indicated that if it were indeed true that African Americans were poised to wage their own direct action struggle, "it may be through the Negroes that the unadulterated message of non-violence will be delivered to the world."[50]

Upon return from their journeys, these individuals delivered scores of lectures to eager audiences and conveyed what they had learned in editorials and interviews that emphasized the efficacy of nonviolent direct action and "the striking similarity between the Indian and Negro problems," as one article in the *Norfolk Journal and Guide* put it.[51] When, for example, Benjamin Mays returned from India in 1937, he focused on the effect of Gandhi's efforts on racial pride and moving a subject population past fear. "Mr. Gandhi has gone a long way towards making the Indian people proud of their race and proud of their great history," freeing them from years of domination and imposed racial inferiority, Mays wrote—a lesson that "Negroes in America can understand and appreciate."[52] Mays argued in a series of articles that this newfound pride stemmed from the "new conception of courage" that comes from breaking free of the "imperialism built on racialism" that defined the British presence in India, and learning "to face death, to die, to go to jail for the cause without fear and without resorting to violence." Moreover, because "problem of race is world-wide," as Mays put it (echoing Du Bois), the Indian example had special pertinence for the "natives of South Africa and the Negroes of the United States" who were subject to the most violent forms of "race prejudice." According to him, therefore, the lesson that the world ought to learn from "India's little Brown man" is plain: "when an oppressed race ceases to be afraid, it is free."[53]

In drawing on the language of fear, fearlessness, and pride, Mays presented nonviolent action as a demanding choice of the courageous—a means of asserting dignity, racial pride, and strength while contesting injustice—rather than the default weapon of the weak. Building a nonviolent movement entailed conquering fear of violence, fear of reprisal, fear of death; it entailed identifying and calling out white supremacy as an empire of fear, maintained as much through the frightened cruelty of the oppressor as through the frightened acquiescence of the oppressed. In a world built on racist violence, Mays suggested, the nonviolent might, in fact, have the strategic edge: "the world is accustomed to dealing with men who strike back physically, men who are mentally cruel and men who are saturated with fear."[54] Mays's analysis traveled some distance in supplying an answer to the concern that nonviolent direct action only left the vulnerable open to outright massacre, and it located nonviolence within an empowering and resonant language of self-liberation: for him, the Indian example demonstrated how powerful the seemingly powerless could be when organized along Gandhian lines, wielding nonviolence against the twinned evils of colonialism and segregation. If the language here sounds like Martin Luther King, Jr., it is likely not accidental; Mays would later become one of King's key advisors, beginning with his years at Morehouse and extending through the end of his life.[55]

These cross-cultural exchanges and discursive enterprises of world construction laid the groundwork for early experiments in bringing noncooperation, boycotts, and civil disobedience (back) to bear against Jim Crow. In the early 1940s, James Farmer, a young Gandhian and student of Thurman and Mays, joined forces with Bayard Rustin, a Quaker pacifist, to embark on a new project to build the organizational basis for an American nonviolent movement against Jim Crow. Initially under the auspices of the majority-white pacifist organization, the Fellowship of Reconciliation (FOR), Farmer and Rustin founded the Congress of Racial Equality (CORE), which would eventually grow into one of the primary organizational drivers of civil rights disobedience in the South. Breaking from FOR's straightforwardly antiwar program, Farmer and Rustin viewed racial hierarchy in the United States as central to the broader pacifist agenda and tied to the movements against colonialism in India and elsewhere. This was what Farmer identified as the "race logic of pacifism": the maintenance of white supremacy worldwide generated enormous violence; waging nonviolence against its segregationist and colonialist guises should therefore be the chief preoccupation of Gandhians, pacifists, and partisans of nonviolence.[56] Though CORE's initial forays into nonviolent direct action were rather limited—small sit-ins at a Chicago coffee shop; an attempt to integrate a roller skating rink—both Farmer and Rustin held grander ambitions. Even as the leadership of FOR hedged, Farmer prepared a "Provisional Plan for Brotherhood Mobilization," envisioning a society-wide Gandhian movement through which black civil rights activism could develop a truly mass base. "We must withhold our support and participation from the institution of segregation in every area of American life," Farmer later wrote, "—not as an individual witness to the purity of conscience, as Thoreau used it, but a coordinated movement of mass noncooperation as with Gandhi." Through such a movement, black activism could move beyond "the elegant cadre of generals we now have" and toward "an army of ground troops."[57]

In 1942, just as the Quit India movement was getting off the ground half a world away, Asa Philip Randolph—labor leader and founder of the largest black trade union, the Brotherhood of Sleeping Car Porters—began issuing the call for mass civil disobedience along the lines Farmer envisioned. As a result of his successful bid one year earlier to pressure the Roosevelt administration to desegregate the war industries, Randolph already had something of an organizational structure in place under the auspices of the March on Washington Movement (MOWM) and had emerged as an influential and widely respected national voice for desegregation. Randolph began formulating plans for a disobedience campaign at a series of mass meetings and policy conferences leading up to the summer 1943 "We Are Americans Too" Conference organized by the MOWM. In a speech in San Francisco, Randolph recited the lessons he thought pertinent to the moment: "Negroes must fight for what they get. That they will only get what they take. That they can't take anything without power, economic, political, social, moral and spiritual. That the power comes from organization—the organization of the masses.... That the Negro must depend on themselves to win their rights."[58] Two weeks later in Detroit, Randolph detailed what that self-reliant, organized power might look like:

> Our first job then is to actually organize millions of Negroes, and build them into block systems with captains so that they may be summoned into physical motion. Without this type of organization, Negroes will never develop a mass power which is the most effective weapon a minority can yield. Witness the strategy and maneuver of the people of India with mass civil disobedience and non-cooperation and the marches to the sea to make salt. It may be said that the Indian people have not won their freedom. This is so, but they will win it... India is now waging a world shaking, history making fight for independence. India's fight is the Negro's fight."[59]

In particular, Randolph envisioned a range of strategies across a large-scale campaign, including boycotts of segregated street cars and coordinated dine-ins at restaurants that refused service to black people, starting with those in Washington DC, "seat of the nation's most reactionary and prejudiced elements."[60] He solicited FOR, and particularly Rustin and Farmer, for help in making preparations.

By the start of the 1943, Randolph's proposal for waging nonviolence domestically garnered significant publicity, much of it less than enthusiastic. The debate from the early days of Indian noncooperation reprised itself in the press, as critics raised various objections from the specifically Indian quality of Gandhi's disobedience to the numerical imbalance between black and white Americans, to very real fears about violent reprisals against unarmed black protestors. The *Pittsburgh Courier* declared Gandhian tactics unsuitable for the "temperament of the American Negro" because they had been crafted according to "the way of the Oriental mind."[61] Du Bois, despite the years of work he put into tying African Americans to Indians through common membership within a "colored world" struggling for freedom, now declared firmly: "This is not India," and he insisted that the self-sacrifice required of *satyagraha* was "bred into the very bone of India" but would be "insane" in the United States. The case of African Americans, he conceded "is not happy, but also it is far from desperate."[62] Many expressed support for the concept of civil disobedience but worried that at present "the masses" were not sufficiently trained or disciplined to maintain nonviolence in the face of the violence that would surely be directed at them.[63] Still others, echoing Frazier's concerns from two decades before, worried that civil disobedience would only "release the brutality of the South." One editorial asked, "What makes Randolph or anyone else think [civil disobedience] would succeed in this country, except in offering irresponsible and vicious elements an excuse for slaughtering thousands of colored citizens?"[64]

The difficulty of fathoming mass disobedience in the United States is a powerful reminder, sixty years into the wake churned up behind the civil rights movement, of the fact that grassroots uptake of nonviolent resistance by African Americans was far from inevitable. While years of imaginative transit between India and the US had forged a sense of a "common cause" against "racialism and imperialism," to use King's phrase, and had rendered credible the idea that nonviolence could provide a means to fight both, many viewed British imperialism as almost polite in comparison with Southern segregation: "In India Gandhi is in jail, in Georgia he'd be lynched."[65] With the efficacy of the Indian movement as yet unclear, and with American experiments with nonviolence largely hypothetical—or local and limited—mass nonviolence remained a risky and relatively untested idea.

All of this is more than just the backstory to King's pronouncement of a "common cause" with Indians in 1959. Rather, these paths of transit shaped the contours of how those like King thought about nonviolence and civil disobedience—and why they thought it was a meaningful way to wage an assault on "racialism and imperialism." As we will see, this transnational anticolonial imaginary resonated with and enriched one of the civil rights movement's most important animating languages: that of liberation and self-emancipation.[66] Even so, the story is also more complicated than a direct line between black America and India might suggest. Indeed, King's statements about the "common cause" reflect not a simple lineage, but a further widening of the world of anticolonial struggle in the years after World War II and a shift of its center of gravity from Asia to Africa. King's imagination of the world of nonviolent struggle thus came not just from India but also through the circuits of imaginative transit between the United States, South Africa, and Ghana that occurred throughout the1950s—transit that refashioned the identification of African Americans to Africa and sustained the idea of nonviolence as a viable means of anticolonial resistance. Indeed, although the success of the Indian independence movement had a seismic effect on the shape of this world, the early years of the Cold War took a significant toll on the ties between African Americans and India that had been so diligently crafted and nurtured. Towering figures of black internationalism like Du Bois were sidelined, ostracized, and harassed due to the perception of communist sympathies. In this new environment, architects of the new bipolar international order actively conflated public support for anticolonial and antiracist struggle with support for communism, leaving black activists of all ideological stripes vulnerable to red baiting and persecution. Meanwhile, as Indian leaders transitioned from being anticolonial activists to running the government of a sovereign nation, it became clear that softening their public criticism of Jim Crow might be the price of maintaining a relationship with the United States.[67]

Nevertheless, even as the "old notion of U.S. Negroes being part of a 'colored' global majority aligned with South Asia in particular began to evaporate" in the heat of the Cold War, the rise of nonviolent resistance elsewhere in the "darker world" stood poised to revitalize and enrich the notion of making common cause through disobedience.[68]

In Transit Toward Defiance

In the fallow time of the early Cold War, African American activists continued to explore the idea of adapting Gandhian methods to their own context, partially provoked by and mediated through news about the escalation of South African resistance in the early 1950s and through exchanges between activists across continents. The South African antiapartheid struggle, and particularly the Defiance campaign of 1952, provided a kind of bridge (if a tenuous one) from the black internationalism and "colored cosmopolitanism" that had animated debates over civil disobedience in the years between the world wars and the eruption of grassroots nonviolent direct action in the South. It is but a tenuous bridge, because momentum toward mass disobedience—an idea that seemed so promising in the mid-1940s in the US, as individuals like Randolph and CORE organizers Rustin and Farmer experimented with the Gandhian form—had all but stalled by the early 1950s. Even so, as political scientist Alvin Tillery has argued, in that same moment South Africa became "an important flashpoint in the global confrontation between white supremacy and black equality"—one that held particular significance for African Americans interested in nonviolence.[69]

In 1948, Daniel Malan's National Party swept into power in the Union of South Africa on a plank of hardline Afrikaaner nationalism, based on the promise to legally codify and further entrench a strict regime of racial segregation and white supremacy. Following on the heels of the general election, Malan's government moved to expand and formalize systems of racial classification, segregation, and disenfranchisement, while providing the government broad powers to suppress and criminalize dissent. The new regime of fully legalized apartheid, which affected black South Africans as well as Indians and "Coloureds" (those classified as mixed race), galvanized opposition groups, uniting organizations across racial lines for the first time.[70] Deciding that the "time had come for mass action along the lines of Gandhi's nonviolent protests in India," the African National Congress (ANC) adopted a new program for action, embracing the "weapons" of "immediate and active boycott, strike, civil disobedience, non-co-operation," and worked to forge an alliance with the South African Indian Congress and the Franchise Action Council.[71] The opportunity to use these "weapons" came in 1952, as the 300th anniversary of white settler colonialism in South Africa approached. At the start of the year, the ANC demanded that the government repeal the apartheid laws and announced their intention to launch a nationwide noncooperation campaign should the government refuse to do so by the end of February. The Malan government, for its part, remained intransigent, insisting on the "permanent and not man-made" differences between races, and promising to "make full use of the machinery at its disposal to quell any disturbances and, thereafter, deal adequately with those responsible for inciting subversive activities of any nature whatsoever."[72] And so the campaign of Defiance of Unjust Laws was born.

The plan was simple but ambitious: widespread noncooperation with and direct defiance of segregation laws in order to court arrest and fill the jails beyond capacity, creating administrative and institutional chaos. As historian James Meriwether describes it: "People of color walked into the white sections of post offices; they used white entrances and platforms at railway stations and boarded white railway cars; they entered locations without permit; they stayed out at night without curfew passes."[73] As the arrests compounded—1,500 the first month, climbing to over 8,000 by the end of the year—thousands resolved to forego bail and instead serve out their terms, in hopes of overwhelming the jail system. The campaign never achieved that goal, however. In 1953 riots broke out, giving the government the pretext they needed for severely cracking down on dissent and imposing harsh repercussions on protestors and organizers. Yet Defiance could claim one important success: in the wake of the campaign, the ANC was vaulted to the forefront of the militant antiapartheid struggle, and its membership rolls swelled to more than five times its precampaign numbers—from somewhere below 20,000 to as many as 100,000.[74]

Despite the scale of the ANC's noncooperation, nothing like the avalanche of US news and debate that accompanied the Indian independence struggles followed South African Defiance. Nevertheless, the campaign caught the attention of those who had been at the forefront of experimentation with nonviolence in the 1940s—Farmer, Rustin, and Randolph, along with others from CORE—and managed to spark anew a debate about the use of civil disobedience in the South. Bill Sutherland, a pacifist activist who had helped found New York City CORE, caught wind of the Defiance campaign in 1951, through a chance meeting in London with the South African editor of *The Bantu World*, Jacob Nhlapo: "here was a person," Sutherland later recounted, "who gave me an opportunity to see that—indeed—in one area of the world resistance and the struggle for liberation was going to take the form of a Gandhian's approach."[75] Sutherland excitedly relayed what he had learned to the organizers at CORE, and he mailed some of CORE's literature to ANC leaders in South Africa, initiating direct contact between the African American Gandhians and their South African counterparts, and prompting Rustin's first trip to the continent.[76]

What the CORE organizers saw, through the window of the Defiance campaign, was a continent in motion against the racial order of colonial rule—and a constellation of movements waging the fight nonviolently. As Rustin reported to the readers of the *Baltimore Afro-American* upon returning from his trip to Africa: "The continent of Africa is afire. From the Suez Canal to the Cape of Good Hope, colonial imperialists face unrest, threats, arson, and open rebellion. Their often proclaimed promise of 'freedom in time' is as suspect throughout Africa as the 'time-will-take-care-of-it' theory is among the masses of colored Americans." Though Rustin acknowledged the diversity of tactics being employed on the continent in the fight for "freedom now," in writing that the methods "range from Ghandi-like [sic] non-violence to murder and burning"—the former, a reference to the Defiance campaign; the latter, the armed struggle of the Mau Mau rebellion in Kenya—Rustin made his preferences for the South African style of struggle clear.[77] Sounding notes that would be repeated, all but verbatim, to describe the sit-ins that spread throughout the American South less than a decade later, Rustin pointed to the use of nonviolence in South Africa: "hundreds of men and women, singing a song of freedom, go willingly to prison. They refuse to pay fines. In a well-disciplined campaign of civil disobedience and non-co-operation, they dare to challenge the oppressive Malan government. Yes, from the Mediterranean to the Cape, Africa is afire."[78]

For Rustin, as for Benjamin Mays before him, nonviolent direct action offered the possibility of rising up against a militarily strong oppressor, while minimizing the risk of either brutal annihilation or an ever-escalating cycle of retaliatory violence. Challenging racial hierarchy, colonial power, and the entrenched interests of white supremacy, Rustin believed, would inevitably provoke violence; even the use of nonviolence could not eliminate this probability. But based on his own experience confronting domestic racism, and buoyed by the success of the Indian example and its apparent reverberations through South Africa, Rustin thought that nonviolence might shift the terms of the struggle off of the familiar ground of offensive and defensive violence—the ground that segregationists and colonial powers understood and anticipated—while opening space for liberation.[79] Issuing a reply to Frazier's worries three decades before, Rustin intimated that white fear was the ultimate source of racist, retaliatory violence—and that white fear of armed black movements would only exacerbate this violence. Nonviolence, in contrast, provided an active, assertive form of defiance that could, simultaneously, confront and diffuse that fear.[80] He therefore hoped that African American interest in the South African campaign might provide an opening to make the case for a mass, nonviolent movement against Jim Crow. As Rustin wrote to A. J. Muste, because of the growing public concern over apartheid, "Negroes in America can be more readily brought to an interest in pacifism through an interest in Africa than in any other way."[81]

Indeed, the South African case proved important for what it suggested about nonviolent direct action: that it had force beyond the Indian context, and that it had potential applicability under conditions that looked far more like Jim Crow than anything African Americans saw in the British Raj. Analogies between Jim Crow and apartheid seemed rather straightforward to make—as journalists, activists, and politicians routinely cemented the comparability of the South African and Southern systems of white supremacy by rendering "apartheid" as "Jim Crow" in countless headlines and articles throughout the years.[82] The Malan government's apartheid policies were, after all, easily cognizable as Jim Crow segregation statutes. At a deeper level, however, many identified in apartheid something quite familiar to African Americans: the bedrock of white anxiety—the deep-seated fear of losing power—that motivated racial hierarchy and its violent enforcement.[83] As Rustin would later write of the Mississippi Delta, "Fear in the Delta is Kenya's fear; reaction to fear in the Delta is South Africa's reaction."[84] Even so, many African Americans surveyed what they saw of apartheid and found it, in Mays's words, "worse than anything that ever existed in the Southern United States"—an assessment based, in part, on the Malan government's disinterest in dressing segregation up with liberal rhetoric.[85] Collectively, these analyses set up a peculiar structure of analogy and disanalogy between the US and South Africa—apartheid was both the same and worse. Conceiving of apartheid and Jim Crow as literal translations of each other helped forge an imagination of shared struggle and structural similarity between the South and South Africa, while conceiving of racial hierarchy in the United States as a less severe form of its South African "translation" helped insulate nascent potentialities for nonviolence in the US from their eventual eclipse in South Africa.

As Rustin hoped, as the Defiance campaign wore on, it raised yet again the possibility of civil disobedience closer to home. Mary McLeod Bethune wrote with abiding "satisfaction" in the *Chicago Defender* about the "resistance of the colored peoples of the world to the pressures of racial discrimination, everywhere, but particularly as evidenced in this country and in South Africa," and suggested that these struggles demonstrate the active role individuals must play in their own liberation.[86] Horace Cayton was more explicit still:

> This movement commands world attention. It commands attention because it may presage a new method of struggle for colonial peoples. . . . It might even work in the United States and this possibility intrigues me. Just suppose one bright Monday morning every Negro in the United States woke up and decided not to act like a Negro. Suppose that every colored person conducted himself that day just as if he were white: went into every restaurant, hotel, barber shop, and applied for any job where there was a vacancy. . . . What is happening in South Africa today and what will continue to happen there may prove a lesson to dark peoples throughout the world.[87]

At a moment in which public opinion had seemed to turn in favor of fighting Jim Crow in the courts and through petitioning the government, rather than by mobilizing the masses, the South African example seemed to offer other, more militant possibilities.

This is not to say that South Africa—or India, for that matter—was particularly on Rosa Parks's mind when she initiated a year-long rebellion against Montgomery, Alabama's segregated public transit in 1955—though both she and E. D. Nixon, one of the organizing forces behind the Montgomery Improvement Association, did have their own individual links to Gandhian initiatives to use civil disobedience and direct action against Jim Crow.[88] The Montgomery bus boycott was not caused, in any direct or simple way, by events on other continents; as with much of the action in the development of the civil rights movement, nonviolence was waged from the ground up, on the basis of the long-standing frustration of local communities at the white supremacist structures that ordered their lives. This undeniable reality prompted George Frederickson to remark that "[f]ormal ideology and linkage with struggles going on in other communities, to say nothing of elsewhere in the world, came only after the fact of nonviolent activity at the grass roots."[89] I want to suggest that this is partially right but nevertheless misses an important point. While anticolonial struggle did not *cause* an American uprising against Jim Crow, Parks and others acted in the midst of an "entire world in motion," as A. Philip Randolph once put it, in which debates played out publicly through the course of decades over the terms of anticolonial struggles "elsewhere in the world"—and their relationship to the fight at home. The anticolonial frame was not a theoretical construct devised and imposed entirely by movement leaders from above (or after the fact), but a live context that connected the domestic grassroots to related fields of action across the world. This context shaped the way that many activists talked about nonviolence and disobedience, the way they imagined a universe of global struggle—and located their own place within it. Granting Frederickson's point that South African Defiance did not provide the impetus behind Montgomery does not entail denying the power of an imagination that linked the two as individual pieces of a larger conflict over the fate of white supremacy in all its forms. Indeed, for a vulnerable minority population subject to endemic racist violence, an imaginary of nonviolence that located African Americans fighting as part of a global majority of colonized and oppressed "darker peoples" could serve as an important reservoir of confidence and empowerment.

Nkrumah Was No Foreigner

This is the imagination of struggle that King displayed in his early speeches and sermons in and around the Montgomery campaign as he tried out themes that would continue to shape his career as chief orator for the civil rights movement and as its most famed theorist. In August 1956, shortly after the conclusion of the bus boycott, King assured an audience in Buffalo, New York, of the size and scale of the movement within which Montgomery was but one part. Drawing on a theme he had developed in the early 1950s through numerous sermons, distinguishing a "dying old order" and an emerging "new world order," King connected Alabama to a global majority of "colored people" who had "lived under the yoke of Colonialism and Imperialism," which "dominated [them] politically, exploited [them] economically, segregated and humiliated" them. This formulation—economic exploitation, political domination, and the indignities of segregation—was a routine piece of King's oratory, a phrase he used to capture the dimensions of racial oppression both foreign and domestic, a set of practices shared by both colonialism and segregation, and thus a set of shared experiences tying African Americans to a greater "colored world" beyond national borders.[90] This global majority, King assured his audience, was on the move:

> There comes a time when people get tired of being plunged across the abyss of exploitation, when they have experienced the bleakness and madness of despair.... So with the coming of this time an uprising started and protest started and these people rose up against Colonialism and Imperialism and as a result, out of the 1,600,000,000 colored people in the world today, 1,300,000,000 are free.... [I]f we look back we see the old order of Colonialism and Imperialism thrown upon the seashores of the world and we see the new world of freedom and justice emerging on the horizon of the universe.

Joining this world in motion were African Americans, who had their own knowledge of "the old order." Before recounting the history of slavery and emancipation, King told his audience: "We know the history of this old order in America."[91]

While King—like many African Americans—found common cause with the anticolonial struggle in broad terms, distinctive lines of connection were forged through the means of nonviolence. The late 1950s in particular stood as a moment of promise for the potential of nonviolent direct action as a means of fighting the economic exploitation, political domination, segregation, and humiliation that King diagnosed at the heart of colonialism and Jim Crow alike. And at the center of this optimism stood the newly independent state of Ghana.[92] Under the leadership of the charismatic Pan Africanist Kwame Nkrumah and inspired—in part—by the Indian independence movement, in the late 1940s the Convention People's Party (CPP) had adopted full independence as their goal ("Self-Government Now") and selected nonviolent direct action as the means. "We live by experience and by intelligent adaptation to our environment," Nkrumah wrote in a 1950 pamphlet laying out a program of what he would call "Positive Action." "From our knowledge of the history of man, from our knowledge of colonial liberation movements, Freedom or Self-government has never been handed to any colonial country on a silver platter." Citing the example of India, Nkrumah expressed his intention to use "all legitimate and constitutional means by which we can cripple the forces of imperialism," from legal "political agitation" and "educational campaigns" to "the constitutional application of strikes, boycotts, and non-co-operation based on the principle of absolute non-violence." Like other practitioner-theorists of nonviolence before, after, and concurrent with him, Nkrumah detected in nonviolence the potential for activating the ability of "the masses" to participate in their own "struggle for freedom"—the creation of a "widespread political consciousness and a sense of national self-respect."[93] The resulting Positive Action campaign launched by the CPP triggered a three-week long general strike and boycott of British goods. In response, the British government shuttered Ghanaian newspapers and arrested Nkrumah and other CPP leaders on charges of inciting an illegal strike.[94]

When, on the heels of the conclusion of the Montgomery bus boycott, Ghana won its independence, Martin Luther King, Jr. and Coretta Scott King traveled to Accra as Nkrumah's honorary guests at the independence day celebrations, alongside a broad range of African American notables— including A. Philip Randolph, Howard University President (and enthusiastic Gandhian) Mordecai Johnson, the editors of the *New York Amsterdam News* and *Chicago Defender*, the head of the Associated Negro Press, as well as Shirley Graham Du Bois and Eslanda Robeson.[95] It was actually Bill Sutherland, who had moved to Ghana in 1954 and now worked as personal secretary to Nkrumah's finance minister, who arranged for the Kings to attend the festivities. Sutherland watched the couple take in the spectacle of the flag of an independent Ghana being raised, as Nkrumah delivered his independence day speech, and noted how moved they were, hearing Nkrumah conclude his speech with the words: "Free At Last, Free At Last, Free At Last!" When King stood in front of the Lincoln Memorial six years later and uttered the words, pulled from "an old Negro spiritual," "Free at last! Free at last! Thank God Almighty, we are free at last!," Sutherland "couldn't help but wonder if those thunderous words in Washington D.C. had not come from King's memory of that historic evening in Ghana."[96]

Indeed, for King, the two moments—the long history of African American resistance and resilience in the struggle for freedom, encapsulated for King in the spiritual "Free at Last," and the liberation of the African continent from white colonial control, symbolized by the lowering of the Union Jack in Ghana to Nkrumah's cries of "Free at Last"—were bound up with each other. Upon his return from Ghana, King delivered a sermon in his home parish of Dexter Avenue Baptist Church of Montgomery. There, he recounted the moments after the flag of the newly sovereign nation of Ghana was raised in Accra: "when Prime Minister Nkrumah stood up before his people out in the polo ground and said, 'We are no longer a British colony, we are a free, sovereign people,' all over that vast throng of people we could see tears. And I stood there thinking about so many things. Before I knew it, I started weeping. I was crying for joy. And I knew about all of the struggles, and all of the pain, and all of the agony that these people had gone through for this moment."⁹⁷ Even at this early stage of King's career as an activist and movement leader, this knowledge of struggle, pain, and agony was an intimate one. In the two and a half months that elapsed between the conclusion of the Montgomery bus boycott and King's departure for Ghana, racial terror was unleashed on the black citizens of Montgomery. Homes and churches were bombed; black bus riders were attacked; snipers took aim at passing busses; and Klansman rode through black neighborhoods, intimidating residents. Just as King was leaving the country, the City Commission decided to suspend bus service altogether for several weeks on account of the violence. As King stood, weeping, at the Ghanaian independence celebrations, he was not a man triumphant, in the glow of a decisive success—but embattled, anxious, and holding onto the tenuous threads of fragile, limited, and easily reversible gains.⁹⁸

Leading up to his trip, King and the leadership of the newly formed Southern Christian Leadership Conference sent a series of lengthy telegrams to the Eisenhower administration, pleading with them to address the unchecked brutality directed at black Americans and their allies throughout the South. On January 11, they detailed the scale of the violence in Alabama:

> Christian churches literally have been destroyed by dynamite and T.N.T. Numerous individuals, including women have been beaten on the streets. The homes of Negro and white leaders have been bombed. Men and women, black and white sitting peacefully in buses have been attacked by snipers. A fortnight ago, a 15 year old Negro girl was brutally beaten. A few days ago the legs of a woman eight months pregnant were shattered by a gun fired into a public conveyance. A state of terror prevails.⁹⁹

A month later and without a meaningful response from Eisenhower, they wrote again to report the continued escalation of violence: "We are no longer faced with sporadic violence, but with what appears to be an organized campaign of violence and terror . . . our people, though resolute and courageous, cannot be expected forever to be targets for rifles, shotguns, and for bombs." This second letter, dated February 14, 1957, ended with something of an ultimatum: "If you, our president, cannot come South to relieve our harassed people, we shall have to lead our people to you in the capitol."¹⁰⁰ In fact, King would have to travel to West Africa before he was able to secure a meeting with the federal government. Greeting Vice President Richard Nixon in

Accra, King told him: "I want you to come visit us down in Alabama where we are seeking the same kind of freedom the Gold Coast is celebrating."[101]

Thus, as King watched the independence celebration unfold, the moment held a particular, doubled poignancy marked by the lines of imaginative transit through which King, and the idea of a nonviolent freedom struggle, had traveled to arrive at that time and place: he stood, witnessing the official end of British colonial rule in Ghana—a liberation hard won through largely nonviolent means—when he could not seem to secure a commitment from the American president to publicly denounce only the most recent bout of racial terror.[102] He heard, he told his Dexter congregation, the strains of that same "old Negro spiritual" in the Ghanaians' celebratory cries: "we could hear little children six years old and old people eighty and ninety years old walking the streets of Accra crying: 'Freedom! Freedom!' . . . They were crying it in a sense that they had never heard it before"—and, we might venture, in a sense in which King had never heard it before. Layered over those cries of freedom, King continued, "I could hear that old Negro spiritual once more crying out: " 'Free at last, free at last, Great God Almighty, I'm free at last.' . . . This was the birth of a new nation. This was the breaking aloose from Egypt."[103]

What King saw in Ghana filled him with a renewed sense of possibility for what the tools of civil disobedience and nonviolent action could achieve—the meaning they might hold for the oppressed everywhere. Connecting African Americans to Ghana through the history of slavery, King used the last half of his sermon to relay "three or four things that [Ghana's independence] reminds us of and things it says to us . . . as we ourselves find ourselves breaking aloose from an evil Egypt, trying to move through the wilderness toward the promised land of cultural integration." Echoing Frederick Douglass's insistence that "power concedes nothing without demand," the first lesson King drew was that the path to liberation was necessarily one of self-liberation: "The oppressor never voluntarily gives freedom to the oppressed . . . if Nkrumah and the people of the Gold Coast had not stood up persistently, revolting against the system, it would still be a colony of the British Empire. Freedom is never given to anybody voluntarily." The idea was one that held direct consequences for his Alabama audience, in the fraught context of an ambivalent victory. "[D]on't go out this morning with any illusions," King cautioned. "Don't go back to your homes and around Montgomery thinking that the Montgomery City Commission and that all of the forces in the leadership of the South will eventually work out this thing for Negroes.... If we wait for it to work itself out, it will *never* be worked out! Freedom only comes through persistent revolt, through persistent agitation, through persistently rising up against the system of evil." The evidence of this truth, King suggested, lie not just in Ghana—but also in India and the history of abolition.[104]

King found great hope in the idea that Ghanaians could win their freedom—that they could "break aloose from oppression and violence" using the tools of nonviolent direct action. This was King's second lesson: "here is a nation that is now free through nonviolent means." Yet for all King's optimism that nonviolence could deliver freedom from oppression without unleashing bitterness and reactionary hatred, he had to speak directly to conditions on the ground in 1957 Montgomery. Ghana's third lesson was one that Montgomery's black residents had already learned: "Ghana reminds us that whenever you break out of Egypt, you better get ready for stiff backs. You better get ready for some homes to be bombed. You better get ready for some churches to be bombed. You better get ready for a whole lot of nasty things to be said about you, because you getting out of Egypt." Even so, King concluded, despite the "hours of despair and disappointment," Ghana's independence provided undeniable proof that the "old order of colonialism, of segregation, of discrimination is passing away," and that freedom for African Americans—surely—could not be forever delayed.[105] Such was the power of the Ghanaian moment—that it could, as King told Etta Moten Barnett in Accra, "give impetus to oppressed peoples all over the world," in "Asia and Africa, but also America."[106]

The "Year of Africa" Comes Home

In the context of the late 1950s, it was Accra—not Alabama—that operated as the vibrant center of nonviolent struggle in the world. While Nkrumah is better known for his Pan Africanist aspirations, his vision for a liberated Africa was wedded to the idea that nonviolence was the way to get there. It was in Accra in 1958 that Nkrumah gathered an array of African anticolonial leaders and thinkers—including Tom Mboya from Kenya, Patrice Lumumba from Congo, and Frantz Fanon representing Algeria—together to debate the relationship between liberation, nonviolence, and armed struggle. The All-African Peoples' Conference, Nkrumah hoped, would provide a forum for the collective formulation of "the Gandhian tactics and strategy of the African Non-Violent Revolution" with regard to "Colonialism and Imperialism" and "Racialism and Discriminatory Laws and Practices," in addition to religious and tribal divisions.[107] A year later, Accra again provided the staging ground and the meeting point for an international team made up of Bill Sutherland, Bayard Rustin, Rev. Michael Scott from South Africa, and activists from the British antinuclear movement, as they dispatched to the Sahara Desert in protest of French plans to test an atomic weapon there.[108]

Yet by 1960—widely hailed as the "Year of Africa," as seventeen new nations gained independence—optimism about nonviolent decolonization was quickly waning. Even as Nkrumah assembled plans for a Positive Action Conference, attended by figures from all over Africa and the world (including Alabama), events were quickly revealing the brutal lengths to which colonial powers would go to hold onto the levers of territorial and political control, particularly where the claims of white settler colonies were concerned.[109] Less than a month before the conference, South African police at Sharpeville opened fire on demonstrators protesting the apartheid government's pass laws, killing almost seventy people and wounding nearly two hundred more. In the wake of the massacre, the government declared a state of emergency, retaliating swiftly and fiercely against any signs of dissent and demonstration, and banning the ANC, forcing them underground. At the same time, the Algerian war raged on, as French forces indiscriminately bombed neighborhoods suspected of harboring Algerian fighters, wielding torture, surveillance, and population removal against the insurgency.[110] By the time Nkrumah welcomed his guests on April 7, 1960, by celebrating "the remarkable success" achieved by Positive Action "in the liberation struggle of our continent," citing specifically the inspiring example of South African defiance of the pass laws, his audience was primed to respond with skepticism.[111] Under these conditions, it was Frantz Fanon—in Accra again as representative of the Algerian revolution—who made the more convincing case. As Sutherland later recalled, Fanon "spoke in a quiet and sober voice explaining his view of the regrettable necessity of armed struggle," and telling the proponents of nonviolence: "We tried this method, but the French came into the Casbah, broke down door after door and slaughtered the head of each household in the center of the street. When they did that about thirty-five consecutive times, the people gave up on non-cooperation."[112] A year later, after the murder of Congo's democratically elected leader and the ensuing crisis of postcolonial sovereignty, even Nkrumah had stepped "away from a Gandhist position."[113]

In these same months, however, half a world away and situated in a very different political moment, black students in the United States launched a nonviolent struggle of their own, sitting-in and going to jail in cities and towns across the South.[114] Five days after the Positive Action Conference concluded, the students gathered at Shaw University in Raleigh, North Carolina, to found the Student Nonviolent Coordinating Committee (SNCC).[115] As the young activists gathered, they hammered out a basic set of principles that would orient the organization—among them, that "nonviolence is our creed," and that "we identify ourselves with the African struggle as a concern of all mankind."[116] Six months later, when SNCC reconvened in Atlanta for a conference on "Nonviolence and the Achievement of Desegregation," they invited Alphonse Okuku, student at Antioch College and brother of Kenyan nationalist leader and trade unionist Tom Mboya, to speak about "the great significance of the African struggle for freedom and its relation to our own fight."[117] John Friedman, the Antioch student who suggested an invitation be extended to Okuku, also hoped he might "[convey] the 'spirit'" of SNCC's efforts "to his fellow Africans," keeping alive lines of connection that had long been a source of solidarity, inspiration, and intellectual exchange for African Americans and anticolonial activists the world over.[118]

The ease and obviousness with which the SNCC students viewed the relationship between the Southern sit-ins and a broad, continental anticolonialism was both emblematic of its time and the product of a longer history—a history of imaginative transit between black Americans and the decolonizing world, in which nonviolent direct action emerged as a plausible means of taking part in a freedom struggle that exceeded national boundaries. By 1960, the concerns E. Franklin Frazier posed in the early 1920s about the inability of nonviolence to protect protestors from Jim Crow's extreme brands of violence had not entirely disappeared; indeed, they would resurface in new guises over the course of the following decade. But at this moment, filtered through the "world shaking" and "history making" success of the Indian and Ghanaian movements, and structured along lines of analogy and disanalogy with South Africa, anticolonial nonviolence appeared a promising means of contesting white supremacy's specifically American instantiations. Throughout the twentieth century, from the Indian noncooperation movement through the African revolutions of the 1950s and 1960s and beyond, African Americans at the forefront of the fight for civil rights imagined themselves as part of a common cause, working to end the ravages of white supremacy that were global in scope. Through processes of comparison and analogy, through public debate over means and ends, through travel and exchange with activists across continents, these individuals constructed the notion of nonviolent direct action, and civil disobedience along with it, as a powerful means of self-emancipation and social transformation—one all the more relevant for its anticolonial pedigree. Civil disobedience emerged in the midst of a "colored world" in motion against colonialism *and* segregation, as activists walked the lines of connection between the two. It was no accident, then, that when SNCC Chairman John Lewis spoke about the "serious revolution" being waged in the South in his own March on Washington speech, he stepped beyond domestic borders to frame the fight for enfranchisement and human rights here at home in terms borrowed from South Africa: "'One man, one vote' is the African cry," he told the hundreds of thousands assembled there. "It is ours too. (It must be ours.)"[119]

A Problem for Philosophy

At the start of this chapter I suggested that it is the normative framework of constitutional democracy that renders civil disobedience a "problem for philosophy": it is a form of action that contravenes the moral imperatives of a legitimate order yet does so in the service of aims defensible in democratic and liberal terms, and as such it presents a justificatory puzzle. But if civil disobedience, properly circumscribed and contained within the moral-political boundaries of the domestic political order, raises the philosophical question of how to justify lawbreaking within a constitutional democracy, what do these decades of imaginative transit suggest? What new problem does this history pose for philosophy and political theory?

At a basic level, the lines of imaginative transit detailed here reveal how very limited the mainstream philosophical interest in civil disobedience has tended to be—how narrowly drawn its questions, and therefore its answers. Beginning from the premise that the existing political order is legitimate, desirable, and normatively defensible, theorists of civil disobedience approached the problem of conscientious lawbreaking as one of determining the parameters within which disobedience strengthens rather than erodes the rule of law, constitutional principles, and democratic institutions. This is no small thing: in the midst of the late 1960s and early 1970s, theorists like Rawls and Walzer worked to defend civil disobedience and citizen activism—to find spaces for it within the bounds of liberal-democratic theory—against those who conflated disobedience with crime and dissent with violence. But theirs was also a limited enterprise that too often failed to ask whether activists—and in particular, *the activists most often cited in defense of the mainstream account of civil disobedience*—began from a similar premise, or whether the questions they asked and answered were constructed differently.

Seeing civil disobedience within a global frame, therefore, does not pose a new problem for philosophy, generating a new puzzle in need of normative justification; instead, it reveals liberal-democratic philosophy—its habits of analysis and *ways of seeing*—to be the problem.[120] The practices of theorizing taken up by figures like Rawls looked at mid-century American civil disobedience—a form of activity emerging out of the context of worldwide struggles against varied forms of white supremacist rule—and devised analyses that minimized and domesticated the problem of racial hierarchy and disregarded the global, anticolonial networks sustained by activists in transit as philosophically unimportant. African American civil rights activists were keenly aware of the democratic institutions in their midst—and the ways they were systematically shut out of them; they actively strategized numerous ways to mobilize constitutional principles in defense of their rights as citizens, as individuals, and as a group. But the idea of civil disobedience was not conceived exclusively in domestic terms nor in the putatively race-neutral language of the rule of law, democratic citizenship, or constitutional patriotism. Rather, the immense intellectual labor that sustained a vibrant, decades-long, transnational conversation about nonviolence was animated by the question of what practices, ideas, and forms of power connected the Jim Crow United States to the decolonizing world; it was a conversation that conceived of civil disobedience and nonviolent direct action specifically in terms of their potency for resisting racial domination. The dimensions of this conversation, as I have detailed it here, was both *comparative* and *relational* in analysis: thinking comparatively, activists spanning three continents asked how different sites of racial domination varied—identifying commonalities and contrasts that related to the possibilities of mass resistance; at the same time, thinking relationally, they sought to understand white supremacy as a shared, global condition, operating with a common, reinforcing logic.[121]

This context and these connections matter. As I have suggested, figures from Mays and Thurman to King and Rustin seized on the idea that the fear that held white supremacy in place—the fear of the oppressed, tending toward anguished submission; and the fear and status anxiety of the oppressor, tending toward violent repression—could be powerfully challenged through the creative, strategic use of nonviolent protest and civil disobedience. Only nonviolence, understood not as a form of constitutional appeal but as *decolonizing praxis*, offered a means of black self-assertion, self-emancipation, and empowerment while simultaneously reducing the likelihood of white violent reprisal, backlash, and resentment; only nonviolence could enable citizens themselves to transform a racist political and social order while leaving room for the possibility that one's adversaries, one's oppressors, might themselves emerge changed and not simply defeated or embittered. As the next three chapters detail, this was an idea with real power—but not without its own complications.

3
Incarceration as Liberation

From the time that I began workin I never had a mind to stop but after that happened in Winona, I knew it wouldn't be anything that would stop me other than death. So now it's "Give me liberty or give me death."
—Fannie Lou Hamer, Interview with KZSU radio (1965)[1]

I had reached the point, at which I was not afraid to die. This spirit made me a freeman in fact, while I remained a slave in form. When a slave cannot be flogged he is more than half free.
—Frederick Douglass, *My Bondage and My Freedom* (1855)[2]

We are in an era in which a prison term for a freedom struggle is a badge of honor.
—Martin Luther King, Jr., Statement to the press (1960)[3]

"Ain't No Damn Law"

In a bus terminal parking lot on the morning of June 9, 1963, a group of organizers working on black voter registration—among them, Fannie Lou Hamer, Annell Ponder, James West, June Johnson, Rosemary Freeman, and Euvester Simpson—came face to face with Mississippi justice. Returning from a week-long training workshop in South Carolina, the group was headed back to Greenwood when the bus pulled into the Continental Trailways terminal in Winona for its scheduled mid-morning stop, only to be greeted by a four local lawmen: Mississippi State Highway Patrolman John Basinger, the Montgomery County Chief of Police Thomas Herod, the Winona Sheriff Earl Wayne Partridge, and Deputy Sheriff Charles Perkins. Apparently a white passenger aboard the bus had called ahead to alert the authorities that the group's arrival might bring "trouble" of the integrationist sort. After four of the group attempted to order food at the Staley's Café lunch counter, trouble indeed followed rather swiftly—but not of their own making. When Ponder and her fellow travelers tried to get one of the waitresses to acknowledge their presence and serve them, Herod and Basinger pounced. Billy club in hand, Herod ordered them to get out. Ponder politely protested that the current state of the law recognized and protected their right to be served, to which Herod simply replied, more poignantly than he perhaps knew: "Ain't no damn law."[4]

Exiting the terminal, Ponder and the others tried to regroup and decide what to do. As they were taking down the license plate number of the one of the patrol vehicles, Herod and Basinger angrily rushed out of the café and began arresting them one by one, pushing them into the patrol car. Fannie Lou Hamer, who had remained on the bus while the others were inside, now disembarked at the sight of the commotion, to see if she should proceed on to Greenwood. Her sudden appearance among the group was apparently enough of an offense to prompt her arrest, as well. "Get that black son of a bitch, too!" Herod shouted, referring to Hamer. "Bring her down in the other car." As she was climbing into his police vehicle, Sheriff Partridge kicked Hamer for good measure. The motley crew of lawmen—some in plainclothes, some in uniform—ultimately arrested six of the eight organizers and hauled them all down to the Montgomery County jail.

The activists might have suspected that arrest was only the beginning of their ordeal; the dangers of organizing for black freedom in Mississippi were well known. As Charles Payne details in the opening pages of his masterful account of civil rights organizing in the state, in the century-long span between Reconstruction and the 1960s, Mississippi had defined itself as ground zero for racial terror, boasting of more lynchings than any other state. Moreover, Winona—located just past the eastern edge of the Mississippi Delta, about thirty miles from Greenwood—had served as the headquarters for the area's White Citizens' Council. Though the organization officially eschewed violence in favor of more "respectable" methods of safeguarding white supremacy—in Payne's words, they promoted "the agenda of the Klan with the demeanor of the Rotary"—their economic reprisals and political maneuvers were often backed by an all too credible threat of force.[5] In fact, as civil rights organizing intensified throughout Mississippi in the postwar period, violent retaliation often followed closely behind—a lesson that Hamer, a sharecropper from the heart of Delta country, had already learned well. Less than a year before her Winona arrest, Hamer tried to register to vote; in retaliation, night riders fired upon the home of Mary Tucker, where Hamer was presumed to be staying, along with some forty other homes.[6] Staley's Café itself had served as the setting for at least two prior showdowns over integration, both of which resulted in the arrest and subsequent beatings of the activists involved.[7]

To call such violent enforcement of the color line "extralegal" is perhaps to miss the point—or rather, to oversimplify the matter. Throughout Jim Crow America, violence against black citizens, particularly those suspected of being "agitators" and activists, not only went unchecked; it also transpired with the tacit approval, and sometimes direct involvement, of elected officials and police officers. Violence did not come only from civilians under cover of darkness; it also came at the hands of officers sworn to protect and serve, with no less impunity for the fact of broad daylight. Sheriff Partridge and his fellow lawmen on the scene that morning in June "had good reason to believe that [they] were above the law—local, state, or federal," as Davis Houck observes in his essay on the Winona arrests. "Several brutal beatings and the flagrant flouting of the law simply had met with no adverse consequences." Indeed, Mississippi's governor appeared to endorse and protect such actions.[8] As Hamer had remarked dryly that June morning, standing outside Staley's Café and about to be arrested for the singular offense of being black in public space: "This is what it's like in Mississippi."

Yes, Hamer, Ponder, and the others knew very well that black folks in Mississippi tended to encounter worse than confinement once detained by law enforcement. But perhaps nothing could have fully prepared them for the brutality of the Winona authorities and the vicious, protracted torture they would be subjected to while in their custody. Inside the Montgomery County Jail, after issuing an ominous warning that the group would be taught "how to say 'yes, sir' to a Mississippi white man," June Johnson—then only fifteen years old—was singled out as the first to learn that lesson's details.[9] From the adjacent cells, her coworkers could hear her screams, as she pleaded with the officers. "You all are supposed to protect and take care of us," she insisted. By the time Basinger, Perkins, and local policeman William Surrell were done with her, she later recounted, her clothes had been torn from her body, she was covered in blood, and her eye had been permanently damaged from repeated head trauma. After returning to her cell, she was ordered to wash her clothes and clean the blood from her body—presumably to conceal any evidence of the beating that had just taken place.[10]

James West and Annell Ponder learned their lessons next—West, beaten with a blackjack by two other black prisoners forced to do the dirty work;

Ponder, brutalized by Basinger and Perkins for refusing to say, "yes, sir." But perhaps the worst of it was reserved for Hamer, who was singled out for special punishment due to her leadership role in working for black voter enfranchisement in Sunflower County. Calling the two prisoners, Sol Poe and Roosevelt Knox, into the cell, Basinger armed them with a blackjack and instructed them to "make that bitch wish she was dead."[11] An interview from days after her arrest describes successive waves of physical abuse and sexual assault by the police officers and the prisoners they had conscripted. Her agonized screams seemed only to intensify and inspire further violence. As she explained, "I had to get over there on the bed flat on my stomach, and that man *beat* me—that man *beat* me til he give out. And by me screamin', it made one of the other ones—plainclothes fellow [Perkins], he didn't have on nothing like a uniform—he got so hot and worked up off it, he just run there you know and started hittin' me on the back of my head." Hamer tried her best to use her hands to shield herself from the brunt of the force but to no avail; they simply beat her hands "till they turned *blue*." When the officers gave out, they called on Knox and Poe to take over, one after the other. In the course of the beatings, Hamer's dress worked its way up her legs, exposing her thighs and undergarments. Attempting to preserve her dignity, she moved to pull her dress back down. One of the officers pushed her hand away and pulled her dress up over her back, and pressed Knox and Poe to continue, until at last the officers grew weary from their exertions and bade Hamer return to her cell.[12]

In the intervening hours, word of the arrests had reached Student Nonviolent Coordinating Committee (SNCC) Field Secretary Lawrence Guyot in Greenwood, who quickly assembled a group to drive to Winona. When Guyot confronted the officers and asked about the arrests, charges, and bail, Partridge told him to "get out of Winona and stay gone." Though Guyot tried to comply—he thanked the officers and started walking back out toward his car—the police had other plans. After identifying him as a voting rights organizer and asking whether he knew how to say "yes, sir," Basinger punched Guyot in the face and dragged him into the sheriff's office, where he was shoved up against a wall and forced to remove his clothes. The police then beat him with a blackjack, held a lit slip of paper up to his genitals, and kicked him down a set of stairs. They ultimately charged Guyot with resisting arrest and disturbing the peace.[13]

The beatings ended on Sunday night, but conditions in the jail cell were hardly conducive to the welfare of these seven detainees. The heat was stifling;

the cells were filthy and lacked access to drinking water; the activists were not permitted to make phone calls or access medical care. Within an earshot of Hamer, the officers considered whether it would all be easier if they just "put them sons of bitches in Big Black [River]" so "nobody would ever find them." Even so, the prisoners insisted on defending themselves in whatever way they could. As June Johnson recalled, "The food was terrible, so we all ended up going on a strike. We would sing."[14] That spirit of dignity-in-defiance greeted SNCC worker Ida Mae Holland, when she was finally allowed into the cells to check on her colleagues: "The first person I saw was Annell Ponder. Her face was swollen and she had a black eye. She could hardly talk, but when she saw me, she whispered, 'Freedom.'"[15]

Though less gruesome, the courtroom drama that the seven activists encountered at their "trial" two days later was no less distressing and no less revealing of the dynamics of the Jim Crow legal order. Having overheard the police on Monday night debating what kind of trumped up charges they could manufacture, the group was tried the next day without legal representation and convicted in a matter of minutes of disorderly conduct and resisting arrest. That afternoon, police forced them to sign individual statements claiming that no beatings had taken place while in the care of the Montgomery County authorities. Neither local law nor public opinion were on the activist's side: in 1960, the Mississippi legislature passed House Bill 558—a breach of the peace law that penalized anyone found "with intent to provoke a breach of the peace, or under circumstances such that a breach of the peace may be occasioned thereby" such as persons in "crowds or congregating with others" in a number of public and private settings, including those where sit-ins or other desegregation protests had taken place in the past.[16] Thus, as Winona's paper would later insist, the threat posed to (the racial) order by the mere presence of black activists was both clear and present: "the action of the seven Negroes who were arrested last week at the bus terminal could easily have caused a riot, and their failure to obey law officers could not be overlooked."[17] Though the Kennedy Justice Department would, several months later, file charges against Partridge, Herod, Basinger, Perkins, and Surrell for civil rights violations, none of them would ever be punished for their crimes. "Despite overwhelming physical evidence, testimony by all seven victims, FBI Special Agents, as well as brave witness by the black inmates who'd beaten West and Hamer, and expert prosecutorial strategy and execution by Justice Department attorneys," Houck notes, "an all-male, all-white jury took but 75 minutes to find the five men not guilty on all counts."[18]

When the group finally left the custody of the Winona police one day later, the organizers who came to pay their bonds and secure their release—Dorothy Cotton, James Bevel, and Andrew Young—barely recognized them beneath the swelling and bruises. Yet if the lesson that four days in Winona was supposed to impress was how to politely toe the color line—how to say "yes, sir" to a white man—that lesson was lost on the group. As Hamer would later insist, "If them crackers in Winona thought they'd discourage me from fighting, I guess they found out different. I'm going to stay in Mississippi and if they shoot me down, I'll be buried here. I don't want equal rights with the white man; if I did, I'd be a thief and a murderer."[19]

* * *

Winona in June 1963 might seem an odd place to start a chapter on civil disobedience—both for its relative obscurity in the catalogue of civil rights movement events and, relatedly, for the notable absence of any planned campaign. The group's incarceration in Winona, we might say, was both shockingly routine and utterly uninvited—a glimpse of the everyday viciousness of the Mississippi racial ordinary, to be sure, but one without real lessons for political theorizing about protest. For all their brutal detail, those four days in Montgomery County told a common enough story in Mississippi; it was not even the most extreme incident of racist violence against civil rights activists to occur in the state during that particular weekend.[20] Hamer and her fellow travelers, moreover, did not plan on getting arrested that morning in June—they did not arrive in Winona to roll out a campaign of civil disobedience; to the extent that they intended their use of the bus stop facilities to serve as a test for the Interstate Commerce Commission's 1961 desegregation order, their actions nevertheless fell far short of protest. There were no press there at the Trailways depot to record their arrest; there had been no planned campaign to draw them there.[21] Compared to the iconic, coordinated mass actions that mark the public imagination of the civil rights movement, Winona might register but dimly: a minor—if bloody—local skirmish in a decades-long struggle for freedom.

Yet the events in Winona tell us something critical about the social and political landscape of the Jim Crow regime, as black activists encountered it in the 1960s—about the ordeal of going to jail; about the relationship between criminal justice and the fight for desegregation; and about the analytical lenses that activists developed to understand, critique, and respond to the practices and institutions of white supremacy. The circumstances around the groups' arrests point to the critical continuities between legal and extralegal violence that defined the Jim Crow order—the network of practices and institutions that connect segregated spaces, both public and private, to a system of police force, jails, courts, and vigilante violence, oriented toward the protection and maintenance of white property and white power. While the injustice of segregated public accommodations is often understood as linked to the indignity and humiliation of being denied service based on race, along with the social inequalities created and sustained through such differentiation, the policing—official and unofficial—of segregated space also fed into practices of harassment, criminalization, incarceration, and violence directed at black bodies perceived to be "out of place."[22] The Jim Crow state was structured as a regime of private property owners deputized to police the color line; a regime based not on the monopolization of force by the state but on the democratization of force amongst white citizens, empowered to maintain the status quo with whatever means necessary. Recall that it was a white passenger who initiated the incident by alerting the police about the presence of black organizers on the bus to Winona; it is not farfetched to assume this individual knew the likely consequences of calling the authorities. This too was an act of color-line policing, made possible by the ways ordinary white citizens were empowered to serve as auxiliaries to the more formalized organs of state violence and racial control. "That Tuesday when they had our trial," Hamer emphasized in a 1964 speech in Indianola, Mississippi, "the same policemen that had participated in the beatings was on the jury seat, people. And I was charged with disorderly conduct and resisting arrest."[23] Under these conditions, the boundaries between illegal protest and legally protected action blurred, creating spaces in which activism generally and black activism specifically was always already criminalized.[24] When Hamer later recounted her experiences in Winona before audiences both local and national, it was not as evidence of a local incident with a handful of particularly racist cops, but as part of a "damning indictment of American interracial justice."[25]

Yet activists used experiences such as those in the Montgomery County jail and courthouse in surprising and creative ways—as opportunities to double down on freedom: withholding markers of deference and submission ("yes, sir") from white authorities; singing and striking over jail conditions; gathering evidence and documenting facts, often surreptitiously, to press their case forward; and broadcasting their experiences to build solidarity with and mobilize others. Hamer, in particular, used the Winona story as a key element in public speeches and statements in order to motivate others to—as she put it—"stand up."[26] The experience of arrest and incarceration, born of brutality and the travesty of justice bent in the service of white supremacy, could become a touchstone for activism and a fighting spirit: "there used to be a time when you would hit a Negro—a white man would hit a Negro—the others would go and hide," Hamer told her audience. "But there's a new day now, when you hit a Negro, you likely see a thousand there. Because God care. God care and we care. And we can no longer ignore the fact that we can't sit down and wait for things to change because as long as they can keep their feet on our neck, they will always do it. But it's time for us to stand up and be women and men."[27] In Hamer's retelling, the Winona jail is not the site of her own powerlessness before the brutality of white power; it is her standing ground. While the story she tells undoubtedly attunes her listeners to the costs of activism, she offers it as a testament to the power of ordinary black citizens to fight back and claim the freedom that is rightfully theirs.[28]

This set of ideas—linking together a particular critique of Jim Crow justice to defiant, liberatory action and the building of solidarity—became a cornerstone of evolving and contested activist thinking on the ethics and tactics of civil disobedience through the early 1960s as the grassroots movement took off. In these early movement years, this narrative was meaningfully centered on the jail experience, as a generation of young activists launched an assault on segregated public accommodations through the sit-ins and Freedom Rides and devised a way of making arrest and incarceration a means of protest rather than simply a consequence of it. Through the tactical innovation of "jail, no bail"—the practice of remaining in jail in order to withhold bail monies—student activists of SNCC and CORE reconstructed and transformed the meaning of going to jail and its place within direct action. What had been an experience defined by fear, stigma, and vulnerability became, variously, an enactment of courage, dignity, and freedom; a way of multiplying and extending protest into new arenas; and a means of withholding cooperation from illegitimate power. All of this entailed a structural critique of Jim Crow institutions significantly wider and more complex than the claim against segregated accommodations usually associated with these campaigns. Arrest and punishment were used, therefore, as sites for practices of agency and liberation. Embedded within the particular domestic contexts of Jim Crow, this political orientation was nothing other than the development and deployment of civil disobedience as decolonizing praxis: a form of activism that wedded self-liberation—the cultivation of fearlessness in the face of domination—to the practices of solidarity building, structural critique, and cost levying that sought to enable broader, systemic liberation.

To chart these ideas, I will take temporary leave of Mississippi to follow new lines of transit, only to return at the end of the chapter. In the next section, I engage briefly with the ways in which political and legal theorists have thought about arrest and incarceration quite differently—as a means of containing disobedience's potentially destabilizing effects—before offering an alternative in the form of "comparative freedom."

From Containment to Comparative Freedom

The violent, risky ordeal of going to jail—so powerfully narrated by Hamer—figures into the literature on civil disobedience not as an ordeal at all, but as a means of safeguarding the constitutional order. As I detailed in Chapter 1, acceptance of arrest and legal punishment helps ensure that civil disobedience remains within the framework of law—normatively speaking—even while activists break specific, individual laws. Thus, it has stabilizing effects, both practically and normatively. At a practical level, as some theorists argue, the risk of arrest faced by the disobedient—and the corresponding demand that they face their punishment willingly—functions as a check against insincere, trivial, or destructive protests: only those truly committed to the cause at hand would put themselves in a position to be arrested, tried, convicted, and jailed. According to David Lefkowitz's argument, this gesture of self-sacrifice "contributes to the stability of the state and so to its ability to facilitate morally necessary collective action." The state's ability to punish—or, more narrowly, in Lefkowitz's analysis, *penalize*—those who engage in civil disobedience "makes it more likely that actions with the potential to reduce the state's ability to successfully and efficiently apply laws and policies will take place only when the injustice of existing laws and policies is believed to be significant." The knowledge that one has to face particular costs—in the form of fines or incarceration—forces the protestor to "consider the potential cost to justice of their engaging in such acts. In particular, the more resources the state devotes to dealing with public disobedience, the less it has to use for achieving what a majority of citizens, employing a morally defensible procedure, have determined to be required by justice."[29] The threat of punishment, as well as the requirement of submission to it, thus operates as a mechanism of containment—a limitation on the potential for disobedience to threaten the stability of the state.[30]

The most pervasive explanation of the role of accepting arrest, however, is that it communicates something essential to the broader society. Facing punishment signals sincerity, demonstrating that, although illegal or otherwise disobedient, the act of protest is made in good faith, borne of deep conviction. It dramatizes the moral importance of the matter at hand—the injustice or wrong being protested—and encourages the democratic public to reflect seriously on the protestor's appeal, forcing a reconsideration of the law or policy in question.[31] "Being completely open about one's acts and being willing to accept the legal consequences of one's conduct," Rawls argues, "is a bond given to make good one's sincerity, for that one's deeds are conscientious is not easy to demonstrate to another or even before oneself." In order to do so, and in order to establish the moral basis of our claims in the eyes of the community, "we must pay a price."[32] The dramatic self-sacrifice involved in accepting arrest thus provides a means to establish terms of trust and future cooperation between protestors and broader society, and thus a way to "reassure and to move the majority."[33] This, too, is a kind of mechanism of containment: it ensures that civil disobedience is something other than—more than—the instrumentalization of civic relations. By willingly going to jail, the disobedient protestor not only communicates the sort of commitment to the rule of law that is absent in revolutionaries and rebels; they also demonstrate that they are not trying to overpower their fellow citizens or circumvent legitimate processes of democratic will-formation through a show of force. Due punishment not only ensures that disobedience "does not destroy the order or stability of national or community life"; it also communicates the desire to refrain from doing so.[34]

This view of what accepting arrest might mean—state stability and containment—takes for granted that the state and its normative order is a thing to be preserved. And from this perspective, the insistence that protestors cheerfully submit to arrest and legal punishment appears quite reasonable: it is what an activist must do if they want to be perceived in the right way (as a reformer, not a revolutionary or criminal). And yet here we are faced with Fannie Lou Hamer and her fellow travelers, bloodied in the Winona jail on the night before their sham trial. What kind of allegiance does such a system merit from those it violates, dominates, and abuses?[35] Were Hamer to break the law in protest, should she submit to arrest under this violent, racist order to further stabilize it, affirm the legitimacy of it, and contain the unruly effects of her protest? How might we shift the frame and ask new questions about what accepting arrest—as many civil rights activists did, over and over again—might mean under these conditions? What part does this play in disobedience, re-conceptualized not as constitutional patriotism or fidelity to law, but as decolonizing praxis?

Bernard Boxill suggests a powerful alternative by situating Martin Luther King, Jr.'s account of civil disobedience not within a liberal or democratic theory of political obligation but as part of the black radical tradition. In particular, Boxill follows a different path of imaginative transit—temporal rather than geographic—that connects King backward in time to Frederick Douglass's self-emancipation from the condition of enslavement. Across Douglass's three biographies, he famously narrates his violent struggle against a slave-breaker named Covey—a struggle that not only results in Covey's retreat but also fundamentally transforms Douglass. As Boxill argues, the torture of "breaking" was not mere punishment for disobedience; rather, it was "frequent, severe, unexpected flogging" designed to make the slave lose "his taste or ability to deliberate and choose, and consequently his preference to obey only himself."[36] In resisting Covey's attempt to break him, therefore, Douglass does more than simply fight back; rather, he discovers within himself the capacity to make himself more-than-half free, even while enslaved. "I was changed after that fight," Douglass recounts in *My Bondage and My Freedom*, "I was *nothing* before; I WAS A MAN NOW. It recalled to life my crushed self-respect and my self-confidence, and inspired me with a renewed determination to be A FREEMAN." Though Douglass remains enslaved, he declares himself comparatively free by virtue of his own action and his own imaginative capacities: "It was a resurrection from the dark and pestiferous tomb of slavery, to the heaven of comparative freedom.... I had reached the point, at which I was *not afraid to die*. This spirit made me a freeman in *fact*, while I remained a slave in *form*. When a slave cannot be flogged he is more than half free."[37]

In Douglass's narration, the fight with Covey—the act of resistance through which he refuses to be "broken," overcomes a fear of death, and becomes free "in *fact*"—is thus pivotal: it is the necessary condition for his ultimate escape from slavery. In Neil Roberts's terms, the struggle opens up the possibility for "assertion"—the "forthright implementation of an imagined conviction into action," through which Douglass is able to imagine a *much-more*-than-half-free freedom for himself individually and for the enslaved collectively, and to act on it.[38] For Douglass, the experience opens up the horizon of future possibility, a life beyond the "prison" of mental and physical enslavement:

> The thought of only being a creature of the *present* and the *past*, troubled me, and I longed to have a *future*—a future with hope in it. To be shut up entirely to the past and present, is abhorrent to the human mind; it is to the soul—whose life and happiness is unceasing progress—what the prison is to the body; a blight and mildew; a hell of horrors. . . . The intense desire, now felt, *to be free*, quickened by my present favorable circumstances, brought me to the determination to *act*, as well as to think and to speak.[39]

Comparative freedom locates the fugitive movements between liberty and slavery, and names the forms of action and psychological orientations that enable a separation between the *form* of oppression (its legal, juridical, and political realities) and its *fact* (what oppression does to the agential and imaginative capacities of the person). As Boxill puts it, though Douglass was well aware "that he had not won all of his freedoms and consequently was a slave in form," in struggle he had retained "the ability and pleasure to think, deliberate, and choose for himself."[40]

Boxill connects King's civil disobedience to Douglass's struggle for freedom "in *fact*" as a "similar way for black people to become more than half free and to keep alive the hope of achieving complete freedom." In King's theorization and practice of civil disobedience, Boxill perceives the power of a mass refusal to recognize the authority of the "master's commands," which in turn reinvigorates and reconfirms the ability of ordinary black Americans to act (comparatively) freely. In this, he argues, King went a step further than Douglass, in envisioning a form of action that could become truly *mass* action—raising the possibility that nonviolent mass activism might change more than just those who engage in it. While the enslaved "risked their lives for their own more-than-half freedom," they "did not seem to have supposed that their strategy could set an example for other slaves." In contrast, and though King remained skeptical of the capacities of white citizens for moral transformation, "King could put enough civilly disobedient people to work to hope that their defiance could have good effects on the wider community."[41]

While I will take up this latter concern more fully in the next two chapters, what I would like to emphasize here is the way Boxill's account reorients us toward the activists jailed in Winona and to the question of submitting to arrest after breaking the law in protest. Instead of asking about how the presumptively legitimate state can be maintained, even amidst the disruption of disobedient protest, Boxill encourages us to see like an activist—to ask about the meaning activists attributed to their actions and the effects those actions had.[42] What did it mean for Annelle Ponder to whisper "Freedom" through a jail cell? What would it mean for the students of the sit-in campaigns and the Freedom Rides, whose activism left them vulnerable to expulsion from school, verbal harassment, violent assault, and potential death at the hands of white citizens empowered by a racist state—what would it mean for them to act within and against this context, and then willingly serve jail sentences? What would it mean to do this en masse—not just as an individual act, but as a collective one?

Commenting on the students involved in the sit-ins in a May 1960 article entitled "The Burning Truth in the South," King himself provides the beginnings of an answer—in terms that resonate, directly and powerfully, with Douglass's own narrative:

> Though confronted in many places by hoodlums, police guns, tear gas, arrests, and jail sentences, the students tenaciously continue to sit down and demand equal service ... the spirit of self-sacrifice and commitment remains firm, and the state governments find themselves dealing with students who have lost the fear of jail and physical injury.
>
> Hundreds have already been expelled, fined, imprisoned, and brutalized, and the numbers continue to grow. But with the punishments, something more is growing. A generation of young people has come out of decades of shadows to face naked state power; it has lost its fears, and experienced the majestic dignity of a direct struggle for its own liberation. These young people have connected up with their own history—the slave revolts, the incomplete revolution of the Civil War, the brotherhood of colonial colored men in Africa and Asia. They are an integral part of the history which is reshaping the world, replacing a dying order with modern democracy.[43]

Here, King frames the issue in two ways rendered invisible when we see like a white state: First, he places arrest and jail alongside other risks that civil rights protestors routinely took—expulsion, firing, police brutality, and physical assault or death at the hands of segregationists. These are simply the risks that faced any black citizen who dared step "out of place" under Jim Crow—the risks of facing "naked state power." Second, in referencing the history of imaginative transit that preceded this moment, King frames the meaning of protest not as "fidelity to law" nor as allegiance to the ideals of the constitutional nation-state. Rather, he connects the jailed student activists to liberation struggles across a whole world, one that has long been in motion—from those more-than-half-free slaves who revolted a century before, to the transnational expanse of contemporary anticolonialism.[44] Here, as with facing public and private violence without reprisal or fear, going to jail is linked to an enactment of courage and dignity, and thereby, liberation. And it is this liberation, this demonstration of "majestic dignity" and freedom that will challenge, and ultimately transform, what King elsewhere calls an "evil system," and here deems a "dying order" of domination and inequality—an order with deep roots in the past and global reach. Thus, the inward-facing power of self-emancipation is tied to the outward-facing power of collective action that can change systems and orders. In a newspaper interview just a few days before his article appeared in the pages of *The Progressive*, King put it this way: "We will encourage more students to go to jail, to build a spirit, a cause among Negroes. If we fill up his jails, the white man will have no place to put us."[45]

Read through the work of Chapter 2, and alongside Boxill's and Roberts's elaborations of comparative freedom, King's statements raise the possibility of a dynamic and complex set of meanings carried by the act of going to jail—a possibility I will explore through the campaign of "jail, no bail," waged by student activists in 1960–1961, as they chose to serve out jail sentences rather than securing bail or paying fines. As we will see, the discourse of jail, arrest, and punishment that first arose during the sit-ins in 1960 complicates the idea that accepting arrest is meant to delimit protest, signal state legitimacy, or simply express a moral appeal. Rather, "jail, no bail" worked to multiply protest across new arenas, extend and intensify the critique of interlocking networks of unjust institutions, and leverage jail time as a means of building solidarity while disrupting institutional functioning. As such, "jail, no bail" demonstrates what it means to pursue civil disobedience as a decolonizing praxis, linking the enactment of self-emancipation with processes of solidarity building and crisis-generation.

The Evolution of "Jail, No Bail"

"'Let's go to jail; let's stay in jail.' With these words the student leaders gathered at the Conference on Non-violent Resistance renounced the practice of rushing out of jail when arrested."[46] After a season of sit-in campaigns that began with four students in Greensboro and quickly spread throughout the South, more than 200 student delegates representing over fifty colleges across thirteen states gathered at Shaw University in Raleigh, North Carolina, to strategize and coordinate.[47] Out of this meeting emerged the fledgling SNCC, then conceived as nothing more than a temporary "clearing house" for the ideas and strategies of otherwise completely local, independent campaigns. A limited set of principles would guide this process; among them, the delegates agreed unanimously, would be "the practice of going to jail rather than accepting bail."[48]

By the time of the mid-April conference, the sit-ins had already sent around 1,000 students and activists to jail, mostly for trespassing, disorderly conduct, disturbing the peace, or resisting arrest. The spectacle of well-dressed, well-mannered, and steadfastly nonviolent young students being hauled off to jail by the dozens had done much to put the sit-ins on the map, as an event of intense national interest and historical importance. Only in a few locations, however, had the idea of remaining in jail—rather than paying bail or going out on appeal—been contemplated or attempted as a part of sit-in tactics.

One such place was Nashville, a city home to a sizeable college student population and defined by an "odd mix of racial progressiveness on the one hand and conflict and intolerance on the other."[49] For months in advance of the event that inaugurated the sit-in movement—the now-famous demonstration of four black students at a Woolworth's lunch counter in Greensboro, North Carolina—James Lawson, divinity student at Vanderbilt and field secretary for the Fellowship of Reconciliation (FOR), had been leading nonviolent workshops for students in preparation for a planned anti-segregation campaign of Nashville's own.[50] The sit-ins began on February 13, 1960, at a number of segregated lunch counters downtown and continued for several weeks. Though police initially refrained from action, by the end of the month, they announced that "the grace period was over." After allowing a growing crowd of agitated whites to attack the students with lit cigarettes, rocks, and their fists, the police arrested eighty-one of the demonstrators—but none of the attackers—and charged them with disturbing the peace.[51] When they were convicted of the charge at their trial the Monday the 29th and ordered to pay a fine of fifty dollars per person or serve a thirty-day term in jail, the students surprised everyone by choosing the harsher of the two punishments. Diane Nash, a student at Fisk University and soon to become a critical SNCC organizer, served as spokesperson for the fifteen sit-inners in court that day, John Lewis among them. "We feel that if we pay these fines," she said, "we would be contributing to and supporting the injustice and immoral practices that have been performed in the arrest and conviction of the defendants."[52] Encouraged by their example, an additional sixty individuals arrested for sitting-in followed suit, foregoing the chance to pay the fines and joining their fellow students in jail instead.[53] Inside the jail, the students sang and chanted their refrain: "Jail without bail!"[54] Unlike in other cities, however, a key concession from the mayor cut the students' stint in jail far short of a full sentence.[55]

In Tallahassee, too, eight students chose jail over bail. The same week that Lawson, Nash, Lewis, and hundreds of students in Nashville were sitting-in, the local Tallahassee chapter of CORE sponsored its first sit-in, organizing black students at Florida A&M University and a local high school to demonstrate at Woolworth's and McCrory's, another chain store downtown. After several weeks of almost daily sit-ins and a handful of arrests, a young student organizer named Patricia Stephens led a group of nearly 1,000 A&M students to march, in waves, on the two stores, urging them to "fill the jails if necessary." Along the way, as historians August Meier and Elliot Rudwick detail in their classic biography of CORE, the students met with "club-wielding whites" as well as police, wielding a "tear gas barrage," which ultimately dispersed the crowd.[56] As in so many cities and towns that saw sit-ins, stand-ins, wade-ins, and lie-ins, the eleven arrested demonstrators were charged and convicted of disturbing the peace and unlawful assembly. When faced with the choice of paying a $300 fine or spending sixty days in Leon County Jail, eight of the eleven disregarded their attorney's advice and opted for jail. In a statement issued from jail, later compiled and published by CORE alongside other testimonies from student sit-in participants, Stephens insisted on the importance of remaining in jail: "We could all be out on appeal, but we strongly believe that Martin Luther King was right when he said: 'We've got to fill the jails in order to win our equal rights.'"[57]

The events in Nashville and Tallahassee suggested a new and radical direction for protest strategy but also a demanding one. In August at the CORE-sponsored Interracial Action Institute in Miami, the topic of "jail, no bail" was put on the table as a major item for consideration. While the tactic had much to recommend it, it asked a great deal from protestors, some of whom were more vulnerable than others in jail, and many of whom might not be able to afford long stretches of time away from family or work. Unlike other protest guidelines advocated by the direct action groups of the early 1960s—remaining nonviolent, maintaining a neat appearance, speaking politely and refraining from insults, and so on—forgoing bail was not simply a matter of training, nor was it something that could be required of all demonstrators. The tactic was also anathema to many civil rights activists, particularly those within the NAACP, who had for years labored—often successfully—under the belief that the courtroom, not the jail cell, was the place to wage battle against segregation and racial injustice. Purposely getting arrested was one thing; refusing bail seemed perverse and perhaps dangerous to the cause. Speaking before a crowd at Fisk University in April 1960, Thurgood Marshall, then the head of the NAACP's Legal Defense Fund, made it clear that those arrested should plead not guilty and accept bail: "Once you've been arrested, you've made your point. If someone offers to get you out, man, get out!"[58] Many within the NAACP were growing increasingly concerned about the issue, even as they expressed support for the developing sit-in movement and pledged to cover the legal fees for those arrested.[59] As indicated by a position paper drafted several months later, the NAACP increasingly viewed the tactic with suspicion and anxiety—as an "ill-conceived" "forfeit[ure] of constitutional rights" that risked weakening the "overall legal attack on this spiteful, vicious system," and potentially "stigmatizing our youths with criminal records" in exchange for few, if any, tangible gains.[60]

The activists in Miami, however, came to a different conclusion. They saw in "jail, no bail" a means of placing CORE on the cutting edge of the burgeoning protest movement, and threw their weight behind the idea in principle and in practice.[61] Despite its associated risks, serving out a jail sentence made some amount of practical sense, as it could help CORE and SNCC reduce the need for vast sums of bail money, thereby conserving already limited resources and reducing dependence on the NAACP. But more crucially, it offered activists the ability to "galvanize the local black community into militant protest and awaken the conscience of many northern whites to a degree that mere arrests by themselves could not accomplish," while moving the locus of protest action from the lunch counter to the jail cell itself—and thus, from the site of one injustice (segregated public accommodations) to another related one (the mockery of legal justice dressed up in a coded language of public safety and law and order).[62] "At the Interracial Action Institute," James Robinson wrote in the September 1960 issue of the *CORE-lator*, "we discussed jail versus bail and concluded that in cases of unjust arrest arising from nonviolent protest action, remaining in jail is effective in mobilizing community support. It also forms a direct protest in itself against segregation laws. At the same time, each individual should be left free to determine the extent of the sacrifice he wishes to make." Dedication to this approach was tested, and proven, several days later, at a sit-in action in Miami in which eighteen were arrested. Seven of them ultimately decided to stay in jail—where they found conditions segregated, filthy, and dangerous—until their trial date.[63] With Nashville, Tallahassee, and Miami, the "jail-in" was born.

Through Jail to Freedom

Despite its newfound militant appeal, the idea of using the jail cell as a platform for extending protest was not new. Indeed, it had important precedents and carried particular significance for civil rights activists. As Nicole Rhoton details, not two decades before the emergence of the sit-in movement, conscientious objectors, draft resisters, and pacifist protestors against World War II had attempted to redefine "the path to prison as one of virtue," and transform the prison cell into a "forum for resisters to explore political and philosophical ideas and experiment with tactics of nonviolent direct action."[64] Many of the men jailed for refusing conscription did not accept imprisonment as a way of signaling respect for a system perceived to be legitimate; on the contrary, many viewed their imprisonment as unjust and illegitimate and pushed their protest further by staging various noncooperation campaigns within and against the prison.[65] Campaigns waged from within the prison's walls included antiwar protests and refusals to work for war-related industries, general work and noncooperation strikes against prison conditions, and anti-segregation protests—including a remarkable 135-day strike at the Federal Corrections Institute in Danbury, Connecticut, resulting in the desegregation of the mess hall in August of 1943.[66] And among those leading and participating in such campaigns were names that would loom large in the decades of civil rights work to follow: George Houser, an FOR field worker who co-founded CORE after his release; Joe Guinn, head of the local NAACP youth council in Chicago and co-founder of CORE with Houser; Bayard Rustin, organizer of the 1947 FOR-led Journey of Reconciliation and the 1963 March on Washington; and James Peck, a pacifist and labor organizer who went on to work with CORE as a publicity agent and one of the coordinators of the 1961 Freedom Rides.[67]

Outside this cadre of pacifists, however, the broader valences of going to jail were less positive, if more potent. Arrest and imprisonment carried an understandable stigma, often deeply felt by the young students who inaugurated the sit-in movement. The criminalization of the black community and the racialization of convict labor and crime, particularly in the post-Reconstruction South, created a set of deeply entrenched ideas about the shame and indignity of going to prison—ideas that often tracked alongside class divisions.[68] For a generation of black students, some of them the first in their families to finish high school and attend college, the pressures to avoid arrest—and the movement altogether—were considerable. Some wrote letters to their parents from jail, pleading with them to understand why they had chosen to demonstrate and risk arrest. While some came around, inspired by the dignity displayed by their children in the midst of injury, assault, and arrest, others did not. "I lost my family that spring of 1960," John Lewis recalls in his memoir. "When my parents got word that I had been arrested—I wrote them a letter from the Nashville jail explaining what had happened and that I was acting in accordance with my Christian faith—they were shocked. Shocked and ashamed. My mother made no distinction between being jailed for drunkenness and being jailed for demonstrating for civil rights. 'You went to school to get an education,' she wrote me back. 'You should get out of this movement, just get out of that mess.'"[69]

But arrested civil rights activists had more to fear from a Southern jail than parental reproach or social stigma. In the decades since the Civil War, the criminal justice system had been developed as a powerful institutional tool for safeguarding white supremacy—a means of keeping black people "in their place." The intertwining of unofficial and official violence—lynch mobs aided by the acquiescence, explicit support, and direct involvement of law enforcement personnel and political officials; a network of police, courts, jails, and penal work camps often set to work in the service of racial domination—had helped shape both the perception and reality of imprisonment in the Jim Crow South.[70] These developments, as historian Dan Berger argues, "were constitutive, not incidental." In the period leading up to the "classical" civil rights movement years, "whites freely terrorized blacks through the law— with economic reprisals, with political disenfranchisement—and then used the law to evade punishment." At the same time, "white extralegal violence against blacks . . . was so pervasive as to be functionally and sometimes even technically legal."[71] While lynching had become far less common by the 1960s, the mass arrests following civil rights protests represented a new attempt of the legal system to enforce the color line and to instill activists with fear of the repercussions for rocking the segregated boat. Civil rights workers (both black and white) were particularly at risk once arrested and imprisoned, subject to violence and abuse at the hands of police, prison guards, or other prisoners looking to discipline these "outside agitators" and "troublemakers."[72] In the interaction between black Americans arrested for protest and a legal system intent on preserving the status quo, the reality of Jim Crow justice revealed itself: oppression in the guise of law and order—a systemically pervasive and complex web of laws, customs, and principles that worked to protect (and reinvent) racial hierarchies.

A 1962 commission chaired by Eleanor Roosevelt and convened at the insistence of civil rights groups after the shocking and massive violence attending the Freedom Rides detailed the multiple ways that the legal and criminal justice system were implicated in ongoing racial injustice. Out of the testimonies,

> the pattern emerged: Police intimidation by acquiescence or complicity in white mob violence; by mass arrest of peaceful demonstrators on dubious charges; by brutality on streets and in jails. Judicial intimidation with the purpose of blocking civil rights by mass convictions; by placement of the highest charges, including criminal anarchy, against leaders; by the attempt to bankrupt organizations with astronomical bail and bond; by the attempt to stop civil rights action by injunction, and by isolating leaders in jails. Testimony indicated that police viciousness and judicial intransigence have increased with the new strength of the civil rights movement.[73]

To bring the fight for racial equality and justice to the jail cell, then, pushed protest far beyond the lunch counter, cutting to the heart of the mechanisms of racial control. It signified a radical form of noncooperation and an assertive challenge to systemic injustice—not a single law or policy. It also entailed a significant act of courage.

The emerging sit-in movement—which would feed directly into and considerably shape the civil rights movement campaigns of the 1960s, from the Freedom Rides through voter registration and community organizing in the Deep South—thus did much to challenge and invert the associations between jail and criminality, indignity, fear, and domination. The dynamic combination of Gandhian nonviolent resistance with Christian themes that permeated the national leadership of CORE and the circle of student activists from Lawson's nonviolent workshops celebrated the "unmerited suffering" of the jail-going experience—needed to purify the protestor and convert the hearts and minds of the broader public. Yet at the same time, another ideology was growing up alongside this one, competing with but not necessarily contradicting it.[74] The historical significance of the Southern jail as a space of racial subjugation was gradually being transformed by the activists themselves, shifting the usual negative connotations of being a "jailbird" into something positive and dignified. "Now it is a nice thing to go to jail," the *Baltimore Afro-American* announced in one headline. With the mass arrests that accompanied the sit-ins, "the ordinary jail or hoosegow is suddenly transferred and changed over night from a detention house of evil-doers into a Golgotha where innocent men are crucified for their ideas."[75] The idea of "jail, no bail" celebrated the jail experience as—in King's words—"a badge of honor" rather than a mark of shame; the jail cell, the very manifestation of unfreedom and domination, was artfully remade into a site of liberation, protest, and dignity. In Berger's terms, incarceration was turned into "a spectacle of freedom."[76]

As historian Zoe Colley argues, "Central to this transformation was the evolution of an ideology that embraced 'freedom' as a critical rhetorical component"—an ideology that redefined freedom in the context of incarceration and arrest, and placed the idea of freedom from fear and from subjugation at the heart of the evolving civil rights movement. "Freedom was a state of mind, and something that could be achieved in both an individual and a collective sense. . . . By *choosing* to go to jail, movement participants placed an emphasis upon securing one's mental freedom from fear, even at the cost of one's physical freedom."[77] At its best, the jail experience could be politicizing, liberating, motivating—a source of solidarity amongst activists. "You get ideas in jail," Charles Sherrod told *Harper's Magazine* in October of 1961. "You talk with other young people you've never seen. Right away we recognize each other. People like yourself, getting out of the past. We're up all night, sharing creativity, planning action. You learn the truth in prison, you learn wholeness. You find out the difference between being dead and alive."[78]

Sherrod's words suggest not merely a different interpretation of the meaning of accepting arrest than the one that we find in many political theory discussions of it, but an entirely different orientation to the subject. His words resonate not with Rawls or Lefkowitz but with Boxill, Douglass, and the network of global anticolonial activists who theorized disobedience as a means of cultivating and practicing fearlessness. For the former, accepting arrest performs a crucial function not for protestors but for spectators and the state; it serves, in particular, those political and moral ends that are most valuable to the state and to the majority (e.g., assurance of reformist intent; systemic stability; commitment to civility; affirmation of legitimacy). This perspective obscures both the inward-facing and outward-facing sides of civil disobedience as decolonizing praxis, as well as the relationship between them: the use of jailing as a defiant form of self-emancipation that could build solidarity among activists; and the use of collective jailing as a means of identifying, dramatizing, and interrupting the formal and informal structures of violent, racial rule.

During the "jail, no bail" campaigns of 1960 and 1961, activists leveraged the act of accepting arrest as a means of extending protest into new arenas—the jail cell itself—and to new communities, galvanized by the arrest of nonviolent student protestors. Taking up the call of those like Diane Nash who viewed going to jail as a means of withholding cooperation from an unjust legal system, "jail, no bail" operated as a strategic means of challenging the status quo. By filling the jails, activists would seek to overwhelm the system of "law and order," and thereby use mass jailing as a further assault on Jim Crow. This external struggle for freedom from oppressive institutions was intimately intertwined, moreover, with internal processes of transformation. Activists used imprisonment to build solidarity inside the jail cell; they transformed sites of fear and repression into sites for enacting courage, dignity, and agency. The act of going to jail was neither understood as reaffirming the state's legitimacy nor exclusively as a means of persuasive communication with a broader public of white citizens. Rather, the intentional redefinition of jail "from a place of shame to one of political honor" entailed, essentially, an unlikely but extremely powerful transformation of carceral space, as "the quintessentially private place of dishonor where rights are drastically curtailed and citizens becomes subjects," into a public space in which solidarity building and the capacity for freedom flourished."[79]

In *Civil Rights and the Idea of Freedom*, Richard King identifies four distinct, but overlapping, meanings of freedom at play during the civil rights movement. First, King argues, the standard American account of liberal freedom operated within activists' appeals for the same rights and liberties granted other citizens—those enshrined, for example, in First Amendment rights to free speech, assembly, and petition, as well as in the Reconstruction amendments' guarantees of equality of citizenship and due process of law.[80] This is the idea of freedom at work in the consensus narrative discussed in the first chapter, which presents the fight for civil rights as the fight for the enforcement and realization of legal and political rights and liberties that, essentially, already existed in the American constitutional framework. While not precisely incorrect, such an account fails to register the other vital understandings of freedom that were operative in and through the civil rights movement generally, and in the act of going to jail in protest particularly. In addition to liberal freedom, King argues that activists understood freedom to encompass ideas of autonomy—that is, the "process of becoming free from an old sense of self and from relationships of oppression and dependence" through the enactment of self-respect; the ideal of participatory freedom—the act of creating and maintaining "institutions that enable public participation in the exercise of power"; and finally, the freedom of collective deliverance and the process of self-liberation.[81] While standard accounts of the role of accepting arrest in the civil rights movement emphasize both liberal freedom and participatory freedom, the idea of incarceration as tied to autonomy and collective deliverance—those same forms of freedom taken up by the more-than-half-free slaves—is largely absent.

Yet the emerging ideology of "jail, no bail" is a powerful testament to precisely these ideas of freedom—ideas that tied the immediate experiences of the jailed student activists to a longer history of anticolonial nonviolence. "There was a sense of power, in a place where you didn't feel you had any power," explained one activist. "There was a sense of confronting things that terrified you, like jail, police, walking in the street." Though the precise demands and concrete gains of the movement—for desegregation of schools, public accommodations, housing, or employment; for an end to police brutality and a commitment to economic equality—were important, there was something else of critical value in the enactment of movement activism itself. "We were saying in some basic way, 'I will never again stay inside these boundaries.' . . . I had grown up in a society where there were very clear lines. The older I got, the more I found what those lines were. . . . Across those lines were powers that could do you in, so you just respect them and you don't cross them. The civil rights movement just destroyed that and said that if something puts you down, you have to fight against it."[82] The transformation of fear into courage, incarceration into liberation, meant that subjugation was rejected and agency enacted. The racial order was revealed and disputed not merely on the basis of claim making—the demand for *civil rights*— but as a struggle simultaneously *of* and *for* black freedom. As John Lewis phrased it, "Being involved tended to free you. You saw segregation, you saw discrimination, and you had to solve the problem, but you saw yourself also as a free man, as the free agent, able to act."[83] Such public, collective processes of liberation and deliverance were intimately intertwined with more individual experiences of autonomy, and expressed, as Richard King contends, Hannah Arendt's insistence that "to *be* free and to act are the same."[84] More accurately, perhaps, per Douglass and Boxill, we might say that to act is to be *comparatively free*.

Freedom Rides and Jail-Ins

By the end of 1960, however, the commitment to "jail, no bail" had been more theoretical than actual. Despite SNCC's inaugural pledge and CORE's ongoing enthusiasm for the tactic, throughout 1960 most of those arrested heeded the counsel of parents, loved ones, and lawyers, and left jail as soon as they could afford to post bail. In October at the second SNCC conference in Atlanta, James Lawson raised the issue, reminding everyone of the pledge they had taken in April and urging a return to it. "We lost the finest hour of our movement when so many hundreds of us left the jails across the South. Instead of letting the adults scurry around getting bail, we should have insisted that they scurry about to end the system which had put us in jail. If history offers us such an opportunity again, let us be prepared to seize it."[85]

Two weeks later on October 19, King was arrested along with seventy-seven others for sitting-in at Rich's department store in Atlanta. Much to the students' satisfaction, thirty-eight of them, King included, pursued a policy of refusing to pay fines or bail—"even if it means," King wrote in a letter to Judge James Webb, "remaining in jail a year or even ten years."[86] Though King would ultimately spend days, not years, in jail, the experience prompted him to consider the justification of "jail, no bail" more concretely; he drafted a list of reasons explaining the tactic's meaning and its importance to the black freedom struggle. In "Why We Chose Bail Rather Than Jail," King offers multiple arguments; while some overlap with the way theorists of civil disobedience have characterized the importance of accepting arrest, others move significantly beyond it, pointing toward a strategic use of jail-going as a means of fighting unjust institutions. In all, King lists eight reasons, which include "appeal to conscience of opponent" and the idea that "self-suffering" is the "highest expression of non-violence," but also the use of accepting arrest "to disarm the opponent of one of the chief weapons that he has held over the Negro—mainly the threat of arrest"; the ability to "[put] the opponent on the defensive" and "[weaken] his morale"; and finally a pragmatic consideration of going to jail as "a money saving device" which prevents "needless litigation."[87]

The one-year anniversary of the first sit-ins and the escalation of protest in Rock Hill, South Carolina, gave CORE and SNCC activists the opportunity they had been looking for—a chance to put these ideas about "jail, no bail" more fully into practice. The anti-segregation fight had been going on there in fits and starts for a year, without much success. In the late fall of 1960, Tom Gaither, a CORE activist working in South Carolina and a veteran of the Miami Interracial Action Institute, started laying the groundwork for a jail-in to reinvigorate the local movement in Rock Hill. At the end of January, Gaither had recruited nine students from the local Friendship Junior College to sit-in at McCrory's lunch counter, on the pledge that when arrested, they would take the position of "jail, no bail." No sooner had they taken their seats at the counter when the police arrived and arrested them for trespassing. The next day in court, they all pleaded not guilty; they were nevertheless convicted and sentenced to either thirty days on the York County road gang or fines of $100 each. Nine of the ten opted for hard labor. "We could have paid $100 fines, or we could have posted $200 bail each and gone out pending appeal," Gaither reported. "Instead, we chose to be jailed-in. All nine of us felt that this would strengthen the impact of our protest. Furthermore, instead of the city being $900 richer for the injustice it had committed, it would have to pay the expense of boarding and feeding us for 30 days."[88] The choice of jail had a further effect, seeming to upset the balance of power in favor of the convicted activists, at least for a time: "Surprise and shock filled the courtroom when it became known that we had chosen to be jailed-in. The only thing they had to beat us over the head with was a threat of sending us to jail. So we disarmed them by using the only weapon we had left . . . jail without bail. It was the only practical thing we could do. It upset them considerably."[89] Jailed, the "Friendship Nine," did not relent. They sang spirituals, calling up the ghosts of more-than-half-free slaves a century before, and maddening the guards with the refrain "Before I'll be a slave, I'll be buried in my grave." They went on a hunger strike against cruel mistreatment and engaged in a work slowdown when it became clear they were being forced to do much more work than the other prisoners; at one point, all nine were crammed in a single solitary confinement cell for "refusing to obey orders."[90]

On February 3, the SNCC steering committee reconvened in Atlanta. The events at Rock Hill were at the top of the agenda; ultimately, it was decided that they should recruit a group of students to travel to Rock Hill in solidarity—to sit-in with the intention of getting arrested and joining the Nine in prison. They released the following statement: "There are nine students here serving thirty days on the York County chain gang for sitting in at lunch counters and requesting service. Their sitting-in shows their belief in the immorality of racial segregation and their choice to serve the sentence shows their unwillingness to participate in any part of a system that perpetuates injustice. Since we too share their beliefs and since many times during the past year, we too have sat-in at lunch counters, we feel that in good conscience we have no alternative other than to join them."[91] Four SNCC activists, three of whom were already well-versed in sitting- and jailing-in—Diane Nash, Charles Jones, Charles Sherrod, and a relatively new recruit, Ruby Doris—rushed to Rock Hill, where they were arrested and sentenced to thirty days when they refused to pay their fines. Meanwhile, SNCC and CORE orchestrated a solidarity campaign, coordinating with hundreds of activists to continue dime store sit-ins in Rock Hill and at the McCrory's location in New York City.[92] They also organized a motorcade of 600 to the York County prison farm to support the men from CORE and SNCC serving out their time there.[93]

Though the Rock Hill jail-in remained limited, never expanding beyond the nine CORE and four SNCC members, it confirmed the power of "jail, no bail" for galvanizing the movement. Within the month, the campaign spread to two other cities—first to Lynchburg, Virginia, where a handful were arrested, and then to Atlanta, where seventy-six individuals were ultimately jailed, filling the Fulton County to overflowing in the cell blocks reserved for black prisoners.[94] The possibilities for future actions loomed large; activists started to envision 1961 as the year of the jail-in.[95] When CORE began preparations for a new Freedom Ride through the border states and into the Deep South to test the 1960 Supreme Court ruling in Boynton v. Virginia[96]— finding segregation in the bus terminals and lunch counters that serve interstate travel routes unconstitutional—they resolved to make "jail, no bail" a crucial part of their approach.

James Farmer, national director for CORE, had long been in favor of "jail, no bail" as a way to "make the maintenance of segregation so expensive for the state and the city that they would hopefully come to the conclusion that they could no longer afford it."[97] Anticipating the danger the riders would face—though, perhaps, not yet comprehending its extent—the original plan for the Freedom Ride was a carefully controlled affair. Thirteen activists representing an adequate mix of white and black, North and South, all well-trained in nonviolent resistance, would make the journey from Washington, DC to New Orleans via two different bus lines. Along the way, riders would sit in an integrated arrangement on the buses; at each stop, pairs of activists would attempt to desegregate restrooms, lunch-counters, and waiting rooms. If arrested—or, more accurately, *when* arrested—the riders pledged to take jail sentences over fines or bail.[98] As throughout the sit-ins, there were multiple justifications and understandings of what going to jail meant for these activists. A moral appeal to conscience, a strategic withdrawal of cooperation, and a direct bodily enactment of freedom and collective power intertwined and competed for symbolic primacy amongst the activists, and within each activist. "With our very bodies," Farmer wrote after the rides concluded, "we would obstruct the wheels of injustice; by our eloquence and ineluctable presence we would teach a callous public of the inhumanities its complacency condoned. (How could they resist the truth once they saw it?) To smash the thrall of unconstitutional laws and immoral legal practices we would fill the jails to bursting, if necessary. We would act directly on the institutions and especially on the evildoer, negotiating, persuading, cajoling, giving him no rest."[99] It was also hoped, of course, that the arrests, convictions, imprisonment, and likely physical violence against the Freedom Riders would provoke a reluctant, complicit federal government to intervene—a goal that would prove all too elusive over the course of the movement.[100]

When the first wave of the Freedom Ride ended, notoriously, with one bus bombed outside of Anniston and many riders savagely beaten by a Klan-led mob outside of Birmingham, SNCC saw an opportunity to take up the banner and finish the route through Alabama and Mississippi to New Orleans.[101] Upon hearing radio reports of the bus bombing in Anniston, the Nashville student movement swung into action, calling an emergency meeting to discuss what ought to be done. In the course of a meeting that lasted through the night and into the next morning, it was decided: allowing the Freedom Ride to end in segregationist violence would set a terrible precedent for future campaigns, emboldening white supremacists to action and depressing a civil rights movement on the cusp of becoming a truly national, grassroots mass movement for the first time.[102] Armed with $900 somewhat unwillingly given by the executives on the board of the Nashville Christian Leadership Conference (NCLC), Nash, Lewis, and the rest of the Nashville coordinating committee arranged for ten riders to travel to Birmingham to resume the route—first to Montgomery, then to Jackson, and finally to New Orleans.[103] Thanks to the national press attention to the orchestrated mob violence against the first Freedom Riders, the Nashville students were spared the worst of what Alabama had to offer. They were, nonetheless, arrested immediately upon their arrival in Birmingham on May 17—appropriately, or perhaps ironically, the anniversary of the *Brown v. Board of Education* decision—and held at Southside jail. Pledging to remain in jail despite being held without charge, the students did the only thing they could, the only thing that seemed reasonable to those accustomed to unjust arrest: they went on a hunger strike and tormented their jailers with a constant barrage of freedom songs. When, finally, they were released from jail—on the arrangement that they would be driven by Birmingham police out of Alabama—the students did not go easily. As Lewis later recalled, "We refused to cooperate. We let our bodies go limp, forcing the officers to drag us from the jail out into the night"—out into the vehicles that would take them back, unwillingly, to the Tennessee border.[104]

Undeterred, SNCC arranged transportation back to Birmingham to try again, along with a fresh batch of eleven new Freedom Riders sent from Nashville. With many failed attempts now behind them, the riders finally made their way successfully out of Birmingham; on May 23, after contending with a riot and an all-night siege at First Baptist Church in Montgomery, the bus crossed the state line into Mississippi, followed closely behind by a second bus organized through the joint efforts of several organizations, thanks to the behind-the-scenes efforts of Diane Nash.[105] The riders had barely disembarked in Jackson when they were arrested by local police and charged with incitement, breach of the peace, and disobeying an officer.[106] Between the two buses, twenty-seven riders were arrested. Farmer, among those arrested from the second bus, realized that Jackson might represent the moment they had been waiting for: a chance to fully realize the vision of "jail, no bail." Thus, in court on the 26th, the riders opted to remain in jail for thirty-nine days—the longest they could stay without forfeiting the right of appeal—rather than accepting the NAACP's offer to pay their bail, and rather than accepting the judge's sentence of a $200 fine and a sixty-day suspended sentence.[107] A joint meeting of the SCLC, CORE, SNCC, and the NCLC—the newly formed Freedom Rides Coordinating Committee—held in Atlanta that same day confirmed the new purpose behind the Freedom Rides: "To fill the jails of Montgomery and Jackson in order to keep a sharp image of the issues before the public."[108] They would recruit more riders to seek arrest and imprisonment; they would, in Farmer's words, "fill up the jails, as Gandhi did in India, fill them to bursting."[109]

The resolve of the Freedom Riders to stay in jail seemed to tax the patience of more than a few "liberal" and "moderate" supporters of civil rights. The same day that the Freedom Rides Coordinating Committee issued its statement about "filling the jails," an interview in the *New York Times* took the riders to task for "baiting" Southerners. The article, referring to the Freedom Riders as "roving bands," reported that "some liberal Southerners of both races," along with "moderates" nationwide had begun calling for an end to the Freedom Rides, claiming that they were doing more harm than good to the cause of civil rights. According to one unnamed critic of the Freedom Rides, a liberal "white leader" in a "prominent role in the civil rights struggle," the bus trips and jail-ins "don't appeal to any underlying sympathy among Southerners. This becomes a dare, not a protest."[110]

Already exasperated that the Freedom Rides were continuing, the news that the riders chose jail and not bail did not sit particularly well, either, with President Kennedy. A tense phone call from Kennedy to Martin Luther King, Jr. ended badly, when King refused to try to talk the jailed riders down from their militant stance. Kennedy, for his part, was unmoved by the willingness of the activists to remain in jail: "That is not going to have the slightest effect on what the government is going to do in this field or any other. The fact that they stay in jail is not going to have the slightest effect on me," he told King, according to the transcript of the call taken by one of Kennedy's aides. "Perhaps," King replied, "it would help if students came down here by the hundreds—by the hundreds of thousands." To which a beleaguered Kennedy answered: "The country belongs to you as much to me . . . don't make statements that sound like a threat."[111] While hundreds of thousands of protestors was a mark too high to hit, the example set by the twenty-seven jailed riders mobilized hundreds. By the end of the campaign, 328 individuals would face time in a Mississippi prison—some of them at the Hinds County Jail, others in Mississippi's state penitentiary at "Parchman Farm."[112]

Founded at the turn of the twentieth century on forty-six square miles of plantation land, Parchman Farm was a monument to the post-Reconstruction effort to use the prison to do what slavery no longer could. As historian David Oshinsky details, Mississippi Governor James Vardaman—banking on white fears of social equality—envisioned Parchman in the form of "an effective slave plantation," a means of ensuring that the necessary lessons of "proper discipline, strong work habits, and respect for white authority" were instilled in young black men—lessons that, he feared, the end of slavery had threatened.[113] The place quickly developed a reputation for brutality, and by the 1960s it enjoyed a well-earned ignominious fame throughout the South. But the Freedom Rides had effectively placed their cause within view of the national media—whether or not that media was particularly sympathetic to the calls for jail without bail—and with so many eyes watching, Mississippi Governor Ross Barnett's hands were more than usually tied. This perhaps prevented worse treatment from coming down on the heads of the young SNCC and CORE Freedom Riders imprisoned there—though the guards certainly did what they could to make the civil rights activists' stay a memorable one. At Barnett's orders, the Freedom Riders were kept in strict isolation from one another in the maximum security wing of the penitentiary, restricted from going outside. In the midst of the intense loneliness, boredom, and isolation, the activists did what they could to create some small semblance of public space: they sang freedom songs that reverberated from cell to cell, they went on a hunger strike to protest their mistreatment, they talked back to guards, and refused to obey orders. Guards responded by putting the riders in solitary confinement, confiscating their mattresses, subjecting them to extreme temperatures, insulting and harassing them, and in at least a few cases, shocking them with electric cattle prods. "They tried to turn us into animals," Farmer reported at a press conference upon his release in July.[114]

However, despite the grueling, often cruel and inhumane conditions they faced, particularly at Parchman, all but a few of the riders lived out their commitment to "jail, no bail." Inside the jails all summer long, activists adopted different positions on how the arrested should behave, and there was a wide range of opinions on what exactly the jail experience meant and what was required of activists. A significant point of contention was how activists should think about the outward effects of going to jail—the power of this action to change oppressive social arrangements. Ideas ranged from the rather absolute and religious commitment to nonviolence shared by the radical core of Nashville students, who tended to insist on the transformative power of unmerited suffering, to the hard-edged secular realism of activists like Stokely Carmichael (later, Kwame Ture), who viewed nonviolence as a primarily strategic imperative—a means of throwing the opponent off balance, or preventing institutions from functioning. There was greater consensus, however, on the importance of "jail, no bail" for activists individually and collectively: it was an act of self-liberation, an expression of fearlessness, and a defiant rebuke of a system defined by terror and violence. In Raymond Arsenault's words, "[In] effect, the Freedom Riders turned prison into an unruly but ultimately enlightening laboratory where competing theories of nonviolent struggle could be discussed and tested. In the darkest corners of Parchman, where prison authorities had hoped to break the Riders' spirit, a remarkable mix of personal and political education became the basis of individual and collective survival."[115] The riders had (in Farmer's words) "twisted the tail of the lion" and in so doing, galvanized a national movement.[116]

Of course, behind—and intertwined with—the empowering narratives about the jail experience that activists told, lies a sometimes brutal reality. Echoing parts of Hamer's harrowing Winona experience, Freedom Rider Frank Holloway described what awaited him at Parchman farm: "There were about eight guards with sticks in their hands . . . and the Freedom Rider being questioned was surrounded by these men. Outside we could hear the questions, and the thumps and whacks, and sometimes a quick groan or cry. . . . They beat several Riders who didn't say 'Yes, sir . . . ' Rev. C.T. Vivian of Chattanooga was beaten pretty bad. When he came out he had blood streaming from his head."[117] Not all who went to jail found joy, solidarity, enlightenment, or liberation there; whatever else it was, the experience of the Southern jail was dangerous and frightening—sometimes violent, and often, lonely and monotonous. "All encounters with the criminal justice system were fraught with danger," Berger argues, "both because of what would happen in prison and because of prison's place within the larger geography of white violence."[118] It was this location—the epicenter of racial control—that made "jail, no bail" such a risk; it is also what could make it powerful.

Though Jackson's jails were never completely filled, the months-long campaign did take its toll on Jackson's finances—costing the city, by some estimates, over a quarter of a million dollars in police overtime, prison costs, and legal fees.[119] But the Freedom Rides also saddled CORE with a considerable financial burden. The decision of the arrested riders to appeal their convictions after thirty-nine days meant that the need to raise funds for appeal bonds was not eliminated. There was no reason, it seemed, why extending the black freedom struggle out onto the streets—into lunch counters, waiting rooms, rest rooms, and ultimately jail cells—necessitated giving up the courtroom as a key battleground. In fact, by July, CORE had spent nearly $140,000, much of it in bail bonds and legal expenses. As the rides went on, the court in Jackson began increasing jail time for its convicted riders as well as bail amounts. Moreover, in a surprise move explicitly intended to drain the organization's funds, on August 4 the court ordered that the 196 riders released on appeal needed to return to Jackson for arraignment. They announced that no appeals could be withdrawn and that riders would be tried two at a time—forcing CORE to not only finance multiple trips per rider back to Jackson but hotel stays as well. By the end, the total bond requirement had reached $372,000—a sum so large it nearly succeeded in bankrupting CORE, had it not been for the intervention of the NAACP Legal Defense Fund in November 1961.[120] While it would take years to resolve the cases, the time, effort, and money poured into the legal battles ultimately paid off—in 1965, the Supreme Court reversed the Freedom Rides convictions.[121]

The attempt, largely successful, to fill up Jackson's jails represented the high-water mark of "jail, no bail." While activists would continue to face jail throughout the decade, the importance of remaining there faded over time, in line with other key developments in the movement. Practical considerations were, in part, responsible for its ultimate decline: as discussed in this chapter, the need to pay bail was, in fact, never eliminated, as activists blended partial adherence to the principle of "jail, no bail" with the ability to appeal unjust convictions. The importance of appeal increased over the course of the decade, as more and more courts resorted to excessive bail and harsh sentencing—such as Louisiana's notorious use of its "criminal anarchy" statute, carrying a maximum penalty of ten years of hard labor—against civil rights workers. Additionally, particularly within CORE, there was an increased understanding and appreciation of the uneven risk that a jail term represented across activists differentiated by class, gender, and background; for some, staying in jail represented an unreasonable demand.[122] Finally, as a matter of ongoing, movement-wide tactics, it did not make much practical sense to have the strongest, most seasoned, and committed activists languishing in jail cells across North and South when they were needed more urgently in the field.

But the year and a half of radical activism extending from the sit-ins through the Freedom Rides and ending in a Mississippi prison had a lasting impact on the developing movement, out of which emerged a flexible understanding of the meaning of arrest and imprisonment—one that was as much about principle as it was about tactics. The trajectory from Nashville in 1960 to Jackson in 1961 cemented the place of imprisonment in the drive for racial equality. Within that span of time, activists creatively built on the layers of meaning contained in the Southern jail to challenge systemic injustice, shift the balance of power in their favor, appeal to the conscience of sympathetic communities North and South, and boldly enact a freedom long denied. In effect, as Colley observes, ultimately "jail, no bail" took the movement "inside the prison and ensured that imprisonment was no longer a byproduct of racial protest, but a tactic in itself."[123]

Ethics and Tactics

In mobilizing against white supremacy, civil rights workers took a great many risks other than arrest, among them grave bodily harm and even death, both inside and outside the jail. As a matter of course, they understood that the freedom struggle would entail a willingness to accept the consequences of controversial, contentious political action; legal risks, such as arrest, imprisonment, and conviction, represented only one subset of them. The Freedom Riders, as well as the student sit-in activists before them, prepared themselves not merely for arrest but also for insult, violence, brutality, and even death; in a moment of gallows humor, Freedom Riders referred to the last night before they embarked on buses to the Deep South as the "Last Supper."[124] They were as well prepared as they could have been for the kinds of personal and collective risks they took, but those risks were not couched in legal terms. As I have argued, "jail, no bail" did not unfold according to a logic of containment and stabilization—using submission to arrest to express fidelity to the constitutional order, or to mitigate the systemic challenge posed by disobedience. Instead, "jail, no bail" played out as decolonizing praxis: transforming sites of fear into the proving ground for courage, institutions of subjugation into spaces of liberation. It was in "[facing] naked state power," to recall King's words, that a young generation "lost its fears," and experienced "the majestic dignity of a direct struggle for its own liberation"—a struggle for liberation that was already alive within a world of anticolonial struggles for freedom and within a present past of more-than-half-free slaves. In the arc of these words, the moral importance of legal punishment recedes into the background of a sweeping history being performed and enlarged in the present—a history in which black agents, engaged in one part of a worldwide struggle against white supremacy, transform themselves and the world in the fight for freedom.

The risks of this struggle—from the unjust arrest and the subsequent stay in a jail cell all the way through to segregationist violence and the apparent lack of political will for punishing or preventing that violence—were furthermore connected, by activists, into a narrative about racial injustice in America. Activists identified their experiences in protest and in jail as extending out of a greater, more fundamental injustice rooted deeply in the American system. The police who arrested them, the judges who sentenced them, and the guards who locked them up were connected to an entire structure of law and order which operated to defend racial hierarchies: the Southern segregation statute issued from the same systemic problem as the mass arrests of activists protesting it. In this context, "jail, no bail" was a mechanism not to contain protest, to limit its effects or confine it within modest reforms, but to deny authority and legitimacy to the very institutions of their domination. "Serious revolution," as James Lawson argued in November of 1961, "is total and maintains a question mark over every aspect of society; no institution is taken for granted."[125]

It was in this spirit of "maintaining a question mark" over the interconnected practices of racial domination—of interrogating how they were connected—that activists transformed the trip to jail into a means of withholding further cooperation to an oppressive tangle of laws, practices, customs, and beliefs. It was in this spirit that they used arrest and imprisonment creatively and strategically, as a way of multiplying, extending, and amplifying protest, bringing the fight for equal justice into the heart of the racial order. In so doing, they remade targeted, local protests into far-reaching critiques of "law and order," forged networks of solidarity and bonds of common experience, and emboldened local communities as well as national ones. This is the necessary, outward-facing work of a decolonizing praxis: the ethical work of self-transformation is simultaneously directed externally—working strategically to interrupt and challenge an oppressive world in order to reconstitute it. In the midst of this work, it is crucial to note that white citizens, locally and nationally, were not the only relevant audience for the work of "jail, no bail."

Yet seeing civil disobedience like a white state obscures much of this by systematically diminishing the violence of "law and order" represented by the Southern jail cell as an isolated aberration. Such a focus has the effect of erasing some of the more radical claims of the protestors—and perhaps overlooking some of their most stunning successes. There is little room in the narrative provided by theorists of civil disobedience for the compelling and provocative ideology of freedom through unfreedom—liberation through incarceration—that came out of the sit-ins and Freedom Rides. For the activists themselves, it seems that one of the most important reasons to voluntarily submit to arrest was precisely to demonstrate an end to subjection—to perform an individual and collective power that could not be controlled or cowed by the customarily means of keeping people "in their place." This liberatory action, this crucial inward-facing work of decolonization, "implied that the self-respect achieved through political action came less from white recognition than from the recognition by and among [activists] themselves of this new sense of empowerment."[126]

The power of "jail, no bail" was premised on the inseparability of ethics from tactics: the enactment of liberation and generation of solidarity in the jail cell was linked to, and required, the exercises of collective power that allowed activists to amplify their protest, withhold cooperation, and apply pressure. "Jail, no bail" was thus a practice of comparative freedom, but it was also more than that. The internal transformation of the self (the recovery of the capacities for action, the cultivation of fearlessness) was intimately tied to the relational and systemic transformations made possible by collective disobedience—transformations that promised a freedom much more than half. As Diane Nash indicated to her fellow activists in a statement on the merits of refusing bail, the ethical and tactical dimensions of protest action were mutually constitutive: "Some of the considerations . . . are matters of pure principle; they involve the center of what nonviolence means. Some of them are practical considerations, matters of tactics in our struggle. But it is difficult to draw the line between what is principle and what is tactics, because the two merge together."[127] The line was difficult to draw precisely because the ends were entirely bound up with the means.[128] Seeking and enduring arrest was meaningful for this particular set of activists because it allowed a direct intervention into the conditions of injustice they protested; as such, it enabled a powerful and direct rebuke of racial subjugation. Liberation and the enactment of agency, as processes both internal and external, required the tactical leveraging of collective power against an institution at the heart of racial control in the Jim Crow South: the Southern jail.

To focus attention on these ties is to push back on the implicit assumption that a strategic (rather than moral or reason-giving) orientation threatens to instrumentalize political relations—transforming the public sphere into a space of competition, self-interest, manipulation, and the callous use of others for our own narrow ends. Yet, centering the relationship of tactics to ethics within discourses about civil disobedience—and the re-introduction of disruption, power in numbers, and coercion to the set of tactical possibilities contained therein—only raises the question of what, exactly, is required by a commitment to nonviolence. And so we turn next to Birmingham, Alabama in 1963—to the campaign memorialized as the pinnacle of the nonviolent civil rights movement, the moment when a local campaign for desegregation went national, finally pushing the Kennedy administration to put civil rights at the center of its agenda.

4
Forcing the Better Argument

> In the arena of political and social events, what men feel and believe matters much less than what, under various kinds of external pressures, they can be made to *do*.
> —James Farmer, *Freedom—When?* (1965)[1]

> Politics will, to the end of history, be an area where conscience and power meet, where the ethical and coercive factors of human life will interpenetrate and work out their tentative and uneasy compromises.
> —Reinhold Niebuhr, *Moral Man and Immoral Society* (1932)[2]

> We are going to turn Birmingham up side down and right side up.
> —Martin Luther King, Jr., Mass Meeting at First Baptist Church, Birmingham (1963)[3]

Winning Hearts and Minds

By the time Martin Luther King, Jr. and the Southern Christian Leadership Conference rolled into town in early April of 1963, the city of Birmingham had already made a national name for itself as a segregationist stronghold in which white vigilante violence not only went unchecked but also was actively supported by local police and politicians.[4] The first wave of Freedom Rides, as seen last chapter, came to a bloody and smoldering end as members of the Klan led an attack on the buses near Birmingham, sanctioned and supported by the city and state police. Long before then, though, Birmingham had gained a certain notoriety as a place where workers trying to unionize found themselves whipped, beaten, or killed as "subversives"; and black people who stepped out of line (by moving into houses in formerly white neighborhoods, by organizing against segregation or in favor of labor rights) found their homes and churches bombed—attacks of such frequency that they earned the city the soubriquet "Bombingham."⁵

In the American historical imagination, Birmingham in 1963 stands as a kind of symbol for the segregationist Deep South, and the campaign there a morality play: the forces of obvious good, led by King, withstood the blatant evil of the public safety commissioner, Eugene "Bull" Connor, as he and his police force unleashed dogs and opened fire hoses on nonviolent protestors—among them, children. The images of these events number among the most famous of the entire movement and evidence a strategic success won by the SCLC and Fred Shuttlesworth's local Alabama Christian Movement for Human Rights (ACMHR). While much of what occurred between March and May of 1963 was not planned in advance—the product, instead, of an evolving strategy to meet immediate needs and contingent events—the choice of Connor as an adversary was no accident, and the value of the staged spectacle presented by the Birmingham police's reaction to protestors was all but immediately recognized by organizers. As James Bevel, a key figure in the Birmingham campaign, later recalled, "the greater the resistance in the application of the science of nonviolence, the clearer the issues become for the onlooker." The clash of nonviolent protest with violent retaliation, Bevel suggested, provided the kind of shocking contrast needed to capture white Americans' attention to make them understand the stakes of the struggle: "You have a better means of showing and revealing and bringing out the contradiction when there is an adamant attitude in people about superimposing their attitudes upon other people."⁶

Bevel's distillation of this "science of nonviolence" opens up questions about the communicative power of civil disobedience. What is the "contradiction" that is revealed? Revealed to whom and for what purposes? What is the relationship between nonviolence as a mode of persuasion and the provocation (or use) of coercion and violence? The preceding chapter argued that reconceiving civil disobedience as a decolonizing praxis uncovers its inward-facing dynamics—disobedience as a means of self-emancipation and solidarity building. But the enactment of "jail, no bail" also suggested ways that civil rights activists directed their action outward—toward other publics and audiences, including state actors. Emancipation from racial domination and the transformation of white democracy required more than internal liberation, and more than the nurturing of small, committed communities of those already engaged in activism. It required speaking to and making demands of others in order to build new relations with them.

The idea of civil disobedience as an essentially communicative act is central to the liberal view of it, as I discussed in Chapter 1: it is, as Rawls calls it, a "mode of address" intended to change the minds of fellow citizens and public officials. As such it must remain nonviolent and non-coercive. Though the full implications of this perspective were undertheorized by the mid-century theorists who popularized this perspective, emphasizing the essentially communicative and symbolic quality of civil disobedience eased concerns about its counter-majoritarian nature: if civil disobedience operates chiefly by persuading majorities and public officials to act, there is less concern that such activism functions unilaterally and non-democratically, frustrating laws that are the product of legitimate democratic procedures and express a majoritarian will. This is an important point if the political context is taken to be already meaningfully democratic. Change comes from changing a majority of minds, not from forcing society to bend to one's will; it is aimed at persuasion rather than immediate institutional intervention or the coercive threat of mass disruption. As deliberative democratic theorist William Smith put it, civil disobedience "communicates opposition in the hope that the majority will come to agree with and affirm the concerns of disobedient citizens."[7] In this way, disobedient citizens must act "in such a way that they respect the principles of public deliberation, in particular that deliberation is geared in the first instance towards reason-giving and persuasion, only in the final instance towards strategic compromise, and never towards coercion."[8] That is, the norms of democratic engagement require that citizens attempt to reason with each other and relate to each other as equals capable of being persuaded by eschewing the use of threat or violence. Though a particular act of civil disobedience—a sit-in or traffic blockade—may be spectacular, it has an "*exclusively* symbolic" and thoroughly communicative character.[9] It must operate not through force but through what Jürgen Habermas famously called the "unforced force of the better argument."[10]

There is an undeniably communicative dimension to civil disobedience. And yet problems arise when persuasion is made the unproblematic opposite of coercion—or when persuasion is associated uncritically with "nonviolence," and coercion with "violence." There is no guarantee that a commitment to non-coercion ensures that one's fellow citizens will interpret disobedience in persuasive or communicative terms; the assumption that they will do so presupposes forms of mutual respect and recognition that may in fact be lacking (and whose very lack might have prompted disobedience in the first place). Who else but those that can already take their equal standing for granted—those individuals who are assured of their accepted status as legitimate political actors, as recognized speakers and citizens—can guarantee that their disobedience will be interpreted as sincere and non-coercive, as making serious moral and political claims? Like the charge of "incivility," the accusation that protestors are acting coercively, forcefully, or violently rather than deliberatively is often "a way of masking and managing disruptive demands to inclusion in the public realm." It is, as Linda Zerilli contends, "a familiar means of denying the political (and thus common) quality of those claims and making them sound instead as if they were 'merely subjective' outbursts of one sort or another."[11] Even when marginalized protestors commit themselves to a principle of non-coercion, their lack of equal standing might nevertheless hinder their attempts to be seen and heard as making a reasoned appeal to fellow citizens (a problem I will return to in more detail in Chapter 5).

Thus, the binarization of persuasion/coercion and nonviolence/violence (and the mapping of the first binary onto the second) occludes from view the extent to which conditions of "social peace" are already premised on covert but violent exercises of power. This was a point that Reinhold Niebuhr, whose theology deeply influenced King's political thought, fully appreciated. Under normal conditions, Niebuhr argued in his 1932 *Moral Man and Immoral Society*, the "coercive elements" of power "are covert because dominant groups are able to avail themselves of the use of economic power, propaganda, the traditional processes of government, and other types of nonviolent power." Everyday life, in other words, is structured through rules, norms, and procedures that are in themselves nonviolent but are wielded by the powerful to mask the systemic violence and coercion that characterizes relations of domination. The marginalized are then burdened with the responsibility for upholding a violent order that calls itself peaceful: they are called upon to express their dissent civilly, non-coercively—a shifting conceptual terrain that is itself defined by relations of domination—or not to dissent at all:

> By failing to recognize the real character of these forms of coercion, the moralist places an unjustified moral onus upon advancing groups which use violent methods to disturb a peace maintained by subtler types of coercion. Nor is he likely to understand the desire to break the peace, because he does not fully recognize the injustice which it hides. They are not easily recognized, because they consist in inequalities, which history sanctifies and

tradition justifies. Even the most rational moralist underestimates them, if he does not actually suffer from them. A too uncritical glorification of cooperation and mutuality results in the acceptance of traditional injustices and the preference of subtler types of coercion to more overt types.[12]

What Niebuhr suggests is that the need for protest action is created by the very impossibility of persuasion: when forms of power and domination are so masked by the veneer of normalcy that they appear unquestionable and unremarkable, appeals to reason are unlikely to succeed, and new forms of action are demanded. Mass protest, then, seeks to strip away what Niebuhr calls the "moral conceit" of the status quo, challenging the idea that peace always trumps equality, justice, or democracy.[13] By their very nature and conditions of necessity, these actions cannot function as an ideal of persuasion, nor are they easily analogized to the reasoned speech acts of deliberative exchange. The forms of disruption, confrontation, crisis generation, and coercion detailed here emerge amidst the systemic failure of persuasion: when violence, inequality, and domination have undermined the material, affective, and political bases that might enable forceless communicative exchange; and when those who benefit from the maintenance of *white* democracy have effectively masked its violent, racial, and oppressive character, such that it appears as simply (and legitimately) democratic. Such actions, therefore, are not best understood as persuasion's opposite but as tools that undermine the givenness of the current order, helping to build a world in which persuasion might be possible.

In what follows I focus on two ways that the Birmingham campaign relied upon a productive entanglement of persuasion and coercion. First, picking up on Bevel's comments on the "science of nonviolence," the activists of the SCLC and ACMHR—on the ground and thinking on their feet—developed an approach that used acts of civil disobedience to provoke a coercive and violent response. While these staged confrontations—what sociologist Doug McAdam labeled as the campaign's "strategic dramaturgy"—were important for generating media coverage, and thereby sympathetic attention, the logic behind these interactions is critical.[14] In revealing the ordinarily hidden violence of white supremacy, they called on white audiences to consider their relationship to the violence before their eyes: Did they wish to be associated with it—to be implicated in it—by virtue of a shared, socially privileged position secured by whiteness? Or did they wish to see themselves otherwise—as acting "on the side of justice"? Rather than appealing to a shared set of values already in existence or eliciting the sympathies of a ready-made audience of white allies, the revealing confrontation between nonviolent direct action and violent reaction—what I characterize as the campaign's *tactics of disclosure*—was, as Karuna Mantena points out, "an interpolation, a constructive act."[15] It hailed a white audience not yet present, challenging them to shift the way they understood their place within the racial order and their role in maintaining it.

Second, the SCLC and ACMHR leveraged the power of crowds to interrupt everyday routines and temporarily disable the functioning of municipal institutions. In the early weeks of the campaign, as they struggled to mobilize large enough numbers of local black citizens to voluntarily face arrest and police violence, they staged marches in such a way as to attract hundreds of spectators who, in turn, faced off with Connor's police forces and threatened sustained disorder. Later, at the behest of Bevel and his wife, jail-in organizer Diane Nash, the campaign mobilized hundreds of school children and teenagers to fill the streets, fill the jails, and overwhelm the city's capacity to keep order. These *tactics of disruption* required a recognition that the maintenance of domination relied on the ongoing cooperation of the marginalized—cooperation that could be productively and disruptively withdrawn. This is what Frances Fox Piven calls "interdependent" or "disruptive power," wielded from below and premised on "the ability of people to defy the rules and dominant interpretations governing social relations."[16] These tactics also involved some measure of coercion—physically impeding civilians or state actors, forcibly shutting down institutions or processes, wielding power in numbers and pressure tactics to gain a hearing. Yet these methods of force were required for communication to succeed under conditions of entrenched hierarchy: disruption and coercion were needed to gain any sort of recognition at all—to be seen and heard as subjects worthy of engagement and response, as subjects who demand engagement and response.

In this way, the tactics of disruption and disclosure—and the attendant forms of coercion and disorder that come with them—confound the neat lines that are supposed to separate symbolic demonstration and direct action, persuasion and coercion, the "forceless force" of the better argument and those techniques designed to *force* the better argument. Disruption and disclosure were paired tactics central to the outward-facing operation of a decolonizing praxis: enacted by black subjects refusing to cooperate through submission, the crises engendered by disruption offered the possibility of arresting the racial status quo for long enough that hidden realities could be disclosed and new possibilities considered. A little bit of coercion could open the door to not only persuasion but also to the construction of new white subjects, engaged in the work of building a democratic future.

Planning a Crisis

It was not without reason that Bull Connor appeared to activists in the SCLC and the ACMHR as the ideal foe, and it is not entirely incorrect to recall the clash between Connor's police forces and marching black children in the stark terms of a morality play. It is undoubtedly true that Bull Connor was a brutal figure who helped enforce racism "by the whip, the razor, the gun, the bomb, the torch, the club, the knife, the mob, and many branches of the state's apparatus"—a zealot committed to ensuring that "White and Negro" would never "segregate together," to quote one of his more famous aphorisms.[17] But Birmingham was a place altogether stranger and more complex—and ultimately more American—than an account which begins and ends with Bull can allow. An industrial iron and steel town, after the 1907 buyout of the local Tennessee Coal, Iron and Railroad Company by J. P. Morgan, Birmingham was less an independent city than an industrial colonial outpost of the U.S. Steel Corporation. Throughout the twentieth century, its politics and economics were dominated from afar, by the interests and capital of "absentee barons" in New York and Pittsburgh, whose profits relied on "the low price of labor, which set the South apart from the North and kept Birmingham's workforce tied to the plantation and the separate regional labor market." As historian Glenn Eskew argues, "the use of a discriminatory race wage kept the working class divided along racial lines, with white workers earning more than black workers but both below the national scale."[18] The vitriolic nature of both its class and racial strife, the frequency and official sanctioning of vigilante violence—paid for, early on, by industrial elites—and the entrenched form of segregation in Birmingham, therefore, cannot in good faith be attributed to a perversion of reigning national values, to Southern backwardness or Jim Crow culture. For Birmingham, the greater structure of American politics, capital, and culture in the twentieth century must bear some responsibility.[19]

Bull Connor began his career as a baseball announcer of local fame, and entered politics only after industrial heavyweights and Bourbon political elites (Birmingham's "Big Mules")—in need of some local, grassroots, populist credibility to prevent the New Deal from coming to the "Magic City"—tapped him to be their man (first) in the state House of Representatives and (after that) on the three-man City Commission.[20] The latter position, which he held for twenty-three years between 1936 and 1963—with one four-year gap in his tenure after a 1951 police corruption scandal ousted him briefly from office—defined his career, and earned him a reputation for running the department like a "small-time gestapo," according to one account.[21] It was during his last turn as public safety commissioner, however, from 1956 on, that Birmingham's reputation for racial violence started to catch up with it, finally placing Connor at cross purposes with some of the powerful business interests and grassroots constituents who got him where he was. After the Freedom Ride riot, the downtown real estate interests, led by chairman of the Birmingham Chamber of Commerce, Sidney Smyer, took the view that vigilantes were giving the city a "black eye" which would hinder investment and economic growth, as had happened to Little Rock after 1957—the status quo was risking the loss of its "moral conceit." Stopping "racial incidents" and restraining the city's "violent elements"—recommitting, in Niebuhr's terms, to the uses of "nonviolent power" to mask the underlying violence of continued domination—thus became a priority for a powerful and rising contingent of the business community.[22]

When the SCLC started serious discussions of a Birmingham campaign in January of 1963—responding, at last, to Shuttlesworth's insistence that they come—it looked like Connor might be on his way out. In November of the prior year, a city referendum on the form of government eliminated Connor's position, when a margin of roughly 2,500 voted for a mayor-city council system over the current City Commission system. Connor, however, believed the referendum to be of dubious legality, and, with the help of former state senator and long-time friend James Simpson, pushed the matter before the Alabama Supreme Court, hoping to at least ensure that he could remain in his commission position through the litigation process, and perhaps even until the expiration of his term in 1965.[23] In the meantime, hedging his bets, Connor decided to run for city mayor, with elections scheduled for March. The election pit Connor against Tom King, a local attorney and racial liberal, and Albert Boutwell, a former state senator and lieutenant governor who differentiated himself from Connor by pairing his firm segregationist record with a condemnation of vigilante violence and departures from law and order. Next to Connor, Boutwell looked like a reasonable man; a vote on March 5 had Boutwell the front-runner with 17,434 votes to Connor's 13,780. In the run-off election the next month, held on April 2, Boutwell won handily, with nearly 8,000 votes more than Connor's 21,648.[24]

With the surprise start of the SCLC and ACHMR's joint desegregation push the next day—plans had been kept secret, lest they interfere with the election or provide pro-segregation forces time to strategize—the public reaction was, by and large, one of opprobrium. The initial campaign of sit-ins, pickets, and selective buying, which aimed at desegregating downtown lunch counters and instituting fair hiring practices in local department stores, seemed to some premature, with the new government not yet in office. Throughout April, the national press emphasized Boutwell's "moderate" credentials and took direct action leaders—particularly King—to task for jumping straight to protest. "The day after the election," *Time* magazine chided, "into Birmingham came the Rev. Martin Luther King Jr., hero of the 1956 bus boycott in Montgomery. Without consulting most of the Birmingham Negro leaders, King announced that 'Birmingham is the most thoroughly segregated big city in the U.S. today,' said that he would lead demonstrations there until 'Pharaoh lets God's people go.'" Siding with locals who were quick to cry "outside agitator," *Time* concluded that "King's drive inflamed tensions at a time when the city seemed to be making progress, however small, in race relations."[25] An editorial in the *Washington Post* insisted that "a substantial measure" of victory "had already been won in Birmingham—and in the best possible way, through the operation of the democratic process and the power of the ballot," and it pronounced the demonstrations there unwise and of "doubtful utility." Boutwell's win, the editors felt assured in announcing, made segregation in Birmingham "a past that is dead" and thus no longer in need of protest.[26] For its part, *Newsweek* celebrated Boutwell's victory as the "toppling" of the city's "monument" to segregation and implicated extremists on both sides (King, Connor) for muddying the moderate waters, while the *Wall Street Journal* alternated between military and mob metaphors.[27] The *New York Times* daily wrote of the lack of support for direct action amongst the Birmingham black community and urged in the editorial pages "a cooperative spirit" with the new administration—claiming the new mayor-elect as the bearer of a "more enlightened approach to race relations."[28]

Activists on the ground suspected, however, that Boutwell would be willing to reform Birmingham only far enough to show that segregation had a softer side. From Shuttlesworth's perspective, Boutwell was a Bull in sheep's clothing—merely a "dignified Connor" who would never desegregate willingly, no matter what the papers or local "moderates" had to say about it.[29] Though Birmingham's black vote comprised the entire margin of Boutwell's victory, he appeared only as the lesser of two evils. His campaign was in fact premised on the idea that segregation's longevity was best safeguarded by preventing the violent excesses committed in its name—a possibility that promised only the veneer of reform, bolstered by the disciplining logic of decorum. (As King would remark during a mass meeting in May, "What we don't need in the South is another North.")[30] Even so, it seems that the SCLC and ACMHR organizers of the desegregation effort were rather reticent to let the opportunity to square off with Connor pass them by. What Connor offered was a guaranteed *crisis*: to Shuttlesworth, the "idea of facing 'Bull' Connor was the thing," as he seemed unable to show restraint when faced with protests.[31] In the effort to achieve even its most modest aims—desegregation of lunch counters, restrooms, and water fountains; hiring black applicants for clerk positions in department stores; amnesty for arrested protestors; a reopening of public parks shut earlier in the year; and the establishment of a biracial committee to devise, among other things, a plan for the desegregation of schools—Connor's fierce commitment to guarding the color line would be essential.[32] As Wyatt Tee Walker, executive director of the SCLC, argued in April, "We've got to have a crisis to bargain with. To take a moderate approach, hoping to get white help doesn't work. They nail you to the cross, and it saps the enthusiasm of the followers. You've got to have a crisis."[33]

This proposed relationship between nonviolent civil disobedience and upheaval or repression—the idea that the former is somehow reliant on the latter for efficacy—was, in the early days of the Birmingham struggle, as yet underspecified and under-strategized by organizers. A fuller strategy of confrontation of the sort typically attributed to the shrewd, meticulous planning of King, Walker, and the SCLC—born at Birmingham, redeployed two years later in Selma—would in fact only emerge later, out of the contingencies of the campaign itself.[34] The early plans for the campaign were more limited and aimed at leveraging the economic interests of the service-sector business community against the racial intransigence of political elites. As it was originally conceived, "Project X" would entail a series of well-orchestrated sit-ins paired with a selective buying campaign at the height of the Easter season, and it would thus rely less on the response of the police and the power of spectacle than the ability of businessmen to read the bottom line.[35]

This is not to say that the planned sit-in campaign did not require its own forms of dramatization or that it favored the mechanisms of pure moral suasion over and against those of what Gene Sharp calls "nonviolent coercion"—withholding cooperation or causing disruptions in order to force concessions.[36] It is clear that in planning for the Birmingham campaign, the SCLC and ACMHR anticipated business closures and mass arrests—in fact, they required them for their plan to work. In the weeks prior to the campaign's start date, Walker selected primary, secondary, and tertiary targets, counting the number of lunch seats in each business, and setting up a legal strategy in light of the city's ordinances and bonding procedures.[37] Walker, Shuttlesworth, and King hoped to "fill the jails," as in Jackson, Mississippi, during the Freedom Rides, recruiting hundreds (if not thousands) to seek arrest and imprisonment for the cause—a tactic that carried multiple meanings, as I argued in the preceding chapter. In even more direct terms, moreover, the boycott aimed to put segregation out of business—to make its continuation financially unviable, whether businessmen themselves were persuaded about the moral matter or not. A progress report dated March 30, 1963—on the eve of the project's launch—makes clear the extent to which "police brutality," "unconstitutional arrests," the breakdown of "law and order," the potential for "loss of life," and thus the intervention of federal marshals were not only anticipated but also incorporated into the strategy.[38] By design, then, through the Birmingham campaign the nation would discover in King not "a gentle follower of the way of moderation and sweet reason but . . . a prophet of Old Testament mien whose strategy was to press his adversary to the wall—nonviolently, but to the wall."[39]

This was all proving rather difficult, however, in the early weeks of the campaign. Even as the local and national press vacillated between ignoring the campaign and responding to it as if to an invading army, the leaders were finding it hard to generate enough interest in the campaign. Few, it turned out, were prepared (or able) to go to jail; and among the press, the SCLC and ACMHR found few allies and little sympathy. Most troublesome of all, Connor was playing it cool—ensuring that his men arrested sitters-in in an orderly fashion and without violent incident. After only a handful of days, the campaign was flagging and in real trouble; Walker felt sure they needed to find a way to "make Bull Connor tip his hand."[40] In the first of what would turn out to be several crucial improvisations, the leaders decided to incorporate regular marches through downtown into their protest strategy, set to start on Palm Sunday—April 7, 1963. "The white power may think that things will blow over," King said at the mass meeting at James Baptist Church the night before, "but we are just getting started."[41] And so they were: on

Sunday, Reverend A. D. King of the ACMHR led a small procession of nineteen activists, flanked by hundreds of bystanders, down Sixth Avenue toward City Hall, only to be halted and arrested by police after a few blocks. It was then that things took a turn. The spectators, angered by the abrupt and swift end of the march, became agitated, prompting Connor to call on the K9 squad for crowd control. Leroy Allen, a teenage bystander, fought back; encouraged by yells from the crowd, he struggled with the dog, pulled out a knife, and was knocked to the ground. Several other cops (with dogs in tow), meanwhile, pushed back against the crowd, swinging billy clubs and kicking Allen.[42] Connor stood by: "Look at that dog go," he reportedly said. "That's what we train them for—to enforce the law—just like we train our officers."[43]

Unlike the iconic photo of Birmingham police dogs attacking fifteen-year-old Walter Gadsden that would make front-page news nearly a month later, this moment passed without much national attention. What little coverage the protest garnered was not terribly supportive of the protestors or their questionably nonviolent spectators. The *New York Times* story, for example—buried on page 31—carried the headline, "Police break up Alabama march—Birmingham protest ended as Negro attacks dog," while many publications continued to take the perspective that the protests were an ill-timed, irresponsible mess (when they covered them at all). In the days, hours, and weeks following the April 7 march, however, the significance of what had transpired was not lost on Birmingham organizers. Walker, particularly, saw immediate potential for the tactics of disclosure. "I've got it. I've got it," he told King on the phone.[44] The "accident" of Palm Sunday—the gathering crowds, the angry bystanders, the brutality of the police—could be "parlayed into its most useful application": making visible the violence of the Birmingham regime. As Walker recounted in a 1964 interview with Robert Penn Warren, small "demonstrations that had begun . . . with 15 and 8 and 12 and 20" could "swell to 1500" if spectators had enough time to gather, increasing both the press-worthiness of the event and the likelihood of a confrontation with the police. "Now, this is a little Machiavellian," Walker admitted, but "it was the image of all of these people following just a handful and it was the spectators following [them] upon whom the dogs were turned" that "built the Birmingham movement."[45] In the weeks to come, the line separating spectators from protestors, movement from masses, would become increasingly blurry.

Despite the explosive potential of the events on Palm Sunday, it would take a few weeks for the strategy to really take off. Another march on Good Friday resulted in the arrest of King, Abernathy, and Shuttlesworth, among others, and provided the campaign its first front-page article in the *New York Times*, and a quiet, small form of federal intervention.[46] Two days later, Easter Sunday, brought a repeat performance of the prior week: a march in support of the jailed Good Friday marchers turned violent when police turned on roughly 2,000 spectators who had amassed, and who, again, responded with anger when the activists leading the march were halted and arrested. When patrol wagons drove away from the scene with arrested marchers in tow, bystanders yelled and threw rocks at police, shattering the window of a police motorcycle. Though the canine corps was saved for another day, police used billy clubs and night sticks to disperse the crowd, clubbing a few to the ground. The incident did make the front page of the *New York Times*, under the following headline: "Negroes protesting arrests hurl rocks at police—30 seized—Many clubbed." The photo accompanying the story, depicting a police officer struggling to put a woman into a patrol car, identified those throwing rocks simply as "demonstrators," thereby including all those assembled as members of the movement.[47] A strategy premised on dramatic, disruptive confrontation was taking shape.

And thus, it was out of the contingencies of a flailing Project X that Project C—for "confrontation"—emerged. The darker side of this strategy was clear from the start, as James Forman—then the executive secretary of SNCC—makes evident in a less-than-flattering account of the Birmingham campaign in his memoir, *The Making of Black Revolutionaries*. When he arrived at the SCLC's Birmingham headquarters at the Gaston Motel, on the evening after the Palm Sunday march, he discovered Walker and a handful of others celebrating the day's unexpected turn. "We've got a movement. We've got a movement," they said, jumping up and down elatedly. "We've had some police brutality. They brought out the dogs. They brought out the dogs. We've got a movement!" It was, in Forman's view, "very cold, cruel, and calculating to be happy about police brutality coming down on innocent bystanders, no matter what purpose it served."[48] As the organizers understood, the stakes in Birmingham were quite high, and the battle all but impossible to win against an enemy capable of keeping its violence and brutality latent or just out of the public eye. But Forman's critique highlights some of the dilemmas posed by the entanglement of nonviolent action with violent reaction and calls for a clearer account of the tactics in play: What are the stakes of asking the already vulnerable, already brutalized, to put their bodies on the line in order to publicly demonstrate brutalization? Who is the audience for the demonstration, and what are its purposes?

Disclosure and Disruption

The Good Friday march and subsequent arrests marked the movement's most famous instance of civil disobedience: violating a federal court injunction. Thanks to police surveillance of the SCLC-ACMHR's mass meetings, the police were apprised of King's intention to march (and thus face arrest) and moved swiftly to prevent King, Walker, Shuttlesworth, and 135 others—including King's brother, A. D., and Ralph Abernathy of the SCLC—from marching. The injunction was issued on the basis of their participation in prior civil disobedience: "plans or projects commonly called 'sit-in' demonstrations, 'kneel-in' demonstrations, mass street parades, trespasses on private property after being warned to leave the premises by owners of said property, congregating in mobs upon the public streets and other public places, unlawfully picketing private places of business in the City of Birmingham, Alabama; violation of numerous ordinances and statutes of the City of Birmingham and the State of Alabama," and so on. The Palm Sunday march was particularly cited in the injunction—specifically the fact that the SCLC-ACMHR "foster[ed], encourage[d] and cause[d] a mob consisting of approximately 700 to 1,000 Negroes to congregate upon the public streets," at which point they become "unruly," requiring the intervention of the canine corps. With these events as evidence, the injunction claims "an undue burden and strain upon the manpower of the Police Department," particularly as the "actions and conduct" cited "are calculated to cause and if allowed to continue will likely cause injuries or loss of life."[49]

As is well known, King and the others decided to march; and just like clockwork, King, Abernathy, and forty-four others were arrested and charged with parading without a permit. Refusing to get out on bail in the tradition of "jail, no bail," King remained imprisoned after the others left. He passed the time by furiously drafting a rejoinder to a statement by eight white clergymen in Birmingham, who accused the campaign of being both "unwise" and "untimely." Scrawled on the margins of the *Birmingham News*—to be deciphered and transcribed by Walker on the outside—King addressed the clergymen and a broader audience of "white moderates," who seemed to be more committed to critiques of movement tactics than demonstrations of support for its goals. "I have almost reached the regrettable conclusion," King wrote in his reply, "that the Negro's great stumbling block in his stride toward freedom is not the White Citizens' Counciler or the Ku Klux Klanner, but the white moderate, who is more devoted to 'order' than to justice; who prefers a negative peace which is the absence of tension to a positive peace which is the presence of justice; who constantly says: 'I agree with you in the goal you seek, but I cannot agree with your methods of direct action.'"[50] King's full response would be published as the "Letter from a Birmingham City Jail" the following June, after the immediate fires of the campaign had died down, to gain national notoriety and prestige "only in the afterglow."[51]

In the "Letter," King diagnosed the problem of the "white moderate" as one of cultivated moral blindness and anesthetization to the suffering and oppression of others—a problem, he said, of "vision."[52] Members of the "oppressor race" find it difficult to relate to the "deep groans and passionate yearnings of the oppressed race" because they have not experienced and do not often see the manifold realities of racial injustice—from the "vicious mobs [who] lynch your mothers and fathers at will and drown your sisters and brothers at whim" to the "hate-filled policemen [who] curse, kick, and even kill your black brothers and sisters"; from the everyday interpersonal rituals of submission and humiliation to the systemic operation of racial capitalism.[53] Indeed, this not-seeing is a learned skill: it is the "shallow understanding" of those encouraged to deny their own complicity in injustice to preserve an idea of the polity—and of themselves—as "people of goodwill."[54] As he would later explain in the introduction to *Why We Can't Wait*, King's 1964 autobiography of the Birmingham movement, such a perspective was fostered nationally, at a society-wide level, through the systematic whitening of history—the production of a national narrative "by the white writers" of "pale history books," censored to exclude any thorough accounting of American white supremacy and expunged of the evidence of three centuries of black struggle against it.[55] The national narrative, and therefore civic identity, of white Americans was premised on a half-truth at best—one that required the evasion and dismissal of what black citizens knew: "for two hundred years, without wages, black people, brought to this land in slave ships and in chains, had drained the swamps, built the homes, made cotton king and helped, on whiplashed backs, to lift this nation from colonial obscurity to commanding influence in domestic commerce and world trade." What black Americans knew, King argued, was that despite this history, and despite some of the trappings of formal emancipation, "equality had never arrived."[56] Under these epistemic conditions, white moderates were quick to decry black protest as unnecessary, aggressive, and illegitimate disturbances of a social order that they were primed to view as more just and democratic than it was. They had been well educated to play their part as white citizens within a white state.

In response, King offered a breakdown of the Birmingham campaign's strategy to confront and reorient the "vision" of white moderates through the *tactics of disclosure* and the *tactics of disruption*.[57] White moderates (those unwilling to embrace explicit white supremacy, but equally uncommitted to the fight for racial justice) had to learn to see the status quo for what it was—an indefensible, "obnoxious negative peace" that masked ongoing violence and demanded that black Americans accept the conditions of their own oppression. They had to understand that under these conditions, the ritual defense of the rule of law or democratic procedure only works to shore up the forms of domination that are pursued and normalized under the sign of democracy.[58] What was unlearned, unseen, or willfully ignored had to be made visible and knowable in a new way; the vehicle for this altered vision was nonviolent direct action and civil disobedience, wielded as a form of "political pedagogy," as Brandon Terry has aptly put it.[59] Where the eight clergymen charged the Birmingham movement with bringing "unwise" and "untimely" chaos to the city, King countered that those "who engage in nonviolent direct action are not the creators of tension," but merely those who "bring to the surface the hidden tension that is already alive," so it can be "seen and dealt with."[60] The idea suggested by the Palm Sunday and Easter Sunday marches was that nonviolence, countered dramatically with violent force by agents of the state or white citizenry, would put the routine brutality and degradation of white supremacy on display—and would do so in such stark, undeniable terms that white moderates would be forced to reckon with what it meant for their own self-understanding. "Instead of submitting to surreptitious cruelty in thousands of dark jail cells and on countless shadowed street corners," King later wrote, the tactics of disclosure would "force [the] oppressor to commit his brutality openly—in the light of day—with the rest of the world looking on."[61]

The point of disclosure was not just about trying to attract media attention, though print and television media were key to the campaign's ability to reach white citizens and lawmakers nationally, as well as international audiences. The idea was rather to reveal the ongoing structures of domination through a dramatic confrontation with them, while simultaneously undercutting the usual dynamic of a publicly justifiable reprisal. What Piven and Cloward suggest with respect to the poor equally applies here: vulnerability to constant coercion is part of what it means to be oppressed, a reality that is all the more evident in the public's acceptance of police repression against them:

> The very labels used to describe defiance by the lower classes—the pejorative labels of illegality and violence—testify to this vulnerability and serve to justify severe reprisals when they are imposed. By taking such labels for granted, we fail to recognize what these events really represent: a structure of political coercion inherent in the everyday life of the lower classes.[62]

In order for white audiences to see this structure, as well as honestly grapple with its implications, it was imperative that the movement's tactics deny them the comfort of believing that the violence faced by activists was legitimate—just the operation of the democratic state ensuring peace and safety for all, with a bit of force when necessary. Executed properly, King argued that the tactics of disclosure caused a sort of "paralysis," as white citizens and state officials experienced the loss of their ability to respond to the crisis in the usual way, with the usual justifications, arguments, and dismissals. In this moment, King hoped they would be forced to craft a new way of thinking about the confrontation before their eyes and their relationship to it. Black protestors, having transformed the jail cell from "a dungeon of shame to a haven of freedom and human dignity," would use disobedience to flip the carceral logic of white supremacy on its head: this time, it would be the "power structures" that would be "caught—as a *fugitive from a penitentiary*," and "*imprisoned* in a luminous glare."[63] With the spotlight trained on them, the question for white moderates and political leaders would then become whether they wished to continue to accept the violent racial order and thereby continue to be complicit in it.

At the same time that King described the transformative possibilities for disclosure, he also defended the necessity of the *tactics of disruption*. Echoing Frederick Douglass, King observed that the material and psychological rewards enjoyed by those who are dominant tend to be jealously guarded: "Lamentably, it is an historical fact that privileged groups seldom give up their privileges voluntarily. Individuals may see the moral light and voluntarily give up their unjust posture; but, as Reinhold Niebuhr has reminded us, groups tend to be more immoral than individuals."[64] Gesturing beyond his audience of white citizens taking in news of the drama on their televisions and in the morning paper, King contended that those supposedly moderate figures in local and national government—the Boutwell and

Kennedy administrations—would need to be *compelled* to act, as well. Their responses to the problems of segregation, police brutality, and racialized violence could not wait for—or rely upon—the ethical and political transformation of white citizens, the prospects of which remained uncertain, however necessary; a decolonizing praxis could not work exclusively through the mechanism of rousing the "white moderate" to a new consciousness. After all, one time-tested method of putting off black demands for freedom and racial justice was to claim that little could be done until the hearts and minds of white citizens came around.[65] Consequently, King identified disruption as a means through which the oppressed could force a renegotiation of the terms of social and political life with power holders. As he explained to the clergymen, such a renegotiation would have to come through pressure and coercion, albeit nonviolent: "The purpose of our direct-action program is to create a situation so crisis-packed that it will inevitably open the door to negotiation."[66]

The tactics of disruption required recognizing the ways in which local and federal authorities relied on the appearance of peaceful order to preserve democratic legitimacy, political power, and capitalist gain. For federal authorities, the issue was bound up with the American image in the midst of Cold War politics. As King remarked a few weeks later during a mass meeting, it was only once daily routines were disrupted that Kennedy "got disturbed" about the situation in Birmingham:

> For Mr. Kennedy has to sit around the tables of the world. And sometimes Mr. Khrushchev is on the other side. He is battling for the minds and the hearts of men in Asia and Africa. . . . they're not gonna respect the United States of America if she deprives men and women of the basic rights of life because of the color of their skin. Mr. Kennedy knows this.[67]

In pressuring the federal government to intervene in Birmingham—and beyond that, to take active steps on civil rights legislation—King understood the value of confrontations like the one on Palm Sunday and the photographic evidence they could yield. Similarly, for local authorities, the timing of the selective buying and sit-in campaign in Birmingham was timed to threaten Easter revenues while putting pressure on a new administration; the mass marches that began on Palm Sunday simply signaled a ratcheting up of that essential concept. Disruption was thus a crucial mechanism for unsettling the equilibrium that held white supremacy in place: the assumption that the most significant threat to ongoing stability and order came from the force of "the segregationists' 'Never'" rather than "the Negroes' 'Now.'"[68]

Disclosure and disruption—as the outward-facing dynamics of a decolonizing praxis—were thus intimately linked to the inward-facing enactment of self-emancipation. Engaging in these tactics required a recognition of the ways in which the status quo, with its veneer of normalcy, legitimacy, and orderly peace, was conditional on the ongoing compliance of the oppressed. While King drafted his "Letter" from within the walls of the Birmingham Jail, James Bevel took over his speaking role at the April 12 mass meeting and spent his speech reminding the attendees of their implicit power. Likening the passivity encouraged by domination to a kind of sickness—a metaphor King himself also favored—Bevel urged everyone to recognize their own agency: "Bull Conner doesn't have it in his power . . . to free the Negroes or enslave them," he said.[69] Rather, it was a matter of whether people wanted to be "healed"—to "be free": "Now all the newspapers, and all the television cameras, and all the white policemen sitting up wondering what you going to do. Because they wondering, too, whether you're going to be free. . . . And if you answer the question, said, 'Yes, we want to be free,' it's nothing they can do about it."[70] The newspapers, the police, the government, and white citizens were finally watching; it was up to the black citizens of Birmingham to decide what to do with that attention, to alter their vision.

"Turn on Your Water, Turn Loose Your Dogs"

By the end of the April, enthusiasm for the campaign was once again flagging. Rifts in the black community, separating the activist core in ACMHR from the middle-class network of community leaders, businessmen, and clergy whose support they needed, had dogged the campaign from the beginning. Despite King's best efforts, many shared the opinion of Emory O. Jackson, editor of Birmingham's black newspaper, the *Birmingham World*, who called the protests "both wasteful and worthless."[71] There were problems, too, with the movement's core constituency. The jails were nowhere near full: volunteers for arrest were hard to come by—not surprising, given the Birmingham police's well-earned reputation, and the likelihood of losing one's job for associating with the movement. William Kunstler, a white civil rights activist and attorney working with the SCLC, recalls in his memoir a particularly bleak mass meeting at the end of April: "I watched in dismay as both King and Ralph Abernathy exhorted a packed church for almost an hour in order to persuade a dozen people to volunteer to go to jail."[72] Police reports on an April 24 mass meeting tell a similar story.[73] Furthermore, without drama to keep them there, the national media were packing up and moving on. "We've got to get something going," King said on April 29 at an emergency meeting of SCLC and ACMHR organizers. "The press is leaving, we've got to get going."[74] It was time to see if Connor's hand could be tipped once again.

The idea came from Bevel, training and recruiting Birmingham's youth alongside his wife and fellow organizer, Diane Nash. With adults vulnerable to social and economic sanction, Bevel suggested the movement organize schoolchildren instead. The idea, Bevel later suggested, was that unlike adults, children and young people would not be so "indoctrinated into [the] kind of violence and suppression" that would make them too fearful to demonstrate or too pessimistic that activism could meaningfully change anything. Additionally, Bevel saw that involving children was a powerful way of involving adults: "A lot of people were afraid to come to mass meetings . . . [because] the Alabama Bureau of Investigation would be around taking pictures and harassing people. So when the children became involved, they became involved . . . . And our position was, rather than . . . get your children out of the movement, join the movement with your children."[75] Bevel and Nash had already spent weeks organizing Birmingham youth: leading parallel mass meetings for teenagers, hosting workshops on nonviolence, and recruiting new organizers by talking to them about the ways segregation left them vulnerable to violence and robbed them of equal public resources for their schools.[76] At the same late-April mass meeting that garnered so few volunteers, it was thanks to this work—along with the efforts of Dorothy Cotton, Andrew Young, Bernard Lee, and Isaac Reynolds—that a significant portion of those volunteers were kids, "some of which," the police report from the meeting tells us, "were as young as eight or nine years old."[77]

Despite a (perhaps momentary) lapse of decorum in the Gaston Motel after Palm Sunday, neither the SCLC nor the ACMHR were cavalier about the danger their activists faced. Moreover, as Adam Fairclough argues, the tactics of disclosure and disruption sought not to maximize bloodshed but tension; in the midst of Project C, the goal was not "*deadly* violence" but "*dramatic* violence."[78] Again, one of the premises of nonviolent-but-coercive direct action was that it provoked a response, but it did not elicit the harshest, most fear-driven violence from whites. But the line they walked was a perilously fine one: the crowd's anger upon which they relied was not in their control, nor was the level of police repression or white retaliatory violence. And the idea of asking children to walk into the fray, to lead the movement down that thin line, was not one quickly or carelessly endorsed. Convinced, however, that the children both understood the reasons for marching and the risks, King reluctantly consented to what *Newsweek* would call the "children's crusade"—though not until after he had witnessed its efficacy.[79] The confrontation between Connor and children would surely disclose the cruelty of racial domination in the starkest possible terms, while the numbers of enthusiastic, youthful volunteers made sustained disruption—fomenting a citywide crisis while limiting the retaliatory options of the police—a real possibility for the first time. Even so, the need to put children and teenagers at the forefront hinted at the difficulties of using protest to transform the problem of white vision. It was only because "whites were unfazed by the obvious injustices of American society and the maltreatment of Birmingham's nonviolent adult blacks" that the movement was forced to "give them child marchers to make the cruelties of the Jim Crow South more vivid."[80]

On the morning of May 2, over 1,000 teenagers and children skipped school and went to the Sixteenth Street Baptist Church instead, ready to march, ready to be arrested. With King missing in action—holed up in his hotel room, wrestling with the dilemma over whether to let schoolchildren march—Bevel and Walker sent the kids marching eastward from the church, toward City Hall, a dozen at a time, making it unclear to the police precisely how many juvenile marchers they should be expecting. Annetta Streeter Gary, who was sixteen at the time of the Birmingham campaign, recalls the ensuing scene this way:

> We went out in groups. As soon as one group cleared, then another group would go. The idea was that they were not going to be able to handle all of us. They did not have enough police to stop us. Kelly Ingram Park, as far as you could see, was just people, people everywhere . . . I remember that I started crying when I looked up and saw all of the people. I guess it was just the idea of what was about to take place, the things that we had heard about, that Dr. King had talked about, how the movement was just moving forward. It was just overwhelming.[81]

A flummoxed Connor called in the fire department and hastily erected police barricades in the blocks surrounding the park, in an effort to restrict the marchers to the black section of town. A few groups made it past the barricades and into downtown; Connor personally oversaw their arrests. All told, 600 were arrested that afternoon. By four days later—May 7, the final day of marches—the number would climb to some 2,500, split between city and county jails and, when those overflowed, the fairgrounds.[82]

The second day of children's marches witnessed as many as 1,500 youthful volunteers, greater numbers of spectators, and a police department vowing not to be blindsided again, ensuring that barricades and fire trucks were in place around Kelly Ingram Park well in advance of the afternoon protest. A little after one o'clock, groups of children streamed out of Sixteenth Street toward downtown; coordinating the action via walkie-talkies, a few groups were sent in the opposite direction, as decoys to lure the police in the wrong direction. Apparently without King's knowledge, Walker also dispatched a handful of activists to call in false alarms, requiring that police officers or fire trucks would be diverted from the scene of the protest, thus spreading Connor's forces thin. "I had to do what had to be done. At times I would accommodate or alter my morality for the sake of getting the job done ... I did it consciously. I felt I had no choice. I wasn't dealing with a moral situation when I dealt with a Bull Connor," Walker would later say. Summarizing the logic of disclosure and disruption, he concluded: "We did with design precipitate crises, crucial crises in order to expose what the black community was up against."[83]

Such a crisis emerged the next day—after an hour of arrests, and no place to detain many more, Connor ordered Glenn Evans, head of the patrol division, to turn his hoses on the protesters. *Newsweek* reported the incident: "Some cowered. Some sat, hands behind their heads. Some sprawled on the pavement, awash with spray.... Finally, they damped down the demonstrators." But then, as had happened numerous times before, the 1,500 spectators who had gathered to watch and cheer the children on grew angry and found the hoses turned on themselves, too. "Negroes jeered and danced and mockingly turned their backsides to the spray. Rocks arced out of the crowd, and bottles and bricks were pitched from a rooftop. A chunk of concrete hit a photographer's ankle. Other missiles nicked two firemen."[84] The pressure on the hoses was upped until the spray could peel away clothing and the bark on trees, knock over demonstrators, or send them flying through the air. And then the dogs were called out. Twenty-three-year-old Milton Payne was bitten by a dog, as was Henry Shambry; a teenager named Walter Gadsden was greeted by the bared teeth of a German shepherd as he tried to cross the street—yielding the most (in)famous photo from Birmingham. Rocks and bricks rained down on the police from the angry crowd of spectators-turned-demonstrators until the protests were halted at 3 p.m., due to concerns over the quickly escalating level of violence.[85] That night at the mass meeting at Sixteenth Street, King encouraged the assembled crowd that the tactics of disclosure and disruption were working: "Just let them get their dogs, and let them get the hose, and we will leave them guttered with their own barbarity. We will leave them standing before their God and the world splattered with the blood and wreaking with the stench of their Negro brothers." Soon, King said, they would have to say: "'We're going to have to bring an end to our excesses, for this can't stop these people.'"[86]

Saturday witnessed a rematch between spectator-demonstrators and the police, when teenage marchers were prevented from leaving the churches by police cordons, disappointing and angering the 3,000 watching and waiting nearby. They dared the police to use hoses and dogs; the police obliged and were met by a barrage of bottles, rocks, and bricks.[87] A march to the city jail on Sunday, in contrast, faced off with police—"Turn on your water, turn loose your dogs, we will stand here till we die," one activist reportedly shouted. They were ultimately allowed to proceed to a nearby park, where they conducted a prayer meeting.[88] Monday, a day which saw over 1,000 arrests, returned to a familiar pattern, when a bottle thrown by a spectator set officers on alert, readying their fire hoses and trying to disperse the crowd. With jails overflowing, Birmingham seemed ready to explode.

The mounting tension, rising violence, and mobilized children finally caught the attention of President Kennedy, motivated at long last by his "deep fear of domestic violence and disorder," and seeing in Birmingham "the specter of black retaliation, of a violent black revolt touching off a sanguinary race war."[89] Within the first two days of the "children's crusade," the president dispatched Burke Marshall, assistant attorney general in charge of civil rights, and Joseph Dolan, assistant deputy attorney general, to Birmingham to urge an end to demonstrations and jump-start negotiations. Though recognizing the "very real and deep injustices" faced by Birmingham blacks, a statement from Robert Kennedy read, the means and the methods they used to combat them were suspect, particularly the "dangerous business" of using children in marches. It was, Kennedy urged, "in meetings, in good faith negotiations," that the SCLC and ACMHR should press their case, "not in the streets."[90]

Indeed, it is little remembered how controversial the Birmingham campaign was in its time, and how much criticism, resistance, and discomfort it generated, even as the tide of national press coverage turned in favor of the demonstrators and against the forces of Birmingham law and order. The idea of sending kids and teenagers out to protest was a particular sticking point, as was the strategy of triggering crisis and repression. Regarding the "children's crusade," charges of opportunism and callous instrumentalism came quickly and from all corners—from Boutwell ("people who are not residents of this city, and who will not have to live with the fearful consequences, [have] come to the point of using innocent children as their tools") on through to Malcolm X ("real men don't put children on the firing line").[91] In centrist *Time*'s estimation, in Birmingham "there had been no winners in a war that had no heroes. Bull Connor was by no means Birmingham's only shame.... Yet at the same time, Negro Leader King could be criticized for using children as shock troops and for inciting protests even as a new, relatively moderate city administration was about to take over Birmingham."[92] Later in the summer, with Birmingham not yet comfortably distant in the rearview mirror and the March on Washington still on the horizon (looking, to many, more menacing than is imaginable in the hindsight of history), David Lawrence put to paper what many "white moderates" in the US felt: Why, he asked, "have so many Negro ministers become active leaders and managers of street 'demonstrations' that have resulted in disturbance of the peace, arrests, bloodshed and death? Do [they] really feel that people of other races cannot be impressed with the merits of their cause except through so-called 'nonviolent' demonstrations which so often lead to violence?"[93]

As detailed earlier in the chapter, King would always maintain, in the "Letter" and elsewhere, that his nonviolent troops were not responsible for the upheaval, violence, and tension that often followed in their wake. Walker, King, and others were willing to admit that the efficacy of nonviolence relied upon violence—on the likelihood that police officers, officials, or white crowds would respond with brutal force, in full public view and for all the world to see. But they denied *causal responsibility* for this violence; as we have seen, the idea of the tactics of disclosure is that such protests merely *expose* it. Violence, King claimed, was systemic to the racial order in the United States, often hiding behind the veneer of civil peace and law and order. Indeed, black citizens protesting racial injustice not only disclosed the existence of this violence but often also revealed key aspects of its functioning—the intertwining of private and public violence, the interweaving of social, economic, and political forms of oppression, and—to the activists' bitter disappointment—the frequent unwillingness of national politicians and moderate allies to come to their aid. But the lingering, skeptical question from "white moderates"— and the quick accusation of illegitimate movement violence—highlights the messy intertwining of violence and nonviolence, and the difficulties of countering the habits of vision cultivated through whiteness.

Even so, the tactics of disruption were on full display on May 7, the last day of protests—the day that finally faced Sidney Smyer and the white negotiators with the need to make some concessions to SCLC-ACMHR. On that day, Dorothy Cotton and James Forman put "Operation Confusion" in action, sending kids in groups toward downtown along different routes, while Walker sent out volunteers to report false alarms. With the police surprised and confused, the plan worked, and hundreds of youths began streaming into downtown, a swelling crowd of spectators behind them. According to media accounts, "2,500 to 3,000 persons rampaged through the business district," "charg[ed] in and out of department stores," and brought traffic to a standstill while police stood by and watched, powerless to prevent it.[94] Meanwhile, just inside the chamber of commerce, a group of eighty-nine members of Birmingham's white elite were meeting with Burke Marshall, trying to figure out what kind of token reforms would be enough to end the demonstrations. When they stopped to take a lunch break, as Eskew writes, "they discovered bedlam in the streets."[95] As Marshall recalled, "There were fire engines going by all the time, sirens screaming; reports would come in from the police chief and the sheriff that they didn't think they could handle the situation for more than a few hours."[96] As the afternoon wore on, tensions flared into violence, as police attacked spectator-demonstrators, first downtown, and then again back at Kelly Ingram Park. The violence, described by some as a riot, reached its peak when the hoses and dogs once again emerged, and the notorious Alabama State Troopers waded into the crowds, beating the protestors back with clubs. A blast from a hose sent Shuttlesworth to the hospital.

That night, the negotiation teams met to work out a tentative agreement. What they came up with, and what King and the SCLC later accepted (without Shuttlesworth's assent), was both vague and lackluster: King, as Claude Sitton wrote, "accepted promises of progress from white business and civic leaders in lieu of immediate action."[97] The negotiations had been closed, with the identities of the white negotiators kept secret, giving both sides the ability to claim different interpretations of the nature of the accord.[98] The promises announced were less than activists had hoped: in exchange for a moratorium on demonstrations, the Birmingham economic elite agreed to appoint a biracial committee (without agreeing upfront to set a school desegregation timeline); to make token black hires in their stores within ninety days (with vague promises for future hires on an undisclosed timeline); and to desegregate public accommodations at an unspecified point in the future.[99] A demand that the city hire black police officers, raised by the campaign once the black spectators began clashing with the lily-white police force, got nowhere at all. More depressing still, the political leadership of Birmingham failed to acknowledge or endorse even these minimal "points for progress," as the SCLC-ACMHR called them. Mayor Boutwell had this to say: "I'm unwilling to make decisions virtually at gunpoint or as the result of agitation" and while faced with unlawful attempts to "overthrow this government."[100]

The Birmingham chapter ended not, however, with this whimper of an accord, but with the bang of renewed racial violence. On May 11, in an attempt to assassinate Martin Luther King, Jr., the Klan bombed the Gaston Motel and the house of King's brother, A. D., setting off a three-hour riot that enveloped nearly thirty blocks of the city and involved an estimated 2,500 participants. The sun rose on a city still smoldering, as Kennedy sent in the Alabama National Guard in case violence should erupt once again.[101] King, traveling back to Birmingham from Atlanta, went from pool hall to pool hall, asking people to voluntarily forfeit any weapons and trying to raise morale. "There may be more blood to flow on the streets of Birmingham before we get our freedom, but let it be our blood instead of the blood of our white brother. The agreements that have been made will be met. There will be integration in Birmingham in the next few weeks."[102] As it turned out, King should not have promised so much. A biracial committee was not even appointed until months later; it met irregularly for a while until it was dissolved the year after; public accommodations desegregation only came in 1964, as forced compliance with the Civil Rights Act; a wave of protests that same year forced the hiring of five black clerks in downtown stores; and not until 1966 did Birmingham see its first black policeman.[103] King was right about the schools: they desegregated in the fall of 1963. He was also right about the blood, though: the reactionary bombing of the Sixteenth Street Church killed four children, and the subsequent police brutality and retaliatory violence took two more.

Of course, the Birmingham campaign claimed a victory and a stage apart from the local one. In a televised address on June 11, Kennedy observed that "events in Birmingham and elsewhere have so increased the cries for equality that no city or State or legislative body can prudently choose to ignore them," and he proposed before a national audience civil rights legislation to desegregate public accommodations and fight employment discrimination. When Kennedy spoke of the moral crisis facing the nation, he retrospectively authorized a subset of the claims made by protestors in the months prior. His speech conferred official legitimacy on the struggle at Birmingham; but in the same moment, Kennedy also attempted to draw the tactics of disclosure and disruption to a close, constraining their meaning to a fight against explicitly racist laws, and announcing a return to progress through ordinary procedures of law and legislature. Indeed, Birmingham had set loose an incredible wave of 700 civil rights protests and 15,000 arrests across 200 American cities in the month since May. "The fires of frustration and discord are burning in every city, North and South, where legal remedies are not at hand." Kennedy continued:

> Redress is sought in the streets, in demonstrations, parades, and protests which create tensions and threaten lives. We face, therefore, a moral crisis as a country and as a people. It cannot be met by repressive police action. It cannot be left to increased demonstrations in our streets. It cannot be quieted by token moves or talk. It is a time to act in the Congress, in your State and local legislative body and, above all, in all of our daily lives.[104]

Kennedy's speech called on Americans to consider their conscience in light of racial realities in America, yet it also made plain the ways that the tactics of disruption motivated Kennedy's shift toward national legislation. The moral crisis would not be such a crisis if "fires of frustration" were not already burning hot that summer. Protests "threaten disorder, and threaten lives," and the ongoing racial strife in cities North and South threatened America's image abroad. Famously, of course, Kennedy had been "horrified" by the photographs of Birmingham, a detail that myriad newspaper stories recounted and numerous academic studies repeated.[105] But, as taped recordings of White House meetings reveal, his horror had distinctly geopolitical overtones. "What a disaster this picture is," he said in a meeting in May, referring to the photo of the police dog attacking Gadsden. "That picture is not only in America but all around the world." It was crucial, after Birmingham, to move black protest "into the courts and out of the streets," lest the "Negroes . . . push things too far."[106] Whether going "too far" would be defined by the choice of tactics, the duration of protests, or the content of claims, remained for the moment unclear. What was fully apparent, however, was that the crisis of order that unfolded in Birmingham's wake—instigated and orchestrated by protestors—mattered a great deal, both enabling change while revealing its limits.

The Lessons of Birmingham

The tactics devised by activists in the midst of the Birmingham campaign complicate the relationship between persuasion and coercion, nonviolence and violence: from leadership figures like King, Walker, Shuttlesworth and Bevel, to the spectator-demonstrators whose numbers and righteous rage made the campaign possible, to the teenagers and children who mobilized in the first weeks of May, the activists of the Birmingham campaign understood the challenge before them as one of *forcing* the better argument. They needed to orchestrate protest in a way that challenged rather than affirmed the boundaries of what was politically possible—that disclosed ignored realities, withdrew cooperation from dominating social relations, and used the force of disruption to elicit concessions from those who were not eager to make them. The techniques of crisis-generation—disclosure and disruption—were, in a real sense, communicative: they communicated a set of ideas about the latent violence of American racial orders, the interwoven structures of private and public racism that defined them, and the implication of "moderates" in their maintenance. Yet the success of these communicative aims necessarily relied on forms of violence, repression, and coercion—in the guise of police brutality that disclosed an entire system of oppression; in the anger of spectator-demonstrators that carried the implicit threat of more violence to come; in the force of federal marshals sent, belatedly, to prevent further vigilantes and riots; and in the nonviolent coercion brought by disruption and mass noncooperation.[107]

Despite the limited and ambivalent gains in the city of Birmingham itself, the tactics of disclosure and disruption won real victories at the federal level that should not be diminished. But the campaign also revealed, in new and poignant ways, some of the contradictions of the outward-facing dimensions of a decolonizing praxis. As we have seen, the efficacy of the campaign relied on the willingness of nonviolent protestors to subject their bodies to violence without retaliating. But equally, the campaign required the agency of spectators—spectators who became, at least momentarily, demonstrators—who held no such commitments. From the Palm Sunday march through the "children's crusade," it was the thousands of amassed "onlookers" who ensured that Connor's police force responded with force and were overwhelmed when they did. These spectator-demonstrators, as I have called them, "show[ed] up" throughout the campaign; but they did so, as Robin D. G. Kelley contends, "*on their own terms*": they "had no intention of filling the jails" but were nevertheless "clearly demonstrating their utter contempt for the police, in particular, and racist oppression, in general."[108] Even as Walker and others planned on the outpouring of this contempt, however, they felt their communicative aims—the need for a stark contrast between nonviolent demonstrators and violent police officers—imperiled by it. The tactics of disclosure would not work if the campaign could not make a violent white response to black protest appear shockingly illegitimate; but this outcome was by no means easy or assured, given that white supremacy is based on the routine legitimation of antiblack violence.[109] Consequently, SCLC and ACMHR activists often emphasized that those throwing rocks, jeering and taunting the police, and flashing knives at police dogs were emphatically *not* part of the movement; they were discursively dismissed as "some few spectators" who had no part in the campaign.[110]

In King's view, the spontaneous rage of the spectator-demonstrators in Ingram Park—taunting, throwing bricks, fighting back—could never provide the same "*aesthetic* force" of nonviolent coercion. King would later lay out the logic more fully in his responses to the riots of the mid- and late-1960s, as well as to the critiques of nonviolence issued from within Black Power—a logic Brandon Terry beautifully elucidates:

> On King's account, the aesthetic experience of witnessing the inarticulate insurgency of ghetto rioting induces "understandable" feelings of menace and fear, which, in their overwhelming impact upon the senses, provoke reactionary and racist responses. The exacerbation of fear, and the spectacle of chaotic rebellion, becomes grist for racist ideology, which charges that blacks lack the capacity for civil participation and justifies repression and rightlessness by treating black dissent as an existential threat to society.[111]

This logic, recall, was at the heart of the decolonizing praxis forged through imaginative transit; it was the lynchpin of the response to E. Franklin Frazier's worry that black nonviolence would only invite massacre. The idea was that *only* nonviolence could meaningfully confront racial hierarchy while removing the justification for such retaliatory, racist violence. But while King might have been correct in his judgment that violence—or the perception of it—would only feed the justificatory practices that bolster white supremacy, the Birmingham campaign's reliance on the spectator-demonstrators and simultaneous need to discredit them suggests the contradictions inherent in attempting to confront the problem of white vision.

Indeed, the events of April and May 1963 worked on white American conscience in complex ways, delivering mixed results. While King, in the aftermath of Birmingham, was remade by national American media—from an agitator of revolts unwise and untimely into a "prophet of moderate reform," the reasonable and sane alternative to black voices still more militant—the means and methods of the black freedom struggle were becoming increasingly suspect.[112] In the months after Birmingham, a series of national polls detailed the contours of the complicated, contradictory, and fraught perceptions of the "Negro revolution," viewed by white Americans. Though a bare majority recognized some right to demonstrate, most felt that demonstrations had hurt more than helped the cause of civil rights, and that the particular tactics used were problematic: 67% nationwide found lunch counter sit-ins unjustifiable; 55% disagreed with the use of boycotts against discriminating businesses; 91% were opposed to "lie-ins" at construction sites in protest of hiring discrimination. Perhaps the most surprising finding is that 56% of whites nationwide, and 75% of white Southerners, viewed the act of going to jail in protest as illegitimate—not as a sign of respect for the law or a moral act of persuasion. Only the March on Washington passed the test as acceptable means.[113]

Overall, and by significant margins (two to one), the white individuals polled by Harris and Associates thought "Negroes [were] moving 'too fast,'" and that they were demanding more than they were "ready" for. Another poll found that roughly six out of ten white Americans outside of the South felt that their fellow black citizens were already being treated "about right" or even "too well."[114] At a time when the vast majority of black Americans supported the civil rights movement (and its means), the numbers revealed good reason for their dwindling hope in the moral resources of "white moderates."[115] Despite widespread support for the principles of equality, justice, and freedom underpinning civil rights demonstrations and black demands, the affirmation of principles almost always came with a caveat and an equivocation—a firm "yes" to principles of racial equality, attached to a nagging "but . . . " But: "they're pushing too hard." But: "they're asking too much." But: "their demonstrations are disgraceful and disruptive." But: "they're holding a gun to our heads." This is what Steward Alsop and

Oliver Quayle termed "the other side of the but" in the pages of the *Saturday Evening Post*:

> There is a very marked difference between the two sides of the but. On the "yes" side there is an abstract desire to see justice done to the American citizen whose skin happens to be black. But the desire is abstract; it is not deeply felt. On the other side there is the question: "How will it affect *me*?" And if the answer is that Negro advance may endanger social status, or a job, or the value of a house, the desire for abstract justice evaporates quickly, and the desire to "keep the colored in their place" appears instead.

In comparison to an abstract commitment to justice for theoretical others who remain elsewhere, Alsop and Quayle concluded, the desire for the stability and certainty of the status quo "can be very deeply felt" indeed.[116]

In its immediate context and aftermath, Birmingham—and the wave of protests it inspired—elicited feelings of shame and disgust among many white Americans, who experienced sincere outrage over the images of Southern police brutality generated by civil rights protests. But it also provoked a sense of fear, alienation, and profound discomfort about what might happen when the televised revolution arrived in a neighborhood closer to home. The simple insistence that civil disobedience operate through persuasion overlooks the reality that a great deal of confrontation, disruption, and coercion were necessary to win even modest concessions where racial equality was concerned. And it evades the difficult fact that, beyond an abstract endorsement of equal rights, no broad agreement existed in the United States about what defined the problem of racial inequality and racialized unfreedom, and what remedies would be required, let alone legitimate. What the survey data reveals is the extent to which white ambivalence over racial equality shaped and determined the debate over protest ethics: prevailing ideas about what means were acceptable and reasonable were entirely bound up with the question of what ends were desirable—and thus the unsettled question of whether, in the eyes of white civilians and politicians, black equality was really worth the costs exacted by protest and upheaval. As Inge Powell Bell observed in her early study of CORE's use of nonviolent direct action, "doubts about the Negro's right to equality were reflected by doubts about the legitimacy of using strong means for attaining this end. . . . To argue that nonviolence was necessary to the movement because it won allies among

Northern white liberals is another way of saying that the justice of the Negro's claim was not fully accepted."[117]

In June of 1963, Bayard Rustin said that "Birmingham has taught white America many lessons—not the least of them that Negroes were serious when they said they would fill the jail until Southern cities were impoverished and that social dislocation is a reality that confronts all segregated institutions." But there were lessons for cities nationwide, as well: "It ought now to be perfectly clear that Negroes will not wait another twenty-five years. No longer can white liberals merely be proud of those well-dressed students, who are specialists in non-violent direct action; now they are confronted with a Negro working class that is demanding equal opportunity and full employment."[118] Those were demands that spoke as much to urban centers in the "North" (that is, cities across the Northeast, industrial Midwest, and Sun Belt) as they did to cities in the heart of the Jim Crow South; and they presaged the coming of "a season of doubt" over the question of how far white Americans would be willing to go to address the reality of racial domination—particularly, Rustin emphasized, "when the cause was not so clearly dramatized or its location so comfortably distant."[119]

Rustin's question would turn out to be a difficult one.

5
The Techniques of Disavowal

The challenge, now, is to the rest of the country. . . . The question is, how will the white people respond? See, what will they focus on? Will they focus on the fact that the Negroes shouldn't be down there [protesting]? And some of them are unruly? And some of them approach violence? And some of them do this, and some of them do that? Or, will they . . . focus on their just grievances, and say, "Okay, this is what we've got to do. We've got to move over here and begin to accommodate them." That kind of call is going out across the country now.
—Bob Moses, Speech on Freedom Summer at Stanford (1964)[1]

I do think that one of the things that has been absolutely crucial to American history can almost be summed up in the metaphor of a black corpse or a black presence or a black horde which everyone in one way or another agreed not to look at. . . . As a Negro, I cannot afford to ignore or deny or overlook it, but the white American necessity is precisely to deny, ignore, and overlook it.
—James Baldwin, "Liberalism and the Negro— A Round-Table Discussion" (1964)[2]

The End of Innocence

In the summer of 1963—arguably at the height of the Southern civil rights movement—Charles B. Turner, Jr. announced that the "honeymoon between white liberals and the Negroes" was over.[3] It was a full year before the phrase "white backlash" would become a regular feature in newspapers and magazines all over the country; a full year before the 1964 Harlem riot would initiate a series of long, hot summers, bringing many white Americans face to face with the prospect of an urban black rebellion. In the wake of Birmingham's national reverberations, and on the heels of the March on Washington and the drafting of the 1964 Civil Rights Act, it might seem like an odd moment (at least in retrospect) to question the white liberal public's commitment to civil rights. But Turner's observations turned out to be prescient. "The marriage" between while liberals and black civil rights activists, Turner argued, had flourished only under a particular set of historical conditions that were, in fact, premised on black subordination—"a time when integration involved more theory than practice, and a time when Negroes couldn't afford to ask questions, let alone make demands of their friends."[4] As direct actionists continued to press their case in the streets North and South, demanding not just a seat at a Southern lunch counter but also equal access to quality integrated housing, education, and employment nationwide, many erstwhile friends of the civil rights movement seemed to lose their stomach for equality in the face of its real costs. "The liberal's anguish stems from one of those tenacious liberal illusions: that, contrary evidence notwithstanding, they could achieve integration at no cost or inconvenience to themselves," Turner diagnosed. "They expect to achieve equality for all Americans without pain or strain, and then emerge as innocent as they began."[5]

Turner was not the only one who began to notice the fraying edges of the New Deal-turned-civil-rights coalition. His essay was one of a growing genre of commentary on the increasingly apparent tensions between black activism and white liberalism—tensions that were amplified as white public attention shifted to urban centers outside the South.[6] At a roundtable forum devoted to the topic in March 1964, Dr. Kenneth Clark—sitting in the audience—intervened to dispute the claim made by philosopher Sidney Hook (one of three white panelists) that white Americans bore no collective guilt for the crime of racism. The problem with white liberalism, Clark contended, was that it was more fully defined by attachments to whiteness than to liberal ideals. "I think one of the important things Negro Americans will have to do is learn how they can deal with a curious and insidious adversary—much more insidious than the out-and-out bigot." Echoing the words of James Baldwin—the fourth and only black panelist—Clark explained the "affliction" of white liberalism: "It is an insidious type of affliction because it attempts to impose guilt upon the Negro when he has to face the hypocrisy of the liberal. The Negro doesn't have to feel guilty when he faces out-and-out bigotry." White liberalism, as Clark saw it, was bound to respond to black claims defensively, and even aggressively, and then demand that black Americans bear the moral blame for white reaction. The problem is that whiteness claims a right to comfort—a right presumed to be fundamental: "Professor Hook is, in effect, saying: 'Jim [James Baldwin]: don't make me uncomfortable.... Don't make me have to look behind my own façade."[7]

This practice of avoiding discomfort—of maintaining innocence and resisting the need to look behind the façade—is the subject of this chapter. Civil rights disobedience, as I have demonstrated in the preceding chapters, was a multifaceted strategy for decolonizing America's white democracy. Its reception, development, and practice played out at different levels: individually, as a method of self-emancipation and personal transformation; locally, as a means of building solidarity, disrupting everyday routines, and pressuring state and municipal officials; nationally, as activists staged crises that caught public attention, disclosed the latent violence supporting segregation, and demanded responses from federal policymakers; and globally, among a network of activists experimenting with civil disobedience and nonviolent activism as a means of confronting forms of white supremacy. Woven throughout these various layers are ideas about the intersubjective potential of civil disobedience—a technique for arresting the attention of spectators, engaging new audiences, interrupting civic relations and institutions defined by hierarchy, dramatizing new political claims, and thus creating the space for reconstituting the polity. This hopeful politics, practiced and advanced by stalwart theorist-practitioners in CORE, SNCC, SCLC, and a host of local organizations, was on display—in all its messy potential—in Mississippi jail cells and on the streets of Birmingham. Yet, in Birmingham and elsewhere, its most radical possibilities were frustrated again and again by the depths of white investment in racial hierarchy. Ultimately, the promise of civil disobedience as more than a politics of cost levying depends on the habits of vision and epistemological frameworks of the citizens who see, interpret, and respond to it—habits and frameworks that the movement's disruptive disclosures challenged but did not fully transform.

This chapter continues—and complicates—the argument of Chapter 4 by engaging with a largely forgotten episode from the civil rights movement: radical activists of the Brooklyn chapter of CORE planned to stall hundreds of cars on the highway leading to the 1964 World's Fair. The stall-in represents a key moment in the history of the civil rights movement because critical debates over strategy and tactics, violence and nonviolence, legal and extralegal forms of action, integration and equality, and the role of "white liberals" and "white backlash" in the black freedom struggle all coalesced around it.[8] At first glance, the contrast with Birmingham appears stark: on the one hand, an event that occupies as central a place as any in the pantheon of civil rights protests; and on the other hand, an event that is remembered with disdain—as an ill-conceived, irresponsible, and potentially violent failure—when it is remembered at all. Tamar Jacoby's judgment of the stall-in in her book *Someone Else's House: America's Unfinished Struggle for Integration* sums up a pervasive view: "the year's most spectacular flop," a "protest for protest's sake . . . aimed at everyone and no one in particular," and portent of a damaging trend toward militancy, extremism, and separatism at a time when "the white establishment was trying finally to deliver on the nation's promises, moving, albeit haltingly, to grant at least formal equality to black citizens."[9] In other words: not just a failed protest, but also one both dangerous and gratuitous in conception—a slap in the face of earnest allies, a danger to the real work of civil rights, and an assault on innocent bystanders who neither created nor had meaningful responsibility for remedying structures of racial injustice. If the Birmingham campaign, in the popular memory, offers a testament to the power of a nonviolent appeal to conscience—the apotheosis of courageous civil disobedience—then the Brooklyn CORE stall-in tells the tale of its degradation.

This reading of the stall-in is formed by the same epistemic context that ensured the protest's preemptive defeat—a context in which racialized ways of knowing and seeing the political world shape the judgments about what qualifies as legitimate civil disobedience, what appears as persuasive or sympathetic, and what counts as civil or nonviolent. In my view, what separates Birmingham's Project "C" from Brooklyn CORE's stall-in is not a consequential difference in their tactics. Rather, the divergent public responses to these two campaigns reveals the interpretive and perceptual practices constitutive of white supremacy—what I have characterized as seeing like a white state—that shape citizens' and policymakers' assumptions about the nature of racial injustice, responsibility for remedying it, and the proper means of action for doing so.[10] Drawing on the work of James Baldwin, Charles Mills, and Elizabeth Spelman, this chapter reads public reactions to the stall-in as evidence of the discursive work of maintaining "white ignorance" against the direct challenges of civil disobedience's decolonizing praxis. Brooklyn CORE's stall-in posed a radical claim: the consumer pleasures offered to some were linked to racialized deprivations for others; and therefore all Americans were implicated in the crime of racial injustice. In response, white politicians, journalists, and citizens responded with discursive strategies—*techniques of disavowal*—that helped them discredit the stall-in and its organizers, and thus maintain the façade of their own innocence and moral standing.

As such, the story of the stall-in poses a challenge to many activists' own hopes for what civil disobedience could accomplish in transforming racial hierarchy.

Stalled Freedom

When "master builder" Robert Moses conceived of the 1964 New York World's Fair, he imagined a grand homage to the kinds of freedom enabled by free enterprise, new technology, and consumer convenience—"an Olympics of progress and healthy rivalry, a vast Colosseum [sic] dedicated to new friendships . . . [and] the hopes and aspirations of a new world."[11] But with less than a month to go before opening day, the Brooklyn chapter of the CORE announced plans for a fair exhibit of their own: hundreds, if not thousands, of stalled cars on the highways leading to the fairgrounds, tying up traffic for hours and preventing hundreds of thousands of eager fair patrons from entering the gates. Isiah Brunson, a soft-spoken twenty-two-year-old and chairman of Brooklyn CORE, explained it this way: "We are having the stall-in to shut off traffic at the World's Fair because the city and the state have seen fit to spend millions and millions of dollars to build the World's Fair, but have not seen fit to eliminate the problems of Negroes and Puerto Ricans in New York City."[12] Unless the City of New York made rapid progress on long-standing demands for quality, integrated schools, nondiscrimination in housing and employment, and a civilian review board to oversee cases of police brutality in black and Puerto Rican neighborhoods, CORE would choke off the arterial highways connecting the city to the Fair—and thus, the city to much anticipated tourist dollars.

Organizers envisioned the stall-in as a way to "create a large enough traffic jam so that women and men trapped on the highways that ran through some of New York City's most impoverished areas would be forced to observe, up close, the effects of institutional racism."[13] While Brooklyn CORE's operation was small, it was precisely the kind of dramatic direct action tactic that had endeared the chapter to Brooklyn locals.[14] Echoing—but significantly radicalizing—the lesson that Birmingham activists learned about transforming spectators into demonstrators, CORE organizers like Oliver Leeds hoped that the tactic of the stall-in would offer the opportunity for disempowered citizens to become activists. As Leeds explained to the press, the significance of the stall-in was that it was not a centrally orchestrated project, carefully planned and controlled by the organization. Rather, it was meant as a tactic that offered "the man on the street" the ability to act on his own and for himself. Referencing the simmering frustration of black New Yorkers and the imaginative appeal of the stall-in as a tactic, Leeds suggested that this decentralized strategy would be its strength: "From what I've heard in Bedford-Stuyvesant, neither CORE nor anyone else is going to be able to stop him. That's the beauty of the whole operation."[15]

In its most elaborate version, plans for the stall-in entailed not just the stalling of thousands of cars but also the coordinated blockage of all avenues of entry to the Fair. While some volunteers would "drive awhile for freedom," forcing traffic off the highways and onto surface streets through borough ghettos, others could "join the World's Fair civil rights exhibit" by blocking the doors to Fair-bound subway cars or pulling their emergency breaks; still others would create pedestrian traffic jams at the fairground gates by paying the $2.50 admission fee in $2.49 worth of pennies. Some suggested that live rats, collected in the apartment buildings of Bedford-Stuyvesant and Harlem, be released into the crowds during President Johnson's opening ceremonies speech—a tactic pioneered by rent-strike leader Jesse Gray, who organized tenants to bring rats (dead and alive) from their homes to court as evidence of the conditions in which they lived. For his part, Gray proposed operating bus tours from the fairgrounds—presumably picking up those wading through the bottlenecks caused by the stall-ins—to the city's infamously dilapidated tenements, for what he would later call "New York's Worst Fair."[16]

Local and national press jumped on the story, devoting column inch after column inch to the protest—helping to make the stall-in one of the best publicized and most criticized protests that never occurred. Commentators were quick to condemn the protests as unreasonable, dangerous, and even violent, while angry letters to the editor—and to the offices of CORE and the World's Fair Corporation—poured in.[17] In a series of deft rhetorical moves, in the hands of journalists, citizens, and politicians, the stall-in proposal was easily transformed into the specter of an unquestionably violent protest; the means of nonviolent coercion and disruption likened to the brutality of segregation's staunchest defenders; and the systematic denial of decent housing, schools, jobs, and public services to the poor and black quickly analogized to the "hardship" and "inconvenience" endured by drivers stuck in a traffic jam on their way to the Fair. "The mischievous scheme . . . to tie up traffic on the major arteries leading to the World's Fair on opening day is well calculated to do the utmost possible damage to the cause of civil rights," claimed an editorial in the *New York Times*. "It is madness to assume that creating a big traffic jam and inconveniencing people on their way to work, to business, or to recreation will somehow make them more sympathetic to the rights of the Negro."[18] The *New York World-Telegram* charged that CORE was "using the same type of rude and lawless tactics employed by their worst enemies."[19] These themes were repeated, reiterated, and redeployed in countless letters, insisting that "if the Negro wants his rights, he should not deprive the white man of his," as one individual put it.[20] On this logic, violating the presumptive "right" of white citizens not to be inconvenienced for a day was likened to the regime of racial terror imposed on black citizens, as if the two were somehow equivalent.

Politicians were not far behind in their condemnations. Senators Hubert Humphrey and Thomas Kuchel—key congressional leaders in the drafting and ultimate passage of the 1964 Civil Rights Act—urged "good manner[ed] tactics" (like the March on Washington) and warned that "illegal disturbances, demonstrations which lead to violence or injury, strike grievous blows at the cause of decent civil rights legislation." Revealing, perhaps, how very short the reach of history is—given the direct connection between mass protest and the very legislation they were trying to shepherd through Congress—the senators lectured Brooklyn CORE that "civil wrongs do not bring civil rights. Civil disobedience does not bring equal protection under the laws. Disorder does not bring law and order."[21] Humphrey, in fact, went a step further: in direct reference to Birmingham, he said, "the scenes of dogs and policemen with clubs being used against peaceful demonstrations caused great public outcry. But if extremists in the civil rights movement decide to inconvenience hundreds of thousands of people, it's going to have the same reaction in reverse."[22] In language reminiscent of that used by Birmingham officials, Richard Wagner, then mayor of New York, likened the protests to a "gun held to the heart of the city," which threatened more harm than "anything that Dixiecrat Senators can do in Washington, or that the forces of bigotry can do in this city."[23] A bit too eager to seize on public rifts in the civil rights movement, all were quick to distinguish the majority of "responsible Negro leaders" who remained true to nonviolence and kept their eyes on the prize (the civil rights bill) from those irresponsible few willing to bring "unnecessary inconvenience to others" to get their way—or at least get their names in the papers.[24] The consensus was in: the stall-in was both violent and ridiculous—vindictive, uncivil, and certainly illegitimate; and also, petulant, insincere, and meaningless.

Less discussed was the fact that the proposed civil rights bill—then stalled behind a segregationist filibuster in the Senate—would be of limited utility for New York City's black communities on issues of education and employment, and absolute irrelevance with regard to housing and police brutality. In the first place, the public accommodations title, a cornerstone of the bill and a key achievement of the Southern civil rights movement, did not address the nature of segregation outside the South, which by 1964 was no longer demarcated by "Whites Only" signage or statutes designating access to hotels, restrooms, buses, and lunch counters. And although the 1964 Civil Rights Act did ultimately include provisions for fighting segregation in education and discrimination in employment, many saw reason for skepticism.[25] The absence of legally mandated school segregation had not done anything to improve the quality of education across black neighborhoods in New York, let alone integrate the schools. In terms of employment, although New York had been an early adopter of anti-discrimination legislation—the first state in the nation to pass a law banning racial discrimination in hiring, in 1945—communities of color in the city still faced lily-white unions and systemic underemployment. As in urban areas across the country, black residents of New York were in a perfect position to appreciate the cruel intertwining of racial and class oppression, and the self-reinforcing effects of inferior access to quality housing, education, and employment.

All the press attention on the plans for the stall-in brought notoriety and publicity to the protest, but it also ensured a swift and coordinated response from the city and the World's Fair Corporation. Famously unsympathetic to civil rights claims, Robert Moses's response to the press was characteristically dismissive: "The fair will not become a stage for irresponsible interference with visitors, secondary boycotts and demonstrations not related to the proper conduct of the fair."[26] Behind the scenes, meanwhile, and in conjunction with the New York Traffic Commissioner Henry Barnes, a new law was swiftly passed stipulating a maximum penalty of thirty days jail time and a $50 fine for any driver who might run out of gas on the highways of New York. Though officials insisted that the law had nothing to do with the stall-in, and was instead a commonsense measure adopted by many other municipalities and states to keep traffic clear on major roads and highways, the passage of the law proved that New York could wield the law against unwanted protest just as readily and as easily as any town in the solid South. The Queens district attorney managed to get an injunction against the protest, while the New York World's Fair Corporation took advantage of its status as a private rather than public entity in order to prohibit all "demonstrations, parades, congregations, picketing or other similar acts on the Fair site" without "written permit" of the corporation—permission that they would consistently refused to grant, even to protests much more tame, traditional, and legally protected than the stall-in.[27] Additionally, and at Moses's urging, the city promised to keep a massive force of police, tow trucks, and a helicopter airlift at the ready along the major Fair throughways—a testament to how quickly and effectively money, time, muscle, and means could be put together by the ruling powers in New York when there was the political will to do so.[28]

Thus, though quickly backed by CORE chapters in the Bronx, Harlem, Manhattan, Long Island, and Yonkers, along with college chapters at Queens College and Columbia University, the protest was not to be. National CORE opposed the stall-in, on the grounds that it violated CORE's established Rules for Action. They alleged that organizers had failed to try to negotiate with the city first; had not focused their protest on a single, clear target; and had planned an action that prevented other chapters from pursuing more traditional protest tactics at the Fair—the picketing of particular pavilions, for example, of the sort hastily planned by National CORE as an alternative to the stall-in.[29] When the Brooklynites proceeded with their plans anyway, in defiance of National Chairman James Farmer's explicit instructions, the chapter was formally suspended.[30] Without the backing—and the logistical capacity—of the national organization, the local chapters had little ability to pull off a 2,000-car stall-in. While Brooklyn CORE was not the feckless, inept, and reactionary organization that the press portrayed it to be, their past campaigns had been locally focused, and they had never tried to organize something on the scale of the stall-in before; in reality, they had neither the reach nor the means to do so.[31] Brunson, concluded one disappointed New York City civil rights leader, "is no Bayard Rustin."[32] Perhaps more to the point, however, the imposition of criminal fines and jail time for potential stallers-in likely had a chilling effect on those would-be volunteers looking to put their cars—and their cause—on exhibit.

The morning of April 22, under the gray and drizzling New York skies, journalists awaiting a massive highway tie-up found—to their rather smug delight—few cars and little traffic.[33] At the fairgrounds, a rather orderly procession of several hundred activists organized by Farmer picketed several state and corporate pavilions and were arrested; a less orderly attempt to keep subway doors from closing on one train ended quickly, as police, swinging their clubs and injuring seven, forcibly removed protestors.[34] At President Johnson's speech during the opening ceremonies, a group of college students heckled, taunted, and chanted their way through the president's claim that "We"—Americans, that is—"do not try to disguise our imperfections and our failures. No other nation in history has done so much to correct its flaws."[35] But a stall-in there was not. On the other hand, neither were there huge crowds waiting to partake in the Fair's many futuristic wonders. Although Moses had anticipated opening day would bring one-quarter million patrons through the Fair gates, by the mid-afternoon, scarcely more than 60,000 had visited Tomorrow-land. The bad weather was undoubtedly a factor. But so was the press around CORE's protest.[36] "I was out there and there were a number of other members of Brooklyn CORE that didn't try to stall anything," recalled Major Owens, a Brooklyn CORE member who later became the chapter's chairman. "But we didn't have to. The bluff worked so beautifully until there were no cars."[37] The stall-in may have fizzled, but it hardly failed.

Disrupting White Comfort

However radical it may have seemed, the tactic of the stall-in did not represent a total break with what came before it. As it developed through tactical experimentation and "political thinking in the streets," civil disobedience as a decolonizing praxis was built on the creative and tenuous combination of disruption, disclosure, and a bodily confrontation with spectators, citizens, and officials that involved them in the action. To be sure, with the stall-in, Brooklyn CORE proposed to radicalize tactics like the sit-in, the jail-in, and even the strategic crisis-generation of the Birmingham campaign: the audience it aimed to reach was wider, its message of culpability more wide-ranging, and the potential for disruption more profound. Yet the difference is in degree, not kind.

In essence, Brooklyn CORE's plans amounted to a call for mass civil disobedience of the kind that Martin Luther King, Jr. would issue in the last year of his life, as part of the Poor People's Campaign. Facing the entrenched conditions of Northern racism and urban poverty, in 1968 King argued that nonviolence must be adapted to respond to "heightened black impatience and stiffened white resistance":

There must be more than a statement to the larger society, there must be a force that interrupts its functioning at some key point.... Mass civil disobedience as a new stage of struggle can transmute the deep rage of the ghetto into a constructive and creative force. To dislocate the functioning of a city without destroying it can be more effective than a riot because it can be longer lasting, costly to the larger society but not wantonly destructive.[38]

In the spring of 1964, Brooklyn CORE was perhaps ahead of the curve in envisioning civil disobedience in this way—as a creative means for channeling the rage and frustration produced by racialized urban poverty in order to address the needs of neglected black and Puerto Rican communities. But by opening day of the World's Fair, the New York City CORE chapters, and Brooklyn CORE particularly, had already fought rounds of battles with the city government over sanitation, housing, schools, union employment, and police brutality, with only the most modest of concessions to show for it. They were already contending with the conditions of "heightened black impatience" and "stiffened white resistance" and were strategizing new means to meet the moment.

By the summer and fall of 1963, stall-ins already seemed to be in the air. In July, Louis Lomax—author of *The Negro Revolt*—suggested just such a thing in a lecture at Queens College: "Imagine the confusion," he told his audience, "if 500 people get in their cars, drive towards the Fair grounds, and run out of gas."[39] At the same time, radical activists from SNCC and CORE were brought on board to the idea of a March on Washington only by the possibility that the march might operate as a part of a massive campaign of civil disobedience—"A protest rather than a plea. Stage sit-ins all across Washington. Tie up traffic. Have 'lie-ins' in local airport runways. Invade the offices of southern congressmen and senators. Camp on the White House lawn. Cause mass arrests. Paralyze the city."[40] A few months later, in his keynote address at the annual convention of the SCLC—now, post-Birmingham, post–March on Washington, newly counted among those "responsible" organizations which knew the difference between legitimate protest and unwarranted disruption—Wyatt Tee Walker all but proposed a nationwide stall-in. Echoing a plan proposed by Diane Nash in the wake of the Sixteenth Street Church bombing that killed four children, Walker floated the idea of a massive campaign of disobedience: "Is the day far-off that major transportation centers would be deluged with mass acts of civil disobedience; airports, train stations, bus terminals, the traffic of large cities, interstate commerce, would be halted by the bodies of witnesses nonviolently insisting on 'Freedom Now'?" Such a protest, had it ever come to pass, would have far outstripped the World's Fair protest both in radicalism and in levels of disruption.[41]

Ironically, given his very public opposition to the World's Fair stall-in, James Farmer had defended just this sort of disruptive tactic one month prior to the Fair, when the Harlem chapter of CORE held a sit-in on the Triborough Bridge, dumping garbage collected from two neighborhood schools on the road, and tying up traffic for twenty minutes while trying to show angry motorists a small slice of life in many of the city's black neighborhoods. Predictably, the action generated some bad press. This "perversion of the integration drive," like the stall-in after it, "trample[d] on the rights of all citizens," aroused hostility in "even the most sympathetic of communities," and proved once and for all that "sit-ins and demonstrations . . . are self-defeating in such cities as New York, Chicago, and Boston, where Negroes do have legitimate means of making their wants and needs felt."[42] In *Freedom—When?*, Farmer argued that, against the negative editorials and "those complaining about 'amateurish' demonstrations," the Triborough action was meant "to inform a comfortable and complacent public about the reprehensible condition of two Harlem schools." Every citizen of New York, he continued "should know what goes on inside the ghetto walls they skirt each day!"[43] Beyond the specifics of that protest, moreover, in these passages Farmer provided a compelling justification for strategies that cause public discomfort, provoke hostility, and work to disrupt the daily lives of other citizens. Farmer posed the following rhetorical question: "What good is it to discomfort and anger people who themselves can do nothing about Harlem conditions? What except bad can come of such provocations?" He then offered this reply:

> No one of us at CORE ever claimed the garbage dump alone would solve the education problem in New York City or even a significant part of it—as if only those demonstrations which single-handedly solved problems were justified. What we do claim is that city officials will not move to improve the quality and racial balance of the schools until (a) both officials and the general public realize that conditions are unconscionable, and (b) both realize that they cannot skirt the issue without risking some dislocation.[44]

In short, Farmer defended the Triborough trash dump in the terms of disclosure—staging a display of "unconscionable" conditions—and the disruption that it requires—the status quo cannot continue without discomfort and "dislocation" for the public and politicians alike. The point was to make manifest a reality that was being consistently disavowed and demonstrate the consequences of continuing disavowal.

With this in mind, Farmer also warned of giving too much credence to fears about whatever backlash may result from the disruption and disorder of protest. Indeed, he identified the practice of criticizing civil rights protest on the grounds that it may make white citizens angry as itself a tool of white supremacy—a device used to maintain racialized structures of power. The limits of dissent should not be pegged to the maintenance of white comfort, and the agenda for racial justice should not be premised on the exchange of civility for empathy. Giving in to the disciplinary force of such criticisms, Farmer argued, simply "trains black men to pin their sense of priorities on the tail of current white feelings, or more precisely, what are perceived to be current white feelings."[45] The entire discourse around white backlash and "polite" protest—what Juliet Hooker has recently theorized as a politics of white grievance, readily mobilized whenever racial dominance and political mastery are under threat—preemptively delegitimizes any form of protest that upsets a white public habituated to the norms and practices of white supremacy.[46] Thus, for Farmer, white backlash discourse could only frustrate the transformative potential that activists had long identified in civil disobedience—including the possibility that white citizens may find themselves changed through an instructive experience with discomfort.

This latter idea was indeed central to Brooklyn CORE's stall-in plans. Well aware of the huge capital investments the city had made to bring the Fair back to New York City, activists saw the stall-in as a way to put financial pressure on the city to address their concerns. But they also framed their protest broadly, as a means of arresting the attention of white citizens by temporarily denying them comfort and upsetting their expectations for consumer pleasure. In the weeks before opening day, Leeds asked the press why "people should enjoy themselves" at the Fair—an event designed to showcase American progress and wealth—in the midst of widespread black suffering across the nation.[47] Echoing the idea of using protest as a tool for discomfort, another member of Brooklyn CORE put it this way: "We're going to try very hard to see that whoever gets to the Fair is pretty uncomfortable getting there. We must disrupt the white man's easy going and pleasant life. We must let him know that since we're not comfortable, he won't be comfortable."[48]

It was easy for politicians and the press to frame these statements as vengeful—a random and indiscriminate lashing out at blameless fair-goers who had no responsibility for discriminatory housing, education, employment, or policing. But as CORE organizers like Brunson insisted as they replied to the letters pouring in to their offices, the point was not revenge.[49] Rather, these activists saw that the "white man's easy going and pleasant life" was premised on the systematic neglect of black communities: public and private resources were seemingly abundant for the former, even while cities claimed insufficient power and money to address the latter. White citizens, then, as beneficiaries of a system that prioritized their pleasure over the fundamental demands of racial justice, needed to come face to face with their own culpability—and their own power, as privileged citizens, to demand change. SNCC organizer Bob Moses unpacked this logic for a white audience at Stanford University, just two days after the Fair's opening: "The whole idea of New York City spending millions of dollars—the city spent $30 million, Ford spent millions of dollars, U.S. Steel spent millions of dollars, all private industry [is] spending millions of dollars to build a fair to show people how they will live in the year 2000, with beautiful glass buildings and moving sidewalks." Moses remarked on the "fantastic" irony of it all—the enormous outlay of wealth and the pageantry of consumer abundance, while black residents fought for jobs and organized rent strikes "because there are rats running up and down their walls." Yet few seemed interested in thinking about the relationship between these two realities: "All everyone was concerned with was, 'Don't mess up our World's Fair.'" The stall-in, in turn, posed a reasonable question: "Whose World Fair?"[50]

Far from an illegitimate assault on innocent bystanders who deserved their freedom from inconvenience, the plans for the stall-in suggested that culpability for racial injustice was society-wide. Indeed, this is a premise that they shared with the activists at the forefront of civil rights disobedience in the South. The Birmingham strategy, as we have seen, was premised on an implicit connection between the virulent, violent racism of Southern segregationists and the wavering, conditional support of white liberal politicians and citizens. The paired tactics of disruption and disclosure were designed to erode the distinction between those who wield overt racial violence and those who tacitly accept it, or willfully ignore it—drawing out the brutality of segregation in order to force an ethical dilemma for those white Americans who gave lip service to racial equality. King insisted from within his cell in the Birmingham Jail that those who prioritize order over justice are equally culpable for the maintenance of oppression; civil disobedience must find ways of forcing such an acknowledgment. As I argued in the last chapter, this is a distinct project from simple moral suasion: it requires more than just calling on white Americans to recommit to principles they already hold—or even calling on them to commit to new principles. It requires new agents, capable of seeing the world (and their responsibilities to it) quite differently.

Such a transformation would take time. But activists argued that the necessary first step was unsettling the expectation that white enjoyment should be protected and prioritized amidst racialized deprivation. The disruption of the stall-in might create an opening to dramatize the necessary relationship between the two, forcing white Americans to either actively commit to real democratization or more affirmatively assert their investment in hierarchy. At a minimum, the organizers hoped to make it impossible for white fairgoers and city officials to continue to ignore CORE's long-standing demands. But the more ambitious proposition was that the stall-in might push white Americans to reflect on the ways their own material comfort and consumer pleasure was linked to the structural neglect, economic exploitation, and political disempowerment of black communities. As in Birmingham, the tactics of disclosure and disruption were meant to confront and unsettle the ways of seeing and unseeing, knowing and not knowing, that routinely prevented such reflexivity, and that safeguarded hierarchy.[51]

Yet, read alongside the real (though limited) successes of the Birmingham campaign, the thwarted stall-in offers lessons about white supremacy's resiliency and the difficulties of civil disobedience's transformative, outward-facing ambitions. To better understand these dynamics, I suggest we look more closely at the problem of "white ignorance" and the discursive means used to discredit and delegitimize the stall-in—what I refer to here as *techniques of disavowal*.

Ignorance Fights Back

One month before the stall-in, James Baldwin stood on a New York City stage and was pressed by his interlocutors to defend his skepticism about white commitments to racial justice. In response, he offered the metaphor of a "black presence" that white Americans have collectively "agreed not to look at."[52] The problem, as Baldwin suggested during the roundtable and in his contemporaneous essays, is not just that white America is guilty of immense destruction, but that white citizens systematically deny that they are its authors—they need to deny that they are its authors. As he put it in the letter to his nephew that opens *The Fire Next Time*, "they do not know it and do not want to know it," and it is this "innocence which constitutes the crime."[53]

Here, Baldwin is complicating the relationship between knowledge and responsibility, guilt and innocence. It seems reasonable to suggest that we cannot be fully responsible for causing harm if we did not know our actions were harmful, or if we lacked the necessary information for acting differently. Ignorance preserves both innocence and moral standing: our actions caused harm but we did not know, so we are innocent of willful wrongdoing; we would have acted differently if only we had known because we are not the kind of people who believe in deliberately causing harm. Baldwin argues that white Americans adopt precisely this stance—confessing ignorance, eschewing responsibility, and preserving innocence—under conditions in which the evidence of harm is abundant and readily apparent: "The point is that these crimes are committed, and have been committed for generations now, in the name of white Americans. So you can't now say, 'My neighbor can be lynched and he's also innocent,' and still say you're not responsible."[54] For white Americans, the knowledge of domination is not lacking; it is simultaneously acknowledged and rejected. Baldwin's wording here is suggestive: white Americans do not look, but also they have *agreed* not to look; they do not know, but also they do not *want* to know. The agreement to avert one's eyes and the desire not to know reveal the situation for what it is: not a lack of knowledge or sight, but—in the terms George Shulman suggests—a *disavowal* of what is already known and what can be readily seen.[55] Not looking and not knowing are ongoing commitments. They are choices and activities that are made possible by the very knowledge they deny.

This sense of ignorance as an active stance—as more than a cognitive deficit or the absence of knowledge—is reflected in Charles Mills's and Elizabeth Spelman's accounts of "white ignorance." As Mills articulates, white ignorance is not a lack of information, but a socially produced system of knowledge that requires active management and maintenance. More specifically, white supremacy produces and reproduces an epistemic context in which the conceptual categories of perception, memory, and action are shaped by the simultaneous justification and erasure of domination: the conceptual distinction between human and "savage," civilized and uncivilized, citizen and subject "*is driving the perception, with whites aprioristically intent on denying what is before them.* So if Kant famously said that perceptions without concepts are blind, then here it is the blindness of the concept itself that is blocking the vision."[56] These maneuvers are actively validated by those vested with epistemic authority. White ignorance is not a deficit, but the production of perceptual and interpretive frameworks that inform how citizens see and know—generating what Martin Luther King, Jr. recognized as a problem of white "vision."[57] It is thus a stubborn problem, not easily undermined by marshalling counter-evidence. Instead, Spelman suggests that it is not a "*belief* subject to warrant or nonwarrant, but a *commitment* subject to approval or disapproval, encouragement or discouragement, support or abandonment."[58] Under white supremacy, forms of approval and encouragement are readily available, and consequently, white ignorance is "*an ignorance that resists*," that "*fights back*" and "*refuses to go quietly*."[59]

In many ways, the decolonizing praxis of civil disobedience—in its inward- and outward-facing aspects—responds to this epistemic context. The tactics of self-emancipation represented by the jail-in took stock of the way the status of ethical and political personhood was denied black Americans—a denial built into everyday rituals of domination and submission, violence and fear. Self-emancipation refused the imposition of fear, the expectation of continued submission, and the relegation to diminished personhood. Freedom—or, at least, comparative freedom—was not a grant of rights by the powerful, but the enactment of this refusal by the dominated. The tactics of disruption and disclosure, meanwhile, were necessitated by the failures of persuasion under these conditions. It would not be enough to insist, rationally and reasonably, that black Americans were citizens and deserved the rights of citizens; it would not be enough to show that racism was pervasive and harmful. The problem of ongoing racial domination was not that white Americans were unaware of it; the problem was that the social order was structured to approve, encourage, and support collective avoidance of it. The shock of disruption, the bodily confrontation that disclosed latent violence—these forms of action were intended to force white Americans to confront what they did not wish to know and agreed not to see, jeopardizing the innocence and moral standing secured by ignorance. Disruption and disclosure aimed to make it impossible, at least momentarily, to continue not looking and not knowing.

Campaigns like the one in Birmingham supplied powerful evidence of the merits of this strategy. Disruption and disclosure worked in May of 1963—at least in some fashion—resulting in a cascade of nationwide protests and Kennedy's belated support for national civil rights legislation.

Yet Birmingham's successes contained hints about their contingent nature and suggested ways in which white ignorance might ultimately fight back. In Kennedy's June speech, discussed in the previous chapter, he took up the language of the civil rights movement, granting that the disruptive and disclosive events in Birmingham and across the country had made it impossible for governmental bodies to continue to ignore their claims. Yet, as I suggested, Kennedy's language was one of retroactive legitimation and prospective delegitimation: he authorized the protests that preceded that moment as the legitimate "cries for equality," while aiming to draw the time for demonstrations to a close. Seeking further "redress . . . in the streets" would "create tensions and threaten lives." This latter admonishment was as much for legislators who delayed or opposed redress as it was for activists who fought for a fuller freedom beyond the lines of legislation.[60] A year later, the activists of Brooklyn CORE, like so many others, acted in a context shaped by this discursive act—and by the fact that national legislation was working its way through the chambers of Congress (though stalled by segregationist filibuster, and though representing only some aspects of the demands and claims of civil rights activists themselves). The possibilities for protest in 1964 were shaped by the ways that direct action was both affirmed and rejected, legitimated and delegitimated, by the legislative process then underway.

The lines between legitimate and illegitimate forms of protest were drawn differently, and with different stakes, by activists themselves. Yet their boundary disputes likewise reflect the dilemmas and contradictions generated by the epistemic context of white supremacy. As I articulated toward the end of Chapter 4, the Birmingham campaign's discursive need to disown the spectator-demonstrators on whom they relied exposes the fraught terrain on which civil disobedience was staged. It suggests a sharp awareness amongst activists of the powerful ideational resources available for discrediting black protest—or, in the terms of this chapter, the many ways that white ignorance stands prepared to resist. Similarly, the controversy over Brooklyn CORE's tactics within national civil rights organizations—the concern that the stall-in represented a tactical mistake that would alienate allies, threaten legislation, or delegitimize the movement as a whole—reflects a shared uncertainty about the prospects for transforming white citizens through civil disobedience, and acute concerns about the potentially regressive response to disobedience if it failed to do so.

In what follows, I describe three linked discursive maneuvers—what I characterize, following Shulman, as *techniques of disavowal*—that were mobilized in the weeks after the stall-in was announced: *disaggregation, escalation*, and *disqualification*.[61] These techniques, in various ways, simultaneously affirmed and rejected the protestors' demands, at once acknowledging and denying responsibility for addressing them. These techniques successfully insulated white citizens and political officials from engaging with the deeper, more expansive forms of collective and individual culpability at stake in the stall-in, beyond the narrowest terms of national civil rights legislation—preserving white innocence and moral standing. At the same time, they repositioned political elites and white liberal opinion as the true guardians of civil rights: they, not black protestors, would ensure the terms of equal citizenship. Civil disobedience would only serve to damage the prospects of black equality, and—many hastened to mention—the rights and comforts white citizens had every reason to expect.

The technique of *disaggregation* worked to fracture the geographies and sites of racial domination, so that the claims of the Southern movement were exceptionalized, and the arenas of individual protests disconnected. Senator Humphrey's reference to the Birmingham campaign cited earlier ("the scenes of dogs and policemen with clubs being used against peaceful demonstrations") was not incidental: the attempt to discredit the tactics of disruption in New York—the stall-in and the earlier Triborough Bridge blockade—often began by distinguishing the problems of the urban "North" from those of the South. One editorial in the *New York Times* suggested that the activists of CORE read a recent article by historian Oscar Handlin to better understand "the equal rights problem" they faced: "His conclusion is that sit-ins and street demonstrations are the sole recourse in those areas of the South where Negroes are still excluded from political decisions and due process of law." In contrast, in New York and other Northern and Midwestern cities, "Negroes do have legitimate means of making their wants and needs felt." Resorting to disruptive acts of civil disobedience is the work of "ultra-zealots" within the ranks of the movement, whose tactics "tear the community apart."[62] Similarly, *LIFE* magazine distinguished protests against the "obvious indecencies of the South" to those waged against the "complicated second-stage frustrations of joblessness, ghetto housing, poor schools and poverty," which—though a national problem—were not specifically related to Jim Crow. The issues identified by Brooklyn CORE were "the result of a wide social sickness," and protest against them would only degenerate "into a generalized tormented rage against the whole blank front of 'the Man's' society," a series of "self-defeating brawls and tantrums."[63]

The disaggregated geography of Southern exceptionalism designates the South as a separate, uniquely problematic space—riven by racial prejudice and out of step with national, constitutional norms.[64] Indeed, and despite years of civil rights organizing, mobilizing, and protesting in cities in the industrial Northeast, Midwest, and West Coast, the idea that Northern racism bore any resemblance to its Southern counterpart remained anathema to most Americans, thanks in part to the designation of Northern segregation as de facto rather than de jure, and by the realities of racial separation in America's cities. Amidst a narrative that identified America's racial woes not in national structures but in Southern exceptionalism, de jure segregation was cast as an anachronistic remnant of a backward past that had to be rooted out; de facto segregation was, in contrast, legally "innocent," caused not by "any systemic policy of racial exclusion fostered by law or administrative policy" but by the aggregation of individual, private, free-market choices.[65] Poverty and underfunded schools may have been, in the words of *LIFE*'s editorial writer, the signs of a "wide social sickness," but it was a nebulous and diffuse sickness—one without specific cause or attributable chains of responsibility. It was not the kind of thing one could protest meaningfully.

The social problem of de facto segregation, from this perspective—the underfunded schools, limited access to jobs, and confinement within immiserated neighborhoods that defined the black Northerner's plight—was not appropriately addressed by aggressive government action since the federal government did not (at that moment) mandate that African Americans live, school, or work separately. This narrative naturalized racial inequality in New York, placing it, as Matthew Lassiter argues, "beyond the scope of judicial remedy" and freeing policymakers, politicians, businessmen, and private citizens from "any historical or contemporary responsibility"—an idea belied by the very real, and rather recent, history of discriminatory federal, state, municipal, and private action, particularly with regard to housing.[66] Thus, the separation of de jure segregation (as a discrete legal injustice with a clear remedy) from de facto segregation (as a diffuse social problem without an obvious solution) placed policy remedies in the North on the wrong side of American values of individual freedom, consumer choice, and free-market individualism. While increasingly, national public opinion favored federal intervention and mandated integration in the South, despite encroachment on some free-market liberties and individual preferences, in the North, an active disavowal of culpability tipped the scales the other direction. In sum,

Baldwin once quipped, "De facto segregation means that Negroes are segregated but nobody did it."[67]

As the invocation of Southern exceptionalism rendered free-market choice innocent of racial injustice, it intertwined with an additional disaggregative discourse—one that severed each arena of claim-making from all others. Critics of the stall-in demanded a clear, singular grievance tied to the site of protest—perhaps not an unreasonable expectation, if racial domination in one arena had little to do with racial domination in another, or if piecemeal and site-specific protests had yielded real results. But Brooklyn CORE's experience suggested otherwise.[68] And what the World's Fair promised was a context in which activists could present the totality of their demands—not one by one, as separable, discrete issues, but all together as a single, disclosive "civil rights exhibit."

In response, journalists, politicians, and citizens insisted that even if New York had a race problem, the Fair could not possibly be a meaningful site of protest against it. The subject of protestors claims simply had nothing to do with the World's Fair, and Brooklyn CORE's years of work in putting their demands before the city had nothing to do with the plans for the stall-in. "The World's Fair has not been discriminating against anybody," read one telling column published in the *Times*. "It is not a seat of government. It has no authority to bring about civil rights reforms or correct wrongs in the social order. Its theme, 'Peace through Understanding,' in itself suggests sympathy with the just aspirations of all peoples. To make it the scene of various demonstrations, as Brooklyn CORE and perhaps other groups apparently intend to do, is to send the marchers to the wrong address."[69] Protestors, in other words, were making a problematic claim, foolishly directed at an unrelated audience, and irresponsibly implicating the innocent—delivering the wrong address, at the wrong address.

Thus, the technique of disaggregation worked to uncouple the claims and tactics of the Southern movement—now legitimized through federal legislation—from events and grievances in cities like New York, while separating spheres of claim-making from each other—and designating some spheres as specifically off-limits. Disaggregative responses defined the problem of racial injustice as the product of clear, intentional, and legalized discrimination and assumed that government alone held the responsibility for addressing it. Ordinary citizens—in their roles as fair-goers and consumers—played no part in the construction of racial hierarchies, and it was simply wrong to force them to be subject to the inconvenience and disruption of a protest. Yet it was this very set of assumptions that the stall-in attempted to target and critique: to press the idea that a culture of consumerism and the everyday habits of white citizens were implicated in the racial order, and to insist that—as Brian Purnell puts it—"all members of society were responsible for maintaining racist structures *and* for eventually eradicating them."[70] The plans for the stall-in urged a particularly poignant confrontation with an alternative construction of segregation, racism, and the quiet mechanisms of their maintenance: *everyone* was party to American racial orders, and everyone was jointly responsible for them. The "innocent" fun of the Fair was not in fact innocent, because it symbolized the forms of investment willingly undertaken by the City of New York—consumer pleasure—alongside the willful failure to invest in black well-being on equal terms.

Though most responded to the stall-in with anger and reproach, a few readers of the New York papers saw what stall-in organizers hoped they might: "Far be it from me to assert that the situation in New York is exactly what it is in the South," wrote one individual in a letter to the editor. "But our present indignation does seem very similar to that of white Southerners when they are confronted by militant civil rights movements in their own states. Should we not, in this light, re-examine the implications of what we are so sanctimoniously saying about the 'stall-ins' "?[71] More sardonically, but no less poetically, another letter writer from Los Angeles scoffed: "Tsk, tsk, tsk—the whites dislike traffic jams. I'll bet they'd like Harlem even less."[72] These responses, however, were few and far between. The structural injustice of segregation and racial domination that thrives without legal mandate, which is naturalized as the product of morally defensible individual choices, implicates all white citizens in the maintenance of the structure; yet these same features provide available scripts and frameworks for shielding white citizens from recognizing their moral and political culpability. Broad disavowal appears justified; civil disobedience looks illegitimate—gratuitous, irresponsible, and dangerous.

While the technique of disaggregation imposed limitations on the proper arenas for claim-making, the technique of *escalation* undercut the legitimacy of tactics by conflating disobedience with violence, and inconvenience with serious harm. *Escalation*, as a discursive strategy, relied and built on disaggregation: if the claims of Brooklyn CORE were disconnected from the (now legitimized) Southern movement, and if the arena of conflict was inappropriate (the marchers had been sent to the "wrong address"), then their tactics appeared similarly disproportionate, self-indulgent, and dangerous. While Mayor Wagner drew on the metaphor of a mugging to liken the stall-in to a "gun" pointed at the city, others were more direct in designating the stall-in an act of violence. In the statement by Senators Humphrey and Kuchel, they move quickly from a condemnation of illegal protest to a condemnation of violence: "Violence is the very antithesis of law and order," threatening the legal mechanisms necessary for securing civil rights. The stall-in (now cemented as "violent" because it was "illegal" as well as "unruly") violated the standards of decorum set by the Southern civil rights movement—a "peaceful crusade" of "good manners, forbearance, and devotion."[73]

As much as the stall-in broke with some conventions—perceived or actual—defining civil rights protest, it was as much of a stretch to call it "violent" as it was to reimagine events like Birmingham as a "peaceful crusade" that automatically won Northern sympathies because of good manners and a commitment to remain within the bounds of law. As Bob Moses argued in his speech at Stanford, the forms of force involved in the stall-in were no different from those of the sit-in:

> The principle around which you desegregated lunch counters was, you went in, sat in at those lunch counters and said to the whole town, "Either you serve me or nobody gets served." ... Now, in effect, the people who were leading the stall-ins were saying to New York City, "Either you pay attention to our very real, trying problems or nobody, nobody can function in this city, we're going to tie you up."[74]

The response of local and national politicians to the stall-in therefore required a self-serving reimagining of the tactics of the Southern movement and the federal, political response to them—transforming the disruption of the former into an unrealistic standard of decorum, and reimagining the belated, limited commitments of the latter as a consistent, thoroughgoing defense of racial equality. This, too, protected white moral standing while evading responsibility.

Escalation operated, in part, by drawing the contrast between the stall-in and the (Southern) sit-in as starkly as possible—a technique that ironically placed Brooklyn CORE in alignment with defenders of white supremacy rather than the student sit-ins. The tactics of the stall-in were likened to segregationist violence, and the inconveniences imposed by a traffic jam were akin to grave bodily harm and serious rights violations. Wagner accused the stall-in of "strengthening the forces of prejudice and discord" in New York and of doing "more harm" to the cause of civil rights than anything "the forces of bigotry can do in the city."[75] The evidence for the apparent, vengeful violence of the stall-in was suggested by the conflation of inconvenience and discomfort with the denial of fundamental rights. Tying up traffic to the World's Fair was not a means of fighting for rights; it was a means of denying them to white citizens. Humphrey's and Kuchel's formulation of "civil rights" and "civil wrongs" identified the freedom to attend a fair without being delayed by protest and the comfort of driving on a highway undeterred by traffic as precisely the kind of "rights" that could not be threatened, no matter how worthy the cause. A WLIB radio editorial offered that "the ordinary citizen, white or Negro, has the right to travel to the fair free of any harassment" and suggested that traffic can potentially cause collisions posing danger to "life and limb"—thereby making the case that the certain inconvenience represented by the stall-in amounted to an infringement of rights, and that the hypothetical car accidents that might result from a traffic jam amounted to violence.[76] Responses by politicians, editorialists, and numerous letter writers—whose opinions poured in to the CORE offices and to local and national press outlets—confirmed Brooklyn CORE's contention that under white supremacy, white comfort is safeguarded as an essential, inviolable right. "As a white who believes in civil rights," wrote Leonard Novick from Brooklyn, "I can see the Negro only hurting his chances for equality by staging these ridiculous strikes. . . . If the Negro wants his rights, he should not deprive the white man of his."[77]

The conflation of disruption with violence and convenience with a fundamental right justified a criminalized, punitive, and violent response to the World's Fair protests—those that did not take place as well as those that did. As discussed, the city moved quickly to criminalize running out of gas on the highway, imposing fines and jail time for those caught stalling-in—or simply stalling out. On opening day, police did not hesitate to wield their billy clubs freely against those caught holding subway doors open, leaving some activists beaten and bloodied. Meanwhile, some letters to the editor— many from white citizens, as well as a few from black citizens—detailed their own suggestions for an appropriate response by the state and by law enforcement: "If this madness ever materializes," one individual from Queens who identified as only "FED UP" wrote, "I suggest that all participants be herded into paddy wagons on charges of unlawful assembly, illegal detainment of people trying to travel, disturbing the peace, loitering, inciting to riot, and being plain fools."[78] Some imagined darker consequences and felt free to issue threats of sweeping racial violence. Henry Frederick wrote to CORE in mid-April to insist that if "the colored people of Brooklyn want to be and act like parasites," then "they should be exterminated."[79] Another individual, who identified herself as Lorna Jenkins, "a <u>Real Negro</u>," suggested in a postcard to CORE that all cars caught stalling-in should be impounded for a year, with $500 fines imposed on the drivers. Those found for delaying subway travel "of decent peoples" should be put in jail for "1 year and a day." She filled in the return address space with a personal note for the activists of Brooklyn CORE: "Your abuse should have received horse whipping on each & every one of you rats."[80]

Jenkins's angry response—her impulse to criminalize and punish CORE's protest—may be surprising. Yet as Mills argues, the epistemic context of white supremacy forms the perceptions of *all* citizens, not only white citizens.[81] Even so, the stakes of protecting white ignorance differ markedly for white and nonwhite citizens. Playwright Lorraine Hansberry's account of her own reaction to the stall-in is instructive here. As she told an audience on June 15, 1964: "I was in a bit of a stew over the stall-in, because when the stall-in was first announced, I said, 'Oh, My God, now everybody's gone crazy, you know, tying up traffic. What's the matter with them? You know. Who needs it?'" She explained that her initial negative reaction was linked to her social position and upbringing—being part of "a generation of Negroes that comes after a whole lot of other generations" to finally join the ranks of the upper middle class. She described her father as a "real 'American' type American: successful businessman, very civic-minded," who worked his way up and fought through the courts for his family's right to live in Washington Park, a Southside Chicago neighborhood with a racially restrictive covenant.[82] His efforts exemplified for Hansberry "the way of struggling that everyone says is the proper way to do it." Feeling protective of that struggle and its hard-won but fragile achievements, the stall-in frightened and exasperated her; it seemed to violate the way things ought to be done. But Hansberry indicated that her initial reaction was transformed as she watched the reaction from white liberals in Washington, DC and New York, typified in the recurrent, threatening warning: "'You Negroes act right or you're going to ruin everything we're trying to do.'" She contemplated her father's trajectory further, and the unsatisfying fruits borne of fighting white supremacy and segregation the "proper" way:

> The problem is that Negroes are just as segregated in the city of Chicago now as they were then and my father died a disillusioned exile in another country. . . . And I wrote to the [*New York Times*] and said, you know, "Can't you understand that this is the perspective from which we are now speaking? It isn't as if we got up today and said, you know, 'what can we do to irritate America?'" . . . It's because that [*sic*] since 1619, Negroes have tried every method of communication, of transformation of their situation from petition to the vote, everything. We've tried it all. There isn't anything that hasn't been exhausted. . . . And now the charge of impatience is simply unbearable. I would like to submit that the problem is that, yes, there is a problem about white liberals.[83]

Hansberry, who like Baldwin several months prior, was participating in a town hall event on the topic of white liberals and black activism, concluded her comments by emphasizing the "different viewpoint" that comes from being "kicked in the face so often."[84] Her fear, skepticism, and anger at first hearing about the stall-in was animated by different concerns than those motivating her fellow white citizens. Her reaction was the product of knowing and seeing the things that white citizens evaded, avoided, and disavowed. She knew her own material comfort and social standing were precarious, contingent on the whims of a white public that did not like being confronted. As she later remarked in her journal, reflecting on the "explosive" conversation during the town hall, "Negroes are so angry and white people are so confused and sensitive to criticism."[85]

Hansberry's shorthand summary of the predominant response to the stall-in by liberal politicians—"act right or you're going to ruin everything we're trying to do"—aptly characterizes the third technique of disavowal: *disqualification*. Disqualification reaffirms the speaker's commitments to the goals of civil rights protest, and it expresses dismay that the current (violent, outrageous, inappropriate) tactics disqualify those ends and those who wield them. The use of means such as the stall-in give good reason *not* to address the issues of employment, housing, education, or police brutality because the actors demanding redress do not have the moral standing to make demands at all—their actions prove it. In a democracy, public policy cannot respond to a threat; progress on civil rights depends on the ability of black citizens to perform civility, restraint, and decorum.

What white letter writers expressed with explicitly racist vitriol, liberal politicians like Wagner, Humphrey, and Kuchel phrased more delicately.

Wagner affirmed his understanding of the "deep-seated resentments" of his "fellow New Yorkers of the Negro race." He emphasized how hard he tried to "put myself in the place of these people who have these feelings" and how much progress New York City had made in pursuing civil rights—more, he said, than any other city. Then he issued a warning: illegal, "irresponsible" tactics that interfere "with the right of public access to homes, hospitals, places of work and the use of public highways" will halt the progress being made—serving as a "handicap and brake upon our efforts." The only way to move forward was to respond "to need and not to threats"—and he would be the arbiter of such needs.[86] Humphrey and Kuchel positioned themselves similarly: no matter the "long suffered indignities," there was no excuse for breaking the law and causing public disruption. Most outrageously, these protests got in the way of the real, substantive fight for civil rights taking place in Congress: "No one can condone a violation of law. The main reason we are advocating the civil rights bill is because too many states and too many individuals are defying the law of our Constitution and are denying the constitutional rights to our fellow citizens." Civil disobedience, in other words, cannot achieve its stated ends. "Indeed," Humphrey and Kuchel concluded, such protests "are hurting our efforts in Congress to pass an effective civil rights bill."[87]

The technique of disqualification erased black agency and denied the efficacy of protest. What Wagner, Humphrey, and Kuchel seemed to suggest was that black citizens were not actually the primary agents in the fight for their own freedom. The civil rights bill—which Humphrey and Kuchel particularly affirmed as the essence of the struggle—had little to do with the civil disobedience in the streets. At best, disobedience represented a distant moral drama (playing out in the backward South, and confirming American exceptionalism by identifying the exception that proved the rule). At worst, it amounted to a grievous violation of the real work of securing civil rights (endangering a white right to convenience in the progressive North, where "real" racist violence and "real" segregation were not a problem). Brooklyn CORE should leave civil rights in the capable hands of the experts: the process must an orderly, legislative one, and white politicians should be at the helm.

Taken together, the techniques of disaggregation, escalation, and disqualification served to fully legitimate a dismissive, punitive, and paternalistic attitude toward the stall-in: its tactics deserved nothing short of disdain, and its demands could not truly be serious given the tactics. It was a satisfying and comforting message—a reassurance that there was nothing of substance to see in the stall-in, and nothing to be learned from the insistence that all white Americans bore direct responsibility for racial injustice. White citizens really were innocent, after all; they really were good people, with sound moral commitments to equality and justice. The world was fair, or fair enough; and all was as it should be.

The Fantasy of Progress

What might politicians, spectators, and "innocent bystanders" see in the stall-in, were they to see it otherwise? What might we see in it, if we look at it again, adopting—for the moment—a willingness to see it as Brooklyn CORE activists might have? After all, if the New York World's Fair seemed to break with an established pattern of civil rights protest venues, it nevertheless offered no shortage of reasons—from the practical to the purely symbolic—to think it an obvious choice for a CORE demonstration. First, it is not exactly accurate to say that civil rights groups had no claim of discrimination against the Fair or that the Fair had no power to bring about the desired reforms—particularly in the area of employment. Several civil rights groups, including the NAACP, had been battling Robert Moses since the early days of Fair development over black and Puerto Rican employment, to which Moses reacted in a manner quite familiar to civil rights activists across the country: by dismissing them as the bogus claims of agitators and "professional integrationists," which he would not or could not address.[88] The Fair was also a five-year-long public works project of unprecedented scale, requiring the cooperation and manpower of the unionized building trades—the same industry that Brooklyn CORE and other New York groups had been struggling in vain to integrate.[89]

However, it was the symbolic power of the Fair and the image of the future it projected—not just their direct discrimination claims against the unions, nor the undoubted potential of the Fair as a media event—that captured the activists' attention. The New York City chapters of CORE had been struggling for years to make the reality of life in the ghettos of Bedford-Stuyvesant, Harlem, and other impoverished black and Puerto Rican neighborhoods visible to the rest of the city's residents through rent strikes, school boycotts, and protests at construction sites—not to mention the garbage dumps at the Triborough Bridge and, a year earlier, Borough Hall.[90] The Fair presented a perfect opportunity: as Herbert Callendar of the Bronx chapter of CORE explained: "The World's Fair portrays an image of peace, tranquility and progress—the American dream. We want to show that there is also an American nightmare of the way Negroes have to live in this country."[91] In fact, despite the difference over the specifics of strategy, this is precisely the kind of appeal made by National CORE in the leaflets and literature it generated for its own World's Fair pickets, which offered up the contrast between the "real world of discrimination and brutality" endured by black Americans and the "fantasy world of progress and abundance" on display at the Fair.

Indeed, it is hard not to appreciate the perfect irony of creating a traffic jam as a protest of Robert Moses's Fair. Moses: the man who believed cities should be "created by and for traffic" and who wasn't afraid to bulldoze a few neighborhoods to prove it; mastermind and architect behind New York's congested highway system; and urban planner most notoriously associated with the dubious "urban renewal" and "slum clearance" programs of the 1950s (termed "Negro removal" by James Baldwin).[92] As Robert Caro writes in his famed biography of Moses, *The Power Broker*: "To build his highways, Moses threw out of their homes 250,000 persons—more people than lived in Albany, or Chattanooga, or in Spokane, Tacoma, Duluth, Akron, Baton Rouge, Mobile, Nashville, or Sacramento. He tore out the hearts of a score of neighborhoods."[93] On its own, the World's Fair earned an early reputation for being the sort of traffic disaster to which the stall-in could only aspire, thanks to construction on the fairgrounds and the surrounding highways. *Time* magazine claimed that, by 1962, the Fair was renowned mostly for the "bumper-to-bumper embolisms" caused by the highway expansion project, turning Queens into "the world's biggest parking lot" at a cost of hundreds of millions of dollars.[94] Even after construction had been completed, the Fair was automobile- and highway-centric, angling for middle-class patrons coming in by car.[95]

Inside the fairgrounds, what would be criticized as the "Hard-Sell Fair"—a place defined by its "tacky, plastic, here-today-blown-tomorrow look, as if it were a city made of credit cards"—made the contrast between the American dream and its nightmare shadow more spectacularly visible. Due to a conflict between Moses and the Paris-based organization that officially sanctioned World's Fairs, most European nations opted not to participate in the 1964–1965 Fair. Consequently, Moses sold the most prominent pavilion spaces at the Queens site to corporations, not countries. Moses's Fair was a celebration of an infinitely consumable—but ultimately disposable—world: its dozens of buildings were made to last two years and no longer, before being demolished at a considerable cost. There, General Electric's "Carousel of Progress" celebrated the conquering of the home by household electronics while the Ford Motor Company's "Magic Skyway" took patrons on a journey from "the world that was" to the "world that will be" via Mustang convertible. And, most poignant of all, at the Fair's most popular exhibit, General Motors' Futurama, spectators witnessed the wonder of a highway-ringed "City of Tomorrow," a "utopian metropolis" free from "slums or parking problems," while in a far-off jungle, a "road-builder" brought "progress and prosperity" by clear-cutting forests while leaving an elevated highway in its wake.[96]

Denizens of neighborhoods marked for "urban renewal" might well have recognized the "road builder" as none other than Robert Moses—though, in their experience, prosperity was not forthcoming, and slums remained very much a reality. And so with the entirety of the future according to the World's Fair: it represented a temporality of present and future progress both out of step with the reality of inequality in 1964 America, and simultaneously implicated in it. This is a central reason the stall-in was as controversial, divisive, and upsetting as it was: it threatened to interrupt a certain imaginary of progress, democracy, and freedom (wide open as the highway, headed toward the infinite horizon) with the perpetually, systemically stalled reality of racial injustice, in which there were no innocent bystanders.

By its own design, the Fair was meant to represent, exhibit, predict and promote. It hocked visions of progress as product-placement and spoke in the honeyed tones of a 646-acre advertisement for better living—a slum-less, traffic-free and strangely un-peopled city of the future, all in the midst of the slum-ridden, traffic-clogged, and population-dense New York City of the present. In the midst of this tableau, more than a few snapshots offer themselves up as perfect metaphorical encapsulations of the moment—of the Fair or its host city, of civil rights and race relations, of white America in the mid-1960s, working overtime to maintain its idea of itself. But for this particular story about the clash between the America packaged and sold by the Fair and the one prevented from protesting at its gates, few can compare to the animatronic Abraham Lincoln standing in the Illinois Pavilion.

Designed and created by the Walt Disney Corporation specifically for the World's Fair, and at Robert Moses's urging, a mechanical simulacrum of the Great Emancipator was not only summoned from beyond the grave but was also reincarnated a Cold War liberal. During the 1964 and 1965 seasons, spectators at "Great Moments with Mr. Lincoln" watched with amazement as a stunningly life-like Lincoln rose from his seat, turned his head ever so slightly, and delivered some sober words of wisdom—a short oration on liberty stitched together from excerpts of several different speeches. He began his speech thus: "The world has never had a good definition of the word liberty, and the American people, just now, are much in want of one. We all declare for liberty; but in using the same word we do not all mean the same thing."[97] These words, from an 1864 speech Lincoln gave in Baltimore, are true enough to history—at least if your main concern is that Lincoln actually said them. But context matters, and in this case the words left out of the mechanical Lincoln's speech are far from incidental. The human Lincoln, the historical Lincoln, speaking in the midst of the Civil War and on the heels of the massacre of black troops and their officers at Fort Pillow, went on to explain his reflections on the meaning of liberty in the following terms, redacted from the World's Fair rendition:

> The shepherd drives the wolf from the sheep's throat, for which the sheep thanks the shepherd as *liberator*, while the wolf denounces him for the same act as the destroyer of liberty, especially as the sheep was a black one. Plainly the sheep and the wolf are not agreed upon a definition of the word liberty; and precisely the same difference prevails to-day among us human creatures, even in the North, and all professing to love liberty. Hence we behold the processes by which thousands are daily passing from under the yoke of bondage, hailed by some as the advance of liberty, and bewailed by others as the destruction of all liberty. Recently . . . the wolf's dictionary has been repudiated.[98]

The full speech performed at the show was free of any reference to slavery and the American racial order. Instead, the Fair's Lincoln cautioned his 1964 audience of the dangers of enemies within, exhorted fierce reverence for the rule of law, and urged steadfastness in the face of "false accusations" and the "menaces of destruction." Strung together just so, Lincoln's words were a salve to the troubled Cold War mind—a firm endorsement of staying the course, and a reassurance against the legitimacy of the tumult in the streets.[99]

Confronted with this strange, transhistorical robot, I cannot help but compound one metaphor with another to recall the image of the mechanical Turk that opens Walter Benjamin's "Theses on the Philosophy of History." Benjamin's automaton is dressed like a Turkish chess player and controlled by a "wizened" master chess player, a dwarf hidden from view through an optical illusion. The game is rigged; the automaton is "to win each time" by selling his opponent the idea of progressive time: reason made perfect through human history, and a future triumphant, unburdened by the wreckage of past and present. This is, of course, the dream of Moses's Fair, Disney's Lincoln, and mid-century American liberalism. But it is also a myth. "[A] storm is blowing from Paradise," Benjamin tells us later in Thesis IX—a storm that propels the "angel of history" headlong "into a future to which his back is turned, while the pile of debris before him grows skyward. This storm is what we call progress."[100] This is the poignant lesson urged by the stall-in protest that never was: what is called progress has been, in some not-so-distant corners of the polity, just outside the fairgrounds, as a matter of fact—a human disaster. The "pile of debris" left by CORE on the Triborough Bridge and on the steps of Borough Hall appears, no less than the stall-in, was one small attempt to make visible that fact, to force a confrontation with it. As Benjamin suggests, we ignore it at our own peril.

Despite President Johnson's (no doubt) earnest words at the opening ceremonies—forecasting for the future America an "[unwillingness] to accept public deprivation in the midst of private satisfaction"—the Fair itself seemed to speak more loudly of white citizens' willingness, and even eagerness, to do just that. Reverend Milton Galamison—in whose church pews activists solidified plans for the stall-in—perhaps said it best, in a sermon several weeks after the Fair's lackluster opening day. Recounting President Johnson's speech about the sweeping progress represented by the Fair, Galamison wondered aloud what kind of progress the president might have in mind: "Several hundred young people from across the country were arrested for demonstrating inside the fair. Several youngsters were arrested and brutalized by police for sitting on the subway track. But there stood the President talking about progress." Perhaps, Galamison mused, Johnson was referring to the technological marvels inside the fairgrounds—the "new telephones with push-button dialing" or "the automobiles of tomorrow" or a new kind of "sun-tan lotion" on display. "Whatever he was talking about he was not speaking the same languages as the hundreds of people who gathered at the fair to protest and to go to jail."[101] What does progress mean if it is built on the backs of the dominated? What is the value of consumer comfort if it depends on racialized immiseration? Why should black citizens feel invested in a future that does not see or include them—that is premised on continued commitments to not seeing and not knowing the wreckage of racial hierarchy? These were Galamison's questions, and they were Brooklyn

CORE's, too. "Obviously," Galamison emphasized, "in alluding to the scientific wonders of the fair the president was talking about what we *have*. The demonstrators were trying to call attention to what we *are*. There is an instructive difference."[102]

It is this difference that the techniques of disavowal deftly reject—avoiding an uncomfortable encounter with the everyday rule of racial hierarchy and its segregated epistemologies, shielding the order that is from the one that might be.

Epilogue

To Build a New World

Two Fires

The trouble started late on the evening of June 16, 1964, when members of the Ku Klux Klan set fire to a church outside of Philadelphia, Mississippi. Mount Zion Church was slated to host one of many new "freedom schools" across the state—grassroots institutions designed to empower and organize local black youth through an alternative curriculum focused on black history, civic education, and nonviolent resistance.[1] Hoping to salvage their early progress in the area, two CORE organizers—James Chaney and Michael Schwerner—traveled to Neshoba County to check in with the Mount Zion parish and secure housing for project volunteers. What happened next is well-known: Chaney, Schwerner, and Andrew Goodman, a summer volunteer who had accompanied them on the trip, found themselves in the hands of the local sheriff, and promptly thereafter, the Klan. When they failed to call their local headquarters that night, the CORE staff knew to expect the worst.[2]

It was six weeks before the FBI located their bodies, buried deep in an earthen dam on a local farm. Goodman and Schwerner, both white New Yorkers, had each been shot once in the head; Chaney, black and from nearby Meridian, had been subjected to a brutal beating and castration before being shot three times. As the lynching of three young civil rights workers drew national attention and prompted intense public outcry, the federal government and the FBI continued to insist there was nothing they could do to protect civil rights workers in the South. Meanwhile, activists wondered if the bodies of their fellow organizers would have been found at all had Schwerner and Goodman not been middle class and white. It was a devastatingly reasonable question: in the midst of the investigation, the FBI stumbled across the bodies of eight additional black victims, including a fourteen-year old by wearing a CORE T-shirt, whose disappearance and likely murder had generated no such national outrage and prompted no serious investigation.[3] The conjunction of these gruesome deaths with the passage of the Civil Rights Act—what should have been a key moment of victory in a decades-long nonviolent struggle—only exacerbated the anger and frustration on the ground. Speaking at the Oxford Union later that year, Malcolm X summed up a pervasive mood among many civil rights activists: "Civil rights bill down the drain. No matter how many bills pass, black people in that country, where I'm from, still our lives are not worth two cents. And the government has shown its inability, or either its unwillingness to do whatever is necessary to protect life and property where the black American is concerned."[4]

One month to the day after Mount Zion burned to the ground, and more than a 1,000 miles away, the death of Jerome Powell at the hands of police set Harlem and Bedford-Stuyvesant ablaze with the "fire this time." Powell, a fifteen-year-old African American from the Bronx, was shot three times by Lieutenant Thomas Gilligan, a white police officer, off-duty and in plain clothes, as Powell exited an apartment building on the Upper East Side. Powell died instantly, and as a crowd gathered and police sent in scores of reinforcements, tensions mounted. What followed was a week of sustained protests across Harlem and Bed-Stuy, as hundreds gathered daily to demand that the police and the mayor's office hold Gilligan accountable, all the while suspecting—correctly, it turned out—that they would not. Civil rights organizations attempted to channel the fury of the crowds into nonviolent protest. The day of Powell's funeral, CORE transformed a previously scheduled event—a rally demanding federal action in response to the disappearance of Chaney, Schwerner, and Goodman in Mississippi—into a protest demanding justice for Powell. Yet this event, like others, turned riotous as police responded to crowds with a toxic mix of aggression and panic, compounding the initial incident of police brutality with manifold others, while calling up the now infamous images of Southern law and order.[5] As one leaflet that circulated during CORE's July 18 protest put it, "we don't have to go to Mississippi because Mississippi is here in New York."[6] After six days, police reported nearly 500 arrests, millions of dollars in property damage, and twenty-some injured officers. They failed to report the numbers of civilian casualties.[7]

These events profoundly shook activists' faith in nonviolent direct action. "What was the point," Brian Purnell asks, summarizing the dilemma that groups like Brooklyn CORE found themselves in, "of using nonviolent, direct-action protest to win access to jobs, housing, and quality public education if power brokers in government and unions turned a blind eye and a deaf ear or blamed black people's culture and behavior for causing the very social and economic conditions civil rights activists sought to change?"[8] What was the point when law enforcement or deputized white citizens could still kill black citizens with impunity? What could civil disobedience really do, in this context? It seemed neither enough to force the government to safeguard black life nor to spur the kind of thoroughgoing transformation that would be required to secure black liberation. The dramatic violence produced by the tactics of disruption and disclosure had not been sufficient to force a full ethical and political reckoning, and the deadly violence produced by white supremacy showed no signs of abating.[9] In myriad ways, the techniques of disavowal helped the white public sever the connections between New York City and Mississippi, while contributing to a growing political backlash against the forms of dissent that targeted both. The time for civil rights disobedience seemed to be coming to an end.

The shift from civil rights to Black Power, from integration to self-determination, and from civil disobedience to self-defense is often marked with the turn to colonialism as the interpretive frame for naming white supremacy in the United States. In their 1967 book *Black Power: The Politics of Liberation,* Kwame Ture (Stokely Carmichael) and Charles Hamilton famously argued that "black people in this country form a colony, and it is not in the interest in the colonial power to liberate them."[10] While acknowledging that the metaphor was an imperfect one—there is no distant metropole; the mode of capitalist extraction is focused on labor, not raw materials; black Americans are citizens with formal legal rights—for Ture and Hamilton, as for a growing number of black activists in the mid- to late-1960s, the idea of internal colonialism still captured the essentially oppressive and exploitative relations that defined the American racial order. Whatever the imperfections of the metaphor, the power of the "internal colony" was in the way it renewed connections to decolonial projects across the globe—animating a new imaginative geography that linked the US to Cuba, China, Vietnam, and Palestine, and suggesting alternative means of struggle. In this context, Black Power activists contended that nonviolence was too easily co-opted as a technique of colonial management: white citizens and political powerholders demanded black nonviolence without thinking twice about wielding violent repression themselves; they demanded civility while acceding to only the most token reforms; and they stood ready to criminalize, punish, and incarcerate activists who refused this bargain. While the praxis of Black Power did not necessarily mean—to all who cultivated it—armed rebellion or guerilla warfare, Ture and Hamilton were clear about the exhausted potential of dramatic displays of nonviolent protest. White Americans had proven themselves, time and again, incapable "of the shame which might become a revolutionary emotion."[11] Consequently, nonviolence would only propagate the idea that there was little risk to maintaining a racist order: "Those of us who advocate Black Power are quite clear in our minds that a 'non-violent' approach to civil rights is an approach black people cannot afford and a luxury white people do not deserve. It is crystal clear to us—and it must become so with the white society—*that there can be no social order without social justice.*" In fighting for social justice, there must be a credible threat to "fight back."[12]

Indeed, by the middle of the decade, the mainstream, public discourse around civil disobedience was already working to subsume black struggle into a narrative of American exceptionalism, as events like the March on Washington and the Birmingham campaign became part of the techniques of disavowal—a way to discipline activists who appeared to defy the given script for properly civil protest. The dismantling of the formal, legal architecture of Jim Crow—which was only a part of what activists were fighting for—was made to stand in for the whole of transformation, as liberal politicians declared victory and demanded an end to the unrest, lecturing black Americans not to appear ungrateful for what they had been given. In this conjuncture, Ture and Hamilton may have been right that civil disobedience had become too enmeshed in efforts to *resist* transformation to remain (in that moment) a meaningful practice of fighting for it. But it is important for us, as readers nearly sixty years removed, to recognize the distinction between the successful co-optation of civil disobedience and its lived histories. Civil rights disobedience was borne of the connections between anticolonial struggles across the world, and it was never about quiescence or preserving the social order.

Seeing Like an Activist

Extending out of a longer history of imaginative transit within and across a world of anticolonial movements, the activists of the short civil rights movement constructed a vibrant practice of civil disobedience as a means of decolonizing America's white democracy. The United States shared with all colonial contexts a system of rule based on the political disempowerment, economic exploitation, and ritual degradation of a racialized population—a system held in place by fear and violence. Fear and violence acculturated the oppressed into fatalism and acquiescence; fear and violence acculturated the oppressors into blindness, denial, and false superiority. But the American settler colony was also a specific context, presenting particular problems, in that the work of decolonization would have to transform white citizens rather than expel them. They, too, as a significant numerical majority, needed to be a part of an emancipatory future; but they could not contribute to building that future unless they allowed themselves to be transformed in the process.

The enactment of civil disobedience, in its courageous defiance, in its displays of solidarity, and in its symbolic *and* material power, offered a means of self-emancipation—a way of remaking the colonized self in the very spaces that most viscerally defined the problem of colonization: spaces of incarceration and confinement, spaces of racial terror and control, spaces of routine humiliation and deference. At the same time, civil disobedience would do its decolonizing work outwardly, on white structures, relations, and persons: intervening in practices of domination, disrupting daily functioning, arresting public attention, and disclosing the otherwise ignored realities of systemic, violent, racial rule, so that white citizens were forced to confront their complicity. Given white psychic and material investments in hierarchy, activists knew that any form of defiance would meet with resistance, and likely violent resistance. Yet, guided by the example of nonviolence as a tool of anticolonial liberation abroad, civil disobedience offered a means of using the inevitability of this violence against itself. The provocation of civil disobedience, met with a disproportionate and brutal reaction, would reveal white rule to itself—shattering the veneer of democratic legitimacy and moral integrity that stabilized the political life of the white state.

Civil rights activists devised their plans and enacted their strategies with aspirations of emancipation and transformation, animated by the possibility that collective action could change the world. Tellingly, they did not frame civil disobedience as a problem of justification: *Under what conditions is it legitimate for democratic citizens to break the law in protest?* As I have argued, the framework of justification presumes that a legitimate, defensible order already exists where one does not; it imagines dissenters as citizens who enjoy recognition as equal members. They are speakers and actors whose words and deeds are legible, audible, and cognizable within the idioms and frames of the system as it exists. Their disobedience critiques injustice, and in so doing, stabilizes an already extant (though imperfect) liberal democracy.

Approaching the problem of civil disobedience in this manner, therefore, aids in the discursive work that secures white supremacy by obscuring it behind the language and logics of a democracy. In contrast, civil rights activists saw that a legitimate, democratic order had yet to be built, and envisioned their activism as the bridge leading from the world they inhabited to the one they desired. As inhabitants of a system of racial hierarchy, they lacked status as equal members; their action had to do the work of constructing a new set of social relations, free from domination. "I think when we talk about growing up in a better world, a new world," one SNCC activist told Howard Zinn, "we mean changing the world to a different place."[13]

Building this world was not only about the systems of control and domination that structured the United States but also about contesting the global order of white supremacy by targeting its local (but linked) instantiations. Seeing civil disobedience like a white state—or, perhaps more accurately, like a white democracy—severs the work of activism in the United States from contexts that political theorists and political scientists alike categorize separately: authoritarian regimes, colonial states, and other "non-democracies." As we have seen, this not only bolsters an account of racial injustice in the United States as a limited, aberrational problem readily fixable within constitutional democracy's existing normative and legal resources; it also fractures the imaginative geographies constructed by activists in transit, denying that there is anything to be learned from the more expansive ways activists envisioned the problem and its place in the world. As Loubna El Amine has recently argued, this bifurcated world—liberal democracies, versus everywhere else—refuses "the idealism of a solidarity that extends beyond the borders of one country, to encompass, if only indirectly, other peoples with similar fights."[14] In other words, it not only distorts interpretations of the activists of the past and the ties of solidarity they constructed; it also constricts present-day capacities for discerning and participating in such solidaristic efforts in the contemporary moment. As with the ties between Jim Crow and colonialism, the links activists forge between Occupy Wall Street and Tahrir Square, or between Indigenous water protectors at Standing Rock, Black Lives Matter in Ferguson, and the fight for a free Palestine, are not just incidental facts about these struggles, irrelevant to the normative interpretation of activism across disconnected contexts.[15] Approaching protest as a matter of justification often fails to ask what activists are *doing* when they connect their own fights to those of others across the world—what kind of political theories and analyses they are bringing to bear on the world, and what kinds of worlds they are bringing into being through such imaginative transit.

As an alternative practice of political theorizing, seeing like an activist does not mean uncritically adopting the frameworks, perspectives, or claims of activists as our own. Instead, it encourages a more capacious understanding of the creative work of theorizing—attending to the ways that the perceptual and interpretive categories of political life are themselves produced in action and in specific material contexts, exploring the connections between the practices of academic theorizing and the discursive work of maintaining (or challenging) structures of domination, and interrogating the uncritical performances of power that categorize some as producers of knowledge and others as its objects—or its raw materials. "Social movements generate new knowledge, new theories, new questions," as Robin D. G. Kelley has eloquently observed. "The most radical ideas often grow out of a concrete intellectual engagement with the problems of aggrieved populations confronting systems of oppression." This is fundamentally an imaginative, contentious, and collaborative practice of political theorizing—one that can enliven and challenge academic practices of thinking as much as our own sense of the possible. As Kelley continues: "We must remember that the conditions and the very existence of social movements enable participants to imagine something different, to realize that things need not always be this way."[16]

This shifted perspective likewise reveals the limitations that troubled activists' visions. In imagining the dramatic, disclosive, and disruptive work of civil disobedience as a means of combatting white ignorance and eliciting white transformation, civil rights activists underestimated the depth of white ideological identification with, and material investment in, their own supremacy. The early, heady successes of civil rights disobedience in staging explosive confrontations were aided by the very discursive techniques that would frustrate their potential: the construction of the South as a separate, exceptional space; the idealized vision of nonviolent activism as bound by existing norms of civility; the constriction of vision that rendered a demand for democratic decolonization as a plea for constitutional reform. Seeing civil disobedience like activists helps us take account of the shortcomings of the frameworks they devised and exposes the enormity of the unfinished work left in the movement's wake. As Juliet Hooker has argued, "the failure of the victories gained by the civil rights movement to eliminate structural disparities in wealth and the criminal justice system raise important questions about the limited ability of liberal democracy to truly address racial justice."[17]

Given those failures, demanding repeated, heroic displays of nonviolent suffering from black activists perpetrates a double harm: transforming a history of defiant resistance into a demand for peaceful acquiescence and well-mannered petitioning, while requiring that "those who have already suffered the lion's share of the losses inflicted by racism" continue to suffer still more, as the price for a white moral awakening that may never materialize.[18] One path out of this impasse, Hooker suggests, is to reconstruct the struggles of the past in different terms (as I have tried to do here), not to provide a new model that can be imposed on the present, but to allow us to think more expansively about defiant protest as a practice of liberation—one that appears dangerous or uncivil precisely in the moment when it challenges, rather than reaffirms, liberal democracy's bounds.

The Past in the Present

Faced with racial politics in the United States in the decade of Black Lives Matter—amidst successive waves of protest spurred by the deaths of a series of unarmed black men, women, and children at the hands of police officers and deputized white citizens "standing their ground"—we might be forgiven for giving into the unsettling sensation that history is repeating itself. In the days, weeks, and months following the fatal police shooting of Michael Brown, an unarmed black teenager shot by a white police officer in Ferguson, Missouri, in August 2014, protestors took to the streets insisting that "Black Lives Matter"—and stirring a renewed national debate about race, police brutality, and the persistence of the kinds of inequalities (political, social, economic) the civil rights movement of the 1960s aimed to transform. As protestors in Ferguson clashed with heavily armed police forces, the optics of the struggle evoked a past that was never fully or safely past. Iconic scenes from the civil rights movement appeared anew in Ferguson— the spectacle of a mostly white police force, armed to the teeth, facing off against black protestors demanding redress for yet another death; the police dogs used as crowd control. Ferguson was Birmingham in 1963, Ferguson was Harlem in 1964, Ferguson was Watts in 1965.[19] In June 2020 it was happening again, after a video showing Derek Chauvin, a white Minneapolis police officer, knelt for eight full minutes on the neck of a black man, George Floyd, while he pleaded, begged for air, and called out for his deceased mother. Amid a gathering crowd screaming for Chauvin to stop, Floyd died, repeating the last words of Eric Garner, another black man killed by police six years earlier: "I can't breathe."[20] When mass protests erupted in Minneapolis and subsequently in cities and towns across the entire country, the familiar comparisons returned: it was 1964, 1965, or 1968 again.[21] The past was back; the past had never gone away.

Such comparisons capture a powerful sense of temporal doubling—the sinking suspicion that the 1960s are happening again and again, and that reports of Jim Crow's death have been greatly exaggerated. A multitude of contemporary realities seem to speak to an America stalled in time, from intransigent residential and educational segregation, to persistent gaps in income and wealth between black and white Americans, to the police brutality and disregard for black life on evidence in cities and towns across the country. But for all the connections between the past and the present, the idea of repetition—of being exactly where we were, and thus of seeing exactly the same protests we have seen—can be politically dangerous. Ironically, it seems to suggest both an ahistorical permanence to the structures of racial domination (they never change) while also counseling a return to civil rights protest as the sure solution (it is always enough). Indeed, when protests in Ferguson escalated into violence in the fall of 2014, Eric Holder—then U.S. attorney general—was not the first of many to draw on the shared civil rights past to counsel nonviolence: "I would remind demonstrators of our history that . . . the way in which we have made progress in this country is when we have seen peaceful, nonviolent demonstrators that has led to the change that has been the most long lasting and the most pervasive."[22] The same script played out in 2020, as political figures across party lines called on protestors to live up to the "spirit" and the "legacy" of Martin Luther King, Jr. and Rosa Parks.[23]

What political visions—indeed, what *futures*—are ruled out by insisting, over and over again, that today's activists perform an endless repetition of civil rights protest—particularly its most *civil*-ized, *domestic*-ated version? The activists and organizers of the contemporary Movement for Black Lives are not replicators of a civil rights template; they work both *within* and *against* a lineage of black struggle. They live and act in tension with it. As Charlene Carruthers, national director of the Black Youth Project 100 (BYP100), explains: "Activists love and hate the civil rights movement and its best-known strategies. We groan at the idea of 'another march' but will call for mass mobilizations in the aftermath of the killing of one of our own. . . . We love and hate to dig into histories. As Black people, there's so much to love and hate from our histories. Regardless, they are ours. Acknowledging and wrestling with all they entail not only advances our knowledge; they also give us the juice we need to secure our collective liberation."[24] Carruthers calls for a more expansive history—multiplying the stories told about a black radical past, and the critical perspectives those stories take—to ground, inform, and inspire organizing and activist strategies today.

But she also points to the ways in which the lessons of this history must be "reimagined," not just "revived," in order to speak to the specificity of the present context. "Black people are living under the heels of a neoliberal state, a global crisis of capitalism, and further entrenchment of anti-Blackness through policy and culture alike," Carruthers writes. The structure of today's racial regime is the product of the past, not a frozen replica of it. "It is a time of unprecedented levels of state surveillance, unequal and questionable definitions of terrorism, and an obscene expansion of the military-industrial context"—conditions that have arisen since the 1960s, and which were in some ways constructed to demobilize and contain the multitude of uprisings against racism, capitalism, and colonialism that arose during the decade.[25] The New Deal order, with its limited but real social welfare provisions, has been thoroughly racialized and hollowed out—associated with "handouts" for undeserving minoritized populations to justify extreme retrenchment. Rampant privatization has come hand in hand with the construction of an intensified carceral state: expanded surveillance, militarized policing, and mass incarceration, overwhelmingly targeting impoverished and racialized communities.[26] At the same time, the existence of a real black political elite in cities across the country speaks to the uniqueness of a post-civil rights racial order, in which high-profile, individualized black achievement masks pervasive, structural disparities. "When a Black mayor, governing a largely Black city, aids in the mobilization of a military unit led by a Black woman to suppress a Black rebellion," Keeanga-Yamahtta Taylor observes, "we are in a new period of the Black freedom struggle."[27]

The decolonizing praxis of the civil rights movement responded, imaginatively and imperfectly, to the structural realities of mid-twentieth-century white supremacy as activists saw them. The current moment demands no less: an activist praxis that assesses, reveals, and confronts the present. In the spirit of not just reviving but also actively *reimagining* the bounds of the tradition, the activists that make up the diverse coalition within the Movement for Black Lives have refused the bargain that earlier activists like King and Farmer made when they disavowed rowdy black "spectators" or groups whose actions fell outside the established frame for disciplined nonviolence. Like their civil rights predecessors, today's activists have "chosen the tactic of disruption," as Patrice Khan-Cullors, co-founder of #BlackLivesMatter, put it. But they have also chosen "the tactic of challenging respectability" by legitimizing expressions of black rage and pain, by rejecting facile references to civil rights icons of the past, and by centering those who had been pushed to the margins of earlier freedom struggles by virtue of class, gender, sexuality, or criminal history.[28] They refuse the demand for perfect performances of nonviolence, for the production of "respectable" black victims, as the price of white empathy or structural redress. Ironically, then, when commentators call out the Movement for Black Lives for failing the test of civil rights civility, they are not just misconstruing the legacies of civil rights disobedience. They are also dismissing the very thing that makes the contemporary movement powerful, creative, and of its time.

The ultimate point of seeing like an activist is not, then, to simply replace one reading of civil rights disobedience (fidelity to law, or constitutional patriotism) with another (decolonizing praxis). Rather, it is to orient us toward activists as political theorists, engaged in the creative work of analyzing and acting within the present on its own terms—working in transit and in solidarity with activists across the boundaries of our existing political categories, and devising the forms of action that promise to build a new world out of the wreckage of this one.

Notes

Introduction

1. See e.g., Charles DiSalvo, "Abortion and consensus: The futility of speech, the power of disobedience," *Washington & Lee Law Review* 48 (1991): 219–234. Martin Luther King, Jr. and the civil rights movement were invoked with relative frequency in partisan congressional debates over penalizing pro-life protestors at health clinics. See Francesca Polletta, "Legacies and liabilities of an insurgent past: Remembering Martin Luther King, Jr., on the House and Senate floor," *Social Science History* 22, no. 4 (Winter 1998): 479–512.
2. See e.g., Daniel J. Wakin, "Arrest me, please (but jail? No thanks): Rediscovering the price of protest," *New York Times*, June 3, 2001, 35; "WTO protests," *Los Angeles Times*, December 3, 1999, 8; Bruce Chapman, "Fallout—What's in a name? A disservice to the truth," *Seattle Times*, December 12, 1999.
3. See e.g., Bernard Harcourt, "Political disobedience," in *Occupy: Three Inquiries in Disobedience* (Chicago: University of Chicago Press, 2013), 45–92; Daniel B. Wood & Gloria Goodales, "Does Occupy Wall Street have any leaders? Does it need any?" *Christian Science Monitor*, October 10, 2011; Herb Boyd, "OWS and the civil rights movement," *New York Amsterdam News*, November 24, 2011, 32; Gloria Browne-Marshall, "'OWS' and the civil rights movement," *Boston Banner*, December 15, 2011, 5.
4. See e.g., Jamie Chandler, "Snowden's uncivil disobedience," *US News & World Report*, June 18, 2013; Daniel Foster, "Snowden is not MLK: There is a difference between civil disobedience and lawbreaking," *The National Review*, June 13, 2013; Ruth Marcus, "Edward Snowden is no hero," *Washington Post,* July 18, 2013; Nick Cohen, "Edward Snowden shouldn't play the coward," *The Spectator*, June 24, 2013.
5. John Sexton, "Vox: Riots, arson, and shootings aside, Black Lives Matter is pretty peaceful," Breitbart.com, September 3, 2015; Brianna Ehley, "Huckabee: MLK would be 'appalled' by Black Lives Matter movement," Politico.com, August 19, 2015; Barbara Reynolds, "I was an activist in the 1960s," *Washington Post*, August 24, 2015. See also Conor Friedersdorf, "Will Black Lives Matter be a movement that persuades?" *The Atlantic*, September 24, 2015; Simone Sebastian, "Don't criticize Black Lives Matter for provoking violence," *Washington Post*, October 1, 2015.
6. Jeanne Theoharis, *A More Beautiful and Terrible History: The Uses and Misuses of Civil Rights History* (Boston: Beacon, 2018), xiv.
7. Barack Obama, remarks at the "Let Freedom Ring" ceremony commemorating the fiftieth anniversary of the March on Washington for Jobs and Freedom, August 28, 2013, Washington, D.C., online by Gerhard Peters and John T. Woolley, American Presidency Project, http://www.presidency.ucsb.edu/ws/?pid=104025.

8. Barack Obama, remarks at the fiftieth anniversary of the Selma to Montgomery marches, March 7, 2015, Selma, Alabama, https://www.whitehouse.gov/the-press-office/2015/03/07/remarks-president-50th-anniversary-selma-montgomery-marches.
9. Jacquelyn Dowd Hall, "The long civil rights movement and the political uses of the past," *Journal of American History* 91, no. 4 (March 2005): 1233.
10. Candice Delmas, *A Duty to Resist: When Disobedience Should Be Uncivil* (New York: Oxford University Press, 2018), 29.
11. Guy Aitchison, "(Un)civil disobedience," *Raisons Politiques* 1, no. 69 (2018): 7. Notable exceptions to this dynamic of centrality/marginalization include recent, excellent work on Martin Luther King, Jr.'s understanding of civil disobedience. See Barbara Allen, "Martin Luther King's civil disobedience and the American covenant tradition," *The Journal of Federalism* 30, no. 4 (Fall 2000): 71–113; William Scheuerman, "Recent theories of civil disobedience: An anti-legal turn?" *The Journal of Political Philosophy* 23, no. 4 (December 2015): 427–449; Brandon M. Terry and Tommie Shelby, eds., *To Shape a New World: Essays on the Political Philosophy of Martin Luther King, Jr.* (Cambridge and London: Belknap, 2018); James M. Patterson, "A covenant of the heart: Martin Luther King Jr., civil disobedience, and the beloved community," *American Political Thought* 7, no. 1 (Winter 2018): 124–151; Scheuerman, *Civil Disobedience* (Cambridge: Polity, 2018), Chapter 1; Alexander Livingston, "'Tough love': The political theology of civil disobedience," *Perspectives on Politics* 18, no. 3 (September 2020): 851–66; Livingtston, "Power for the powerless: Martin Luther King, Jr.'s late theory of civil disobedience," *Journal of Politics* 82, no. 2 (2020): 700–713; Erin Pineda, "Martin Luther King, Jr. and the politics of disobedient civility," in *Cambridge Companion to Civil Disobedience*, edited by William Scheuerman (New York: Cambridge University Press, 2021). While this work has undoubtedly influenced my own, there remains very little scholarly attention to the theory and practice of civil disobedience by civil rights activists *beyond* King, and in that sense the civil rights *movement* remains exceptionally marginal. This dynamic within political theory echoes the skew of an earlier era of civil rights historiography, which focused predominantly on King (and a small handful of national leaders) to the exclusion of others—particularly the thousands of grassroots activists who powered and sustained the movement.
12. Hugo Bedau, ed., *Civil Disobedience: Theory and Practice* (New York: Pegasus, 1969), 19.
13. John Rawls, "The justification of civil disobedience," in *Civil Disobedience: Theory and Practice*, 247.
14. Jürgen Habermas, "Civil disobedience: Litmus test for the democratic constitutional state," *Berkeley Journal of Sociology* 30 (1985): 109. For a critique of the ways Habermas's account fails to do justice to its own radical and emancipatory potential, see Çiğdem Çıdam, "Radical democracy without risks? Habermas on constitutional patriotism and civil disobedience," *New German Critique* 44, no. 2 (August 2017): 105–132.
15. Habermas, "Litmus test," 107–108.

16. Daniel Markovits, "Democratic disobedience," *Yale Law Journal* 114 (2005): 1897–1952.
17. William Smith, *Civil Disobedience and Deliberative Democracy* (Abingdon: Routledge, 2013), 60.
18. Smith, "Democracy, deliberation and disobedience," *Res Publica* 10, no. 4 (December 2004): 375. For other deliberative accounts of civil disobedience, see Jean Cohen and Andrew Arato, *Civil Society and Political Theory* (London: MIT Press, 1992); James Bohman, *Public Deliberation: Pluralism, Complexity, and Democracy* (Cambridge, MA: MIT Press, 2000), Chapters 3 and 5. More expansive accounts are offered by David Estlund, "Deliberation down and dirty: Must political expression by civil?," in *The Boundaries of Freedom of Expression and Order in American Democracy*, edited by Thomas R. Henley (Kent, OH: Kent State University Press, 2001), 49–67; and Archon Fung, "Deliberation before the revolution: Toward an ethics of deliberative democracy in an unjust world," *Political Theory* 33, no. 3 (June 2005): 397–419.
19. Smith, "Democracy, deliberation and disobedience," 363.
20. The phrase, of course, belongs to Habermas, *Theory and Practice*, translated by John Viertel (Boston: Beacon Press, 1988), 240.
21. My characterization of Brownlee and Celikates as offering "inclusive" accounts is indebted to Delmas, *A Duty to Resist*, Chapter 1.
22. Kimberley Brownlee, *Conscience and Conviction: The Case for Civil Disobedience* (Oxford: Oxford University Press, 2012).
23. Robin Celikates, "Rethinking civil disobedience as a practice of contestation—Beyond the liberal paradigm," *Constellations* 23, no. 1 (2016): 37. See also Celikates, "Democratizing civil disobedience," *Philosophy and Social Criticism* 42, no. 10 (2016): 982–994; Celikates, "Constituent power beyond exceptionalism: Irregular migration, disobedience, and (re)constitution," *Journal of International Political Theory* (2018): 1–15.
24. Celikates, "Rethinking civil disobedience as a practice of contestation," 39.
25. Delmas, *A Duty to Resist*, 42. For a contrasting view, arguing that "uncivil disobedience"—and in particular the use of violence in the name of democratic principles—represents a dangerous fantasy (that of eclipsing the law entirely with popular will), see Jennet Kirkpatrick, *Uncivil Disobedience: Studies in Violence in Democratic Politics* (Princeton: Princeton University Press, 2008).
26. Harcourt, "Political disobedience," 46–47. Structurally, Harcourt's argument maps onto that made by Markovits for "democratic disobedience." For a similar maneuver with respect to the categories of direct action and nonviolent action, see Smith, "Disruptive democracy: The ethics of direct action," *Raisons Politiques* 1, no. 69 (2018): 13–27; Aitchison, "Coercion, resistance, and the radical side of non-violent action," *Raisons Politiques* 1, no. 69 (2018): 45–61.
27. David Lyons, "Moral judgment, historical reality, and civil disobedience," *Philosophy & Public Affairs* 27, no. 1 (1998): 31–49; Celikates, "Rethinking civil disobedience."
28. Markovits, "Democratic disobedience," 1901.
29. Terry and Shelby, "Introduction: Martin Luther King, Jr. and political philosophy," in *To Shape a New World*, 3.

30. I take the phrase "political thinking in the streets" from Kathy Ferguson, *Emma Goldman: Political Thinking in the Streets* (Lanham, MD: Rowman & Littlefield, 2011).
31. Hall, "The long civil rights movement," 1233, 1235.
32. Though widely influential, Hall's article outlining the "long civil rights" perspective was not the first to issue this critique of the ideological uses and abuses of civil rights history. Critical race theorists such as Kimberlé Crenshaw and Derrick Bell traced the mobilization of a triumphalist legal narrative of civil rights in the 1990s. Additionally, of course, not all of the histories now included under the purview of the "long civil rights movement" came in the wake of Hall's agenda-setting article; many of those works seeking to draw attention to the labor, local, Northern (and Western), and global dimensions of the movement likewise came before. See, e.g., Nelson Lichtenstein and Robert Korstad, "Opportunities found and lost: Labor, radicals, and the early civil rights movement," *Journal of American History* 75, no. 3 (1988): 786–811; Robin D. G. Kelley, *Hammer and Hoe: Alabama Communists During the Great Depression* (Chapel Hill: University of North Carolina Press, 1990); John Dittmer, *Local People: The Struggle for Civil Rights in Mississippi* (Urbana and Chicago: University of Illinois Press, 1994); Charles Payne, *I've Got the Light of Freedom: The Organizing Tradition and the Mississippi Freedom Struggle* (Berkeley: University of California Press, 1996); Penny Von Eschen, *Race Against Empire: Black Americans and Anticolonialism, 1937–1957* (Ithaca and London: Cornell University Press, 1997); Jeanne F. Theoharis, Komozi Woodard, and Matthew Countryman, eds., *Freedom North: Black Freedom Struggles Outside the South, 1940–1980* (New York: Palgrave Macmillan, 2003); Theoharis and Woodard, eds., *Groundwork: Local Black Freedom Movements in America* (New York and London: New York University Press, 2005). On the narrativization of the civil rights movement in light of the "long civil rights movement" perspective, see Terry, "Which way to Memphis? Political theory, narrative, and the politics of historical imagination in the civil rights movement," PhD diss., Yale University, 2013.
33. Hall, "The long civil rights movement," 1234.
34. As Hall argues with reference to Mary Dudziak's work, "seen through the optic of the long civil rights movement," the emergence of the civil rights movement in the mid-1950s "looks less like a product of the Cold War and more like a casualty." See Hall, "Long civil rights movement," 1249; Mary L. Dudziak, *Cold War Civil Rights: Race and the Image of American Democracy* (Princeton: Princeton University Press, 2011).
35. See e.g., Lichtenstein and Korstad, "Opportunities found and lost"; Hall, "The long civil rights movement"; Dudziak, *Cold War Civil Rights*. For a critical appraisal of the "long civil rights movement" framework, see Eric Arnesen, "Reconsidering the 'long civil rights movement,'" *Historically Speaking* 10, no. 2 (April 2009): 31–34.
36. Shatema Threadcraft and Brandon M. Terry, "Gender trouble: Manhood, inclusion, and justice," in *To Shape a New World*, 210.
37. Thomas Holt, "The catastrophe that launched a social movement, or why did the civil rights movement begin when it did, as it did?" Unpublished manuscript (in author's possession).
38. I am thankful to anonymous reviewers at Cambridge University Press for helping me frame these questions.

39. King quoted in Birmingham Police Report, Mass meeting of ACMHR at First Baptist Church (April 8, 1963), April 10, 1963, box 13.2, coll. 268, Theophilus Eugene "Bull" Connor Papers, 1959–1963, Birmingham Public Library, Birmingham, AL (hereafter Connor Papers).
40. Kimberlé Crenshaw and Gary Peller, "Reel time/real justice," *Denver University Law Review* 70, no. 2 (1993): 289.
41. Lawrie Balfour, *Democracy's Reconstruction: Thinking Politically with W. E. B. Du Bois* (New York: Oxford University Press, 2011), 5–6.
42. As I explain in Chapter 1, this idea is a reference to, but substantial modification of, what James C. Scott means by "seeing like a state."
43. The use of a Rawlsian framework does not itself render a theorist vulnerable to seeing like a white state. Indeed, most recently, Tommie Shelby has compellingly argued that Rawls's theory of justice offers powerful resources for theorizing racial justice. Yet notably, Shelby does what Rawls did not: he centers the problem of racial hierarchy as fundamental and poses the question of justice from the perspective of the oppressed. Thus, Shelby's starting point is *not* that all citizens suffer roughly equal burdens and owe essentially equivalent duties; but that pervasive, systemic racial injustice produces significantly unequal burdens and thus different ethical obligations. See Tommie Shelby, *Dark Ghettos: Injustice, Dissent, and Reform* (Cambridge and London: Belknap, 2016).
44. David Scott, *Conscripts of Modernity: The Tragedy of Colonial Enlightenment* (Durham and London: Duke University Press, 2004), 4.
45. Rawls, "The justification of civil disobedience," 251.
46. Bernard Boxill, "The roots of civil disobedience in republicanism and slavery," in *To Shape a New World*, 58–77.
47. Jarrett Lovell, *Crimes of Dissent: Civil Disobedience, Criminal Justice, and the Politics of Conscience* (New York and London: New York University Press, 2009), 3.
48. Terry, "After Ferguson," *The Point* 10 (June 2015), https://thepointmag.com/politics/after-ferguson/.

Chapter 1

1. Michael Thelwell, "The August 28th march on Washington: The castrated giant," in his *Duties, Pleasures, and Conflicts: Essays in Struggle* (Amherst: University of Massachusetts Press, 1987), 72. Thelwell's essay first appeared in *Présence Africaine* 21, no. 49 (1964).
2. Tony Milligan, *Civil Disobedience: Protest, Justification, and the Law* (New York and London: Bloomsbury, 2013), 25. William Scheuerman likewise points to this underlying commonality across otherwise distinct philosophical interpretations of civil disobedience. As he writes, "competing models of civil disobedience, despite their sizeable disagreements, also make use of a joint conceptual language, even as they employ that language for different purposes." This language includes a common script for the actions that define civil disobedience: "*civility, conscientiousness, nonviolence,*

and *publicity*"—as well as, I would argue, an acceptance of arrest and legal punishment. Scheuerman, *Civil Disobedience* (Cambridge: Polity, 2018), 7.

3. See, for example, Daniel Markovits, "Democratic disobedience," *Yale Law Journal* 114 (2005): 1897–1952; Bernard Harcourt, "Political disobedience," *Critical Inquiry* 39, no. 1 (Autumn 2012): 33–55.
4. Goldwater cited in Michael Flamm, *Law and Order: Street Crime, Civil Unrest, and the Crisis of Liberalism in the 1960s* (New York: Columbia University Press, 2005), 33.
5. See Milton Eisenhower et al., *To Establish Justice, to Insure Domestic Tranquility: The Final Report of the National Commission on the Causes and Prevention of Violence* (Washington, DC: US GPO, 1969).
6. Eisenhower et al., *To Establish Justice*, 101–104.
7. Eisenhower et al., *To Establish Justice*, 103–104.
8. Eisenhower et al., *To Establish Justice*, 102.
9. Eisenhower et al., *To Establish Justice*, 103.
10. Jerome Skolnick, *The Politics of Protest: Violent Aspects of Protest and Confrontation, a Staff Report to the National Commission on the Causes and Prevention of Violence* (Washington, DC: US GPO, 1969), 11–12.
11. I use "riot" when referring to protests that centrally involve property destruction. Despite the normative baggage of the term, I find it preferable to both the more general alternatives (e.g., "uprising," "rebellion"), as well as the more specific ones (e.g., "violent protest"). While "violent protest" nicely captures the political intelligibility of riots, it pre-emptively defines actions like property destruction as violent, and places the responsibility for interpersonal harm or injury on protestors rather than other involved actors (i.e., police). As I argue in this chapter as well as in Chapter 5, what counts as violent and who is seen wielding violence is a political question—one chiefly at stake in these events. On the political intelligibility of riots, see Sina Kramer, *Excluded Within: The (Un)Intelligibility of Radical Political Actors* (New York: Oxford University Press, 2017), Chapter 7.
12. *Congressional Record* 1959: 18382, 18385; *Congressional Record* 1960: 3982, quoted in Naomi Murakawa, "The origins of the carceral crisis: Racial order as law and order in postwar American politics," in *Race and American Political Development*, edited by Joseph Lowndes, Julie Novkov, and Dorrian Warren (New York and London: Routledge, 2008), 241. See also Vesla Weaver, "Frontlash: Race and the development of punitive crime policy," *Studies in American Political Development* 21 (Fall 2007): 240–242.
13. Murakawa, "Origins of the carceral crisis," 243. See also Weaver, "Frontlash," 240.
14. Barry Goldwater, "Peace through strength: Private property, free competition, and work," *Vital Speeches of the Day* (1964): 744, 746. See also Weaver, "Frontlash," 242–243.
15. J. Edgar Hoover, "Message from the director," *FBI Law Enforcement Bulletin* 34, no. 11 (November 1965): 1.
16. Hoover, "Message from the director," *FBI Law Enforcement Bulletin* 35, no. 11 (November 1966): 1–2.

17. See Hazel Erskine, "The polls: Demonstrations and race riots," *Public Opinion Quarterly* 31, no. 4 (Winter 1967–1968): 676, 670.
18. Richard Nixon, "A commitment to order," NBC Radio Network, Thursday, March 7, 1968. Transcript published in Nixon, *Nixon Speaks Out: Major Speeches and Statements by Richard M. Nixon in the Presidential Campaign of 1968* (New York: Nixon-Agnew Campaign Committee, 1968), 32.
19. Nixon, "A commitment to order," 37.
20. Weaver, "Frontlash."
21. I do not mean to suggest that there was no disagreement between theorists over issues of definition and justification; indeed, there were many. Yet as I will argue later in the chapter, throughout the 1960s and early 1970s, some important points of consensus emerged, despite various disagreements. For an excellent reconstruction of these points of divergence and convergence amongst liberal philosophers—and an interpretation of their importance for the development of liberal political philosophy—see Katrina Forrester, *In the Shadow of Justice: Postwar Liberalism and the Remaking of Political Philosophy* (Princeton and Oxford: Princeton University Press, 2019), Chapter 2.
22. Documents in the Rawls and Bedau archives add further support to Bedau's broad influence in the area of disobedience, particularly on Rawls. Correspondence between Bedau and Rawls through the 1960s indicates that Bedau's bibliography and early essays provided a necessary starting point for Rawls's own investigations of political obligation and civil disobedience later in the decade. See box 1, General correspondence, 1955–1968, Hugo Adam Bedau Papers, Tisch Library, Tufts University; box 7, folder 6, Papers of John Rawls, Pusey Library, Harvard University (hereafter Rawls Papers); box 34, folder 6, Rawls Papers.
23. Hugo Bedau, "On civil disobedience," *Journal of Philosophy* 58, no. 21 (October 1961): 654.
24. Bedau, "On civil disobedience," 661.
25. Bedau, "On civil disobedience," 660, 659.
26. Bedau, "On civil disobedience," 662–664. According to Bedau, the search for a principle that would "identify the sufficient and necessary conditions, applicable in all situations, under which one's obedience (or disobedience) is justified" is unlikely to succeed. As he writes, "Unfortunately, I do not see how any such principle could be produced, or that it would be of any use once it was available. Any principle that could do the job required, being a principle of conduct, would itself be open to the very kind of demurs and controversy it was designed to settle" (663).
27. The mid-century literature on civil disobedience in liberal philosophy, democratic theory, and legal theory is substantial. See, e.g., Richard Wasserstrom, "Disobeying the law," *Journal of Philosophy* 58, no. 21 (October 1961): 641–653; Sidney Hook, *The Paradoxes of Freedom* (Berkeley: University of California Press, 1962); Alexander Bickel, *Politics and the Warren Court* (New York: Joanna Cottler, 1965), Chapter 5; Burke Marshall, "The protest movement and the law," *Virginia Law Review* 51, no. 5 (1965): 785–803; Carl Cohen, "Civil disobedience and the law," *Rutgers Law Review* 21, no. 1 (1966): 1–18; Abe Fortas, *Concerning Dissent and Civil Disobedience* (New York: New American, 1968); Bedau, ed., *Civil Disobedience: Theory and Practice*

(New York: Pegasus, 1969); Hannah Arendt, "Civil disobedience," in her *Crises of the Republic* (New York: Harvest, 1970), 51–102; Michael Walzer, *Obligations: Essays on Disobedience, War and Citizenship* (Cambridge, MA: Harvard University Press, 1970); Carl Cohen, *Civil Disobedience: Conscience, Tactics, and the Law* (New York: Columbia University Press, 1972); Marshall Cohen, "Liberalism and disobedience," *Philosophy and Public Affairs* 1, no. 3 (1972): 283–314; Peter Singer, *Democracy and Disobedience* (New York and London: Oxford University Press, 1974); Ronald Dworkin, *Taking Rights Seriously* (Cambridge, MA: Harvard University Press, 1978); Dworkin, *A Matter of Principle* (London: Harvard University Press, 1985); Paul Harris, *Civil Disobedience* (Lanham, MD: University Press of America, 1989). Howard Zinn provides an early critique of the narrowness of this literature in *Disobedience & Democracy: Nine Fallacies* (New York: Vintage, 1968). More recently, see David Lyons, "Moral judgment, historical reality, and civil disobedience," *Philosophy and Public Affairs* 27, no. 1 (1998): 31–49; Robin Celikates, "Rethinking civil disobedience as a practice of contestation—Beyond the liberal paradigm," *Constellations* 23, no. 1 (2016): 37–45; Celikates, "Democratizing civil disobedience," *Philosophy and Social Criticism* (March 2016): 1–13; Forrester, *Shadow of Justice*, Chapter 2.
28. John Rawls, "Legal obligation and the duty of fair play (1964)," in *John Rawls: Collected Papers*, edited by Samuel Freeman (Cambridge and London: Harvard University Press, 1999), 117.
29. As Forrester demonstrates, Rawls's account of obligations and disobedience narrowed over time: whereas his early theorization of the "duty of fair play" tied the legitimacy of disobedience to failures of reciprocity within cooperative schemes (leaving a potentially wide terrain for justifiable disobedience), his turn to the criterion of the majority's "sense of justice" both individualized and constrained the boundaries of dissent. See Forrester, *Shadow of Justice*, 64–71.
30. Rawls, *A Theory of Justice* (Cambridge, MA: Harvard University Press, 1971), 363.
31. Rawls, *Theory of Justice*, 355.
32. Rawls, *Theory of Justice*, 363.
33. Rawls, "The justification of civil disobedience," in *Civil Disobedience: Theory and Practice*, 249.
34. Rawls, *Theory of Justice*, 355.
35. Rawls, *Theory of Justice*, 355.
36. Rawls, *Theory of Justice*, 372.
37. Lyons, "Moral judgment," 36–37.
38. This is exactly what concerns Lyons: as he argues, the US under Jim Crow cannot possibly qualify as the kind of state in which political obligation can be presumed. See Lyons, "Moral judgment."
39. Rawls, *Theory of Justice*, 375, 373.
40. Rawls, *Theory of Justice*, 364.
41. Rawls, *Theory of Justice*, 367–368.
42. Rawls, *Theory of Justice*, 374, 373.
43. Rawls, *Theory of Justice*, 372.
44. Rawls, *Theory of Justice*, 371–373.

45. Rawls, "The justification," 253.
46. Rawls, *Theory of Justice*, 387–388.
47. Rawls, *Theory of Justice*, 386–387, 390. Rawls calls this latter situation a "strictly partitioned consensus" (388).
48. I do not mean to suggest here that Rawls sees no place for militant, and even revolutionary, action; indeed, he readily admits that when the state loses all claim to being "fundamentally just" (or nearly so), there might be good reason to revolt. Rawls's account, however, must necessarily place revolt outside the bounds of liberal-constitutional politics: they are not actions of the sort that can be properly characterized by a procedural concept of legitimacy.
49. Rawls, *Theory of Justice*, 352.
50. Andrew Sabl, "Looking forward to justice: Rawlsian civil disobedience and its non-Rawlsian lessons," *Journal of Political Philosophy* 9, no. 3 (2001): 311.
51. Sabl, "Looking forward to justice," 312.
52. Walzer, *Obligations*, 17, 61. On the development of Walzer's account of obligations and disobedience, and in particular his differences with Rawls, see Forrester, *Shadow of Justice*, 53–59.
53. Cohen, *Civil Disobedience*, 44–45.
54. As Jennifer Welchman has argued, the move to interpret civil disobedience as essentially or primarily communicative represented a real shift in how it was categorized and understood, as well as the historical movements and events that qualified as examples of it; and yet it is a shift that occurred with seemingly little argument or discussion, let alone justification. Jennifer Welchman, "Is ecosabotage civil disobedience?" *Philosophy and Geography* 4, no. 1 (2001): 99–103. While Welchman attributes this shift to philosophers' anxieties about justifying "indirect" disobedience—a claim that I find plausible on the basis of the textual evidence—I see it as primarily stemming from concerns about the counter-majoritarian nature of civil disobedience (the possibility of direct intervention in, and frustration of, policies and laws adopted through legitimate democratic procedures), which many critics (and not a few defenders) of disobedience viewed as antidemocratic and thereby problematic.
55. Habermas's account of civil disobedience is instructive in this regard: while defending the constitutive indeterminacy of disobedience and elsewhere embracing the "anarchic" character of the unstructured public sphere, Habermas similarly theorizes civil disobedience as a constitution-stabilizing practice—one which leaves the constitutional state "wholly intact," and remains nonviolent and purely "symbolic." See Jürgen Habermas, "Civil disobedience: Litmus test for the democratic constitutional state," *Berkeley Journal of Sociology* 30 (1985): 100–103. Çiğdem Çıdam, "Radical democracy without risks? Habermas on constitutional patriotism and civil disobedience," *New German Critique* 44, no. 2 (August 2017): 105–132. A more recent deliberative account of civil disobedience which in many respects echoes the definitional imperatives of the older liberal account is in William Smith, *Civil Disobedience and Deliberative Democracy* (Abingdon: Routledge, 2013).
56. Martin Luther King, Jr., *Why We Can't Wait* (Boston: Beacon, 2010), 95.
57. Rawls, *Theory of Justice*, 364, n. 19.

58. Rawls, Handwritten notes, "CD & the complications of our federal system [three types of cases]," ca. 1966, box 7, folder 6, Rawls Papers. In these notes, Rawls follows the account of the sit-ins provided by Bickel, *Politics and the Warren Court*, Chapter 5. See also Rawls, Handwritten notes, "Paradigm cases of CD acts (whether justified or not)" and "Points Re CD," ca. 1966, box 7, folder 6, Rawls Papers; Rawls, "Notes for Political Obligation (II)," March 24, 1967, box 7, folder 7, Rawls Papers.
59. Rawls, Lecture notes, "Seminar VI, Civil Disobedience," ca. 1969, box 34, folder 12, Rawls Papers.
60. Rawls, *Political Liberalism* (New York: Columbia University Press, 1993), l.
61. Rawls, *Political Liberalism*, 250, n. 39. See also Rawls, "The idea of public reason revisited," in *Political Liberalism*, 464.
62. See Walzer, "The politics of the New Negro," *Dissent* VII (Summer 1960): 241–242; "A cup of coffee and a seat," *Dissent* (Spring 1960): 111–120.
63. To be sure, the more radical version of King is hardly news to those working within African American political thought and has arguably had a long-standing presence within black public spheres and social-political discourse.
64. Sabl, *Ruling Passions: Political Offices and Democratic Ethics* (Princeton, NJ: Princeton University Press, 2002), 202. Original emphasis removed.
65. Sabl, *Ruling Passions*, 204–205.
66. Sabl, *Ruling Passions*, 211.
67. James C. Scott, *Seeing Like a State: How Certain Schemes to Improve the Human Condition Have Failed* (New Haven, CT: Yale University Press, 1998).
68. In particular, the conditions of a coercive, authoritarian state paired with an incapacitated civil society—conditions that transform a rather routine modernist faith in progress, standardization, and simplification into human tragedies of enormous proportions—are of an entirely different order than the dynamic that I see operating within theoretical treatments of civil disobedience.
69. Seeing like a state, in the particular sense in which I am using it, thus entails the stance of "reformist reform," as French theorist Andre Gorz put it. "A reformist reform is one that subordinates its objectives to the criteria of rationality and predictability of a given system and policy. Reformisim rejects those objectives and demands—however deep the need for them—which are incompatible with the preservation of the system." In contrast, "a not necessarily reformist reform is one that is conceived not in terms of what is possible from within the framework of a given system and administration, but in view of what should be made possible in terms of human needs and demands. . . . A non-reformist reform is determined not in terms of what can be, but what should be." See Andre Gorz, *Strategy for Labor: A Radical Proposal*, translated by Martin A. Niclaus and Victoria Ortiz (Boston: Beacon, 1967), 7–8; see also Ruth Wilson Gilmore, *Golden Gulag: Prisons, Surplus, Crisis, and Opposition in Globalizing California* (Berkeley and Los Angeles: University of California Press, 2007), 242. I am grateful to Ali Aslam for provoking this connection.
70. Sheldon Wolin, *Politics and Vision: Continuity and Innovation in Western Political Thought* (Princeton and Oxford: Princeton University Press, 2004) 17–18.
71. Danielle Allen, "Invisible citizens: Political exclusion and domination in Arendt and Ellison," in *Political Exclusion and Domination*, edited by Melissa S. Williams and

Stephen Macedo (New York and London: New York University Press, 2005), 55. Note how close Allen's description of an "exclusion" account is to Sabl's careful reconstruction (and partial defense) of Rawls's analysis of civil disobedience. Here Sabl explains his more precise interpretation of what Rawls means by the "nearly just" or "fundamentally just" society: "a *piecewise just* society is one in which justice is prevalent—indeed, it may in the limit case be practiced perfectly or almost perfectly—in relations within a powerful 'in' group, but is practiced to a very small degree, if at all, in dealings with an excluded or oppressed group." See Sabl, "Looking forward to justice," 311–312.

72. Allen, "Invisible citizens," 58.
73. On the deep roots of the "aberrational" account of racial hierarchy in the liberal and social contract tradition, see Charles Mills, *The Racial Contract* (Ithaca and London: Cornell University Press, 1997); *Black Rights/White Wrongs: The Critique of Racial Liberalism* (New York: Oxford University Press, 2017).
74. Joel Olson, *The Abolition of White Democracy* (Minneapolis: University of Minnesota Press, 2004).
75. I will return to the issue of acknowledgment and disavowal in Chapter 5.
76. Mills, "Rawls on race/race on Rawls," *Southern Journal of Philosophy* 47 (2009): 161–184; Mills, "'Ideal theory' as ideology," *Hypatia* 20, no. 3 (Summer 2005): 165–184; Mills, "White time: The chronic injustice of ideal theory," *Du Bois Review* 11, no. 1 (Spring 2014): 27–42.
77. Even while I draw from Mills's critique of Rawls and contract theory, I sidestep his dispute with Tommie Shelby over whether Rawls's theory can itself offer resources for projects of racial justice (with ideal and nonideal theory working as necessary complements to each other, as Shelby contends), or whether it must be radically transformed in order to do so (jettisoning the ambitions of ideal theory entirely, as Mills argues). Despite the merits of both Mills's and Shelby's contributions to this argument, their dispute centers on a question I do not take up: the specific philosophical and social justice purchase of ideal versus nonideal theorizing. I am interested here in the particular political context and specific questions that shaped Rawls's account, and what they reveal about the predominant framework for theorizing civil disobedience. That is, I am more invested in understanding how the narrow bounds within which Rawls approached civil disobedience—a question of legitimate lawbreaking in a nearly just society—crowded out other possible interpretive frames, including the ones espoused by activists themselves. See Tommie Shelby, "Rawls and social justice: Rawlsian considerations," *Fordham Law Review* 72, no. 5 (2004): 1697–1714; Mills, "Retrieving Rawls for racial justice? A critique of Tommie Shelby," *Critical Philosophy of Race* 1, no. 1 (2013): 1–27; Shelby, "Racial realities and corrective justice: A reply to Charles Mills," *Critical Philosophy of Race* 1, no. 2 (2013): 145–162; Shelby, *Dark Ghettos: Justice, Dissent, and Reform* (Cambridge and London: Belknap Press, 2016).
78. Gunnar Myrdal, *An American Dilemma: The Negro Problem and Modern Democracy*, Complete 20th Anniversary Edition (New York, Toronto, and London: McGraw-Hill, 1964), lxxii.
79. Myrdal, *American Dilemma*, 3.

80. Myrdal, *American Dilemma*, xxiv. According to David Southern, Myrdal adopted the idea of an "American Creed" prior to beginning his study, after his first trip through the South in 1938. It was a concept with which a number of Myrdal's collaborators had significant disagreements. See David Southern, *Gunnar Myrdal and Black-White Relations: The Use and Abuse of "An American Dilemma," 1944–1969* (Baton Rouge: Louisiana State University Press, 1987), Chapter 2.
81. Myrdal, *American Dilemma*, 13.
82. Myrdal, *American Dilemma*, lxxvii, lxxi. Original emphasis removed.
83. On this point, see Oliver Cox, "An American dilemma: A mystical approach to the study of race relations," *The Journal of Negro Education* 14, no. 2 (Spring 1945): 132–148; Ralph Ellison, "An American dilemma: A review," in *The Death of White Sociology: Essays on Race and Culture*, edited by Joyce A. Ladner (Baltimore, MD: Black Classic Press, 1988), 81–95; Nikhil Pal Singh, *Black Is a Country: Race and the Unfinished Struggle for Democracy* (Cambridge, MA: Harvard University Press, 2004), 151–154.
84. Myrdal, *American Dilemma*, 48.
85. Myrdal, *American Dilemma*, lxxv; Ellison, "An American dilemma," 82–83, 93–95.
86. Myrdal, *American Dilemma*, 13.
87. Myrdal, *American Dilemma*, 1004.
88. Vincent Harding, "History: White, Negro & Black," *Southern Exposure* 1, nos. 3 & 4 (Winter 1974): 55.
89. David M. Kennedy, *Freedom from Fear: The American People in Depression and War, 1929–1945* (New York: Oxford University Press, 2001), 762.
90. Kennedy, *Freedom from Fear*, 763.
91. Myrdal, *American Dilemma*, 24.
92. Rawls, "Nature of Political and Social Thought and Methodology, 1960–1964," 7, box 35, folder 10, Rawls Papers.
93. Walzer, "The obligations of oppressed minorities," *Commentary* 49, no. 5 (May 1970): 79. In Walzer's view, it is thus civil disobedience itself that generates the obligation to obey. Though oppressed citizens cannot be bound by laws they had no part in creating, civil disobedience works by exploiting hypocritical rules to show that they are not *just* hypocrisy. "Now insofar as [activists] do this, or rather, insofar as they do it with some success, they begin the process of transforming their citizenship into something real (something valuable as well). That means also that they begin acquiring obligations within the democratic state where they work and to its citizens among whom they find allies and supporters" (79).
94. Walzer, "What does it mean to be an 'American'?" *Social Research* 71, no. 3 (Fall 2004): 642; Walzer, "The communitarian critique of liberalism," *Political Theory* 18, no. 1 (February 1990): 14.
95. Walzer, "The communitarian critique," 14.
96. Kimberlé Crenshaw et al., "Introduction," in *Critical Race Theory: The Key Writings that Formed the Movement*, edited by Kimberlé Crenshaw, Neil Gotanda, Gary Peller, and Kendall Thomas (New York: New Press, 1995), xiv.
97. Crenshaw et al., "Introduction," xvi.

98. Thelwell, "March on Washington," 72.
99. King, *Why We Can't Wait*, 95.
100. King, *Why We Can't Wait*, 89–90.
101. While I read King differently, William Scheuerman has offered a non-Rawlsian reinterpretation of civil disobedience as "fidelity to law," rooted in King's writings. See William Scheuerman, "Recent theories of civil disobedience: An anti-legal turn?" *The Journal of Political Philosophy* 23, no. 4 (December 2015): 427–449; Erin Pineda, "Martin Luther King, Jr. and the politics of disobedient civility," in *Cambridge Companion to Civil Disobedience*, edited by William Scheuerman (New York: Cambridge University Press, 2021) . On the development of King's thinking about civil disobedience from Montgomery through the end of his life, see Introduction, n. 11.
102. Mary Dudziak, *Cold War Civil Rights: Race and the Image of American Democracy* (Princeton and Oxford: Princeton University Press, 2000), 252.
103. To some extent, the diverse forms of discursive, organizational, and mobilizational labor entailed by devising a diagnostic social theory, connecting it to prognostic means of resolution and redress, providing an account of the meaningfulness of action, and prompting involvement amongst diverse constituencies is conceptualized by social movement theorists as the work of "framing." However, while much of the literature on "framing" and "frame alignment" tends to treat the ideas of social movement actors in a somewhat narrow fashion—as the work of proposing and marketing particular frameworks that are more or less resonant with various audiences—in what follows, I try to construct a wider framework, one which takes seriously the idea of activists as engaged in the work of political theorizing, not simply marketing. Additionally, in contrast to much of the social movement theory literature, I am not primarily concerned here with explaining social movement emergence or success. There is a large literature on framing; for the classic statement and an overview, see David Snow et al., "Frame alignment processes, mobilization, and movement participation," *American Sociological Review* 51, no. 4 (August 1986): 464–481; David Snow and Robert Benford, "Ideology, frame resonance, and participant mobilization," *International Social Movement Research* 1 (1988): 197–218; Benford and Snow, "Framing processes & social movements: An overview and assessment," *American Sociological Review* 26 (2000): 611–639.
104. The reference to "opportunities found and lost" is to Robert Korstad and Nelson Lichtenstein's eponymous article on labor in the "long civil rights movement." Here, I borrow the phrase for different, and perhaps opposed, purposes: not to demonstrate the structural possibilities eclipsed with the advent of civil rights organizing in the 1960s, but to argue for how a detailed attention to activist's strategies can recuperate the radical possibilities implied by civil rights disobedience, while also illuminating its limitations. See Robert Korstad and Nelson Lichtenstein, "Opportunities found and lost: Labor, radicals, and the early civil rights movement," *The Journal of American History* 75, no. 3 (1988): 786–811.
105. Allen, "Invisible citizens," 61.

Chapter 2

1. A. Philip Randolph, Address in Madison Square Garden, June 16, 1942, box 39, folder 1, A. Philip Randolph Papers, Manuscript Division, Library of Congress, Washington, DC (hereafter Randolph Papers).
2. James Weldon Johnson, "Gandhi a prisoner," *New York Age*, March 25, 1922, 4.
3. Ntozake Shange, "Mood indigo," in *A Daughter's Geography* (New York: St. Martin's Press, 1983), 13.
4. Hannah Arendt, "Civil disobedience," in her *Crises of the Republic* (Harcourt Brace: New York, 1972), 83.
5. John Rawls, "Legal obligation and the duty of fair play (1964)," in *John Rawls: Collected Papers*, edited by Samuel Freeman (Cambridge and London: Harvard University Press, 1999), 117. See also Peter Singer, *Democracy and Disobedience* (Oxford: Clarendon, 1973).While liberal theorists view this framework predominantly through the concept of the rule of law, democratic theorists reach a similar conclusion by viewing law as the product of processes of "will formation" and deliberative exchange. In principle, this democratic view leaves room for disobedience beyond the domestic; however, many accounts remain focused on civil disobedience within the bounds of—in Habermas's words—a "constitutional state that remains wholly intact." See Jürgen Habermas, "Civil disobedience: Litmus test for the constitutional democratic state," *Berkeley Journal of Sociology* 30 (1985): 95–116. For an excellent, recent rethinking of civil disobedience as a "practice of contestation" rather than a form of constitutional discourse, see Robin Celikates, "Rethinking disobedience as a practice of contestation—Beyond the liberal paradigm," *Constellations* 23, no. 1 (2016): 37–45.
6. Candice Delmas, *A Duty to Resist: When Disobedience Should be Uncivil* (New York: Oxford University Press), 39. See also Chapter 1.
7. Richard G. Fox, "Passage from India," in *Between Resistance and Revolution: Cultural Politics and Social Protest*, edited by Richard G. Fox and Orin Starn (New Brunswick and London: Rutgers University Press, 1997), 65. The question of origins—of a form that is "originally Indian"—is itself misleading, insofar as Gandhi's own philosophical influences were famously eclectic and wide-ranging.
8. On this, see Alexander Livingston, "Fidelity to truth: Gandhi and the genealogy of civil disobedience," *Political Theory* 46, no. 4 (2018): 511–536. Livingston demonstrates how Gandhi constructed a genealogy of *satyagraha*—connecting Socrates to Thoreau to his own activism in South Africa—for political and philosophical purposes distinct from those of the liberal–legal philosophies that later adopted it. As Livingston writes, "Gandhi's experiments in making civil disobedience travel were in the service of a radical critique of violence that interrogates the deepest presumptions of the very liberal legalism that claims his genealogy of civil disobedience as its own" (513). Livingston's attention to the global transit of civil disobedience—and the distinct, discernible political projects to which specific geographies are attached—resonates with the arguments of this chapter.
9. While I find that "imaginative transit" best suits my purposes, some scholars of black transnationalism adopt the term "translation" to describe related practices. Taking

stock of the fact that "the level of the international is accessed unevenly by subjects with different historical relations to the nation," Brent Hayes Edwards argues that "the cultures of black internationalism can be seen only *in translation*"—that is, "by attending to the ways that discourses of internationalism *travel*, the ways they are translated, disseminated, reformulated, and debated in transnational contexts marked by difference." The work of imaginative transit, I hope, captures something similar—though with emphasis on embodied motion rather than literary translation. See Edwards, *The Practice of Diaspora: Literature, Translation, and the Rise of Black Internationalism* (Cambridge: Harvard University Press, 2003), 6–7. I am grateful to an anonymous reviewer for Cambridge University Press for pointing me toward the affinities with Edwards's work.
10. Aziz Rana, "Decolonizing Obama," *n+1 Magazine* 27 (Winter 2017), https://nplusonemag.com/issue-27/politics/decolonizing-obama/.
11. Penny Von Eschen, *Race Against Empire: Black Americans and Anticolonialism, 1937–1957* (Ithaca and London: Cornell University Press, 1997), 186.
12. Sudarshan Kapur, *Raising Up a Prophet: The African-American Encounter with Gandhi* (Boston: Beacon, 1992); Gerald Horne, *The End of Empires: African Americans and India* (Philadelphia: Temple University Press, 2009); Sean Chabot, *The Transnational Roots of the Civil Rights Movement: African American Explorations of the Gandhian Repertoire* (Lanham, MD, and Boulder: Lexington Books, 2012); Nico Slate, *Colored Cosmopolitanism: The Shared Struggle for Freedom in the United States and India* (Cambridge and London: Harvard University Press, 2011).
13. Thanks to Alex Livingston for helping me articulate this claim more specifically and forcefully.
14. On this front, it is quite revealing to note that the debate over the use of nonviolent direct action and mass civil disobedience that erupted through the African American press in the early twentieth century was ignited by Indian anticolonial mobilization half a world away, and not the women's suffrage movement much closer to home.
15. Thanks to Barbara Cruikshank, Adam Dahl, Ali Aslam, and Pat Coby for pushing me to make the stronger version of this claim.
16. Jodi Byrd, *Transit of Empire: Indigenous Critiques of Colonialism* (Minneapolis and London: University of Minnesota Press, 2011), xxii.
17. Byrd, *Transit of Empire*, xxiii–xxiv. Many thanks to an anonymous reviewer at Cambridge University Press for suggesting these linkages to me, and to Ali Aslam for encouraging me to put them to paper.
18. Hugo Bedau, "On civil disobedience," *The Journal of Philosophy* 58, no. 21 (October 1961): 654.
19. For an argument for separating civil disobedience from nonviolent direct action from a democratic/republican perspective, see Guy Aitchison, "Coercion, Resistance and the Radical Side of Non-Violent Action," *Raisons Politiques* 1, no. 69 (2018): 45–61.
20. As Sean Scalmer writes, "Western press coverage of Gandhi is like a mountain shelf: a sudden and small peak in the early 1920s; a deep valley; a towering summit over 1929–32, perhaps double the size of its nearest neighbours; an incomplete fall; a plateau; and then a smaller peak in the early 1940s, lasting until Gandhi's death in 1948.

Each peak relates to a period of popular struggle for Swaraj: the 'non-co-operation' movement from 1919, the salt satyagraha from 1930, and the 'Quit India' campaign launched in 1942." Scalmer, *Gandhi in the West: The Mahatma and the Rise of Radical Protest* (New York: Cambridge University Press, 2011), 44. While Scalmer's analysis only considers the mainstream press, the pattern of peaks and valleys more or less holds true for the African American press. A pioneering account of the reception of Gandhi and the Indian independence movement in the black press is provided by Kapur, *Raising Up a Prophet*. The two sections that follow in the text are substantially indebted to Kapur's work.
21. Chabot, *The Transnational Roots of the Civil Rights Movement*, 29. Chabot provides an excellent, if brief, overview of Gandhi's main campaigns from South Africa through Quit India in Chapter 2, 19–41.
22. In the end Gandhi only served two years, due to poor health. On Chauri Chaura and its effects on Gandhi's understanding of mass collective action, see Karuna Mantena, "Mass satyagraha and the problem of collective power," in *Political Imaginaries: Rethinking India's Twentieth Century*, edited by Manu Goswami and Mrinalini Sinha (forthcoming).
23. George Frederickson, *Black Liberation: A Comparative History of Black Ideologies in the United States and South Africa* (New York and Oxford: Oxford University Press, 1995), 231. See also August Meier and Elliot M. Rudwick, *Along the Color Line: Explorations in the Black Experience* (Urbana: University of Illinois Press, 1976), Chapter 14.
24. A. L. Jackson, "The onlooker: Mahatma Gandhi," *Chicago Defender*, December 24, 1921, 16.
25. Johnson, "Gandhi a prisoner," 4.
26. Kapur, *Raising Up a Prophet*, 56.
27. Scalmer, *Gandhi in the West*, 20–26.
28. Scalmer, *Gandhi in the West*, 87. The concept of "hyper-difference" comes from Fox, "Passage from India." Even in coverage that attempts to render Gandhi less foreign, Gandhi is analogized to Jesus Christ—making him more cognizable for American audiences, perhaps, but equally otherworldly and out of reach for the politics of ordinary citizens.
29. I take the phrase "empire of Jim Crow" from the work of historian Gerald Horne, who in turn borrowed the phrase from former US Secretary of State Condoleeza Rice. See Horne, *The End of Empires*, 17.
30. E. Franklin Frazier, "The Negro and non-resistance," *The Crisis* 27, no. 5 (March 1924): 213–214.
31. Du Bois prefaced Frazier's reply by noting, "We have received one or two letters protesting against the spirit of this article which we have submitted to Mr. Frazier. His answer seems to us so eminently clear and sound that we are publishing it here as an editorial." *The Crisis* 28, no. 2 (June 1924): 58.
32. During the Watchfire demonstration suffragists burned copies of President Wilson's speeches outside the White House and across the street in Lafayette Park. The initial demonstration lasted several days and resulted in the arrest of eleven women, who

were charged with violating a statute prohibiting the building of fires in public places after sunset. Doris Stevens chronicled the Watchfire demonstration in her book on the militant suffragists and noted Ellen Winsor amongst those arrested. See Doris Stevens, *Jailed for Freedom* (New York: Boni and Liveright, 1920), 305–313, 370.
33. Ellen Winsor to W. E. B. Du Bois, March 2, 1924, in *The Correspondence of W. E. B. Du Bois, Volume 1: Selections 1877–1934*, edited by Herbert Aptheker (Amherst: University of Massachusetts Press, 1973), 283–284.
34. Du Bois to Winsor, April 12, 1924, in *Correspondence of W. E. B. Du Bois*, 284. Winsor later replied, expressing confusion as to "what 'races and peoples' are receiving Gandhi with 'unanimity,'" pointing to Gandhi's relative obscurity in Western contexts. Winsor to Du Bois, April 20, 1924, W. E. B. Du Bois Papers, Ms. 312, Special Collections and University Archives, University of Massachusetts, Amherst (hereafter Du Bois Papers).
35. Tannenbaum, *Darker Phases of the South* (New York: GP Putnam & Sons, 1922), 162–163. Interestingly, Frazier also connects the logic of racial rule in the American South with racialized colonial domination in India, Ireland, and the Belgian Congo, as well as the genocidal settler colonialism of the United States.
36. Frazier, "The Negro and non-resistance," *The Crisis* 28, no. 2 (June 1924): 58–59.
37. Kapur, *Raising Up a Prophet*, 70.
38. Martin Luther King, Jr., "My trip to the land of Gandhi," in *The Papers of Martin Luther King, Jr., Volume V: Threshold of a New Decade, January 1959–December 1960*, edited by Clayborne Carson (Berkeley and Los Angeles: University of California Press, 2005), 233.
39. Slate, *Colored Cosmopolitanism*, 65.
40. On Du Bois's role in these conversations, see Slate, *Colored Cosmopolitanism*; Horne, *End of Empires*; and Kapur, *Raising Up a Prophet*. On Du Bois's internationalism more generally, see Brenda Gayle Plummer, *Rising Wind: Black Americans and U.S. Foreign Affairs, 1935–1960* (Chapel Hill and London: University of North Carolina Press, 1996); Von Eschen, *Race Against Empire*; Carol Anderson, *Eyes Off the Prize: The United Nations and the African American Struggle for Human Rights, 1944–1955* (New York: Cambridge University Press, 2003); Jonathan Rosenberg, *How Far the Promised Land: World Affairs and the American Civil Rights Movement from the First World War to Vietnam* (Princeton and Oxford: Princeton University Press, 2006).
41. Du Bois to M. K. Gandhi, February 19, 1929, in *Correspondence of W. E. B. Du Bois*, 402–403. Du Bois also wrote to the Nobel Prize–winning Indian poet, Rabindranath Tagore, and subsequently published Tagore's reply in the October 1929 issue of *The Crisis*, noting it as "another one of the international messages among the colored peoples of the world." Tagore wrote, in part: "We have been engaged in cultivating each his own individual life, and within the fenced seclusion of our racial tradition. We had neither the wisdom nor the opportunity to harmonize our growth with world tendencies. But there are no longer walls to hide us. We have at length to prove our worth to the whole world, not merely to admiring groups of our own people. We must justify our own existence. We must show, each in our own civilization, that which is

the universal in the heart of the unique." See Du Bois, Announcement of Tagore statement in the *Crisis*, ca. 1929, Du Bois Papers; *The Crisis* 36 (October 1929): 333–334.
42. Gandhi to Du Bois, May 1, 1929, in *Correspondence of W. E. B. Du Bois*, 403.
43. "To the American Negro, a message from Mahatma Gandhi," *The Crisis* 36 (July 1929): 225.
44. Du Bois's gloss on Gandhi's time in South Africa is striking, given Gandhi's explicit concern in South Africa to dissociate the Indian fight against discrimination from the cause of the African majority. In another article Du Bois claimed Gandhi "espoused the cause of the black natives, and was willing to lay down his life for his own convictions." Du Bois thus subtly elided the historical and racial/ethnic complexity of the South African case—as well as Gandhi's early, explicit ethnocentrism—to present Gandhi as a leader in fighting both racism and imperialism broadly, a leader of "dark" peoples. As Slate argues, it was only through the influence of years of interaction with African Americans that Gandhi overcame this ethnocentrism and became a true participant in "colored cosmopolitanism" himself. See Du Bois, "The wide, wide world: Mahatma Gandhi," *New York Amsterdam News*, October 28, 1931, 8; Gandhi, *Satyagraha in South Africa* (Ahmedabad: Navajivan Trust, 1928); Slate, *Colored Cosmopolitanism*, Chapter 4.
45. "To the American Negro," 225.
46. Du Bois, "The wide, wide world: India," *New York Amsterdam News*, October 7, 1931, 8.
47. "Empire at stake," *Pittsburgh Courier*, May 17, 1930, 12.
48. O. R. Burns, "How'd the Sox come out today," *Chicago Defender*, September 20, 1930, 14.
49. The most detailed report of these trips is in Kapur, *Raising Up a Prophet*, Chapter 4 and Horne, *End of Empires*, Chapters 6 and 7. See also Chabot, *Transnational Roots of the Civil Rights Movement*, 74–76; Slate, *Colored Cosmopolitanism*, 112–118. For an account of these exchanges and their ultimate effect on Martin Luther King, Jr.'s conception of love, see Livingston, "'Tough love': The political theology of civil disobedience," *Perspectives on Politics* 18, no. 3 (September 2020): 851–866.
50. Thurman and Gandhi quoted in Kapur, *Raising Up a Prophet*, 88–90.
51. "Howard University professor talks with Mahatma Ghandi [sic]," *Norfolk Journal and Guide*, May 9, 1936, 5.
52. Mays, "Gandhi rekindled spirit of race pride in India, Dr. Mays finds," *Norfolk Journal and Guide*, May 29, 1937, A9.
53. Mays, "The color line around the world," *Journal of Negro Education* 6 (April 1937): 140–142; Mays, "Gandhi rekindled the spirit of race pride," A9.
54. Mays, "Gandhi and non-violence," *Norfolk Journal and Guide*, May 22, 1937, 8. Livingston likewise identifies Gandhian *satyagraha* as a practice of cultivating fearlessness and thereby freedom. See Livingston, "Fidelity to truth," 519–524.
55. Indeed, it seems that King adopted one of Mays's own stories about the trip to India as his own. Mays recounted the uncomfortable, but eye-opening, experience of learning that he, as a black man, was an American "untouchable." King appears to have related this story as his own in a 1965 sermon—not an uncommon practice in sermon

writing (within King's tradition of the "folk pulpit"), and an interesting example of how the years of exchange between African Americans and India continued to shape the terms of struggle in the US. See Slate, *Colored Cosmopolitanism*, 227–228. On King's place in the "folk pulpit" tradition and his use of sources, see Keith D. Miller, *Voice of Deliverance: The Language of Martin Luther King, Jr. and Its Sources* (Athens and London: University of Georgia Press, 1992).

56. James Farmer, "The race logic of pacifism," *Fellowship* 8, no. 2 (February 1942): 8.
57. Farmer, *Lay Bare the Heart: An Autobiography of the Civil Rights Movement* (New York: Arbor House, 1985), 100.
58. Randolph, "The Negro's fight for democracy now," Speech for Golden Gate mass meeting, September 11, 1942, 13, box 39, folder 2, Randolph Papers.
59. Randolph, Keynote address at National Policy Conference, March on Washington movement, September 27, 1942, Detroit, Michigan. Text of keynote reprinted in *Negro Protest Thought in the Twentieth Century*, edited by Francis L. Broderick and August Meier (Indianapolis, IN: Bobbs-Merrill, 1965), 201–210. Quoted text at 207, 210.
60. "Randolph plans 'civil disobedience campaign patterned after Ghandi's [sic]," *New York Amsterdam News*, January 9, 1943, 1; "Randolph to adopt Gandhi technique," *Chicago Defender*, January 9, 1943, 4.
61. "Citizens repudiate non-violence program," *Pittsburgh Courier*, April 24, 1943, 4.
62. Du Bois, "As the crow flies," *New York Amsterdam News*, March 13, 1943, 10.
63. James Farmer, ed., "Is civil disobedience the answer to Jim Crow?" *Non-Violence Action Bulletin*, nos. 2–3 (1943): 5–22.
64. "Civil disobedience," *Pittsburgh Courier*, January 23, 1943, 6.
65. Farmer, "Is civil disobedience the answer," 14.
66. See Chapter 3. To be clear, my claim is not that anticolonialism supplied the *only* source of the language of liberation. Rather, it added an additional dimension to the existing, indigenous traditions extending out of liberation theology and black radical thought.
67. Horne, *End of Empires*, Chapter 12; Slate, *Colored Cosmopolitanism*, Chapter 6.
68. Horne, *End of Empires*, 201. On the effect of the early Cold War on the black internationalism and anticolonialism, see Von Eschen, *Race Against Empire*; Plummer, *Rising Wind;* Anderson, *Eyes Off the Prize;* Singh, *Black is a Country*. On the development of African American identification with Africa, see Harold Isaacs, *The New World of Negro Americans* (New York: Viking, 1963); Du Bois, *The World and Africa: An Inquiry into the Part Which Africa Has Played in World History* (New York: International, 1965); Bill Sutherland and Matt Meyer, *Guns and Gandhi in Africa: Pan African Insights on Nonviolence, Armed Struggle, and Liberation in Africa* (Trenton and Asmara: Africa World Press, 2000); James Meriwether, *Proudly We Can Be Africans: Black Americans and Africa, 1935–1961* (Chapel Hill and London: University of North Carolina Press, 2002); Francis Njubi Nesbitt, *Race for Sanctions: African Americans Against Apartheid, 1946–1994* (Bloomington: Indiana University Press, 2004); Kevin Gaines, *American Africans in Ghana: Black Expatriates in the Civil Rights Era* (Chapel Hill: University of North Carolina Press, 2006); Alvin

Tillery, *Between Homeland and Motherland: Africa, US Foreign Policy, and Black Leadership in America* (Ithaca, NY: Cornell University Press, 2011).
69. Tillery, *Between Homeland and Motherland*, 110.
70. Frederickson, *Black Liberation*, 237–246; Meriwether, *Proudly We Can Be Africans*, 91–96.
71. Nelson Mandela, *Long Walk to Freedom: The Autobiography of Nelson Mandela* (New York: Little, Brown, 2008); "Programme for Action," Statement of Policy adopted at the ANC Annual Conference, December 17, 1949, African National Congress Collection, *South African History Online*, http://www.sahistory.org.za/collection/11597 (hereafter ANC Archives).
72. Private Secretary to the Prime Minister to ANC, January 29, 1952, ANC Archives. The ANC replied to the Malan's letter, writing that the "African people yield to no one as far as pride of race is concerned, and it is precisely for this reason that they are striving for the attainment of fundamental rights in the land of their birth." ANC to Prime Minister Malan, February 11, 1952, ANC Archives.
73. Meriwether, *Proudly We Can Be Africans*, 102; see also Nesbitt, *Race for Sanctions*, 17–20; Frederickson, *Black Liberation*, 246–247.
74. Frederickson, *Black Liberation*, 247–249. On the penalties imposed by the Malan government, see Meriwether, *Proudly We Can Be Africans*, 118.
75. Sutherland and Meyer, *Guns and Gandhi in Africa*, 148.
76. John D'Emilio, *Lost Prophet: The Life and Times of Bayard Rustin* (New York: Free Press, 2003), 167; Sutherland and Meyer, *Guns and Gandhi in Africa*, 148–150; Meriwether, *Proudly We Can Be Africans*, 111–112; Gaines, *American Africans in Ghana*, 103–104. Out of that initial exchange, CORE organizers launched Americans for South African Resistance (AFSAR) to petition the US government to take a stand against apartheid, under the leadership of Rustin, Farmer, and Sutherland, and Randolph, along with CORE co-founder George Houser and Howard University President Mordecai Johnson, among others. Ultimately renamed and reorganized as the American Committee on Africa (ACOA), Martin Luther King, Jr. joined the ranks of its leaders in 1957 after he returned from Ghana. On AFSAR and the ACOA, see Meriwether, *Proudly We Can Be Africans*; Nesbitt, *Race Against Sanctions*. On King's involvement in anti-apartheid activism, see Lewis Baldwin, *Toward the Beloved Community: Martin Luther King Jr. and South Africa* (Cleveland, OH: Pilgrim Press, 1995).
77. Bayard Rustin, "All Africa is aflame," *Baltimore Afro-American*, November 22, 1952, A5. In the report he prepared for the Fellowship of Reconciliation, which funded the trip, Rustin was explicit about these references, dismissing the Mau Mau rebellion as "arson, murder, and Ju-Ju." Nevertheless, even as he pressed the case for nonviolence as an alternative, Rustin's public pronouncements stopped short of forceful criticism of the Mau Mau. Indeed, as he made plain in one public interview, there was a certain amount of hypocrisy in condemning violent revolution against white supremacy and settler colonialism so long as Jim Crow remained. See Rustin, Report on trip to Africa, October 20, 1952, folder "Correspondence: 1947–1952," Bayard Rustin Papers, Manuscript Division, Library of Congress, Washington, DC (hereafter

Rustin Papers); Rustin, KECA Broadcast, January 21, 1953, quoted in D'Emilio, *Lost Prophet*, 174.
78. Rustin, "All Africa is aflame," A5.
79. D'Emilio, *Lost Prophet*, 166–167.
80. King would later mobilize this analysis of assertive nonviolence in specifically masculinist terms. As Brandon Terry and Shatema Threadcraft show, King's attempt to position nonviolence as an alternative to violent resistance entailed inverting the associations between masculinity and violence (thereby reassociating masculinity with nonviolent praxis), while dissociating courage and heroism from violence (thereby showing that violence is rooted in fear and fatalism). The gendered analysis of nonviolence, however, shaped who could be centered in narratives of nonviolent struggle. While King—a heterosexual, married, middle-class father and a preacher—could be positioned as representing the "right" kind of nonviolent masculinity, fears about Rustin's sexuality meant that he was forced into the background. Similarly, King and others marginalized women's contributions to the theory and practice of nonviolence—even as, in places like Montgomery, black women "made the boycott" and much of the movement. On this, see Terry and Threadcraft, "Gender trouble: Manhood, inclusion and justice," in *To Shape a New World: Essays on the Political Philosophy of Martin Luther King, Jr.*, edited by Brandon M. Terry and Tommie Shelby (Cambridge and London: Belknap, 2018), 205–235; D'Emilio, *Lost Prophet*.
81. Rustin to A. J. Muste, quoted in D'Emilio, *Lost Prophet*, 171.
82. E.g., "Capetown commuting on 'Jim Crow' basis," *New York Times*, August 17, 1948, 8; "Segregation protested: South Africans demonstrate against Jim Crow law," *New York Times*, September 6, 1948, 3; Albion Ross, "Johannesburg like home to American," *New York Times*, February 2, 1953, 8.
83. See, for example, Mary McLeod Bethune, "U.S. democracy and Mrs. Bethune have reached another milestone," *Chicago Defender*, July 19, 1952, 10; Mays, "Malan's government in South Africa seems unwilling to learn," *Pittsburgh Courier*, April 19, 1952, 9.
84. Rustin, "Fear in the Delta," 2, folder: Civil Rights, 1940s–1950s, Rustin Papers.
85. Mays, "Malan's government in South Africa," 9.
86. Bethune, "Words of South African racists are compared to 'Mein Kampf,'" *Chicago Defender*, July 26, 1952, 10.
87. Horace Cayton, "South African natives giving entire world a solemn warning against racial bias," *Pittsburgh Courier*, April 19, 1952, 6.
88. E. D. Nixon was one of A. Philip Randolph's lieutenants and was involved with and greatly influenced by Randolph's attempt to mobilize a nationwide civil disobedience campaign in the 1940s. During the summer of 1955, Rosa Parks had attended a two-week training session at Tennessee's Highlander Folk School. There, she participated in training that drew on Gandhi's ideas about nonviolent civil disobedience led by Ram Manhoar Lohia, a Gandhian socialist.
89. Frederickson, *Black Liberation*, 253.

90. King, "The vision of a world made new," September 9, 1954, in *The Papers of Martin Luther King, Jr., Volume VI: Advocate of the Social Gospel, September 1948–March 1963*, edited by Clayborne Carson (Berkeley and Los Angeles: University of California Press, 2007), 182–184; King, "Discerning the signs of history," June 26, 1955, in *King Papers VI*, 216–219; King, "When peace becomes obnoxious," sermon delivered on March 18, 1956 at Dexter Avenue Baptist Church, in *The Papers of Martin Luther King, Jr., Volume III: Birth of a New Age, December 1955–December 1956*, edited by Clayborne Carson (Berkeley and Los Angeles: University of California Press, 1997), 207–208; King, "The rising tide of racial consciousness," address at the Golden Anniversary Conference of the National Urban League, September 6, 1960, in *King Papers V*, 499–508; King, "The Negro looks at Africa," in *In A Single Garment of Destiny: A Global Vision of Justice*, edited by Lewis Baldwin (Boston: Beacon, 2012), 80–82. In an interview he gave while in Ghana in 1957 with pacifist Homer Jack and Rev. Michael Scott, a white minister involved in the anti-apartheid struggle, King put it in slightly different terms: "there is no basic difference between colonialism and segregation, although naturally there are surface differences . . . at bottom both segregation in American and colonialism in Africa were based on the same thing—white supremacy and contempt for life." See Homer Jack, "Conversation in Ghana," *The Christian Century* 74 (April 10, 1957): 447.

91. King, "Birth of a new age," address delivered on August 11, 1956, at the fiftieth anniversary of Alpha Phi Alpha in Buffalo, in *King Papers III*, 339–341. The language King uses here to describe anticolonial movements is a near verbatim repetition of the language he used just two months prior to describe the "Montgomery story." See King, "The 'New Negro' of the South: Behind the Montgomery story," June 1956, in *King Papers III*, 283.

92. On the importance of Ghana's independence for African Americans, see Meriwether, *Proudly We Can Be Africans*, Chapter 5; Tillery, *Between Homeland and Motherland*, Chapter 4; Gaines, *American Africans in Ghana*, Chapter 3.

93. Kwame Nkrumah, "What I mean by Positive Action," in *Revolutionary Path* (London: Panaf Books, 1973), 93–94.

94. On the movement for Ghanaian independence, see C. L. R. James, *Nkrumah and the Ghana Revolution* (Westport, CT: Lawrence Hill, 1977); Nkrumah, *Revolutionary Path*; Nkrumah, *The Autobiography of Kwame Nkrumah* (Edinburgh: Thomas Nelson, 1957).

95. Both W. E. B. Du Bois's and Paul Robeson's passports had been revoked due, in no small part, to their anticolonial and transnational activism.

96. Sutherland and Meyer, *Guns and Gandhi in Africa*, 34.

97. King, "Birth of a new nation," sermon delivered at Dexter Avenue Baptist Church, April 7, 1957, Montgomery, AL, in *The Papers of Martin Luther King, Jr., Volume IV: Symbol of the Movement, January 1957–December 1958*, edited by Clayborne Carson (Berkeley and Los Angeles: University of California Press, 2000), 158–159.

98. David Garrow, *Bearing the Cross: Martin Luther King, Jr. and the Southern Christian Leadership Conference* (New York: Harper Collins, 1986), Chapter 1; J. Mills Thorton, *Dividing Lines: Municipal Politics and the Struggle for Civil Rights in Montgomery, Birmingham, and Selma* (Tuscaloosa: University of Alabama Press, 2002); Jeanne Theoharis, *The Rebellious Life of Mrs. Rosa Parks* (Beacon: Boston, 2013).

99. To Dwight D. Eisenhower, January 11, 1957, in *King Papers IV*, 99–101.
100. To Dwight D. Eisenhower, February 14, 1957, in *King Papers IV*, 132–134.
101. "M. L. King meets Nixon in Ghana," *Pittsburgh Courier*, March 9, 1957, 2; Thaddeus Stokes, "Dr. King says he may meet with Nixon," *Atlanta Daily World*, March 29, 1957, 1. There is a story about Nixon in Ghana that—whether true or not—perfectly encapsulates this sentiment. At a dinner party, Nixon apparently asked the black man sitting next to him what it felt like to be free. The man replied: "I wouldn't know. I'm from Alabama." Quoted in Hugh Tinker, *Race, Conflict, and the International Order: From Empire to United Nations* (New York: Macmillan, 1977), 84.
102. This, indeed, is the shockingly modest request in the two cited letters: that Eisenhower come to the South to deliver a civil rights speech and see firsthand the state of black life under Jim Crow.
103. King, "Birth of a new nation," 158–159.
104. King, "Birth of a new nation," 161.
105. King, "Birth of a new nation," 162–164.
106. Interview by Etta Moten Barnett, March 5, 1957, in *King Papers IV*, 156.
107. Provisional Agenda of the All African People's Conference, reprinted in Nkrumah, *Revolutionary Path*, 132.
108. On the 1958 All Africa People's Conference and the Sahara Protest Team, see Gaines, *American Africans in Ghana*, Chapter 3; Sutherland and Meyer, *Guns and Gandhi in Africa*, Chapter 2; Jean Allman, "Nuclear imperialism and the Pan-African struggle for peace and freedom," *Souls* 10, no. 2 (2008): 83–102. On Accra as the center of debates over nonviolence and decolonization, see Jeffrey Ahlman, "The Algerian question in Nkrumah's Ghana, 1958–1960: Debating 'violence' and 'nonviolence' in African decolonization," *Africa Today* 57, no. 2 (Winter 2010): 67–84. I am grateful to Adom Getachew for pointing me to Jean Allman's essay.
109. Civil rights leader and minister Ralph Abernathy attended the Positive Action Conference, representing the Montgomery Improvement Association.
110. Meriwether, *Proudly We Can Be Africans*, 181–184; Allman, "Nuclear imperialism"; Ahlman, "The Algerian question."
111. Nkrumah, Speech by the Prime Minister of Ghana at the Opening Session of the Conference on Positive Action and Security in Africa, April 7, 1960, *Positive Action Conference for Peace and Security in Africa: Resolutions and Manifesto* (Accra: Community Centre, 1960), 4.
112. Sutherland and Meyer, *Guns and Gandhi in Africa*, 41.
113. St. Clair Drake quoted in Allman, "Nuclear imperialism," 96.
114. The weight of Fanon's analysis of anticolonial revolution and the Algerian context would not reach most Americans, including SNCC activists, until five years later, with the arrival of the American edition of *Wretched of the Earth*, published by Grove Press in 1965. This edition, which reproduced for much larger audiences Constance Farrington's 1963 translation, came out a few months before the Watts riots and was widely marketed as required reading for radical activists. On the role that Fanon played for Black Power and civil rights activists, see Rychetta Wilkins, *Black Power,*

Yellow Power, and the Making of Revolutionary Identities (Jackson: University Press of Mississippi, 2012), Chapter 1.

115. On the sit-ins, see Chapter 3.
116. Recommendations of the Findings and Recommendations Committee, April 1960, Minutes: Aug. 1, 1960–Oct. 30, 1968 (Folder 252253-003-0903), Subgroup A, Series III, Student Nonviolent Coordinating Committee Papers, 1959–1972, Martin Luther King, Jr. Center for Nonviolent Social Change, Atlanta GA (hereafter SNCC Papers).
117. Conference Program, "Nonviolence and the achievement of desegregation," October 15, 1960, 1960 Conferences (Folder 252253-001-0698), Subgroup A, Series V, SNCC Papers. Okuku's presence at the SNCC conference came to my attention thanks to the amazing work of Fanon Che Wilkins on SNCC's internationalism. However, Wilkins incorrectly places Okuku at the April conference at Shaw, rather than in Atlanta. See Fanon Che Wilkins, "The making of black internationalists: SNCC and Africa before the launching of Black Power, 1960–1965," *The Journal of African American History* 92, no. 4 (Fall 2007): 468.
118. John Friedman to Jane Stembridge, September 10, 1960, Correspondence: Oct. 14–16, 1960 (Folder 252253-011-0401), Subgroup A, Series V, SNCC Papers. Alphonse Okuku's presence in the US and at Antioch was already a product of those years of exchange. In 1959, the Southern Christian Leadership Conference hosted Tom Mboya, during which time he got to know both King and Rustin, who helped arrange for Okuku to attend college in the United States. Rustin later recalled that Okuku lived with him for a while when he first arrived.
119. John Lewis, "Speech at March on Washington, 1963", in *African American Political Thought, Volume 2: Confrontation vs. Compromise, from 1945 to the Present*, edited by Marcus D. Pohlman (New York and London: Routledge, 2003), 483.
120. I am grateful to Lida Maxwell for offering me this useful formulation.
121. See David Theo Goldberg, "Racial comparisons, relational racisms: Some thoughts on method," *Ethnic and Racial Studies* 32, no. 7 (September 2009): 1271–1282. What the movement of ideas about anticolonialism and nonviolence suggests, however, is that a comparative enterprise and a relational one need not be mutually exclusive. As I remarked at the beginning of the chapter, both the relational and comparative analyses at stake here elide the problem of American settler colonialism, through the collapse of racialization and colonization that imaginative transit made possible. See Byrd, *Transit of Empire*.

Chapter 3

1. Oral history interview with Fannie Lou Hamer by KZSU Radio Station, Stanford University, 1965, KZSU Project South Interviews, Department of Special Collections and University Archives, Stanford University, Stanford, CA. Digital transcript available at https://searchworks.stanford.edu/view/zb317wv2717.
2. Frederick Douglass, *My Bondage and My Freedom* (New Haven: Yale University Press, 2014), 198.

3. King, "Statement to the press at the beginning of the Youth Leadership Conference," Raleigh, NC, 15 April 15, 1960, in *The Papers of Martin Luther King, Jr., Volume V: Threshold of a New Decade, January 1959–December 1960*, edited by Clayborne Carson (Berkeley and Los Angeles: University of California Press, 2005), 426–427.
4. The details of the account that follows are drawn from Kay Mills, *This Little Light of Mine: The Life of Fannie Lou Hamer* (New York: Dutton, 1993), Chapter 4; John Dittmer, *Local People: The Struggle for Civil Rights in Mississippi* (Urbana and Chicago: University of Illinois Press, 1994), Chapter 8; Chana Kai Lee, *For Freedom's Sake: The Life of Fannie Lou Hamer* (Urbana and Chicago: University of Illinois Press, 2000), Chapter 3; Davis W. Houck, "Fannie Lou Hamer on Winona: Trauma, Recovery, Memory," in *Social Controversy and Public Address in the 1960s and Early 1970s: A Rhetorical History of the United States, Volume 9*, edited by Richard J. Jensen (East Lansing: Michigan State Press, 2017), 1–38; "The Winona incident: An interview with Annelle Ponder and Fannie Lou Hamer, June 1963," in Pat Watters and Reese Cleghorn, *Climbing Jacob's Ladder: The Arrival of Negroes in Southern Politics* (New York: Harcourt Brace, 1967), 361–375; Fannie Lou Hamer, *To Praise Our Bridges: An Autobiography* (Jackson, MS: KIPCO, 1967); June Johnson, Interview by Tom Dent, Tom Dent Collection, box 137, item 13, side 2, Amistad Research Center, Tulane University, New Orleans, LA; Johnson, Interview by Joseph Sinsheimer, typescript, May 5, 1987, box 1, Joseph A. Sinsheimer Papers, David M. Rubenstein Rare Book & Manuscript Library, Duke University, Raleigh, NC. My account is particularly indebted to Houck's thorough, careful, and authoritative narration of the events in Winona.
5. Charles Payne, *I've Got the Light of Freedom: The Organizing Tradition and the Mississippi Freedom Struggle* (Berkeley: University of California Press, 1995), 35.
6. Todd Moye, *Let the People Decide: Black Freedom and White Resistance Movements in Sunflower County, Mississippi, 1945–1986* (Raleigh: University of North Carolina Press, 2004), 101.
7. Houck, "Hamer on Winona," 30–31.
8. Houck, "Hamer on Winona," 32.
9. Johnson, Interview by Dent.
10. Johnson, Interview by Dent.
11. Houck, "Hamer on Winona," 35.
12. "The Winona incident," in *Climbing Jacob's Ladder*, 369–370.
13. In fact, Guyot's part of the story is a little bit more complicated and a little bit more sinister still. After the first round of beatings, Herod loaded him up in the car and drove him to the Carroll County Jail, where he was held for a night. According to Howard Zinn's account, he was beaten by White Citizens' Council members while in Carroll County. Houck notes that he was "taken out of his cell and paraded before scores of police officers who could now identify this homegrown racial agitator." Guyot was returned to Montgomery County on the morning of Monday, June 10. Only then did he see the six activists already held there, whose release he had been trying to secure. Howard Zinn, *SNCC: The New Abolitionists* (Boston: Beacon, 1964), 95; Houck, "Hamer on Winona," 37.

14. Hamer and Johnson cited in Mills, *This Little Light of Mine*, 60–61. See also Johnson, Interview by Sinsheimer.
15. Endesha Ida Mae Holland, *From the Mississippi Delta: A Memoir* (Chicago: Lawrence Hill, 1997), 244. See also Zinn, "The battle-scarred youngsters," *The Nation*, October 5, 1963.
16. Violation of this law was classed as a misdemeanor offense, with a maximum penalty of a "$200 fine, fourth months in jail, or both." The language of the bill is quoted in William Kunstler, "Law and the sit-ins," *The Nation*, November 4, 1961, 351. As Kunstler notes, though "state and federal judges in Mississippi . . . labeled this and companion statues as non-racial legislation," the bill passed "without debate, by a vote of 113 to 3" as part of an anti-integration package. Right before the vote, when one congressman objected that the statute violated the right to peaceful assembly, one of the bill's sponsor's responded: "You know what the bill's for. There's no need to talk about it" (351). For a broader discussion of the use of the law as "a tool for social control of civil rights efforts" in the South, see Stephen E. Barkan, *Protestors on Trial: Criminal Justice in the Southern Civil Rights and Vietnam Antiwar Movements* (New Brunswick, NJ: Rutgers University Press, 1985), Chapters 3 and 4.
17. "Let us do the job," *Winona Times*, June 20, 1963, 1, cited in Houck, "Hamer on Winona," 40.
18. Houck, "Hamer on Winona," 41. See *U.S. v. Earle Wayne Partridge, Thomas J. Herod, Jr., William Surrell, John L. Basinger, and Charles Thomas Perkins*, 18 U.S.C. 242, 371 (1963). Despite the acquittals, William Harrel Lawson and Scott Alan Smith argued that the case nevertheless provided a key symbolic victory, "represent[ing] a moment when the federal government finally took action by enforcing existing legislation protecting civil rights," thereby marking a shift away from the "laissez-fair attitude and approach" it had taken up to that point. Lawson and Smith, "Defeat in decision, victory in action: A critical legal rhetoric reading of *U.S. v. Partridge et al.* (1963)," *Communication Law Review* 12, no. 1 (2012): 11.
19. Hamer, *To Praise Our Bridges*, 15.
20. The jailed activists in Winona emerged from the Montgomery County Jail on Wednesday, June 12, only to learn that Medgar Evers, NAACP field secretary for Mississippi, had been murdered in his driveway by a member of the White Citizens' Council, Byron De La Beckwith.
21. Perhaps (as Reese Cleghorn and Pat Watters aver), press attention was at that moment focused elsewhere—squarely on the figure of George Wallace, darkening the doorway at the University of Alabama to prevent its desegregation. See Watters and Cleghorn, *Climbing Jacob's Ladder*, 138.
22. For this reason, the issue of segregated public accommodations, which was a prime focus of the civil rights movement in the late 1950s and early 1960s, is sometimes maligned as a middle-class issue that was—at best—of distant concern to the black working class. At worst, the issue of public accommodations effectively displaced more central issues—economic inequality and criminal justice—that should have taken center stage. There is, of course, truth in this critique; as Martin Luther King, Jr. would later quip, "What good is it to be allowed to eat in a restaurant if you can't afford

the hamburger?" Even so, accounts focused purely on the indignity and humiliation of segregated accommodations miss what the activists discussed in this chapter surely knew: the segregation of restaurants, lunch counters, parks, pools, and the like were not only linked to other forms of racial domination but also enabled and maintained a regime of racialized policing, criminalization, and incarceration. For a recent account focused on the indignity of segregation, see Bruce Ackerman, *We the People, Volume 3: The Civil Rights Revolution* (Cambridge, MA: Belknap Press, 2014). King's quote is referenced in "Showdown for nonviolence," *Look Magazine*, April 16, 1968, 24—though both Bayard Rustin and Whitney Young expressed similar sentiments. See Rustin, "From protest to politics: The future of the civil rights movement," *Commentary* 39, no. 2 (February 1964): 25; Young, *To Be Equal* (New York: McGraw Hill, 1963), 54.

23. Hamer, "We're on our way," speech delivered at a mass meeting in Indianola, MI, September 1964, in *Speeches of Fannie Lou Hamer*, 52.
24. Mississippi House Bill 558 was not *sui generis*. After the emergence of the sit-in campaigns in 1960, numerous Southern states—including Virginia, Georgia, and Louisiana—passed similar laws that attempted to criminalize desegregation protests, either through vague breach of peace statutes or trespass statutes that made it illegal to remain on private property if the owner has asked you to leave. See Barkan, *Protestors on Trial*, 31–33. Such measures, however, merely formalized and codified a social reality already implicit within racial segregation—that, based on little more than the perception of white citizens or officials, black bodies could be designated as "out of place" and thereby criminal.
25. Houck, "Hamer on Winona," 55.
26. Most famously, Hamer detailed her experience in Winona in front of a televised, national audience, when she testified before the Credentials Committee at the 1964 Democratic National Convention. However, she returned again and again to Winona in speeches and statements throughout her life, both before and beyond the 1964 DNC. See *Speeches of Fannie Lou Hamer*.
27. Hamer, "We're on our way," in *Speeches of Fannie Lou Hamer*, 54.
28. An excellent analysis of Hamer's complex rhetorical strategies in the speech "We're on our way" is provided by Houck and Brooks, "Fannie Lou Hamer, 'We're on our way' (September 1964)," *Voices of Democracy* 6 (2011): 21–43; on Hamer's use of the Winona story more broadly, see Houck, "Hamer on Winona."
29. David Lefkowitz, "On a moral right to civil disobedience," *Ethics* 117, no. 2 (2007): 219–220. Lefkowitz denies that the state has a right to *punish* the civilly disobedient and limits legitimate state action to penalization (defined, following Joel Feinberg, as penalty without the moral judgment of wrongdoing implied in punishment). In his case, submitting to penalty, but not punishment, is required for civil disobedience. Ronald Dworkin espouses a similar but more permissive view, advocating for prosecutorial discretion in the face of civil disobedience. He writes, however, not about what civil disobedients ought to do, but about how the law should deal with them. See Joel Feinberg, "The expressive function of punishment," in *A Reader on Punishment*, edited by Anthony Duff and David Garland (Oxford: Oxford University

Press, 1994); Ronald Dworkin, *Taking Rights Seriously* (London: Gerald Duckworth, 1977), Chapter 8. A succinct, persuasive rebuttal of Lefkowitz's defense is provided in Brownlee, "Penalizing public disobedience," *Ethics* 118, no. 4 (July 2008): 711–716.
30. For a different view, see Kimberley Brownlee, "The communicative aspects of civil disobedience and lawful punishment," *Criminal Law and Philosophy* 1 (2007): 179–192. For Brownlee the law is a "communicative system": public processes of mutual justification allow the civilly disobedient and the state to persuade each other of their reasons (for disobeying, in the case of the former, and for punishing, in the case of the latter). Here the object is not precisely containment, but the exchange of reasons in which both the protestor and the state have opportunities to revise or modify their stance—or not. The state may punish a disobedient and try to persuade her against further acts of disobedience; she may comply, or she may seek to communicate that she has not been persuaded by the state's reasons, by challenging the verdict in court or heading back out into the streets in protest.
31. See also Marshall Cohen, "Liberalism and disobedience," *Philosophy and Public Affairs* 1, no. 3 (1972): 286.
32. Rawls, "The justification of civil disobedience," in *Civil Disobedience: Theory and Practice*, edited by Hugo Bedau (New York: Pegasus, 1969) 247–248.
33. Andrew Sabl, "Looking forward to justice: Rawlsian civil disobedience and its non-Rawlsian lessons," *Journal of Political Philosophy* 9, no. 3 (2001): 317.
34. Carl Cohen, *Civil Disobedience: Conscience, Tactics, and the Law* (New York: Columbia University Press, 1972), 44–45.
35. On the political ethics of the oppressed under conditions of systemic injustice, see Tommie Shelby, *Dark Ghettos: Injustice, Dissent, and Reform* (Cambridge and London: Harvard University Press, 2016).
36. Bernard Boxill, "The roots of civil disobedience in republicanism and slavery," in To Shape a New World: *Essays on the Political Philosophy of Martin Luther King, Jr.*, edited by Brandon M. Terry and Tommie Shelby (Cambridge and London: Belknap, 2018), 70.
37. Douglass, *My Bondage and My Freedom,* 197–198.
38. Neil Roberts, *Freedom as Marronage* (Chicago and London: University of Chicago Press, 2015), 78.
39. Douglass, *My Bondage and My Freedom,* 218.
40. Boxill, "The roots of civil disobedience," 73. My use of the term "fugitive," as well as the broader conceptualization of Douglass's account of comparative freedom, is obviously also indebted to Roberts, *Freedom as Marronage*, Chapter 2.
41. Boxill, "The roots of civil disobedience," 76–77.
42. Juliet Hooker likewise urges a shift away from "orthodox liberal accounts of civil disobedience" toward the archive of African American political thought, and emphasizes the way such a shift enables us to pose different questions about dissent. See Hooker, "Disobedience in black: On race and dissent," in *Nomos LXII: Protest and Dissent*, edited by Melissa Schwartzberg (New York: New York University Press, 2020), 45–63.
43. King, "The burning truth in the South," *The Progressive* 24 (May 1960): 8–10.

44. The disjuncture of the "spatial" from the "temporal" in my phrasing is misleading; we can equally position Douglass transnationally. On this, see Juliet Hooker, *Theorizing Race in the Americas: Douglass, Sarmiento, Du Bois, and Vasconcelos* (New York: Oxford, 2019), Chapter 1.
45. Ray Cromley, "Negroes plan to extend 'sit-ins,'" *New York World-Telegram and Sun*, April 26, 1960.
46. Len Holt, "Jail, not bail," *Southern Patriot* 18, no. 5 (May 1960): 4.
47. Martin Oppenheimer, "Genesis of the Southern Negro student movement (sit-in movement): A study in contemporary Negro protest," PhD diss., University of Pennsylvania, 1963, 69.
48. Recommendations of the Findings and Recommendations Committee, April 1960, Minutes: Aug. 1, 1960–Oct. 30, 1968 (Folder 252253-003-0903), Subgroup A, Series III, SNCC Papers.
49. John Lewis, *Walking with the Wind: A Memoir of the Movement* (New York: Simon & Schuster, 1998), 80. An excellent account of the role of the different college campuses in the Nashville student movement can be found in Jeffrey Turner, "The rise of black and white student protest in Nashville," in *Rebellion in Black and White: Southern Student Activism in the 1960s*, edited by Robert Cohen and David J. Snyder (Baltimore, MD: Johns Hopkins University Press, 2013), 129–137.
50. David Halberstam, *The Children* (New York: Random House, 1998), 11 ff.; Taylor Branch, *Parting the Waters: America in the King Years, 1954–1963* (New York: Simon & Schuster, 1988), 278 ff.
51. Halberstam, *The Children*.
52. Harris, "75 students back in jail," *Tennessean*, March 2, 1960; see also Lewis, *Walking with the Wind*, 110; Branch, *Parting the Waters*, 279.
53. Taylor, *Parting the Waters*, 279.
54. John Lewis recalls the choice for jail over fines and bail in his 1998 memoir: "We weren't about to pay bail. We were in jail because of racial segregation in Nashville. Until that segregation was ended, we had nowhere else to be—we *belonged* nowhere else—but in those lunch counter seats or behind bars. We were happy to be in jail for this cause. We welcomed it. If the authorities chose to release us, fine. We would walk out freely and resume the task at hand. But we were not about to *pay* our way out. We were not about to cooperate in any way with a system that allowed the discrimination we were protesting." Lewis, *Walking with the Wind*, 108–109.
55. Mayor Ben West made a deal with the demonstrators, offering to release them from jail and appoint a biracial commission to examine lunch counter desegregation in exchange for a halt in demonstrations. It was not until after the home of the students' lawyer, Z. Alexander Looby, was bombed and Nash led a protest march, 4,000 strong, into downtown Nashville that all downtown lunch counters were ordered to desegregate.
56. August Meier and Elliot M. Rudwick, *CORE: A Study in the Civil Rights Movement, 1942–1968* (New York: Oxford University Press, 1973), 106–107.
57. Patricia Stephens, "Tallahassee: Through jail to freedom," in *Sit-In: The Student Reports*, edited by James Peck (New York: Congress of Racial Equality, 1960). See

also "8 Florida Negroes choose 60 days in jail over fines," *Washington Post,* March 19, 1960, 1; "Students choose jail terms in Tallahassee, Fla.," *Atlanta Daily World,* March 19, 1960, 1.

58. Quoted in Oppenheimer, *Genesis of the Southern Negro Student Movement,* 101–102; Raymond Arsenault, *Freedom Riders: 1961 and the Struggle for Racial Justice* (Oxford and New York: Oxford University Press, 2006), 89; on the relationship between the NAACP and the direct action organizations regarding "jail, no bail," see also Zoe Colley, *Ain't Scared of Your Jail: Arrest, Imprisonment, and the Civil Rights Movement* (Gainesville: University of Florida Press, 2013), Chapters 2 and 3.
59. See NAACP statements and correspondence on sit-ins, box A-289, reel 21, frames 0305-0434, Group III, Series A, Papers of the NAACP (Microfilm), Manuscripts Division, Yale University Library, New Haven, CT (hereafter NAACP Papers).
60. "NAACP position on 'jail, no bail' concept," Memorandum from Gloster B. Current to Roy Wilkins et al., February 9, 1961, box A-290, reel 22, frame 0061, Group III, Series A, NAACP Papers. See also Colley, *Ain't Scared of Your Jail,* 48.
61. Meier and Rudwick, *CORE,* 113.
62. Meier and Rudwick, *CORE,* 116–117.
63. James Robinson, "Jail—not bail," *CORE-lator* 84 (September 1960). All eighteen were convicted of the charges but were given suspended sentences.
64. Meier and Rudwick, *CORE,* 4–6; Nicole Rhoton, "World War II resistors: Creating communities of resistance in prison," *Peace & Change* 36, no. 2 (April 2011): 193. The other four founders of CORE were likewise pacifists: James Farmer, Bernice Fisher, Homer Jack, and James Robinson. Farmer and Robinson applied for, and were granted, conscientious objector status during World War II.
65. See, e.g., Peter Brock, ed., *These Strange Criminals: An Anthology of Prison Memoirs by Conscientious Objectors from the Great War to the Cold War* (Toronto: University of Toronto Press, 2004). See also Rhoton, "World War II Resistors."
66. James Peck, *We Who Would Not Kill* (New York: Lyle Stuart, 1958). *See also,* Rhoton, "World War II Resistors," 205–211.
67. Rhoton, "World War II Resistors."
68. Kim Gilmore, "Slavery and prison—Understanding the connections," *Social Justice* 27, no. 3 (2000): 195–205; Angela Davis, "From the convict lease system to the super max prison," in *States of Confinement: Policing, Detention, and Prisons,* edited by J. James (New York: St. Martin's Press, 2000), 60–74; Colley, *Ain't Scared of Your Jail,* 5–6.
69. Lewis, *Walking with the Wind,* 121.
70. See, e.g., Gilmore, "Slavery and prison"; Davis, "From the convict lease system"; Gail W. O'Brien, *The Color of the Law: Race, Violence and Justice in the Post World War II South* (Chapel Hill: University of North Carolina Press, 1999); Edward Ayers, *Vengeance and Justice: Crime and Punishment in the Nineteenth Century South* (New York: Oxford University Press, 1984); Douglas Blackmon, *Slavery by Another Name: The Re-Enslavement of Black Americans from the Civil War to World War II* (New York: Doubleday, 2008):Khalil Gibran Muhammad, *The Condemnation of Blackness: Race, Crime, and the Making of Modern Urban America* (Cambridge and London: Harvard University Press, 2010).

71. Dan Berger, *Captive Nation: Prison Organizing in the Civil Rights Era* (Chapel Hill: University of North Carolina Press, 2014), 22.
72. While reports of treatment within jails, prisons, and work farms varied widely, the worst fears of the NAACP were often confirmed—as activists faced beatings and other forms of mistreatment and abuse. See n. 11.
73. *Justice? The Committee of Inquiry into the Administration of Justice in the Freedom Struggle* (New York: Congress of Racial Equality, 1962), 2.
74. The idea of unmerited suffering is illustrated nicely by King in this statement to sit-inners in Durham, NC: "I have prayed much over our Southern situation, and I have come to the conclusion that we are in for a season of suffering. Now I pray that, recognizing the necessity of suffering, the Negro will make of it a virtue. To suffer in a righteous cause is to grow to our humanity's full stature. If only to save ourselves from bitterness, we need the vision to see the ordeals of this generation as an opportunity to transfigure ourselves and American society. Let us not fear going to jail. If the officials threaten to arrest us for standing up for our rights, we must answer by saying that we are willing and prepared to fill up the jails of the South. Maybe it will take this willingness to stay in jail to arouse the dozing conscience of our nation." King, "A creative protest," in *King Papers V*, 370.
75. "Now it is a nice thing to go to jail," *Baltimore Afro-American,* March 5, 1960, 5.
76. Berger, *Captive Nation*, 26.
77. Colley, *Ain't Scared of Your Jail,* 30.
78. Charles Sherrod, quoted in Charlotte Devree, "The young Negro rebels," *Harper's Magazine* (October 1961): 134–135.
79. Richard King, *Civil Rights and the Idea of Freedom* (New York: Oxford University Press, 1994), 42.
80. King, *Civil Rights and the Idea of Freedom*, 26.
81. King, *Civil Rights and the Idea of Freedom*, 27–28.
82. Bernice Reagon, Interview by Dick Cluster, in *They Should Have Served that Cup of Coffee* (Boston: South End Press, 1979), 22–23.
83. Lewis in William R. Beardslee, *The Way Out Must Lead In: Life Histories in the Civil Rights Movement* (Atlanta: Center for Research in Social Change, 1977), 8.
84. Arendt, "What is freedom?" in her *Between Past and Future: Eight Exercises in Political Thought* (New York: Penguin, 2006); King, *Civil Rights and the Idea of Freedom*, 25.
85. Anne Braden, "Student movement: A new phase," *Southern Patriot* 18, no. 9 (November 1960): 4. See also Meier and Rudwick, *CORE*, 119; Oppenheimer, *Genesis of the Southern Negro Student Movement*, 95.
86. See G. Sherman, "'Gaol not bail' for sitters-in," *Atlanta Observer*, October 23, 1960, 9; Telegram to Martin Luther King, Jr. from Nashville Non-Violent Student Movement, October 19, 1960, *King Papers V*, 524; King, Draft statement to Judge James E. Webb after arrest at Rich's Department Store, October 19, 1960, *King Papers V*, 522–524. It had not gone unnoticed by student activists in CORE and SNCC that, despite his advocacy of "filling the jails" of the South, King had spent comparatively few days behind bars. King was ultimately released after Attorney General Robert Kennedy famously intervened on his behalf. See Arsenault, *Freedom Riders*, 89–92.

87. King, "Why we chose jail rather than bail," October 1960, *King Papers V*, 525.
88. Thomas Gaither, *Jailed-In* (New York: Congress of Racial Equality, 1961), 3; "10 Negroes seized in Carolina sit-in," *New York Times*, February 1, 1961, 39.
89. Gaither, *Jailed-In*, 8.
90. Gaither, *Jailed-In*, 8; "Jail-ins," *CORE-lator* 87 (March 1961); "8 Negro students are put in solitary," *New York Times*, February 20, 1961, 19; Meier and Rudwick, *CORE*, 118.
91. Minutes, SNCC Meeting, February 3–5, 1961, Atlanta GA, Minutes: Aug. 1, 1960–Oct. 30, 1968 (Folder 252253-003-0903), Subgroup A, Series III, SNCC Papers; "Three protest groups elect jail; call comes from Rock Hill for help," *The Student Voice* 2, no. 2 (February 1961).
92. C. Hampton, "Jail, yes; bail, no," *Baltimore Afro-American*, February 18, 1961, 1. CORE's protestors at the NYC store wore striped prison uniforms while picketing the store.
93. Gaither, *Jailed-In*; Claude Sitton, "4 Negroes jailed in Carolina sit-in," *New York Times*, February 7, 1961, 36.
94. Sitton, "Negro jail drive pressed in South," *New York Times*, February 12, 1961; "It's jail, not bail," *Baltimore Afro-American*, February 18, 1961, 4; "Students prefer jail ins to bail outs," *Southern Patriot* 19, no. 3 (March 1961): 1, 3; "Jail-ins," *CORE-lator* 87 (March 1961); Colley, *Ain't Scared of Your Jail*, 47.
95. "Across the editor's desk," *The Student Voice* 2, no. 2 (February 1961).
96. *Boynton v. Virginia* 364 U.S. 454 (1960).
97. Farmer, quoted in Arsenault, *Freedom Riders*, 94.
98. "Freedom Rides," *CORE-lator* 88 (April 1961); Peck, *Freedom Ride* (New York: Simon & Schuster, 1962), 115.
99. Farmer, *Freedom—When?* (New York: Random House, 1965), ix.
100. Farmer, *Freedom—When?*, 69.
101. "Bi-racial buses attacked; riders beaten in Alabama," *New York Times*, May 15, 1961, 1; Peck, *Freedom Ride*, 124 ff. A detailed account of what occurred is offered in Arsenault, *Freedom Riders*, Chapter 4.
102. Lewis, *Walking with the Wind*, 144–147; Arsenault, *Freedom Riders*, 179–180.
103. Arsenault, *Freedom Riders*, 184.
104. Lewis, *Walking with the Wind*, 149.
105. "Freedom riders attacked by whites in Montgomery," *New York Times*, May 21, 1961, 1; "Montgomery under martial law," *New York Times*, May 22, 1961, 1; Arsenault, *Freedom Riders*, 224.
106. All but the breach of peace charges would ultimately be dropped.
107. *CORE-lator* 89 (May 1961); Peck, *Freedom Ride*, 139–140; F. Halloway, "Travel notes from a Deep South tourist," *New South* 26 (July–August 1961): 5–6.
108. Freedom Rides Coordinating Committee, Report of meeting, May 26, 1961, 2, box 35, folder 2, Southern Christian Leadership Conference Records, 1954–1970, Martin Luther King, Jr. Center for Nonviolent Social Change, Atlanta, GA (hereafter SCLC Papers).

109. Farmer, in Howell Raines, *My Soul Is Rested: Movement Days in the Deep South Remembered* (New York: Penguin, 1983), 109.
110. Sitton, "Dr. King refuses to end bus test," *New York Times,* May 26, 1961, 1.
111. Quoted in Arsenault, *Freedom Riders,* 274–275.
112. Gaither, Final report on Freedom Rider cases, Hinds County, n.d., folder 119: Freedom Rides–Legal and Financial Aspects (April 3, 1961–June 22, 1962), Series 5, Congress of Racial Equality Papers, 1941–1967, Martin Luther King, Jr. Center for Nonviolent Social Change, Atlanta, GA (hereafter CORE Papers).
113. David Oshinksy, *Worse than Slavery: Parchman Farm and the Ordeal of Jim Crow Justice* (New York: Free Press, 1996), 110.
114. "'They tried to turn us into animals': Freedom Riders sleep in own stench in Miss. jail," *Philadelphia Tribune,* July 8, 1961, 1.
115. Arsenault, *Freedom Riders,* 352.
116. James Farmer, *Lay Bare the Heart: An Autobiography of the Civil Rights Movement* (New York: New American Library, 1985), 21.
117. Halloway's account, which appeared in *New South,* is quoted by Zinn, *SNCC,* 65.
118. Berger, *Captive Nation,* 43.
119. Colley, *Ain't Scared of Your Jail,* 58. Though accurate figures are hard to come by, Farmer no doubt significantly overestimates the cost to Jackson—which he states as "over a million dollars." This overstatement is in itself interesting however, from the perspective of civil disobedience theory. If, as theorists suggest, going to jail were meant as a limiting device or (exclusively) as a moral appeal, then why would Farmer represent the victory of filling Jackson's jail in these terms? See Farmer, *Freedom—When?,* 72.
120. One Mississippi official reportedly bragged that they had "busted CORE with our bond requirements." Testimony of Louis Lusky, in *Justice?,* 30; R. H. Parke, "189 riders appeal Jackson conviction," *New York Times,* August 15, 1961, 1; Meier and Rudwick, *CORE,* 142–143; Farmer, *Lay Bare the Heart* 211–212.
121. *Henry Thomas v. Mississippi* (1965).
122. Nash, always among the most radical and fierce of the activists, expressed no small amount of disappointment in the retreat of "jail, no bail" from prominence. When, at five months pregnant, she decided to drop her appeal of an earlier two-year sentence, she justified her actions this way: "Some people have asked me how I can do this when I am expecting my first child in September. I have searched my soul about this and considered it in prayer. I have reached the conclusion that in the long run this will be the best thing I can do for my child. This will be a black child in Mississippi and thus wherever he is born he will be in prison. I believe that if I go to jail now it may help hasten a day when my child and all children will be free—not only on the day of their birth but for all of their lives." Further, in keeping with the analysis of this chapter, she wrote to her fellow student activists to defend not one but multiple reasons why refusing bail is important: "[The] hours that we give to the state for these trials are hours of humiliation and oppression, hours that defile our worth as persons. And then we are asked to pay the bill for this humiliation in court costs. . . . In addition to these basic considerations, there is the very practical matter

of skyrocketing expense of continued and numerous legal actions. Our Deep South states have become very smart about this; they are setting bonds high." Diane Nash Bevel, Statement, April 30, 1962, box 28, folder 19, Martin Luther King, Jr. Papers, Martin Luther King, Jr., Center for Nonviolent Social Change, Atlanta, GA (hereafter King Papers).

123. Colley, *Ain't Scared of Your Jail*, 59–60.
124. Lewis, *Walking with the Wind*, 135.
125. James Lawson, "Eve of nonviolent revolution?" *Southern Patriot* 19, no. 6 (November 1961): 1.
126. King, *Civil Rights and the Idea of Freedom*, 58.
127. Nash Bevel, Statement, King Papers.
128. On this point, see Mantena, "Competing theories of nonviolent politics," in *Nomos LXII*, 83–121.

Chapter 4

1. Farmer, *Freedom—When?* (New York: Random House, 1965), 17.
2. Reinhold Niebuhr, *Moral Man and Immoral Society: A Study in Ethics and Politics* (New York: Charles Scribner & Sons, 1932), 4.
3. King quoted in Birmingham Police Report, Mass meeting of ACMHR at First Baptist Church (April 8, 1963), April 10, 1963, box 13.2, coll. 268, Connor Papers.
4. Two scathing front-page articles in the *New York Times* written by Harrison Salisbury introduced the country to the racial politics of Birmingham in the spring of 1960, if they hadn't already made its acquaintance: Salisbury, "Fear and hatred grip Birmingham," *New York Times*, April 12, 1960, 1; Salisbury, "Race issue shakes Alabama structure," *New York Times*, April 13, 1960, 1. These articles, reprinted by the local Birmingham newspapers, provoked a libel suit against *NYT* from the three-man Birmingham City Commission; see "3 in Birmingham sue the Times," *New York Times*, April 16, 1960, 15. On Birmingham's reputation in the early 1960s, see also James Bevel, Interview by Blackside, Inc. on November 13, 1985, for *Eyes on the Prize: America's Civil Rights Years (1954-1965)*, Washington University Libraries, Film and Media Archive, Henry Hampton Collection.
5. The city's New Deal era anti-labor vigilantism and the bombing of black houses in "Dynamite Hill" and throughout the city (bankrolled and otherwise supported, it should be said, by US Steel, coal operators, and Birmingham's political power elite) are discussed in detail in Diane McWhorter's *Carry Me Home: Birmingham, Alabama—The Climactic Battle of the Civil Rights Revolution* (New York: Simon & Schuster, 2001), as well as in Glenn Eskew, *But for Birmingham: The Local and National Movements in the Civil Rights Struggle* (Chapel Hill and London: University of North Carolina Press, 1997).
6. Bevel, Interview by Blackside, Inc.
7. William Smith, *Civil Disobedience and Deliberative Democracy* (Abingdon: Routledge, 2013), 33.

8. Smith, "Democracy, deliberation and disobedience," *Res Publica* 10, no. 4 (December 2004): 375. For other deliberative and communicative accounts of civil disobedience, see Introduction, n. 18. For critiques of the deliberative account, see Iris Marion Young, "Activist challenges to deliberative democracy," *Political Theory* 29, no. 5 (2001): 670–690; John Medearis, "Social movements and deliberative democratic theory," *British Journal of Political Science* 35, no. 1 (2005): 53–75; Humphrey Stears, "Animal rights protest and the challenge to deliberative democracy," 400–422; Guy Aitchison, "Domination and disobedience: Protest, coercion and the limits of an appeal to justice," *Perspectives on Politics* 16, no. 3 (2018): 666–679.
9. Jürgen Habermas, "Civil disobedience: Litmus test for the democratic constitutional state," *Berkeley Journal of Sociology* 30 (1985): 99, emphasis mine.
10. Habermas, *Theory and Practice*, translated by John Viertel (Boston: Beacon Press, 1988), 240. This phrase is sometimes rendered as "forceless force," further emphasizing its non-coercive nature.
11. Linda Zerilli, "Against civility: A feminist perspective," in *Civility, Legality, and Justice in America*, edited by Austin Sarat (New York: Cambridge University Press), 116.
12. Niebuhr, *Moral Man and Immoral Society*, 233.
13. Niebuhr, *Moral Man and Immoral Society*, 250.
14. Doug McAdam, "The framing function of movement tactics: strategic dramaturgy in the American civil rights movement," in *Comparative Perspectives on Social Movements: Political Opportunities, Mobilizing Structures, and Cultural Framings*, edited by Doug McAdam, John D. McCarthy, and Mayer N. Zald (Cambridge: Cambridge University Press, 1996), 338–355.
15. Karuna Mantena, "Showdown for nonviolence: The theory and practice of nonviolent politics," in *To Shape a New World: Essays on the Political Philosophy of Martin Luther King, Jr.*, edited by Brandon M. Terry and Tommie Shelby (Cambridge and London: Belknap, 2018), 99.
16. Frances Fox Piven, *Challenging Authority: How Ordinary People Change America* (Lanham, MD: Rowman & Littlefield, 2008), 28.
17. Salisbury, "Fear and hatred," 28. Connor quoted in the same piece.
18. Eskew, *But for Birmingham*, 10. The phrase "absentee baron" is borrowed from McWhorter, *Carry Me Home*, 43.
19. As Richard Lentz remarks: "If Birmingham was the citadel of Southern segregation, it also was an industrial city that, Jim Crow aside, was almost as northern as southern in social conditions." See Richard Lentz, *Symbols, the News Magazines, and Martin Luther King* (Baton Rouge: Louisiana State University Press, 1990), 77. This is not to say, as Eskew sometimes appears to, that Birmingham's "colonial economy" and corporate executives were solely responsible for the social and political structures that ruled Birmingham and shaped its racial politics nor to deny any regional specificity to racial and industrial realities in the Jim Crow South. Rather, my point is a more modest one: the economy and politics of Birmingham were tied in crucial ways to national structures and cannot be explained or dismissed as aberrations within a "fundamentally just" system of American democracy. The picture is simply more complicated, and far less (nationally) innocent, than that.

20. McWhorter, *Carry Me Home*, Chapter 1.
21. Quoted in Eskew, *But for Birmingham*, 95.
22. Sidney Smyer and James Head, president of an office supply firm and chairman of the Committee of 100 (a civic group within the Chamber of Commerce), quoted in "Business in Dixie: Many Southerners say racial tension slows area's economic gains," *Wall Street Journal*, May 26, 1961, 1. See also Burt Schorr, "Moderate Alabaman: Why one-time Dixiecrat helped set up race compromise," *Wall Street Journal*, May 23, 1963, 18; Eskew, *But for Birmingham*, 170–180.
23. *Reid v. City of Birmingham*, 150 So. 2d 735 (1963). See also Letter from Connor to Paul B. Hamilton, January 15, 1963, box 13.53, Connor Papers; Letter from Connor to Charles Affleck, January 16, 1963, box 14.52, Connor Papers.
24. "Birmingham vote ends a long rule," *New York Times*, April 4, 1963, 24; Eskew, *But for Birmingham*, 188-192.
25. "The South: Poorly timed protest," *Time*, April 19, 1963. For an analysis of news magazines' coverage of civil rights movement, and in particular King, see Lentz, *Symbols*.
26. "Handwriting on the wall," *Washington Post*, April 14, 1963, E6; "Violence in Birmingham," *Washington Post*, May 5, 1963, E6.
27. "'Bull' at bay," *Newsweek*, April 15, 1963, 29; "Connor and King," *Newsweek*, April 22, 1963, 28–33; "The prize and the risk," *Wall Street Journal*, May 9, 1963, 12; "The mob's blind force," *Wall Street Journal*, May 14, 1963, 16.
28. "Racial peace in Birmingham?" *New York Times*, April 17, 1963, 40.
29. Shuttlesworth quoted in Birmingham Police Report, Mass meeting at St. James Church (April 3, 1963), April 5, 1963, 3, box 13.2, Connor Papers.
30. King quoted in Birmingham Police Report, Mass meeting at Sixteenth Street Baptist Church (May 7, 1963), May 9, 1963, 6, box 13.4, Connor Papers.
31. Shuttlesworth, "Feud at the top," in Howell Raines, *My Soul Is Rested: Movement Days in the Deep South Remembered* (New York: Penguin, 1983), 155.
32. Foster Hailey, "4 Negroes jailed in Birmingham as the integration drive slows," *New York Times*, April 5, 1963, 16.
33. Walker quoted in Reese Cleghorn, "Martin Luther King, Jr.: Apostle of crisis," *Saturday Evening Post* 15 (1963): 16.
34. Versions of this narrative appear in, for example, David Garrow, *Bearing the Cross: Martin Luther King, Jr., and the Southern Christian Leadership Conference* (New York: William Morrow, 1986), 225–286; Adam Fairclough, *To Redeem the Soul of America: The Southern Christian Leadership Conference and Martin Luther King, Jr.* (Athens: University of Georgia Press, 2001), 114–115; Taylor Branch, *Parting the Waters: America in the King Years, 1954–63* (New York: Simon & Schuster, 1988), 114–122. As Eskew argues, these studies make the mistake of relying too heavily on accounts of Birmingham from memoirs and interviews conducted many years after the campaign itself—and thus, along with King and Walker, read back into Birmingham a more cohesive and consistent strategy than was in fact present at the campaign's start in early April. In mid-March, Shuttlesworth wrote to King and Walker, concerned about both the narrowness of the designed campaign and the lack of careful planning

that had been thus far done: "I am concerned," he wrote, "that we have not clearly defined areas of action, point of emphasis, the degree of commitment, and the time and methods by which other groups will be allowed to participate." Shuttlesworth to King and Walker, March 15, 1963, box 22, folder 11, King Papers. See also Eskew, *But for Birmingham*, 210–212; Thomas Jackson, *From Civil Rights to Human Rights: Martin Luther King, Jr. and the Struggle for Economic Justice* (Philadelphia: University of Pennsylvania Press, 2006), 158.

35. Executive staff meeting on Birmingham, January 23, 1963, box 36, folder 15, SCLC Papers; Tentative schedule for Project X in Birmingham, March 14, 1963, box 1, folder 7, King Papers.

36. For Sharp, nonviolent coercion achieves change "against the opponent's will and without his agreement, the sources of his power having been so undercut by nonviolent means that he no longer has control" (69). Eskew seems to assume that the initial, narrower focus of the campaign necessarily meant an early adherence to (and later abandonment of) a commitment to moral persuasion by King and the SCLC. See Gene Sharp, *The Politics of Nonviolent Action, Volume 3: Dynamics of Nonviolent Action* (Boston: Porter Sargent, 1973). Eskew, *But for Birmingham*, 213–216.

37. Tentative schedule for Project X, King Papers; King, *Why We Can't Wait* (Boston: Beacon, 2010), 56; Garrow, *Bearing the Cross*, 234; Eskew, *But for Birmingham*, 211–212.

38. Project "C" Progress Report, March 30, 1963, record ID 6.1.0.1320, Morehouse College Martin Luther King, Jr. Collection, Series 6: Southern Christian Leadership Conference Organizational Records, Robert W. Woodruff Library of the Atlanta University Center, Atlanta, GA.

39. Lentz, *Symbols*, 78. This, too, is a bit too binaristic a portrayal. As this chapter argues, the logic of the Birmingham campaign was surely about pressing the adversary to the wall—but it was not *only* about this, nor are persuasion and pressure well-conceived as mutually exclusive alternatives.

40. Walker, Interview by John Britton, October 11, 1967, typescript 59–60, New York, NY, Ralph Bunche Civil Rights Documentation Project, Moorland-Spingarn Research Center, Howard University, Washington, DC.

41. King quoted in Birmingham Police Report, Mass meeting at St. James Baptist Church (April 6, 1963), April 10, 1963, 2, box 13.2, Connor Papers.

42. Foster Hailey, "Police break up Alabama march," *New York Times*, April 8, 1963, 31; "Arrests break up City Hall march," *Birmingham Post-Herald*, April 8, 1963; James Forman, *The Making of Black Revolutionaries* (New York: Macmillan, 1972), 311; McWhorter, *Carry Me Home*, 329–331.

43. Connor quoted in McWhorter, *Carry Me Home*, 330.

44. Garrow, *Bearing the Cross*, 239.

45. Walker, Interview by Robert Penn Warren, March 18, 1964, typescript 17–18, box 211, folder 3677, Robert Penn Warren Papers, "Who Speaks for the Negro?," Beinecke Rare Book and Manuscript Library, Yale University, New Haven, CT (hereafter Warren Papers).

46. At Coretta King's urging, Attorney General Robert Kennedy intervened on King's behalf when he found out that King was not given the opportunity to call anyone or see

visitors. Walker and King tried to use this—and the fact that the president had called Coretta personally—to their advantage, but the media were rather dismissive of the story. See Transcript of phone call from Martin Luther King, Jr. to Coretta Scott King, April 12, 1963, 1, box 13.3, Connor Papers; McWhorter, *Carry Me Home*, 353.
47. Hailey, "Fighting erupts at Birmingham," *New York Times*, April 15, 1963, 1.
48. Forman, *Making of Black Revolutionaries*, 312.
49. Bill of injunction, City of Birmingham v. Wyatt Tee Walker, Ralph Abernathy, Martin Luther King, Jr., Fred L. Shuttlesworth et al., April 10, 1963, 5–7, box 6, folder 28, Albert Burton Boutwell Papers, Birmingham Public Library, Birmingham, AL. See also Statement regarding Birmingham injunction, April 11, 1963, box "January 1, 1963–May 25, 1963," King Papers; Shuttlesworth, ACMHR statement rejecting injunctions against demonstrations, April 14, 1963, box 1, folder 23, Fred Lee Shuttlesworth Papers, Martin Luther King, Jr. Center for Nonviolent Social Change, Atlanta, GA.
50. King, *Why We Can't Wait*, 96.
51. McWhorter, *Carry Me Home*, 355.
52. King, *Why We Can't Wait*, 101.
53. King, *Why We Can't Wait*, 91–92. By "racial capitalism," I mean to name the historical and analytical intertwining of racial and economic oppression under capitalism: capital accumulation requires and sustains "relations of severe inequality among human groups," and thus produces "loss, disposability, and the unequal differentiation of human value." In this way, Jodi Melamed argues, "racism enshrines the inequalities capitalism requires" (77). It may seem anachronistic to ascribe to King a critique of "racial capitalism"—a term most closely associated with theorist Cedric Robinson's 1983 work *Black Marxism*, and most widely used within contemporary discourse. Yet, as Jared Loggins and Andrew Douglas contend, a coherent critique of what can meaningfully be called "racial capitalism" is available in King's works. See Jodi Melamed, "Racial Capitalism," *Critical Ethnic Studies* 1, no. 1 (Spring 2015): 76–85; Cedric J. Robinson, *Black Marxism: The Making of the Black Radical Tradition* (Chapel Hill: University of North Carolina Press, 2000); Jared A. Loggins and Andrew J. Douglas, *Prophet of Discontent: Martin Luther King, Jr. and the Critique of Racial Capitalism* (Athens, GA: University of Georgia Press, 2021).
54. King, *Why We Can't Wait*, 96.
55. King, *Why We Can't Wait*, 2–3.
56. King, *Why We Can't Wait*, 3.
57. My account of King's articulation of the tactics of disruption and disclosure is indebted to many conversations and exchanges with three fellow travelers: Karuna Mantena, Brandon Terry, and Alex Livingston. See also Introduction, n. 11.
58. King, *Why We Can't Wait*, 96.
59. Terry, "After Ferguson," *The Point* 10 (2015).
60. King, *Why We Can't Wait*, 96-97.
61. King, *Why We Can't Wait*, 34.
62. Frances Fox Piven and Richard Cloward, *Poor People's Movements: Why They Succeed, How They Fail* (New York: Vintage, 1979), 26.

63. King, Speech at mass meeting, Sixteenth Street Baptist Church, April 9, 1963, 20, transcribed by David G. Holmes, Wyatt Tee Walker Collection, University of Richmond Digital Collections, Richmond, VA (hereafter Walker Collection); King, *Why We Can't Wait*, 36, emphases mine.
64. King, *Why We Can't Wait*, 91.
65. King, *Why We Can't Wait*, 150–151.
66. King, *Why We Can't Wait*, 90.
67. King, Speech at mass meeting, Saint John A.M.E. Church, May 10, 1963, 14, Walker Collection.
68. King, *Why We Can't Wait*, 12.
69. Bevel, Speech at mass meeting, Sixteenth Street Baptist Church, April 12, 1963, 32–33, Walker Collection.
70. Bevel, Speech at April 12 mass meeting, 36.
71. "Birmingham, a target city?" *Birmingham World*, April 10, 1963, 6.
72. William Kunstler, *Deep in My Heart* (New York: Morrow, 1966), 189.
73. See Birmingham Police Report, Mass meeting of ACMHR, St. James Baptist Church (April 24, 1963), April 26, 1963, box 13.3, Connor Papers. See also Eskew, *But for Birmingham*, 255.
74. Garrow, *Bearing the Cross*, 247.
75. Bevel, Interview by Blackside, Inc.
76. On Bevel's and Nash's roles in organizing Birmingham youth, see selections from James W. Stewart, Miriam Taylor McClendon, and Shirley Smith Miller in *Foot Soldiers for Democracy: The Men, Women, and Children of the Birmingham Civil Rights Movement* (Urbana and Chicago: University of Illinois Press, 2009); Janice Kelsey, Interview by Laura Anderson and Wayne Coleman, Birmingham Civil Rights Institute Oral History Project Collection, https://bcriohp.org/items/show/28.
77. Birmingham Police Report, Mass meeting (April 24, 1963), 3, box 13.3, Connor Papers.
78. Fairclough, *To Redeem the Soul*, 229.
79. On children in the civil rights movement, particularly their understanding of the stakes and the risks, see Robert Coles, *Children of Crisis: A Study in Courage and Fear* (Boston: Little, Brown, 1967); David Halberstam, *The Children* (New York: Ballantine Books, 1999). On the children in Birmingham particularly, see Horace Huntley and John W. McKerley, eds., *Foot Soldiers*.
80. Martin Berger, *Seeing Through Race: A Reinterpretation of Civil Rights Photography* (Berkeley and Los Angeles: University of California Press, 2011), 108.
81. Annetta Streeter Gary in *Foot Soldiers*, 120.
82. Eskew, *But for Birmingham*, 265–277. For accounts of the conditions children experienced in Birmingham's overflowing jails, see Huntley and McKerley, *Foot Soldiers*.
83. Walker quoted in Garrow, *Bearing the Cross*, 248; Walker, Interview by Britton, 54, 62.
84. "Birmingham, U.S.A.: 'Look at them run,'" *Newsweek*, May 13, 1963, 28. See also Hailey, "Dogs and hoses repulse Negroes at Birmingham," *New York Times*, May 4, 1963, 1.

85. "Police use water, dogs on marchers," *Birmingham Post-Herald*, May 4, 1963; "Negroes renew march—City firemen again hose down rock-throwing demonstrators," *Birmingham News*, May 4, 1963.
86. King, Speech at mass meeting, Sixteenth Street Baptist Church, May 3, 1963, 9, Walker Collection. King is not always clear about *who* the subject of this transformative paralysis is: segregationists willing to use violence directly against black citizens, or "white moderate" citizens and officials at a remove from the confrontation. There is some evolution in his thought over time: where earlier he emphasized the former in his arguments for nonviolence, during the Birmingham campaign, he focused more on the latter, though he did not completely abandon the idea that even a Bull Connor could be transformed.
87. Hailey, "U.S. seeking truce in Birmingham: Hoses again drive off demonstrators," *New York Times*, May 5, 1963, 1.
88. Quoted in Eskew, *But for Birmingham*, 273.
89. Fairclough, *To Redeem the Soul*, 136.
90. Statement by Robert F. Kennedy, May 3, 1963, DI BMPP-018-008, Burke Marshall Personal Papers Digital Clippings File, www.jfklibrary.org/asset-viewer/archives/BMPP-018-008; see also "RFK says protesters' timing wrong," *Birmingham News*, May 4, 1963; "Birmingham, U.S.A.," *Newsweek*, May 13, 1963, 28; "Nation: Dogs, kids & clubs," *Time*, May 10, 1963.
91. Boutwell quoted in Hailey, "Dogs and hoses repulse Negroes at Birmingham," 1; Branch, *Parting the Waters*, 761–762. Malcolm X quoted in M. S. Handler, "Malcolm X terms King's tactics futile," *New York Times*, May 11, 1963, 9.
92. "Races: Freedom—Now," *Time*, May 17, 1963, 25.
93. David Lawrence, "What's become of law and order," *US News & World Report*, August 5, 1963, 104. See also Lentz, *Symbols*, 97.
94. Claude Sitton, "Rioting Negroes routed by police at Birmingham," *New York Times*, May 8, 1963, 1; "Races: Freedom—Now," 25; Forman, *Making of Black Revolutionaries*, 314; Eskew, *But for Birmingham*, 277–279.
95. Eskew, *But for Birmingham*, 277; Walker, Interview by Britton, 54–62.
96. Marshall quoted in Fairclough, *To Redeem the Soul*, 127-128.
97. Sitton, "Birmingham talks reach an accord on ending crisis," *New York Times*, May 10, 1963, 1.
98. See Jackson, *From Civil Rights to Human Rights*, 163.
99. Sitton, "Birmingham talks," 1.
100. Sitton, "Birmingham talks," 14; "The only choice," *Birmingham News*, May 10, 1963.
101. Anthony Lewis, "US sends troops into Alabama after riots sweep Birmingham; Kennedy alerts state's guard," *New York Times*, May 13, 1963, 1; Sitton, "50 hurt in Negro rioting after Birmingham blasts," *New York Times*, May 13, 1963, 1; "Birmingham in control," *Birmingham News*, May 14, 1963; "City council issues stern warning to lawbreakers," *Birmingham News*, May 13, 1963; "Let's keep order ourselves," *Birmingham News*, May 13, 1963; "A time for cool heads," *Birmingham Post-Herald*, May 13, 1963.

102. Birmingham Police Report, Meeting of the ACMHR at Sixth Avenue Baptist Church (May 13, 1963), May 14, 1963, 5, box 13.5, Connor Papers.
103. Eskew, *But for Birmingham*, 326.
104. John F. Kennedy, "Radio and television report to the American people on civil rights," June 11, 1963, online by Gerhard Peters and John T. Woolley, American Presidency Project, http://www.presidency.ucsb.edu/ws/?pid=9271. The estimated numbers of protests and arrests are from Eskew, *But for Birmingham*, 311.
105. "Kennedy gives fiscal views to critics in ADA," *Washington Post*, May 5, 1963, A2. Arthur Schlesinger famously reported that the photos made Kennedy "sick." However, that sentiment, according to Schlesinger, was followed by a crucial "but . . . ": he was sickened by the images *but* was powerless to take action in Alabama. See Arthur Schlesinger, *A Thousand Days: John F. Kennedy in the White House* (Boston: Houghton Mifflin, 1965), 959. The riots after the May 11 bombings apparently played a role in changing Kennedy's mind. As Allen Matusow writes, during the Birmingham riots, "in the space of a few violent hours civil rights for Negroes came to seem no longer the program of zealots, but a policy for moderate men." Allen Matusow, *The Unraveling of America: A History of Liberalism in the 1960s* (New York: Harper & Row, 1984), 88.
106. Berger, *Seeing Through Race*, 58–60; Nick Bryant, *The Bystander: John F. Kennedy and the Struggle for Black Equality* (New York: Basic Books, 2006), 387–389; Jackson, *From Civil Rights to Human Rights*, 168. Kennedy's concern about demonstrations was a theme he pressed throughout the summer in public statements, not just in private oval office meetings. See, for example, transcripts from his summer 1963 press conferences, American Presidency Project, http://www.presidency.ucsb.edu/news_conferences.php?year=1963&Submit=DISPLAY. On the importance of international opinion and Cold War politics for the progression of mid-century civil rights, see John D. Skrentny, "The effect of the Cold War on African-American Civil Rights, 1945–1968," *Theory and Society* 27, no. 2 (April 1998): 237–285; Mary Dudziak, *Cold War Civil Rights: Race and the Image of American Democracy* (Princeton and Oxford: Princeton University Press, 2000); Philip Klinkner and Rogers Smith, *The Unsteady March: The Rise & Decline of Racial Equality in America* (Chicago: University of Chicago Press, 2002), Chapters 7–8.
107. Robin Celikates argues that this is true of civil disobedience more broadly: its symbolic power—and thus, its ability to persuade—is ultimately reliant on its power to confront, disrupt, and unsettle. "Without moments of real confrontation that will in many instances be seen and categorized as violent," civil disobedience would be little more than "a mere appeal to the conscience of the powers that be and their respective majorities." Celikates, "Rethinking civil disobedience as a practice of contestation— Beyond the liberal paradigm," *Constellations* 23, no. 1 (2016): 42–43.
108. Kelley, *Race Rebels: Culture, Politics, and the Black Working Class* (New York: Simon and Schuster, 1996), 90.
109. As King writes in *Why We Can't Wait*: "Where, in the days of slavery, social license and custom placed the unbridled power of the whip in the hands of overseers and masters, today . . . armies of officials are clothed in uniform, invested with authority,

armed with the instruments of violence and death and conditioned to believe that they can intimidate, maim or kill Negroes with the same recklessness that once motivated the slaveowner. If one doubts this conclusion, let him search the records and find how rarely in any southern state a police officer has been punished for abusing a Negro" (24).
110. King, *Why We Can't Wait*, 116.
111. Terry, "Requiem for a dream: The problem-space of Black Power," in *To Shape a New World*, 306.
112. On King's image during and after Birmingham in the national press, see Lentz, *Symbols*, Chapter 3.
113. Not surprisingly, the numbers are even higher in each category in the South. Among Southern whites, 84% disapproved of sit-ins; 66% disapproved of boycotts; 94% opposed lie-ins; and 75% opposed going to jail in protest. See "The Negro in America," *Newsweek*, July 29, 1963; "What the white man thinks of the Negro revolt," *Newsweek*, October 21, 1963; William Brink and Louis Harris, *The Negro Revolution in America* (New York: Simon & Schuster, 1964).
114. "What the white man thinks," 45; Stewart Alsop and Oliver Quayle, "What Northerners really think of Negroes," *Saturday Evening Post*, September 7, 1963, 21.
115. Regarding black Americans' ambivalent views toward "white moderates," Harris poll reports that 31% of "rank-and-file" blacks nationwide felt white moderates were "more harmful" than helpful, while 40% of black leaders felt that way. 47% nationwide (53% of Northerners; 42% of Southerners) felt that there was no real difference between white racial attitudes North and South.
116. Alsop and Quayle, "What the Northerner thinks," 19.
117. Inge Powell Bell, *CORE and the Strategy of Nonviolence* (New York: Random House, 1968), 44.
118. Bayard Rustin, "The meaning of Birmingham," *Liberation* (June 1963): 8–9.
119. Lentz, *Symbols*, 95.

Chapter 5

1. Robert P. Moses, "Speech on Freedom Summer at Stanford University," April 24, 1964, American RadioWorks: Say It Plan, Say It Loud—A Century of Great African American Speeches, http://americanradioworks.publicradio.org/features/blackspeech/bmoses.html.
2. James Baldwin, Nathan Glazer, Sidney Hook, and Gunnar Myrdal, "Liberalism and the Negro: A round-table discussion," *Commentary* 37, no. 3 (March 1964): 38.
3. Charles B. Turner, "The black man's burden: The white liberal," *Dissent* (Summer 1963): 215.
4. Turner, "The black man's burden," 215. On this point, see Adolph Reed, "Race and the disruption of the New Deal coalition," *Urban Affairs Review* 27 (1991): 326–333.
5. Turner, "The black man's burden," 216.

6. See, e.g., Loren Miller, "Farewell to liberals: A Negro view," *The Nation*, October 20, 1962, 235–238; Murray Friedman, "The white liberal's retreat," *The Atlantic*, January 1963, 42–46; Loren Miller, "Freedom now—But what then?" *The Nation*, June 29, 1963, 539–542; Nat Hentoff, *The New Equality* (New York: Viking Press, 1964); Charles Silbermann, *Crisis in Black and White* (New York: Vintage Books, 1964). See also Carol Horton, *Race and the Making of American Liberalism* (Oxford and New York: Oxford University Press, 2005), 159–165.
7. Baldwin et al., "Liberalism and the Negro," 39.
8. The best and most thorough treatment of this incident is in Brian Purnell's wonderful book *Fighting Jim Crow in the County of Kings: The Congress of Racial Equality in Brooklyn* (Lexington: University of Kentucky Press, 2013), which is based on his dissertation research on Brooklyn CORE. See also, August Meier and Elliot M. Rudwick, *CORE: A Study in the Civil Rights Movement, 1942–1968* (New York: Oxford University Press, 1973), 255–258; Craig Turnbull, "Please make no demonstrations tomorrow: The Brooklyn Congress of Racial Equality and symbolic protest at the 1964–65 World's Fair," *Australasian Journal of American Studies*, 17, no. 9 (July 1988): 22–41; Tamar Jacoby, *Someone Else's House: America's Unfinished Struggle with Integration* (New York and London: Free Press, 1998), Chapter 1; Craig Wilder, *A Covenant with Color: Race and Social Power in Brooklyn* (New York: Columbia University Press, 2000), Epilogue; Lawrence Samuel, *The End of Innocence: The 1964–1965 New York World's Fair* (Syracuse, NY: Syracuse University Press, 2010); Joseph Tirella, *Tomorrow-Land: The 1964–1965 World's Fair and the Transformation of America* (Guilford, CT: Lyons Press, 2014).
9. Jacoby, *Someone Else's House*, 25–31.
10. Thus, in this chapter I connect what political theorists do when they adopt or integrate these interpretive and perceptual practices into their theorizing—thereby "seeing like a white state"—with the habits of thought and ways of seeing taken up by citizens and state actors in the midst of upholding white supremacy.
11. Robert Moses, "Halfway to the Fair," Remarks at the University Club of New York City, March 10, 1962, box 133, folder 1962, Robert Moses Papers, New York Public Library, New York, NY (hereafter Moses Papers). In fact, the 1964 Fair site sat atop the 1939–1940 Fair site, which had prior to that been the Corona dump.
12. "CORE's two young militants who won't be deterred," *New York Herald Tribune*, April 19, 1964; Joan Hanauer, "CORE 'lie-in' at Fair site," *New York Journal-American*, April 5, 1964, 1; Telegram from Isiah Brunson to Mayor Wagner, April 9, 1964, box 5, folder 10, Arnold Goldwag Brooklyn Congress of Racial Equality Collection, Brooklyn Historical Society, Brooklyn, New York (hereafter Goldwag Collection).
13. Purnell, *Fighting Jim Crow*, 259. My understanding of the stall-in is deeply indebted to Purnell's work—both his published materials and the interviews with CORE organizers that he conducted, now archived at the Brooklyn Public Library.
14. On this, see Purnell, "'Drive awhile for freedom': Brooklyn CORE's 1964 stall-in and public discourses on protest violence," in *Groundwork: Local Black Freedom Movements in America*, edited by Jeanne Theoharis and Komozi Woodard (New York and London: New York University Press, 2005), 50–52.

15. Ralph Blumenfeld, "Barnes: CORE Fair plan will paralyze city," *New York Post*, April 10, 1964.
16. The idea for paying admission in pennies came from a community member who attended a mass meeting at Rev. Milton Galamison's church in April. On stall-in plans, see Purnell, *Fighting Jim Crow*, Chapter 8. On Jesse Gray, see Mandi Isaacs Jackson, "Harlem's rent strike and rat war: Representation, housing access, and tenant resistance in New York, 1958–1964," *American Studies* 47, no. 1 (Spring 2006): 53–79.
17. Numerous letters and telegrams regarding the stall-in are housed in the following archival collections: box 126, folder for April 9–16, 1964, Moses Papers; box 1, folder 16, Goldwag Collection; box 3, folder 7, Goldwag Collection.
18. "This helps civil rights?" *New York Times*, April 11, 1964. See also, e.g., "Muddy thinking," *New York Journal-American*, April 10, 1964; "Stand in, no; stand up, yes," *New York Times*, April 23, 1964; WLIB radio editorial, "What is the purpose?" April 18–19, 1964, typescript, box 5, folder 10, Goldwag Collection.
19. "Enemies of civil rights," *New York World-Telegram and the Sun*, April 17, 1964; Robert C. Ruark, "Lawlessness must be overcome," *New York World-Telegram and the Sun*, April 27, 1964.
20. Leonard Novick to the editor, "Tactic against injustice," *Time*, May 1, 1964, 11.
21. E. W. Kenworthy, "Rights bill heads caution Negroes," *New York Times*, April 16, 1964, 1.
22. Humphrey quoted in "Nation: Civil rights," *Time*, April 24, 1964, 18.
23. "Wagner stall-in statement," *New York Times*, April 21, 1964, 31; David Halberstam, "Mayor says stall-in holds 'a gun to the heart of the city,'" *New York Times*, April 21, 1964, 1.
24. Kenworthy, "Rights bill," 24; "Responsible tactics will win rights sooner," *LIFE*, May 1, 1964, 4; "Negro statesmanship," *New York Times*, April 17, 1964.
25. In the end, the employment and school titles of the 1964 Civil Rights Act were far less effective than those dealing with public accommodations. See Bruce Ackerman, *We the People, Volume 3: The Civil Rights Revolution* (Cambridge, MA: Belknap Press, 2014), Chapters 8 and 9.
26. Robert Alden, "CORE maps tie-up on roads to fair," *New York Times*, April 10, 1964, 1.
27. Press release, New York World's Fair Corporation, April 21, 1964, box 85, folder A-4.0, World's Fair 1964–1965 Corporation Records, New York Public Library, New York, NY (hereafter World's Fair Records); Confidential memo from Stuart Constable to Robert Moses, June 21, 1963, box 85, folder A-4.0, World's Fair Records.
28. Marshall Peck and James Sullivan, "New traffic rule gives city teeth to fight stall-in," *New York Herald Tribune*, April 14, 1964, 1; Dave Balch, "Court order bars stall-in," *New York World-Telegram and the Sun*, April 20, 1964. The sanitation department, however, backed the stall-in and refused their towing services to the city. See Junius Griffin, "Sanitation union backs 'stall-in,' won't tow cars," *New York Times*, 15 April 1964, 1; Telegram from Isiah Brunson to John J. Delury, president of Sanitation Local 831, International Brotherhood of Teamsters, n.d., box 5, folder 10, Goldwag Collection.

29. See "CORE Rules for Action," *Civil Rights Movement Archive*, http://crmvet.org/docs/corerules.pdf
30. Telegram from James Farmer to Isiah Brunson, April 9, 1964, box 5, folder 10, Goldwag Collection; Letter from James Farmer to Isiah Brunson, April 10, 1964, Brooklyn Chapter files, folder 103: Brooklyn CORE (Apr. 18, 1962–Mar. 25, 1966), Addendum, 1944–1968, CORE Papers; Press statement from James Farmer, April 10, 1964, Brooklyn Chapter files, folder 103, Addendum, 1944–1968, CORE Papers; Memo to Steering Committee of National Action Council from James McCain and James Farmer, April 11, 1964, Brooklyn Chapter files, folder 103, Addendum, 1944–1968, CORE Papers; Minutes of the National Action Committee meeting, May 1–3, 1964, Philadelphia, PA, box 5, folder 10, Goldwag Collection.
31. See, e.g., Purnell, *Fighting Jim Crow*, 258; Major Owens, Interview by Brian Purnell, December 12, 2003 (typescript), 6–7, box 3, folder 3.8.1, Civil Rights in Brooklyn Collection, Brooklyn Public Library, Brooklyn, NY (hereafter Civil Rights in Brooklyn Collection).
32. "Brunson no Rustin," *New York Amsterdam News*, May 9, 1964, 8.
33. "Stall-in stalls," *Newsday*, April 23, 1964; "The flop," *Time*, May 1, 1964, 22–23; David Nevin, "The show goes on, the spoilers lose the day," *LIFE*, May 1, 1964, 35.
34. Nevin, "The show goes on"; Peter Kihiss, "7 injured in IRT station," *New York Times*, April 23, 1964, 1.
35. This line appears to be an impromptu drop-in provoked by the protests, as it does not appear in the text of Johnson's prepared remarks quote. See Lyndon B. Johnson, "Remarks at the opening of the New York World's Fair," April 22, 1964, online by Gerhard Peters and John T. Woolley, American Presidency Project, http://www.presidency.ucsb.edu/ws/?pid=26179. The drop-in is quoted in Tirella, *Tomorrow-Land*, 199.
36. "Attendance way off," *New York Amsterdam News*, April 25, 1964, 1. Moreover, by some estimates, the demonstrations cost the fair dearly in the form of overtime police pay. See "Says fair protest bill $250,000," *New York Amsterdam News*, May 2, 1964, 15.
37. Owens, Interview by Purnell, 6.
38. Martin Luther King, Jr., *The Trumpet of Conscience* (Boston: Beacon, 2010), 15–16.
39. Lomax quoted in "Going too far," *New York Journal-American*, July 12, 1963.
40. John Lewis, *Walking with the Wind: A Memoir of the Movement* (New York: Simon & Schuster, 1998), 202–203. See also Michael Thelwell, "The August 28th March on Washington: The castrated giant," in his *Duties, Pleasures, and Conflicts: Essays in Struggle* (Amherst: University of Massachusetts Press, 1987), 57–73; James Forman, *The Making of Black Revolutionaries* (New York: Macmillan, 1972), 331–337.
41. Wyatt Tee Walker, Keynote address delivered at 7th Annual Convention of SCLC, Richmond, VA, September 25, 1963, box 203, folder 3588, Warren Papers. After the Birmingham bombing, Nash developed a plan for the creation of a "nonviolent army." Her plan called for a massive campaign of civil disobedience, including a "refusal to pay state and local taxes; a general work stoppage, and the interruption of all communication with Montgomery, the Alabama state capital, by sitdowns on highways, airfield runways, and railroad tracks." It also called for "the tying up of all telephone

lines by harassing the central switchboard of the state capital." See "Dr. King calls Birmingham a blow to nonviolence," *New York Times*, September 25, 1963; Report from Birmingham from Diane Nash to Martin Luther King, Jr., September 17–20, 1963, box 141, folder 8, SCLC Papers.
42. "Disservice to civil rights," *New York Times*, March 8, 1964.
43. James Farmer, *Freedom—When?* (New York: Random House, 1965), 37.
44. Farmer, *Freedom—When?*, 37–38.
45. Farmer, *Freedom—When?*, 46. Not surprisingly, King refused to join his colleagues across the national civil rights organizations in condemning the stall-in, even while he considered it a "tactical error." In a memo to Farmer and others, King echoed his arguments from "Letter from a Birmingham Jail," insisting that direct action cannot be measured against the likelihood of white alienation. "I hear a lot of talk these days about our direct action program alienating former friends. . . . If our direct action programs alienate so-called friends, even if the program happens to be a tactical error like the 'stall-in,' they never were real friends." John Lewis, and with him SNCC, also refused to sign a statement denouncing the protest, while Farmer revised his position in an interview with Robert Penn Warren two months later. See Memo from King to Dorothy Height, Wiley Branton, James Farmer, John Lewis, A. Philip Randolph, Roy Wilkins, Whitney Young, and Jack Greenberg, April 21, 1964, 1–2, box 27, folder 38, King Papers; Press statement from John Lewis, April 17, 1964, box 5, folder 10, Goldwag Collection; Farmer, Interview by Warren, June 11, 1964, box 209, folder 3639, Warren Papers.
46. Juliet Hooker, "Black protest/white grievance: On the problem of white political imaginations not shaped by loss," *South Atlantic Quarterly* 116, no. 3 (July 2017): 483–504.
47. Blumenfeld, "CORE Fair plan will paralyze city."
48. Charles Rabb, "Frustration breeds plan for stall-in at Fair," *Washington Post*, April 19, 1964.
49. Letter from Isiah Brunson to Mrs. Anne S. Holzer, n.d., box 5, folder 9, Goldwag Collection.
50. Moses, "Speech on Freedom Summer."
51. While I describe this project as one of transforming white citizens—in line with the language that civil rights activists themselves used—what was centrally at stake was the abolition of white citizenship as such. As Joel Olson argues, white citizenship "does not simply exclude some persons from enjoying democratic rights. It does much more: it produces a particular conception of democracy that not only denies active participation and social equality but cannot even imagine them." If the decolonizing work of civil disobedience offered a thoroughgoing transformation of American democracy and its citizens, whiteness—as a social position and a framework for ordering the world—could have no place in a shared future of multiracial democracy. I am thankful to an anonymous reviewer for helping me articulate this idea. See Joel Olson, *The Abolition of White Democracy* (Minneapolis: University of Minnesota Press, 2004), 63.
52. Baldwin et al., "Liberalism and the Negro," 38.

53. Baldwin, *The Fire Next Time* (New York: Dial Press, 1963), 19–20.
54. Baldwin et al., "Liberalism and the Negro," 38. As Lawrie Balfour argues, Baldwin's understanding of innocence is as "a kind of disconnection. Embodied in the dream of clean hands and clean breaks, innocence impedes engagement with the difficulties of living." Balfour, *The Evidence of Things Not Said: James Baldwin and the Promise of American Democracy* (Ithaca and London: Cornell University Press, 2001), 88.
55. George Shulman, "Acknowledgement and disavowal as an idiom for theorizing politics," *Theory & Event* 14, no. 1 (2011).
56. Charles Mills, "White ignorance," in *Race and Epistemologies of Ignorance*, edited by Shannon Sullivan and Nancy Tuana (Albany: State University of New York Press, 2007), 27. Emphasis in original.
57. As Spelman puts it, "whites lack awareness of and interest in what it is about them and their institutions that has wreaked such havoc in the lives of blacks." Consequently, "they have not developed the imaginative skills that would allow them to envision a world in which such horrible powers would have been tamed." Elizabeth Spelman, "Managing ignorance," in *Race and Epistemologies of Ignorance*, 120. Of course, nonwhite citizens are likewise formed by this epistemic context, as King and others well knew; but they are formed differently. See Mills, "White ignorance."
58. Spelman, "Managing ignorance," 130. Emphasis in original.
59. Mills, "White ignorance," 13. Emphasis in original.
60. My analysis of this speech and the position taken by Kennedy is shaped by William Sewell's interpretation of the taking of the Bastille. As Sewell argues, patriots in the National Assembly retroactively claimed the violence at the Bastille as the legitimate instantiation of "the people," thereby conferring legitimacy on revolutionary, popular violence. At the same time, however, they tried to separate the resistance of the people from the unjustified license of the mob. As Sewell argues: "The elaboration of the new concept of revolution and its definitive identification with the taking of Bastille occurred when the National Assembly was forced to delimit ever more strictly what forms of political violence might be deemed legitimate. Once an act of popular violence was recognized as the very foundation of political legitimacy, it became imperative to distinguish that one transcendent founding moment from other violent actions that might on the surface seem comparable; otherwise, the state would be forever vulnerable to the whim of any crowd that claimed to act on behalf of the people. . . . The problem of bringing the revolution to a close was thus posed at the very moment of its birth." See William Sewell, "Historical events as transformations of structures: Inventing revolution at the Bastille," *Theory and Society* 25 (1996): 859–860. See also Jason Frank, *Constituent Moments: Enacting the People in Postrevolutionary America* (Durham, NC: Duke University Press, 2010).
61. My theorization of these techniques was broadly inspired by Michel-Rolph Trouillot's account of "formulas of erasure" and "banalization" in the interpretation of the Haitian revolution as a non-event, as well as Kimberlé Crenshaw and Gary Peller's analysis of "disaggregation" in the footage of Rodney King's beating and in the subsequent court case. Trouillot, *Silencing the Past: Power and the Production of History*

(Boston: Beacon, 1995), Chapter 3; Kimberlé Crenshaw and Gary Peller, "Reel time/real justice," *Denver University Law Review* 70, no. 2 (1993): 283–296.
62. "Disservice to civil rights," *New York Times*, March 8, 1964.
63. "Responsible tactics will win rights sooner," *LIFE*, May 1, 1964.
64. The technique of disaggregation (and specifically the geography of Southern exceptionalism) stands as a direct rebuke of the imaginative transit of civil disobedience. Where civil rights activists worked to link a colonialism and segregation—integrating disparate contexts into a global geography of white supremacy and nonviolent direct action—disaggregation severs the US from the world, and the South from the rest of the US. Southern exceptionalism fundamentally relies on a background assumption of American exceptionalism: the South is problematic because it does not fall in line with the Myrdallian Creed—that which makes the US uniquely hospitable to freedom, equality, and democracy.
65. " . . . and in New York's schools," *New York Times*, September 4, 1963, 38. The phrase "innocent segregation" belongs to Matthew Lassiter, "De jure/de facto segregation: The long shadow of a national myth," in *The Myth of Southern Exceptionalism*, edited by Matthew Lassiter and Joseph Crespino (Oxford and New York: Oxford University Press, 2010), 28.
66. Lassiter, "De jure/de facto segregation," 28–29. On the history of Northern segregation, and in particular the role played by federal policy, state action, and real estate practices, see Douglas Massey and Nancy Denton, *American Apartheid: Segregation and the Making of the Underclass* (Cambridge, MA: Harvard University Press, 1993); Thomas Sugrue, *Sweet Land of Liberty: The Forgotten Struggle for Civil Rights in the North* (New York: Random House, 2008); Beryl Satter, *Family Properties: How the Struggle over Race and Real Estate Transformed Chicago and Urban America* (New York: Henry Holt, 2010); David M. P. Freund, *Colored Property: State Policy & White Racial Politics in Suburban America* (Chicago: University of Chicago Press, 2010); Sugrue, *The Origins of the Urban Crisis: Race and Inequality in Postwar Detroit* (Princeton: Princeton University Press, 2014).
67. Baldwin quoted in Silberman, Crisis in Black and White, 10.
68. Purnell, *Fighting Jim Crow*.
69. "This helps civil rights?," *New York Times*, April 11, 1964.
70. Purnell, *Fighting Jim Crow*, 269.
71. Arno Vosk to the editor, "People on our side?" *New York Post*, April 21, 1964. This observation—that Northerners bemoaned protests in their backyard while supporting similar protests in the South—was most loudly and most frequently made by Southern segregationist politicians for their own political purposes.
72. Judith L. Goodman to the editor, "Tactics against injustice," *Time*, May 1, 1964, 11.
73. Kenworthy, "Rights bill," 24. Incidentally, Rawls mentions the stall-in specifically in his notes on civil disobedience, using it to epitomize the sort of coercive disobedience that violates his conditions for appealing to the majority's sense of justice. Tactics like the stall-in qualify as "quasi-force & terrorism." Following Alexander Bickel, he

further remarks that they are a "test of strength" that are "part of the politics of disorder & conflict," as they are "in certain respects violent, or not non-violent." See Rawls, Handwritten notes, "CD & the complications of our federal system [Three types of cases]," n.d., box 7, folder 6, Rawls Papers.
74. Moses, "Speech on Freedom Summer."
75. "Wagner stall-in statement," *New York Times*, April 21, 1964, 31.
76. "What is the purpose?" WLIB radio editorial.
77. "Tactics against injustice," *Time*, May 1, 1964, 11.
78. Clippings of letters to the editor, box 1, folder 16, Goldwag Collection.
79. Letter to CORE from Henry Frederick, April 11, 1964, box 3, folder 7, Goldwag Collection.
80. Postcard to Percy Gilmore from Lorna Jenkins, April 23, 1964, box 1, folder 16, Goldwag Collection.
81. Mills, "White ignorance," 22.
82. Carl Hansberry took his case to the Supreme Court, which in November 1940 delivered a unanimous opinion in his favor—rejecting the specific covenant imposed by the Kenwood Improvement Association, but declining to rule on the constitutionality of racially restrictive covenants as such. See *Hansberry v. Lee*, 311 U.S. 32 (1940).
83. Lorraine Hansberry, "The Black revolution and the white backlash," in *Say It Loud: Great Speeches on Civil Rights and African American Identity*, edited by Catherine Ellis and Stephen Drury Smith (New York: New Press, 2010), 22–23.
84. Hansberry, "The black revolution," 24. The town hall was organized by the Association of Artists for Freedom. Other black panelists for the event included novelists Paule Marshall and John O. Killens; poet and playwright LeRoi Jones; and actors Ossie Davis and Rudy Dee. White panelists included Charles Silberman, editor of *Fortune*; James Weschler, editor at *The New York Post*; and commentator David Suskind. See Harold Cruse, "Artists for Freedom Inc.—Dialogue off-key," in *The Crisis of the Negro Intellectual: A Historical Analysis of the Failure of Black Leadership* (New York: New York Review Books, 2005), 193–205.
85. Hansberry quoted in *Say it Loud*, 21.
86. "Wagner stall-in statement," 31.
87. Kenworthy, "Rights bill," 24.
88. Moses, "Halfway to the Fair."
89. Leaflet, "Stop Discrimination in World's Fair Construction Sites," September 3, 1963, box 5, folder 10, Goldwag Collection; Purnell, *Fighting Jim Crow*, 209–248; Wilder, *Covenant with Color*, 205–206; Tirella, *Tomorrow-Land*, 58–65.
90. Background on "Operation Clean Sweep"—the Brooklyn CORE project that deposited trash from Bed-Stuy on the steps of Borough Hall in an effort to get acceptable trash pick-up service for the neighborhood—can be found in box 1, folder 1.6 and box 3, folder 3.1, Civil Rights in Brooklyn Collection; box 1, folders 5 and 6, Goldwag Collection; Purnell, *Fighting Jim Crow*, chapter 5.
91. Marc Crawford, "Throttle the Fair—the public be damned," *LIFE*, April 24, 1964, 41.

92. Robert Moses, *Public Works: A Dangerous Trade* (New York: McGraw Hill, 1970), 308; Kenneth Clark, "A conversation with James Baldwin," *Freedomways* 3 (Summer 1963): 361–368.
93. Though it remains the definitive biography, the image of Moses that Caro constructs is now being re-evaluated—and found one-sided and wanting—by some historians, most recently in Ballon and Jackson's edited volume. Robert Caro, *The Power Broker: Robert Moses and the Fall of New York* (New York: Vintage, 1975), 19; Hilary Ballon and Kenneth Jackson, eds., *Robert Moses and the Modern City: The Transformation of New York* (New York: W.W. Norton, 2008).
94. "Fairs: Moses in the wilderness," *Time*, October 19, 1962.
95. Tirella, *Tomorrow-Land*, 44; Samuel, *End of Innocence*, 13.
96. C. Gervin Hayden, "The hard-sell Fair," *The Nation*, November 2, 1963, 275–278; "Fairs: The world of already," *Time*, June 5, 1964; "A smasheroo of a World's Fair," *LIFE*, May 1, 1964, 28; Morris Dickstein, "From the thirties to the sixties: The World's Fair in its own time," in *Remembering the Future: The New York World's Fair from 1939–1964* (New York: Rizzoli, 1989), 30.
97. Excerpt from Abraham Lincoln: "Address at Sanitary Fair in Baltimore: A Lecture on Liberty," April 18, 1864, American Presidency Project, http://www.presidency.ucsb.edu/ws/?pid=88871.
98. Lincoln, "Address at Sanitary Fair."
99. The original speeches from which these quotations were taken are as follows: Lincoln, "Address before the Young Men's Lyceum of Springfield, Illinois," January 27, 1838; Lincoln, "Cooper Union address," February 27, 1860, New York, New York.
100. Walter Benjamin, "Theses on the philosophy of history," in *Illuminations*, edited by Hannah Arendt (London: Collin/Fontana Books, 1973), 255–266.
101. Rev. Milton Galamison, "The world of success," June 14, 1964, box 5, folder: Sermons, Dec. 1963–Sept. 1964, Rev. Milton Galamison Papers, Schomberg Center for Research on Black Culture, New York.
102. Galamison, "The world of success."

Epilogue

1. The Mississippi Freedom Summer was coordinated through the Council of Federated Organizations (COFO), an umbrella organization for all the civil rights groups working in the state, including CORE, SNCC, and the NAACP.
2. John Dittmer, *Local People: The Struggle for Civil Rights in Mississippi* (Urbana and Chicago: University of Illinois Press, 1994), 246–248.
3. Dittmer, *Local People*, 248–252.
4. Malcolm X, "The Oxford address at the Oxford Union Debate," in *Malcolm X at Oxford Union: Racial Politics in a Global Era*, edited by Saladin Ambar (Oxford and New York: Oxford University Press, 2014), 178.
5. Janet Abu-Lughod, *Race, Space, and Riots in Chicago, New York, and Los Angeles* (Oxford and New York: Oxford University Press, 2007), 171–175. When surveyed, 53% of the residents of Bed-Stuy indicated Powell's killing as the proximate cause, while a combined 78% indicated that protesting "discrimination" and "deprivation"

was either the "real cause" of the protests or the problem that the protests were "trying to show." See Joe R. Feagin and Paul B. Sheatsley, "Ghetto resident appraisals of a riot," *Public Opinion Quarterly* 32, no. 3 (Autumn 1968): 354.
6. Appellant's Brief, *People of the State of New York v. Epton*, 248 F. Supp. 276 (SDNY 1965).
7. Abu-Lughod, *Race, Space, and Riots*, 175, 178. According to the contemporaneous account produced by two white journalists, nearly 8,000 civilians participated in the protests over the course of the week, and there were 118 injuries among them. Fred C. Shapiro and James W. Sullivan, *Race Riots: New York 1964* (New York: Crowell, 1964).
8. Brian Purnell, *Fighting Jim Crow in the County of Kings: The Congress of Racial Equality in Brooklyn* (Lexington: University of Kentucky Press, 2013), 281.
9. On *"dramatic"* versus *"deadly* violence," see Adam Fairclough, *To Redeem the Soul of America: The Southern Christian Leadership Conference and Martin Luther King, Jr.* (Athens: University of Georgia Press, 2001), 229.
10. Kwame Ture and Charles V. Hamilton, *Black Power: The Politics of Liberation* (New York: Vintage, 1992), 5.
11. Ture and Hamilton, *Black Power*, xvii.
12. Ture and Hamilton, *Black Power*, 53. On this point, Martin Luther King, Jr.'s responses to Black Power are particularly interesting. See Brandon M. Terry, "Requiem for a dream: The problem-space of Black Power," in *To Shape a New World: Essays on the Political Philosophy of Martin Luther King, Jr.*, edited by Brandon M. Terry and Tommie Shelby (Cambridge and London: Belknap, 2018), 290–324.
13. Howard Zinn, *SNCC: The New Abolitionists* (Boston: Beacon, 1964), 14. There are multiple points of contact between the shifted perspective I advocate here and the one central to Lida Maxwell's work on "insurgent truth." Maxwell argues that typical standards of truth and truth-telling look to heroic—usually male, white, and heterosexual—figures who combat the abuse of power with a courageous presentation of "the facts," thereby changing institutions and laws. Instead, Maxwell urges us to look to outsiders who lack the recognition and status to speak truths in this way. In doing so, she suggests the ways that outsider truth-telling acts on the world—"changing the world in more horizontal, material ways—transforming our devices, houses, workplaces, and streets in ways that enable other outsiders to speak of their realities" (135). These "insurgent truths" do not shore up the legitimacy of a world that already exists, but rather "[contribute] to a world that is not fully built" (137). See Maxwell, *Insurgent Truth: Chelsea Manning and the Politics of Outsider Truth-Telling* (New York and Oxford: Oxford University Press, 2019).
14. Loubna El Amine, "Critical exchange: Political and ethical action in the age of Trump," *Contemporary Political Theory* 17, no. 3 (August 2018): 354–355.
15. For work that connects these contexts, see e.g., Ronald Walter Greene and Kevin Douglas Kuswa, "'From the Arab Spring to Athens, from Occupy Wall Street to Moscow': Regional accents and the rhetorical cartography of power," *Rhetoric Society Quarterly* 42, no. 3 (2012): 271–288; Jaskiran Dhillon, "Decolonize this place and radical solidarity: An interview with Natasha Dhillon and Amin Husain," in *Standing with Standing Rock: Voices from the #NoDAPL Movement*, edited by Nick Estes and Jaskiran Dhillon (Minneapolis: University of Minnesota Press, 2019);

Nick Estes, *Our History Is the Future* (New York: Verso, 2019); Steven Salaita, *Inter/Nationalism: Decolonizing Native America and Palestine* (Minneapolis: University of Minnesota Press, 2016).

16. Robin D.G. Kelley, *Freedom Dreams: The Black Radical Imagination* (Boston: Beacon Press, 2002), 8–9.
17. Juliet Hooker, "Black Lives Matter and the paradoxes of U.S. black politics: From democratic sacrifice to democratic repair," *Political Theory* 44, no. 4 (2016): 463.
18. Hooker, "Black Lives Matter," 465.
19. Randy Kennedy and Jennifer Schuessler, "Ferguson images evoke civil rights era and changing visual perceptions," *New York Times*, August 14, 2014, http://www.nytimes.com/2014/08/15/us/ferguson-images-evoke-civil-rights-era-and-changing-visual-perceptions.html.
20. Evan Hill et al., "8 minutes and 46 seconds: How George Floyd was killed in police custody," *New York Times*, May 31, 2020, https://www.nytimes.com/2020/05/31/us/george-floyd-investigation.html. Floyd's last words echoed the murder of Eric Garner by the NYPD in 2014.
21. Julian Zelizer, "It's been five decades since 1968, and things are somehow worse," *CNN*, May 30, 2020, https://www.cnn.com/2020/05/30/opinions/2020-echoes-of-1968-zelizer/index.html.
22. Eric Holder, Statement on the ongoing situation in Ferguson, Missouri, November 25, 2014, Office of Public Affairs, US Department of Justice, http://www.justice.gov/opa/pr/statement-attorney-general-holder-ongoing-situation-ferguson-missouri.
23. See, e.g., Press briefing by Press Secretary Kayleigh McEnany, June 3, 2020, https://www.whitehouse.gov/briefings-statements/press-briefing-press-secretary-kayleigh-mcenany-060320/; Ken Seguira, "Atlanta Mayor Keisha Lance Bottoms addresses city," *Atlanta Journal-Constitution*, May 30, 2020, https://www.ajc.com/news/full-text-read-atlanta-mayor-keisha-lance-bottoms-plea-for-her-city/puDJ3iEafspuLZcbuq9rvO/.
24. Charlene A. Carruthers, *Unapologetic: A Black, Queer, and Feminist Mandate for Radical Movements* (Boston: Beacon, 2018), 45–46.
25. Carruthers, *Unapologetic*, 21.
26. On these developments and how they have shaped the movement for Black Lives, see Keeanga-Yamahtta Taylor, *From #BlackLivesMatter to Black Liberation* (Chicago: Haymarket, 2016).
27. Taylor, *#BlackLivesMatter*, 80.
28. Kahn-Cullors cited in Wesley C. Hogan, *On the Freedom Side: How Five Decades of Youth Activists Have Remixed American History* (Chapel Hill: University of North Carolina Press, 2019), 132–133.

Index

For the benefit of digital users, indexed terms that span two pages (e.g., 52–53) may, on occasion, appear on only one of those pages.

Abernathy, Ralph, 138–39, 140–41, 145–46
Accra, Ghana, 82–84, 85–86, 225n.108
African National Congress (ANC), 75–77
Aitchison, Guy, 5
Alabama Christian Movement for Human Rights (ACMHR), 4–5, 128, 131–32, 135–40, 145–52, 154–55
  See also Birmingham Campaign; Fred Lee Shuttlesworth
All African Peoples' Conference, 81–82
Allen, Danielle, 42, 51–52, 212–13n.71
Allen, Leroy, 137–38
American Creed, 44–46, 214n.80, 250n.64
American Dilemma, An, 44–46, 214n.80
  See also Gunnar Myrdal
American exceptionalism
  in *An American Dilemma*, 44–46
  and disavowal, 177–79, 185, 195, 250n.64
  and liberal theory, 44, 46–49
  and Southern exceptionalism, 13–14, 47–48, 177–79, 185, 198–99, 250n.64
  See also An American Dilemma; Southern exceptionalism
antiapartheid movement, 75–77, 78–79, 86, 222n.76
  See also African National Congress; Defiance Campaign
anticolonialism, 13, 16, 19, 51, 56–59, 60–63, 67–68, 70, 72, 74, 75–78, 79–83, 84–86, 196
  See also colonialism
apartheid, 57, 75–77, 78, 86, 223n.78
Arendt, Hannah, 53–54, 55, 113–14

Atlanta, Georgia, 87, 114–15, 116, 118–19, 152

Baldwin, James, 159, 160–61, 162–63, 173–74, 178–79, 187, 249n.54
Balfour, Lawrie, 17, 249n.54
Bedau, Hugo, 5–6, 24, 30, 31–32, 34, 59–60, 209n.22, 209n.26
Bell, Inge Powell, 157–58
Benjamin, Walter, 189–90
Berger, Dan, 109–11, 121
Bethune, Mary McLeod, 78–79
Bevel, Diane. *See* Diane Nash
Bevel, James, 96, 128, 131–32, 145–47, 154
Birmingham, Alabama, 128, 133–35
  See also Birmingham Campaign
Birmingham Campaign (1963)
  children's crusade, 146–51, 154–55
  as disciplining example, 165, 177
  Kennedy's reaction to, 144, 149, 152–54, 175–76, 243nn.105–6
  King's theorization of, 140–45, 172–73
  planning of, 134–39
  Project C, 137–39, 162–63
  results of, 151–54, 156–58
  role of spectators in, 132, 137–39, 148–49, 151–52, 154–56, 176
  tactics of disclosure in, 131–33, 138–39, 142–43, 145, 146–47, 148–49, 150–51, 152–53, 154–55, 172–73, 175–76
  tactics of disruption in, 131–33, 142, 143–45, 146–47, 148–49, 151, 152–55, 157–58, 175–76
  See also Alabama Christian Movement for Human Rights; Birmingham, Alabama; Letter

Birmingham Campaign (1963) (cont.)
    from a Birmingham Jail; Southern Christian Leadership Conference
Black Lives Matter, 1–2, 197–98, 199–202
Black Power, 56–57, 155, 194–95, 225–26n.114
Black Power: The Politics of Liberation, 194–95
Black Youth Project 100 (BYP100), 200–1
Boutwell, Albert, 134–36, 143–44, 149–50, 151–52
Boxill, Bernard, 19–20, 101, 102–3, 104, 111–12, 113–14
Boynton v. Virginia, 116
Brown, Michael, 1–2, 199–200
Brownlee, Kimberley, 9–10, 230n.30
Brunson, Isiah, 163, 167, 172
Burns, O.R., 69
Byrd, Jodi, 59, 226n.121

Callendar, Herbert, 186–87
Carmichael, Stokely. *See* Kwame Turé
Carruthers, Charlene, 200–1
Cayton, Horace, 78–79
Celikates, Robin, 9–11, 243n.107
Chaney, James, 192–93
Çidam, Çiğdem, 204n.14
civil disobedience
    and acceptance of punishment, 4, 5–6, 9–10, 34–35, 38, 49, 98, 99–101, 104, 123, 229–30nn.29–30
    and civil rights example, 1–4, 10–12, 23–25, 38–41, 47–48
    and civility, 3, 4–6, 9–10, 13–14, 23, 27–28, 31, 34, 37, 38, 39, 43–44, 48–49, 111–12, 129–30, 171, 184, 194–95, 198–99, 201–2
    as communicative, 8–10, 37–38, 128–30, 154–55, 211n.55, 230n.30
    conservative critiques of, 23–25, 27–30, 41–42
    as constitutional patriotism, 4, 17, 38–39, 54–55, 58–59, 89, 202
    as crisis-generating, 20, 49, 104, 131, 135–36, 143–44, 146–47, 149–50, 152–54, 168
    deliberative theories of, 7–10, 38, 129–31, 216n.5
    democratic disobedience, 7–9, 205n.26
    as domestic, 54–57, 58, 88–89, 200–1, 216n.5
    as fidelity to law, 17, 19–20, 34, 47–48, 123, 202 (*see also* John Rawls; *A Theory of Justice*)
    inclusive accounts of, 9–10, 205n.21
    and legitimacy, 4–6, 7, 10, 22–23, 24–25, 37–38, 41–42, 100–1, 104, 111–12, 123–24, 144, 145, 152–53, 196, 211n.48, 249n.60, 253n.13
    liberal theories of, 5–7, 30–40, 46–49, 50, 54–55, 88–89, 99–101, 129
    and moral appeal, 3, 4, 5–6, 9–10, 22–24, 30, 34–39, 46–48, 100, 104, 111–12, 114–15, 117–18, 122–23, 235n.119, 243n.107
    neorepublican theories of, 7–10, 101–2
    and nonviolent direct action, 59–60
    and persuasion, 4, 5–6, 20, 23–24, 30, 34–38, 51–52, 128–33, 156–58, 175, 239n.36
    political disobedience, 10–11, 205n.26
    and political obligation, 8–9, 16, 17, 31–34, 36–39, 41–42, 46–47, 54–55, 210n.29, 210n.38, 214n.93
    and satyagraha, 55, 61–62, 73, 216n.8, 217–18n.20, 220n.54
    script for action, 3, 4, 5–6, 10, 22–23, 34–35, 37, 38, 47–48, 54–55, 99–101
    as stabilizing device, 4, 17–18, 19–20, 22–23, 24–25, 29, 37–38, 40–42, 54–55, 99–101, 111–12, 123, 196–97, 211nn.55–56
    uncivil disobedience, 10, 205n.25
    See also decolonizing praxis; nonviolence
Civil Rights Act of 1964, 159–60, 165–66, 246n.25
civility, 3, 4–6, 9–10, 13–14, 23, 27–28, 31, 34, 37, 38, 39, 43–44, 48–49, 111–12, 129–30, 171, 184, 194–95, 198–99, 201–2
    See also civil disobedience
Clark, Kenneth, 160–61
Cloward, Richard, 142–43

coercion
    as illegitimate means, 4–5, 8–9, 34–35, 129–30
    nonviolent coercion, 49–50, 51–52, 125–26, 136–37, 143–44, 155, 164–65, 239n.36
    as oppression, 142–43
    relationship with persuasion, 20, 128, 129–33, 154, 157–58, 239n.39
    See also nonviolence; persuasion; violence
Cohen, Carl, 24, 30, 37
Cold War, 13–14, 57, 74–75, 144, 188–89, 206n.34
Colley, Zoe, 111, 122–23
colonialism
    internal colony, 58–59, 194–95
    and Jim Crow, 13, 19, 51, 56–59, 62–63, 67–68, 70–71, 80–82, 85–86, 87–88, 89–90, 194–95, 197–98, 219n.35, 222–23n.77, 224n.90, 226n.121, 250n.64
    as regime of fear and violence, 16–17, 19, 51–52, 56–59, 70–72, 77–78, 79–80, 85, 194–95, 196
    settler colonialism, 59, 75–76, 86, 195–96, 219n.35, 222–23n.77, 226.121
    See also anticolonialism; white supremacy
colored cosmopolitanism, 67–68, 75, 220n.44
Committee of Inquiry into the Administration of Justice in the Freedom Struggle, 110
comparative freedom. *See* freedom
Congo crisis, 87
Congress of Racial Equality (CORE)
    connection to Defiance Campaign, 76–77
    early uses of nonviolent direct action, 71–72, 75, 108
    founding of, 71–72
    role in 1964 Harlem riot, 193
    role in Freedom Rides, 116–23
    role in jail, no bail, 19–20, 98–99, 106–8, 115–16
    role in sit-ins, 106–8
    stall-in, 161–68, 171–73, 177–87

Triborough Bridge demonstration, 170–71
Connor, Eugene 'Bull', 128, 133–36, 137–38, 146–50
consensus narrative, 13–14, 15, 23–24, 112–13
constitutional patriotism, 4, 17, 38–39, 54–55, 58–59, 89, 202
Convention People's Party (CPP), 81–82
Cotton, Dorothy, 96
Crenshaw, Kimberlé, 17, 47–48, 206n.32, 249–50n.61
crisis-generation, 20, 49, 104, 131, 135–36, 143–44, 146–47, 149–50, 152–54, 168

decolonization
    democratic, 51, 161, 195–96, 198–99, 248n.51
    global, 85–86, 194–95
    See also anticolonialism; decolonizing praxis
decolonizing praxis
    as alternative theory, 16–17, 19, 51, 89–90, 100–1, 104, 155–56, 161, 195–98, 201–2
    inward-face, 16–17, 19–20, 98–99, 103–4, 111–12, 120–21, 123, 124–25, 128, 145, 175–76, 196
    limitations, 20–21, 59
    outward-face, 16–17, 20, 103–4, 111–12, 120–21, 124–25, 128, 132–33, 143–44, 145, 154–55, 168, 175–76, 196
    and white ignorance, 162–63, 175–77
    product of imaginative transit, 19–20, 57–58, 66–67, 74, 84, 87–90, 101, 103–4, 155–56, 195–96, 197–98
    See also freedom; disclosure; disruption
Defiance Campaign (1952), 60–67, 86
deliberative democracy. *See* democracy
deliberative inertia, 7–8
Delmas, Candice, 3, 10–11, 54–55
democracy
    as already achieved, 17, 32, 36–38, 42–44, 46–48, 55, 58–59, 88–89, 129, 141–42, 196–98, 214n.93 (*see also* American exceptionalism)

democracy (*cont.*)
  deliberative democracy, 7–10, 38, 129–31, 216n.5
  democratic deficits, 7–8
  democratic disobedience, 7–9, 205n.26
  disobedience as threat to, 25–30, 129, 184, 188, 211nn.54–55
  as goal, 16–17, 50–51, 103, 132–33, 196–99, 248n.51
  white democracy, 42, 50, 128, 131, 161, 195–96, 197–98
  and white supremacy, 17–18, 29, 42–44, 142, 196–97
Democratic National Convention (1964), 229n.26
Dexter Avenue Baptist Church, 82–83, 84
disaggregation (techniques of), 176–81, 185–86, 249–50n.61, 250n.64
  See also disavowal
disavowal (techniques of), 20–21, 42, 162–63, 170–71, 173, 191, 193–94, 195
  defined, 174
  related to white ignorance, 174–75
  specific techniques, 176–86
  See also disaggregation; disqualification; escalation
disclosure (tactics of), 20–21, 170–71, 175, 193–94
  in Birmingham Campaign, 131–33, 138–39, 142–43, 145, 146–47, 148–49, 150–51, 152–53, 154–55, 172–73, 175–76
  King's theorization of, 140–45, 172–73
  related to inward-facing dynamics, 125–26, 145
  in stall-in, 168, 171–73
  See also decolonizing praxis; disruption
disqualification (techniques of), 176–77, 184–86
  See also disavowal
disruption (tactics of), 20–21, 169–71, 175, 193–94
  in Birmingham Campaign, 131–33, 142, 143–45, 146–47, 148–49, 151, 152–55, 157–58, 175–76
  in stall-in, 168, 171–73
  King's theorization of, 140–45, 172–73
  related to inward-facing dynamics, 125–26, 145
  See also decolonizing praxis; disclosure
domination
  colonial, 62–63, 69, 80–82, 103–4, 197–98, 219n.35
  as disavowed (*see* disavowal)
  versus exclusion, 42–44, 51, 212–13n.71
  as hidden, 130–31, 134–35, 142–43, 174–75
  maintained by cooperation, 132, 145
  racial, 15, 16–17, 19–20, 42–44, 51–52, 80–82, 89, 103–4, 109–10, 124, 128, 175, 180, 197–98, 200, 219n.35, 228–29n.22
  See also colonialism; Jim Crow; whiteness; white supremacy
Doris, Ruby, 116
Douglas, Andrew, 240n.53
Douglass, Frederick, 84–85, 91, 101–2, 111–12, 113–14, 143–44, 231n.44
Dudziak, Mary, 49–50
Du Bois, W.E.B., 64–66, 68–70, 73, 74, 218n.31, 219n.41, 220n.44

Eisenhower Commission. *See* National Commission on the Causes and Prevention of Violence
Eisenhower, Milton, 25–26
  See also National Commission on the Causes and Prevention of Violence
El Amine, Loubna, 197–98
Ellison, Ralph, 45
emancipation. *See* freedom
epistemic authority, 42, 58–59, 174–75
escalation (techniques of), 176–77, 180–84, 185–86
  See also disavowal
Eskew, Glenn, 133, 151, 237n.19, 238–39n.34, 239n.36
Evans, Glenn, 148–49
Evers, Medgar, 228n.20
exclusion, 36–37, 42–44, 46–48, 51, 212–13n.71
  See also domination

Fairclough, Adam, 146–47
Fanon, Frantz, 85–86, 225–26n.114

Farmer, James, 71–73, 75, 76–77, 116–17, 118–21, 127, 167–68, 170–71, 201–2, 223n.76, 232n.64, 235n.119, 248n.45
fear
   as basis of white supremacy, 19, 51–52, 56–57, 58–59, 65–67, 70–71, 77–78, 89–90, 98–99, 109–10, 113–14, 146–47, 149, 155–56, 157–58, 175, 195–96
   and incarceration, 98–99, 103–43
   liberation from, 19–20, 51, 56–57, 70–71, 77–78, 89–90, 101–2, 103–43, 175
   See also colonialism; freedom; Jim Crow; violence
Fellowship of Reconciliation (FOR), 71–72, 105–6, 222n.77
Ferguson, Missouri, 197–98, 199–200
fidelity to law, 17, 19–20, 34, 47–48, 123, 202
   See also John Rawls; *A Theory of Justice*
Fisher, Bernice, 232n.64
Floyd, George, 199–200, 254n.20
Forman, James, 139, 151
Forrester, Katrina, 210n.29
Fox, Richard, 55, 218n.28
Frazier, E. Franklin, 64–67, 73, 77–78, 81, 87–88, 218n.31, 219n.35
Frederickson, George, 61–62, 79–80
freedom
   and agency or action, 16–17, 49, 98–99, 101–4, 112–14, 116–17, 122–23, 125, 132–33, 145, 175, 196–97
   comparative freedom, 19–20, 101–2, 104, 125, 128, 175
   and fearlessness, 19–20, 51, 56–57, 70–71, 77–78, 89–90, 101–2, 103–43, 175
   and incarceration, 19–20, 98–99, 103–43
Freedom Rides (1961), 3, 11–12, 13–14, 15, 98–99, 102–3, 108, 110–11, 114–23, 124–25, 127–28, 137–38
   Freedom Rides Coordinating Committee, 118–19

Freeman, Rosemary, 91–92
Friedman, John, 87

Gadsden, Walter, 138, 148–49, 153–54
Gaither, Tom, 115
Galamison, Milton, 190–91, 246n.16
Gandhi, Mohandas K, 10–11, 55, 60–67, 68–72, 73–74, 75–76, 118–19, 216nn.7–8, 217–18n.20, 218n.22, 218n.28, 219n.34, 220n.44, 220n.54
Garner, Eric, 199–200, 254n.20
Ghanaian independence movement, 81–83, 84–85
   See also Accra, Ghana; Kwame Nkrumah; Positive Action Campaign
Goldwater, Barry, 23–24, 27–28
Goodman, Andrew, 192–93
Gray, Annetta Streeter, 147
Gray, Freddie, 1–2
Gray, Jesse, 164
Greensboro, North Carolina, 1–2, 104–6
Guinn, Joe, 108
Guyot, Lawrence, 94, 227n.13

Habermas, Jürgen, 5–6, 7–8, 129, 211n.55, 216n.5
Hall, Jacquelyn Dowd, 3, 12–13
Hamer, Fannie Lou, 91–98, 99–101, 121
Hamilton, Charles, 194–95
Hansberry v. Lee, 251n.82
Hansberry, Lorraine, 183–84
Harcourt, Bernard, 10–11, 205n.26
Harding, Vincent, 46
Harlem Riot (1964), 159–60, 193, 252–53n.5, 253n.7
Henry Thomas v. Mississippi, 235n.121
Holland, Endesha Ida Mae, 94–95
Holt, Thomas, 14–15
Hooker, Juliet, 171, 198–99, 230n.42
Hoover, J. Edgar, 28
Horne, Gerald, 57–58, 218n.29
Houser, George, 108, 222n.76
Humphrey, Hubert, 165, 177, 180–82, 184–85

imaginative transit
   compared to "transit of empire," 59, 226n.121

imaginative transit (*cont.*)
  compared to translation, 216–17n.9
  contemporary examples of, 197–98
  definition and significance of, 19, 56–59, 67, 73–74, 84, 87–90, 103–4, 155–56, 195–96, 197–98, 226n.121
  temporal aspects of, 19–20, 101
incivility. *See* civility
Indian independence movement, 60–63, 70–71, 74, 87–88
Indian Noncooperation Campaign (1920–1922), 60–63, 217–18n.20
  See also Indian independence movement
Interracial Action Institute, 106–8

Jack, Homer, 224n.90, 232n.64
Jackson, Alexander Louis, 62–63
Jackson, Mississippi, 1–2, 117–19, 121–23, 136–37, 235n.119
Jacoby, Tamar, 161–62
jail, no bail
  and self-emancipation, 19–20, 98–99, 104, 108–14, 120–21, 122–25, 128, 235–36n.122
  emergence from sit-ins, 104–8, 114–16
  outward dynamics of, 104, 128
  use in Birmingham, 140–41
  use in Freedom Rides, 116–23
  See also decolonizing praxis; freedom
jail-in. *See* jail, no bail
Jim Crow
  and apartheid, 78–80
  and colonialism, 13, 19, 51, 56–59, 62–63, 67–68, 70–71, 80–82, 85–86, 87–88, 89–90, 194–95, 197–98, 219n.35, 222–23n.77, 224n.90, 226n.121, 250n.64
  as control of bodies, 59–60, 96–97, 103–4, 109–10, 229n.24
  as legalized segregation, 13, 47–48, 49–50, 177, 179–80, 195, 228–29n.22
  as regime of exclusion, 23, 33–34, 36–37, 42–44, 46–48, 212–13n.71
  as regime of fear and violence, 16–17, 19, 20–21, 23, 51–52, 56–59, 64, 65–67, 70–72, 73, 77–78, 79–80, 82–84, 85, 87–88, 89–90, 92–97, 109–10, 113–14, 116–18, 119–20, 121, 123–25, 127–28, 130–32, 133–34, 138–39, 141–42, 143–44, 146–47, 150–51, 154, 155–56, 161, 175, 193, 194–96
  as systemic domination, 19–20, 49–50, 51–52, 96–97, 98–99, 123–24, 130–31, 133, 228–29n.22
  See also domination; exclusion; Southern exceptionalism
Johnson, James Weldon, 53, 62–63, 64, 66–67
Johnson, June, 91–95
Johnson, Lyndon, 25–26, 28, 49–50, 164, 167–68, 190–91
Jones, Charles, 116

Kapur, Sudarshan, 63–64
Kelley, Robin D.G., 154–55, 198
Kennedy, John F., 49–50, 95–96, 119, 125–26, 143–44, 149, 152–54, 175–76, 243nn.105–6, 249n.60
Kennedy, Robert, 25–26, 95–96, 233n.86, 239–40n.46
Khan-Cullors, Patrice, 201–2
King, A.D., 137–38, 140
King, Coretta Scott, 82, 239–40n.46
King, Martin Luther Jr., 1–2, 3, 6–7, 10–11, 16–17, 19–20, 25–26, 30, 38–39, 49, 51, 57, 58–59, 67–68, 70–71, 74, 80–85, 89–90, 91, 101, 102, 103–4, 106, 114–15, 119, 127–28, 135–39, 140–47, 148–52, 154, 155–56, 168–69, 172–73, 174–75, 200, 201–2, 220–21n.55, 223n.80, 224n.90, 228–29n.22, 233n.74, 238–39n.34, 239–40n.46, 242n.86, 243–44n.109, 248n.45
  See also Birmingham Campaign; "Letter from a Birmingham Jail"
King, Richard, 112–14
King, Tom, 134–35
Kirkpatrick, Jennet, 205n.25
Kramer, Sina, 208n.11
Ku Klux Klan, 65–66, 92–93, 127–28, 140–41, 152, 192

Kuchel, Thomas, 165, 180–82, 184–85
Kunstler, William, 145–46, 228n.16

Lassiter, Matthew, 178–79
law and order, 24–26, 27, 28, 29, 48–50, 66, 107–8, 109–10, 112, 123–25, 134–35, 136–37, 149–51, 165, 180–81, 193
Lawson, James, 105–6, 110–11, 114, 123–24
Lee, Bernard, 146
Leeds, Oliver, 163–64, 171
Lefkowitz, David, 99–100, 111–12, 229–30n.29
legitimacy, 4–6, 7, 10, 22–23, 24–25, 37–38, 41–42, 100–1, 104, 111–12, 123–24, 144, 145, 152–53, 196, 211n.48, 249n.60, 253n.13
"Letter from a Birmingham Jail," 1–2, 6–7, 38, 49, 141–42, 143–44, 145, 174–75, 248n.45
Lewis, John, 87–88, 105–6, 109, 113–14, 117–18, 231n.54, 248n.45
liberation. *See* freedom
Lincoln, Abraham, 46, 188–90
Livingston, Alexander, 216n.8, 220n.54
Loggins, Jared, 240n.53
Lomax, Louis, 169–70
long civil rights movement, 12–15, 57, 206n.32, 206n.34, 215n.104
Lovell, Jarrett, 20
Lumumba, Patrice, 85–86, 87
lynching. *See* violence
Lyons, David, 10–11, 33, 210n.38

Making of Black Revolutionaries, The, 139
Malan, Daniel, 75–76, 77, 78
Malcolm X, 149–50, 192–93
Mantena, Karuna, 131–32
March on Washington (1963), 2, 87–88, 108, 149–50, 156, 159–60, 165, 169–70, 195
March on Washington Movement (MOWM), 72–73
Markovits, Daniel, 7–9, 10–11, 205n.26
Marshall, Burke, 149, 151

Marshall, Thurgood, 106–7
Martin, Trayvon, 1–2
mass meetings, 72, 135–36, 137–38, 140, 144–46, 148–49, 246n.16
Matusow, Allen, 243n.105
Maxwell, Lida, 253n.13
Mays, Benjamin, 69–72, 77–78, 89–90, 220–21n.55
Mboya, Tom, 85–86, 87
McAdam, Douglas, 131–32
Melamed, Jodi, 240n.53
Meriwether, James, 76
Miami, Florida, 106–8, 115
Mills, Charles, 20–21, 42–44, 162–63, 174–75, 183, 213n.77
Milligan, Tony, 22–23
Mississippi Freedom Summer, 252n.1
Montgomery, Alabama, 82–85, 117–19
  See also Montgomery Bus Boycott
Montgomery Bus Boycott (1956), 39, 58, 62, 79–80, 82–85, 135, 223n.80
Montgomery County, Mississippi. *See* Winona, Mississippi
Montgomery Improvement Association (MIA), 79–80
  See also Montgomery Bus Boycott
Moses, Robert (builder), 163, 166–68, 186, 187–90, 252n.93
Moses, Robert P. (activist), 159, 172, 181
Mount Zion Church, 192, 193
Movement for Black Lives, 1–2, 199–202
Murakawa, Naomi, 27–28, 29
Muste, A.J., 77–78
My Bondage and My Freedom, 91, 101–2
Myrdal, Gunnar, 44–47, 214n.80, 250n.64

Nash, Diane, 105–6, 112, 116, 117–19, 125, 132, 146, 169–70, 231n.55, 235–36n.122, 247–48n.41
Nashville Christian Leadership Conference (NCLC), 117–19
Nashville, Tennessee, 105–8, 109, 117–19, 120–21, 187, 231nn.54–55
National Association for the Advancement of Colored People (NAACP), 62–63, 64, 68, 106–8, 118–19, 121–22, 186

National Commission on the Causes and
    Prevention of Violence (NCCPV),
    25–27, 29, 30–31
New York City, New York, 1–2, 76–77,
    116, 163–68, 170–72, 173–74,
    177–80, 181–82, 183, 185, 186–87,
    188, 193–94
Niebuhr, Reinhold, 127, 130–31,
    133–34, 143–44
Nixon, E.D., 79–80, 223n.88
Nixon, Richard, 28–29, 83–84
Nkrumah, Kwame, 53, 81–83, 84–86
nonviolence
    anticolonial uses of, 19, 51, 56–57, 58–
       59, 60–63, 67–68, 70, 72, 74, 75–78,
       80–83, 84–86, 87–88, 196
    as disabling violent response, 64–65,
       70–71, 77–78, 89–90, 154–56
    nonviolent coercion, 49–50, 51–52,
       125–26, 136–37, 143–44, 155, 164–
       65, 239n.36
    nonviolent direct action, 59–60
    as part of script for action, 3, 4, 5–6,
       10, 22–23, 34–35, 37, 38, 47–48,
       54–55, 99–101
    as related to persuasion, 128–32, 142,
       146–47, 150–51, 154–56, 157–58
       (*see also* persuasion)
    as revealing violence, 138–39, 142–43,
       146–47, 148–49, 150–51, 154–55,
       193–94 (*see also* disclosure)
    as tool of colonial management,
       194–95, 200
    and vulnerability to violence, 64, 65–67,
       73–74, 77–78, 86, 87–88

Obama, Barack, 2–3
Occupy Wall Street, 1–2, 9–10, 197–98
Okoku, Alphonse, 87, 226n.118
Olson, Joel, 42
oppression. *See* domination
Owens, Major, 167–68

Palestine, 194–95, 197–98
Parchman Farm, 119–21
Parks, Rosa, 79–80, 200–1, 223n.88
Payne, Charles, 92–93
Payne, Milton, 148–49

Peck, James, 108
Peller, Gary, 17
persuasion
    as part of script for action, 4, 5–6, 20,
       23–24, 30, 34–38, 51–52, 128–33,
       156–58, 175
    relationship with coercion, 20, 128,
       129–33, 154, 157–58, 239n.39
    See also coercion; nonviolence;
       violence
Philadelphia, Mississippi, 192
Piven, Frances Fox, 132, 142–43
political disobedience, 10–11, 205n.26
political obligation, 8–9, 16, 17, 31–34, 36–
    39, 41–42, 46–47, 54–55, 210n.29,
    210n.38, 214n.93
Ponder, Annelle, 91–92, 93–95, 102–3
Positive Action Campaign, 81–82
Positive Action Conference (1960), 86–87
Powell, Jerome, 193
problem-space, 18
Project C. *See* Birmingham Campaign
public reason, 6–7, 38–39, 51–52
punishment, 4, 5–6, 9–10, 34–35, 38, 49,
    98, 99–101, 104, 123, 229–30n.29
Purnell, Brian, 159, 179–80

Quit India Campaign (1942), 60–61, 72,
    217–18n.20
    See also Indian independence
       movement

racial capitalism, 240n.53
racial injustice. *See* domination; Jim Crow;
    white supremacy
Randolph, A. Philip, 53, 57, 72–73, 75, 76–
    77, 79–80, 82, 222n.76, 223n.88
Rawls, John, 5–8, 10–12, 17, 19, 24–25, 30,
    31–37, 38–39, 43–44, 46–47, 48–
    49, 51–52, 54, 55, 88–89, 100, 111–
    12, 129, 207n.43, 209n.22, 210n.29,
    211n.48, 212n.58, 212–13n.71,
    213n.77, 250–51n.73
    See also *A Theory of Justice*
Reagon, Bernice, 113–14
Reid v. City of Birmingham, 238n.23
riots
    in Birmingham, 151–52, 154, 243n.105

conflated with civil disobedience, 6–7, 23–24, 26–29, 30–31, 88–89, 95–96, 182–83
conflated with crime, 23–24, 26–29, 30–31, 88–89
during Freedom Rides, 118–19, 133–34
in Harlem, 159–60, 193, 252–53n.5, 253n.7
King's view of, 155–56, 169
in South Africa, 76
use of term, 208n.11
Roberts, Neil, 101–2, 104
Robinson, James, 107–8, 232n.64
Rock Hill, South Carolina, 115–16
Rustin, Bayard, 51, 57, 58–59, 71–72, 73, 75, 76–79, 85–86, 89–90, 108, 158, 167, 222–23nn.76–77, 223n.80, 226n.118, 228–29n.22

Sabl, Andrew, 36–37, 39, 212–13n.71
Salt March (1930), 60–61, 217–18n.20
See also Indian independence movement
satyagraha, 55, 61–62, 73, 216n.8, 217–18n.20, 220n.54
Scalmer, Sean, 63–64, 217–18n.20
Scheuerman, William, 207–8n.2, 215n.101
Schwerner, Michael, 192–93
Scott, David, 18–19
Scott, James C., 40–42, 48–49
Scott, Michael, 85–86, 224n.90
seeing like an activist, 18, 20–21, 49–52, 195–99, 202
seeing like a white state, 4, 17–18, 40–49, 55–57, 103–4, 124–25, 162–63, 197–98, 207n.43, 245n.10
segregation. *See* Jim Crow
self-emancipation. *See* freedom
self-liberation. *See* freedom
Selma, Alabama, 1–3, 4–5, 9–10, 11–12, 15, 39, 58, 136
Sewell, William, 249n.60
Shambry, Henry, 148–49
Sharp, Gene, 136–37, 239n.36
Sharpeville massacre, 86
Shaw University Conference, 87, 104–5
Shelby, Tommie, 11–12, 207n.43, 213n.77
Sherrod, Charles, 111–12, 116

Shulman, George, 174, 176–77
Shuttlesworth, Fred Lee, 128, 134–37, 138–39, 140, 151–52, 154
Simpson, Euvester, 91–92
Singer, Peter, 5–6
sit-in campaigns
in Atlanta, 114–15
in Birmingham, 135–37, 144–45
compared to stall-in, 181–82
early uses of, 71–72
and "jail, no bail," 98–99, 102–12, 114–16, 122–23, 124–25
in Miami, 106–8
in Nashville, 105–7
in New York City, 170
plans for March on Washington, 169–70
in Rock Hill, 115–16
in Tallahassee, 106–7
white reaction to, 156, 244n.113
See also Congress of Racial Equality; jail, no bail; Student Nonviolent Coordinating Committee
Sixteenth Street Baptist Church, 147, 148–49, 152, 169–70
Slate, Nico, 57–58, 67–68
slavery, 19–20, 38–39, 61–62, 68, 69–70, 81, 84–85, 91, 101–2, 103–4, 112–13, 119–20, 123, 141–42, 145, 188–89, 243–44n.109
Smith, William, 7–10, 129
Smyer, Sidney, 134–35, 151
Snowden, Edward, 1–2
solidarity, 19, 87, 97–99, 104, 111–12, 116, 121, 124, 125, 128, 161–62, 197–98, 202
Southern Christian Leadership Conference (SCLC)
correspondence with Eisenhower, 83–84
role in Birmingham Campaign, 4–5, 20, 127–28, 131–32, 134–41, 145–49, 151–52, 154–55
role in Freedom Rides, 118–19
stall-in proposal by, 169–70
southern exceptionalism, 13–14, 47–48, 177–79, 185, 198–99, 250n.64
Spelman, Elizabeth, 20–21, 162–63, 174–75, 249n.57

stall-in
  compared to Birmingham Campaign, 161–64, 165, 168, 172–73, 175–76, 177, 181
  compared to sit-in, 181–82
  and disavowal, 176–86
  other proposals for, 169–70
  and white comfort, 171–73
  at World's Fair 1964, 161–69, 171–73, 186–91, 248n.45, 250–51n.73
Standing Rock, 197–98
Stephens, Patricia, 106
Student Nonviolent Coordinating Committee (SNCC)
  anticolonialism of, 87–88, 225–26n.114
  founding of, 87–88, 104–5
  response to stall-in, 172, 248n.45
  role in jail, no bail, 19–20, 98–99, 104–6, 114–16
  role in sit-ins, 104–6
  role in Freedom Rides, 117–21
  role in Winona incident, 91–96
Sutherland, Bill, 57, 76–77, 82, 85–86, 222n.76

tactics of disclosure. *See* disclosure
tactics of disruption. *See* disruption
Tallahassee, Florida, 106
Tannenbaum, Frank, 65–66
Taylor, Keeanga-Yamahtta, 201
techniques of disavowal. *See* disavowal
Terry, Brandon, 11–12, 20, 142, 155, 223n.80
Thelwell, Michael, 22
Theoharis, Jeanne, 1–2
Theory of Justice, A, 32–37
  See also John Rawls
Threadcraft, Shatema, 223n.80
Thurman, Howard, 69–70, 71–72, 89–90
Tillery, Alvin, 75
Turé, Kwame, 120–21, 194–95
Turner, Charles Jr., 159–61

uncivil disobedience, 10, 205n.25 (*see also* civil disobedience; riots)

US v. Partridge et al., 95–96

violence
  armed struggle, 62–63, 65–66, 77–78, 85–86, 194–95
  and colonialism, 16–17, 19, 51–52, 56–59, 70–72, 77–78, 79–80, 85, 194–95, 196
  conducted or condoned by the state, 26, 92–97, 109–10, 119–20, 121, 123–25, 127–28, 130–31, 132, 133–34, 138–39, 141–42, 143–44, 146–47, 148–49, 151, 152, 186, 192–95, 199–200, 243–44n.109
  as democratized, 51–52, 93, 96–97, 109–10
  as disruption of order, 25–29, 30, 35, 46
  and fear, 19, 51–52, 56–57, 58–59, 65–67, 70–71, 77–78, 89–90, 98–99, 109–10, 113–14, 146–47, 149, 155–56, 157–58, 175, 195–96, 223n.80
  and Jim Crow, 16–17, 19, 20–21, 23, 51–52, 56–59, 64, 65–67, 70–72, 73, 77–78, 79–80, 82–84, 85, 87–88, 89–90, 92–97, 109–10, 116–18, 119–20, 121, 123–25, 127–28, 130–32, 133–34, 138–39, 141–42, 143–44, 146–47, 150–51, 154, 155–56, 161, 175, 193, 194–96
  lynching, 64, 66–67, 73–74, 92–93, 107–8, 109–10, 174, 192–93
  perceptions of, 16–17, 130–31, 133–34, 139, 141–44, 149, 150–51, 154, 161, 175, 180–83
  See also nonviolence; riots
Vivian, C.T., 121
Von Eschen, Penny, 57

Wagner, Richard, 165, 180–82, 184–85
Walker, Wyatt Tee, 135–41, 147, 148, 150–51, 154–55, 169–70, 238–39n.34, 239–40n.46
Walzer, Michael, 5–6, 24, 30, 37, 39, 46–47, 54, 55, 88–89, 214n.93
"We Are Americans Too" Conference, 72
Weaver, Vesla, 29
Welchman, Jennifer, 211n.54
West, James, 91–92, 93–94, 95–96

whiteness, 131–32, 150–51, 160–61
  abolition of, 248n.51
  as political category, 42
  and right to comfort, 160–61, 170–71, 173, 176–77, 181–82, 184, 190–91
  transforming white citizens, 4–5, 16–17, 20–21, 51–52, 102, 142–44, 171–72, 176, 177, 195–96 (*see also* white moderate)
  white backlash, 159–60, 161–62, 171, 193–94
  white citizen as ideal, 4, 17–18, 24–25, 42–44, 45, 46–47, 48–49, 186
  white democracy, 42, 50, 128, 131, 161, 195–96, 197–98
  white grievance, 171
  white ignorance, 20–21, 162–63, 173, 174–76, 183, 249n.57
  white moderate, 140–42, 143–44, 149–51, 156–57, 242n.86, 244n.115
  See also seeing like a white state; white supremacy
White Citizens' Council, 92–93, 140–41
white supremacy, 15, 16–17, 19, 48–49, 58, 75–76, 78, 79–80, 123, 142, 161, 181–82, 197–98, 201–2
  defined by fear and violence, 51, 56–57, 58–59, 70–72, 77–78, 87–88, 89–90, 92–93, 131–32, 144–45, 154–56, 193–94
  epistemic context of, 4–5, 20, 24–25, 39–40, 42–44, 141–42, 162–63, 171, 174–75, 176, 181–83, 196–97, 245n.10, 249n.57
  and American democracy, 3, 16–17, 29, 42, 49–50, 96–98, 109–10, 141–42, 194–95, 196–97, 250n.64
  See also colonialism; domination; Jim Crow; whiteness
Why We Can't Wait, 140–45, 243–44n.109
  See also "Letter from a Birmingham Jail"
Winona, Mississippi, 91–98, 100–1, 102–3, 121, 229n.26
Winsor, Ellen, 64–65, 66, 218–19n.32
Wolin, Sheldon, 41–42
World's Fair (1964), 20–21, 161–62, 163–65, 166–68, 172, 179–80, 181–83, 186–89, 190–91
  See also stall-in

Young, Andrew, 96

Zerilli, Linda, 129–30
Zinn, Howard, 196–97, 227n.13

CPSIA information can be obtained
at www.ICGtesting.com
Printed in the USA
BVHW050909250623
666076BV00002B/5